POSTCOLONIAL VIETNAM

A JOHN HOPE FRANKLIN CENTER BOOK

ASIA-PACIFIC: CULTURE, POLITICS, AND SOCIETY

Editors: Rey Chow, H. D. Harootunian, and Masao Miyoshi

Patricia M. Pelley

POSTCOLONIAL VIETNAM

New Histories of the National Past

Duke University Press   Durham and London   2002

© 2002 DUKE UNIVERSITY PRESS
All rights reserved
Printed in the United States of America on acid-free paper ∞
Designed by Amy Ruth Buchanan
Typeset in Minion by Tseng Information Systems, Inc.
Library of Congress Cataloging-in-Publication Data
appear on the last printed page of this book.

In loving memory of

Irene N. and Thomas R.

Contents

Acknowledgments

This book has taken many, too many, years to complete, and over the years I have accrued innumerable debts, which I happily acknowledge here. As a graduate student at Cornell University, I benefited from the insights and criticisms of friends, colleagues, and professors. I would like to thank Jojo Abinales, Donna Amoroso, Benedict Anderson, Myra Best, Đô Văn Gia, Bruce Lockhart, Sherman and Janice Cochran, Walter Cohen, Christoph Giebel, Stephen Graw, Emily Hill, Huỳnh Kim Khánh, George Kahin, J. Victor Koschmann, Micheline Lessard, Shawn McHale, Michael Montesano, John Najemy, Nguyễn Ngọc Kim-Khôi, Virginia Shih, Takashi Shiraishi, James T. Siegel, Jonathan Stromseth, Keith Taylor, Nora Taylor, Thaveeporn Vasavakul, Trịnh Kim-Chi, Christine White, Oliver Wolters, David Wyatt, Emoretta Yang, and Peter Zinoman. In the post-Cornell years, a number of people were gracious enough to read this manuscript in one or more of its earlier versions: David Chandler, Hafid Gafaiti, Rita Smith Kipp, Li Tana, Bruce Lockhart, David Marr, Anatoli Sokolov, and Alexander Woodside. Even though some blunders inevitably remain, these readers have saved me from committing many more, and their comments made me question my assumptions and approach.

I conducted most of the research for this book in three places: the Karl Kroch Library at Cornell, where Margaret Crawford and Allen Riedy were especially helpful; the Institute of Southeast Asian Studies in Singapore, directed then by Kernial Sandhu; and the Institute of History in Hanoi. In addition to thanking Dương Trung Quốc, Nguyễn Hồng Phong, and Văn Tạo, the directors of the Institute, who were always professional and kind, I would like to acknowledge the contributions of Lê Văn Lan, Minh Tranh,

Nguyễn Văn Kự, Phạm Huy Thông, Phan Huy Lê, Trần Quốc Vượng, and Vũ Huy Phúc. All of these people, in Ithaca, Singapore, and Hanoi, made crucial materials available to me and helped me more than I can say.

I have benefited from the financial support of several institutions. The early stages of my research were made possible by the Joint Committee on Southeast Asian Studies of the Social Science Research Council and the American Council of Learned Societies, with funds provided by the William and Flora Hewlett Foundation and the Henry Luce Foundation. I would also like to acknowledge other sources of support, including two National Resource Fellowships, a Foreign Language and Areas Studies Fellowship, and a Martin V. McCoy Jr. Trust Fellowship. I am indebted to Cornell University, whose Southeast Asia Program, Center for International Studies, and Sage Graduate School generously supported my work. At Texas Tech University, Allan J. Kuethe, Chair of the Department of History, and Jane Winer, Dean of the College of Arts and Sciences, made it possible for me to bring this book to a conclusion; James Reckner and Khanh Lê from Texas Tech's Vietnam Center also deserve my special thanks. The friendship of my colleagues at Texas Tech, especially William Gray, Patricia Lorcin, and José Santos, has given me a tremendous boost. I must also thank individuals at Duke University Press who so graciously helped me convert a specialized manuscript into a more readable book, including Executive Editor J. Reynolds Smith, his capable assistant Sharon P. Torian, Series Editor Rey Chow, Assistant Managing Editor Justin Faerber, and Jean Brady whose patience and skill have been invaluable.

Finally, and with great affection, I want to thank the people whose presence has made a wonderful difference in my life: Suanne Pelley, Connor Riggs, Brian Riggs, Thomas Pelley, Sarah Eichhorn, Joan Pelley, Donna Amoroso, and Hafid Gafaiti.

A Note on Diacritics

Because Vietnamese is a tonal language that is unpronounceable and meaningless without diacritical marks, I have included them when they were present in the original text. However, recognizing that nonspecialists may find the diacritics difficult to manage, I have omitted them from terms that are familiar to an English-speaking audience. Widely known toponyms (for example, Vietnam, Hanoi, Haiphong, Hue, Saigon, and so forth) appear without diacritical marks, as do proper names such as Ho Chi Minh, Ngo Dinh Diem, and Vo Nguyen Giap. The major exception to this practice is that proper names familiar to ethnologists, who may or may not be specialists in Vietnamese studies, are written as they normally appear in English. Without doubt this solution is imperfect, but I am convinced that it is preferable to the alternative of omitting the diacritics altogether or, worse yet, using only those that occur in Western languages—the circumflex, for example, and accent marks.

Introduction | Postcolonial Visions

For the purposes of narration and analysis, the idea of "postcolonial" Vietnam is essential but also problematic. In terms of the intention of Vietnamese revolutionaries the postcolonial period was ushered in by the August Revolution of 1945 and announced yet again in Hanoi on September 2, when Ho Chi Minh recited Vietnam's Declaration of Independence before an exuberant crowd of one million Vietnamese. From the perspective of the revolutionaries, the fact that they staged this drama in Hanoi was especially poignant because the French had transformed the city into the headquarters of the colonial regime. The occasion was also significant because it marked and celebrated the emergence of "the people" as a potent political force, for it was tens of thousands of ordinary Vietnamese who brought about the demise of their colonial oppressors. At the level of rhetoric and intention, this moment inaugurated the postcolonial period in the history of Vietnam: it formally concluded more than eighty years of French colonization and marked the end to nearly five years of Japanese occupation. The meaning of this moment — the demise of French Indochina and the emergence of the Democratic Republic of Vietnam (DRV) — was also communicated in symbolic terms. By the time Ho Chi Minh made this historic utterance, Viet Minh revolutionaries had already received the imperial regalia from Bảo Đại, the last of the Nguyễn emperors. They had begun to make the rupture between the colonial past and the postcolonial present clear in practical and logistical terms as well: even before the recitation, they had established many of the basic institutions of government and, in the days and weeks following the declaration, they continued to elaborate the administrative capacities of the new state.

This representation of events, however, is partial in the extreme because it reflects only the experience of the Vietnamese who were allied with the Indochinese Communist Party (ICP) and the Viet Minh. In the aftermath of World War II (and perhaps even at the beginning of the war), Vietnamese of all political faiths recognized that French Indochina was a thing of the past; but not everyone agreed that Vietnam should be governed by Ho Chi Minh and his revolutionary associates. Indeed, one could argue that the un-stated goal of DRV culture in the period after 1945 was to make the revolution "stick," to make it mark the kind of historical upheaval that in 1945 it did not, in fact, represent: the political and social terrain was far more ambiguous and complex. In other words, the idea or chronology that we now take for granted—that the August Revolution of 1945 marked a new beginning in the history of Vietnam—attests to the success of DRV efforts *after* 1945 (and especially after 1954) to reconstruct the events of 1945 in terms of rupture and clarity. In this study of postcolonial Vietnam I accept the now-standard chronology, but my emphasis is on the process through which that narrative became conventionalized.

Within a domestic context, Vietnamese in all parts of the country con-tested the meaning of the August Revolution, questioned the legitimacy of the Viet Minh, and challenged the authority of the Democratic Republic. On their own, however, the disputes among the Vietnamese could not have caused the postcolonial moment to be postponed. On the contrary, one could reason that these sorts of disputes are an essential and intrinsic part of genuine decolonization. But the intervention of foreign powers—Chi-nese Nationalists (GMD), Britain, and France, initially; the Soviet Union and the United States within a short while; and, eventually, the People's Repub-lic of China (PRC)—vitiated what the revolutionaries had so triumphantly proclaimed. In fall 1945, when the Allies (the GMD in the northern part of Vietnam and the British in the southern part) moved in to supervise the Japanese surrender, plans to reestablish French control in the South were already in place. In addition to undermining the revolution militarily, the Allies also sought to undo it through diplomatic offensives. Thus, before the revolution was socially consolidated and before the apparatus of the post-colonial state was fully in place, the momentum was interrupted by Allied attempts to reestablish prerevolutionary patterns or, to be more precise, to create what they disingenuously called a "democratic" state—meaning non-communist, pro-Western, and dependent. By December 1946, revolution-aries were at war—against France, most obviously, but also internally. In

March 1949, the Associated State of Vietnam was established in the southern part of the country with the emperor emeritus Bảo Đại as its head. And yet, as these events unfolded in the South, and at a time when the Associated State actually had more international support than the DRV, the North continued to claim that Vietnam was a single country governed exclusively from the national capital in Hanoi. This was a claim that many Vietnamese rejected. To the extent that the DRV was internationally acknowledged—in 1950 the Soviet Union and the newly constituted PRC officially recognized it—it was understood to encompass only the northern part of the country. In the period after 1945, official culture in the DRV sought to suppress this confusion and these conflicts. And yet, the uncertainty surrounding the events of 1945 persisted.

Years later, when they were pushed to the limits by the Viet Minh siege of Dien Bien Phu, French troops and colonial subjects who fought with them surrendered; and at the Geneva Conference in July 1954, French imperial ambitions in Asia were definitively thwarted. Although northern historians often depicted the "Anti-French Resistance War" (1946–1954) as an example of Vietnamese fighting to free their country from the French, the war was far more complex. Indeed, far from acting en masse in a uniform bloc, "the Vietnamese" were internally divided and they struggled violently among themselves to determine the shape and meaning of postcolonialism. To the extent that they acknowledged these cracks in what was supposed to be a monolithic facade, northern historians dismissively labeled the Vietnamese who opposed them as "reactionaries" or "traitors." Just as the opposition "Vietnamese against French" obscures critical dimensions of the postcolonial experience, the distinctions between "patriots and traitors" or "revolutionaries and reactionaries" camouflage key elements. The point is that although they struggled among themselves and against each other, the Vietnamese were not simply lined up on one side or another of the revolutionary divide. Mere dualisms are too crude to account for what actually transpired. Moreover, explanations that rely on fixed and static notions of the Viet Minh, for example, or assume that alliances remained in place once they were declared, similarly miss what makes the meaning of the postrevolutionary and postcolonial periods so difficult to seize.

When the Viet Minh repossessed the (northern) capital in fall 1954, there were parades and festivals throughout Hanoi to celebrate the restoration of peace after nine years of warfare and to mark the military victory over France. Intellectuals in the DRV presented the events of 1954 as a great vic-

tory, and reasonably so, but the euphoria of 1954 was mixed with an unacknowledged but keen sense of foreboding. As revolutionaries restated and
reaffirmed the break with the colonial past, the Vietnamese (North and
South) were forced to submit to neocolonial kinds of asymmetry. In the
South, the patrimonial presence of the United States negated the possibility
of decolonization in a genuine sense. In the North, where new ties of dependence developed with the Soviet Union and China, Vietnamese attempts
to free themselves from colonial and neocolonial meddling were similarly
fettered. Historians in the DRV criticized neocolonial developments and the
imposition of cold war politics on the people of Vietnam—but only in the
context of the South. Late in 1954, they characterized Ngo Dinh Diem as
the "right hand of the American imperialists and the war-like French," and
early the next year they referred to the "American imperialists who were
threatening the unity of Vietnam." Later that year, DRV officials established
the Front for the Ancestral Land in order to counter the efforts of "Ngo
Dinh Diem and the United States to divide the country."[1] As for northern
leaders, however, who were also entangled in neocolonial and cold war dynamics through their reliance on China and the Soviet Union, historians
presented them as autonomous agents. In short, they refused to acknowledge that Vietnamese politics after the Geneva Conference were even more
muddled than they had been nine years before.

Although the defeat of the French at Dien Bien Phu could not have been
more dramatic, the political consequences of what the Viet Minh had militarily achieved were not so easy to decipher. On the one hand, the Geneva
Accords stipulated that Vietnam was a single state; on the other, they also
established an administrative division between the North and South. Although the agreements emphasized that the two "administrative zones"
would last a maximum of two years, the seventeenth parallel quickly evolved
into a political boundary. While the DRV claimed to represent all of Vietnam, a separate state, identified as the Republic of Vietnam (RVN), had
already been created in the South. In effect, then, there were not two administrative units, but two states and two capitals.

Political and intellectual elites in the DRV did not acknowledge that the
postcolonial moment had been postponed or that the Vietnamese in an inclusive sense had been overwhelmed by cold war agendas. Instead, in 1954
they began to rewrite the past, from remote antiquity to the present. But
they worked with special diligence to reconstruct the events of 1945 and to
reshape the meaning of the nine years of warfare, which they depicted as a

confrontation between the Vietnamese on one side and the French on the other. They also insisted that the defeat of the French in 1954 signaled the restoration of peace and the emergence of the (unified) postcolonial state. To banish the idea that the revolution had been derailed, they concocted narratives of its unassailable coherence. To dispel the fear (and the realization) that they were embroiled in a situation they did not control, they insisted on their own instrumentality and power. Because the situation was so confused, they endlessly tried to make it clear: there was but one Vietnam—the DRV, and but one capital—Hanoi. Inadvertently depicting the ambiguity of this time, some historians described it as the period "when peace had been restored and the North was fighting to reunify the country."[2] Parenthetically, one could add that after the defeat of the United States and the RVN in 1975, the postcolonial period was yet again postponed as the Vietnamese adjusted to new kinds of neocolonial ties. Following the collapse of the Soviet Union in 1991, still new forms of domination emerged. Given the degree to which the interests of foreign capital govern Vietnam today, many Vietnamese are haunted by the thought that the horrendous loss of life and vast ecological damage they have endured over the past fifty years merely set the stage for what they are witnessing today: the reappearance of a wealthy capitalist elite, the reemergence of extraordinary poverty, and the reminder that the destiny of Vietnam is only partially controlled by the Vietnamese.

The point of these details is to clarify that in the case of Vietnam, and in other decolonizing societies as well, one cannot precisely locate the moment when the colonial period is past. Taking a formalist and, from the perspective of the Viet Minh, an intention-centered approach, one can affirm that the colonial period ended in 1945. And yet, almost immediately, because they were again involved in asymmetrical relations of power, the Vietnamese had to push the social, cultural, and even political aspects of decolonization aside. Moreover, even without the machinations of cold war rivalries, one can look for without really finding the purely postcolonial moment. The Vietnamese who orchestrated the revolutionary break from France were often imbued with colonial sensibilities—about the quasi-sacred status of science, for one, and the idea that certain groups of people were destined to dominate and "civilize" others. In other words, well after the French withdrew from Vietnam in 1954, many colonial norms and colonial representations remained in place, either as the objects of unconscious assimilation or as negativities to be rooted out and eradicated.

To summarize my first point, postcolonial culture in the DRV is based on a series of reconstructions, especially of the events of 1945, the period extending from 1946 to 1954, and the period after 1954. It is also based on denials — of the South above all. From 1954 to 1975, southern historians (a designation that probably includes northern immigrants to the South) were extremely prolific. Northern historians only very rarely acknowledged their perspectives, and in the period after reunification in 1976 the stifling of southern voices was even more complete. In a sense, in what follows I am complicit in the attempt to silence the South because I dwell exclusively on cultural productions in the North. My sources, as I have noted, usually refused to recognize the Republic of Vietnam as a legitimate (or even illegitimate) and separate state. Instead, they glossed over this difference, this gap, by clinging to the idea of a single Vietnam ruled unproblematically from Hanoi. But my work is not absolutely complicit. To disrupt what has now become the official narrative of the national past, I examine the fictive dimensions of the North's totalizing claims.

My second point is: the "postcolonial" moment implies a process of decolonization, which I will define here as the extrication of Vietnam from colonial paradigms and structures and the effort to institute new notions and new sources of authority. In short, it refers to the attempt to establish a distance between Vietnam and France precisely because, I would argue, so many aspects of daily life — ranging from the built environment to personal hygiene and styles of dress, from notions of politics and history to ideas about time — stemmed from the French occupation. With the withdrawal of French colonial troops and officials in 1954, the DRV briefly shifted its attention from conducting the war to recovering from it. Postwar reconstruction depended most obviously on the cultivation of food, the rebuilding of cities and towns, and the resumption of industrial production, but it was also much more than restoring the material bases of social life. Reconstruction also required the elaboration of new institutions and the clarification of new social norms. Although this need stemmed from the years of warfare, it was related much more dramatically, as well as more diffusely, to the trauma of colonization.

New national histories constituted a critical part of the process of decolonization. One can argue, indeed, that they formed the very basis of a genuinely new sense of nation. In investigating postcolonial attempts to rewrite the past, my research focuses principally on the work of official historians affiliated with the Research Committee and, later, with the Institute of History.[3] Through lavish commemorative events, changes in the visual cues and symbols of everyday life, and information presented in textbooks and public schools a new sense of the past—crystallized and condensed into memorable bits—was instilled in the people. New histories of the nation were also part of a bigger pattern. From its inception, the committee and, subsequently, the institute, responded to a web of social, political, and cultural dynamics. Party officials often set the agenda for historical research, and although historians did not slavishly adhere to political directives, their activities were circumscribed by the state. Thus, instead of regarding historiography as a conceptual problem unrelated to politics or daily life, I have tried to investigate the links between them, because the historians whose work I discuss were profoundly engaged in a tumultuous setting.

Newcomers to colonial scholarship on Vietnam may see postcolonial texts as needlessly combative; but when they are read as part of a conversation and as a response to what Edward Said has described as the "colonial tradition of disparagement," the content and the tone of postcolonial texts are more easily deciphered.[4] It is probably unfair to generalize about a century of colonial scholarship and to conflate the work of ideologues with that of specialists in religious studies, linguistics, history, anthropology, archaeology, and art history, but colonial scholars and colonial ideologues often shared similar assumptions, and in popular as well as specialized works several common themes emerged.

First, most colonial writers interpreted the French conquest of Vietnam as having been advantageous to the Vietnamese. They wrote about the humanity of France and her great generosity in civilizing a "primitive" people. Not surprisingly, therefore, postcolonial texts emphasized the savagery of the conquest and destructiveness of the French occupation. Second, many colonial writers viewed Vietnam as a smaller, less brilliant version of China. They regarded it as a derivative civilization that had only partially absorbed the once-superior (but now fallen) civilization of China.[5] The postcolonial obsession with origins can be read, at least in part, as a response to the charge and perhaps even the fear of being derivative. The most extensive attempt to decolonize the past (meaning, in this case, to "de-chinese" it) coalesced in the insistence that an unbroken chain of succession linked contemporary generations of Vietnamese to the mythical age of the Hùng kings (traced to the third millennium B.C.E.) and in the effacement of the Hùng kings' traditional (i.e., Sinitic) origins and meaning. Third, whether they looked at the civilization of China or the civilization of France as the source of Vietnam's amelioration, colonial writers frequently failed to see the Vietnamese as historical agents, acting in specific ways in pursuit of specific goals; for them Vietnam was stagnant and passive and could only be brought to life by more vigorous actors.

Like colonial depictions of Vietnam, postcolonial representations were often essentializing, but where colonial texts communicated contempt and condescension, postcolonial ones conveyed images of a dignified past and a self-realized present. In particular, postcolonial texts highlighted the agency and efficacy of the Vietnamese, who both created and responded to the social, cultural, and political conditions of their lives. Countering French narratives of the Vietnamese past, which were mostly shaped by the theme of conquest, postcolonial narratives shifted the emphasis so that the history of Vietnam was structured not by defeat and submission but by resistance and opposition. Even though the colonial past was evidence of Vietnam's weakness vis-à-vis France and seemed to attest to the conflicts and differences that had divided the Vietnamese, postcolonial productions stressed the strength and vitality of Vietnam and its history of unity. But these are only general themes, and in reducing postcolonial representations to pure resistance one misses much of their great richness.

In examining the work of official historians we need to ask why their completion of a new canonical version of the Vietnamese past was so delayed — despite their commitment to it, despite the pressure on them to complete it, and despite their impressive record of publications beginning in 1954. If the Vietnamese themselves had regarded this project as inconsequential, the delay could go unnoticed; but because great intellectual intensity and even a sense of urgency surrounded the problems of history and historical representation the delay raises some intriguing concerns. At this point we must move beyond the dynamic of history/counterhistory and concentrate on those issues that caused the consolidated vision of history to be delayed. And this is my purpose here.

Historical narrative, Hayden White has reminded us, is premised on the belief in a clear set of origins.[6] Thus, in order to decolonize the past — to narrate it in new ways — postcolonial Vietnamese felt compelled to pinpoint origins. They asked: When did the history of Vietnam begin? Only by determining when it began, they reckoned, could they narrate it in a meaningful way. Only after they had a clear sense of origins could they clarify the trajectory of the past and divide it into meaningful segments. Before the question of origins could be resolved, however, official historians had to naturalize the idea of Vietnam. Colonial scholars and colonial administrators recognized a number of geographical, social, and political entities: French Indochina, above all, and its constituent parts: Tonkin (the northern part), Annam (the central part), Cochinchina (the southern part), Cambodia, and Laos. They distinguished between the highlands and deltas, between coastal flats and riverine interiors, but never did they mention "Vietnam." And yet, as Vietnamese scholars launched an assault against French representations, they encountered at the same time the limitations of their own intellectual and emotional habits. At one level, the series of postponements—the inability to bring the new canonical view of the past to fruition—stemmed from the uncertainty over how Vietnam should be defined. In the 1950s, for example, many Vietnamese reflexively believed that "Vietnam" was a particularistic term referring to the land of the ethnic Việt. The process of imagining Vietnam in more inclusive and pluralistic terms was filled with debate and contestation that culminated, at least formally, in 1979 with an official inventory of the fifty-four ethnic groups in Vietnam. For this inclusive vision of Vietnam to become fixed, the Vietnamese had to reject traditional notions of social geography and think in terms of politics and new political boundaries.

The delay in producing a new general history also stemmed from the imperative to write "new history" (lịch sử mới). This rubric was introduced by official historians to describe the new types of analysis and new notions of causality that should bear on new narratives of the past. Fundamentally, new history referred to the inscription of the national past in a framework variously described as Marxist ("marxish"), Marxist-Engelist, Marxist-Leninist, and Stalinist. Despite their many debates on the meaning of these "isms" and their disagreements about their relevance to the history of Vietnam, official historians generally agreed that the new paradigms stressed the linearity as opposed to the circularity of the past: history, they began to insist, moves from one moment to the next in a pattern of evolutionary unfolding. In this evolutionary progression, they agreed, each stage supercedes what came before. Approached in an evolutionary framework, the past could be divided into meaningful segments and written into a broader, more overarching framework as well. While the idea of new history held unmistakable appeal, the process of establishing it was fraught with disputes: official historians simply could not agree on how the past should be periodized. In addition to being developmental, new history also privileged the objective (especially economic) conditions of social change. In other words, causal explanations based on prophecy, omens, or the mandate of heaven were abolished in favor of materialist explanations. But historical materialism, like Marxism or Marxism-Leninism, is famously opaque; even though official historians were eager to innovate, they were often uncertain about how to read the national past according to Marxist structures and categories. Moreover, despite their explicit appeals to a materialist conception of history, official historians often refused to see class conflict or other forms of internal divisions as the motor of history.

In a limited sense, the commitment to new history was purely political. Simply put, official historians were obliged (by party and government decrees) to produce a Marxist history of Vietnam. After all, the interlocutors who mattered at that time were mostly from the Soviet Union and China. But more substantively, Marxist paradigms (or Marxist paradigms as they were codified by Stalin) were also truly alluring because they provided the analytical basis for saying that the history of Vietnam was "normal" and, like the history of any other country, it had predictably moved through a specific set of stages. Marxist historiography made it possible, in other words, to demythologize the history of France and to overcome colonial claims that the history of Vietnam was abnormal and deficient.

It should be noted that although official historians were drawn to normalizing paradigms, they were, at times, also repelled by them; their impulse to insist that Asia (generally) or Vietnam (specifically) truly differed from Europe or France was probably as strong as their inclination to claim they were the same. Reacting against the universalizing models, official historians sometimes presented the Vietnamese past as transcendent and essential, as having escaped the surface contingencies of social life and as standing outside the world of mere events. When they translated the past into pure essence, officials historians tended to dwell on what they regarded as the distinctly Vietnamese tradition of resistance to foreign aggression. Or, still rejecting the linear view of history, they conceived of history as a process — but a process of repetition, not development, in which exemplary moments from the past were periodically restaged. It is from this pointillistic sense of history that the flood of postcolonial commemorative texts emerged. Other anomalies soon arose; for instance, official historians often alluded to Marxism as a method for including mythohistories in "scientific" renditions of the past.

To comment on the tension between nationalism and Marxism is nothing new, but in the case of Vietnam this tension was especially dramatic. Although Marx, Lenin, and Stalin had viewed nationalism as a negative force that could only undermine proletarian solidarity, Vietnamese Marxists were unmistakably nationalistic, and, in an aggressive misappropriation of Stalin, they cited his *Marxism and the National Question* to support their own hypernationalistic endeavors. Moreover, Vietnamese Marxists transformed Marxism from a theory of revolution into a theory of state power and a method for maintaining the status quo. The populist interpretation of Marxism suggests that a revolutionary movement centered on peasants can reconcile this tension. Peasants, in this instance substituting for the missing proletariat, are obviously anticolonial, and therefore nationalistic, and they are socialist to the extent that they oppose colonial oppression.

Not surprisingly, official historians were determined to write "histories of producers" and "histories of the people." But again, there was a tremendous gap between the desire to reconceptualize the past and the kinds of historical representations that were actually offered. In this case, the gap stemmed from conflicting attitudes toward "the people" (*dân tộc*). On some occasions, official historians were inclined to praise "the people" as ardent and pure, but on other occasions they looked at "the people" with skepticism and suspicion: too often, they believed, "the people" were reactionary and swayed by superstition more than science or reason. Moreover, when official historians valorized popular as opposed to elite experiences of history, they had to privilege popular culture as well, and this endeavor was complicated by the fact that popular culture often stood in opposition to constituted authority—whether that authority was in the form of a feudal dynast, a colonial official, or a revolutionary cadre. The attention to popular or vernacular culture also threatened to eclipse the layer of Sinitic culture to which many educated Vietnamese still felt emotionally as well as intellectually attached. Conflicting attitudes toward popular as opposed to elite culture were resolved, in part, by the appeal to national character, national spirit, and national essence. Whereas popular culture was presented as a rejection of elite culture, and therefore highlighted the problem of internal divisions, crystallizations such as the "tradition of resistance against foreign aggression," the "indomitable spirit of the Vietnamese," the "fighting spirit of the Vietnamese," and (later), the "peace-loving spirit of the Vietnamese" allowed internal divisions to recede. Thus, the ideas of popular history and popular culture were often absorbed into the quest for a homogeneous national culture that served the interests of the state. The main purpose of Marxism in Vietnam, especially after 1956, was to consolidate the state—which is not, according to most readings, a revolutionary plan. Even though they rejected traditional historiographical forms, postcolonial historians still operated, in some cases, according to traditional norms. Like the court historians of dynastic times, committee and institute historians viewed historical work as a project of political legitimation.

In seeking to symbolize the nation and state—to make what was abstract and even strange seem familiar—official historians echoed earlier generations of activists, especially those of the 1920s and 1930s. To discourage the Vietnamese from thinking about themselves in purely particularistic terms and to encourage a greater sense of nation, Nguyễn Công Hoan paradoxically likened the nation to a house.[7] Trying to effect a similar transformation, his contemporary Vũ Như Làm also relied on domestic idioms, but he appealed more explicitly to the family: every nation, he claimed, takes the family as its base. Conflating the nation and state, he suggested that the Vietnamese should obey the state as they obeyed their fathers and mothers.[8] Conventional Marxists normally reject nationalism and condemn the reactionary image of the family-state, which naturalizes the idea of hierarchy. In Vietnam, however, after the revolution and the Resistance War, as they sang the praises of the Communist Party, "Marxist" historians depicted the nation and the state as extensions of the family. This predilection cannot be traced exclusively to political designs because vernacular speech as well as Sino-Vietnamese make these figures of speech etymologically correct. The vernacular expression for state—*nhà nước*—is based on the word for "house" (*nhà*) and even "spouse." *Nước* means "water." Similarly, embedded in the Sino-Vietnamese term for state (*quốc gia*) is the root for family (*gia*). The language itself, in other words, and not only the gestures of political and intellectual elites, naturalizes hierarchies: the state, like the nation and the family, stems from primordial norms.

In the broadest sense, in this book I am concerned with the rich hybridity of official histories. In the process of unraveling the strands of this hybrid creation, I try to dismantle some of the clichés that have been attached to the history of contemporary Vietnam and to demonstrate how characterizations such as "orthodox," "communist," "Marxist," "Maoist," and "Marxist-Leninist" have obscured the details and texture of postcolonial times. Similarly, I caution against the inclination to see Vietnam as a product of "pro-Chinese" or "pro-Soviet" affinities (with occasional hints of "neutrality") because these guideposts have too often functioned as analytical traps. The culture and politics of postcolonial Vietnam obviously responded to and reflected the limitations of the cold war, but they also exceeded them. Elements of Vietnamese communism that should be traced to Japan, for example, are often linked only to China. We could point out that when Ho Chi Minh lived in Paris he was in contact with Kyo Komatsu, and much of the vocabulary that the Vietnamese appropriated from Chinese sources was based on Japanese translations of German terms. While official historians often spoke in dogmatic and even authoritarian tones, their language was also opaque and coded; even though they were pressured to reach a consensus and to produce a unanimous view of the national past, they contested each other and even revealed the fluidity of their own views.

It has become a commonplace to remark that the Vietnamese shared an extraordinary sense of unity in the period between 1945 and 1975. I am more interested in internal divisions and the kinds of tensions that the history of unity has neglected and suppressed. Writers who point to the "like-mindedness" of the Vietnamese have confounded the difference between normative and descriptive discourse. When official historians spoke of the "tradition of unity against foreign aggression," they did so *prescriptively*: the Vietnamese *should* have been united when they were, in fact, cataclysmically divided.[9] These prescriptions, this pattern of urging, however, have too often been interpreted as mere description. It is also "normal" to assume that the Vietnamese shared a common vision of their collective past. Rather than trace that historical consciousness (if that is what it should be called) to specific circumstances, there is a tendency among historians to describe it in transcendent and even mystical terms. To the extent that there is or was a shared sense of the past, it emerged, I believe, from the didacticism of the 1950s, 1960s, and 1970s, when official historians tried to cultivate it by exploiting the pedagogical power of commemorative texts and events.

The immediate goal of anticolonialism in Vietnam was to get rid of the French. But the vaster process of decolonization—reauthenticating the nation—was as much about China as it was about France. At the same time, decolonization also implied a simultaneous process of recolonization, as the DRV set out to contain the non-Việt parts of Vietnam through education, military service, and massive relocations, often to New Economic Zones. Decolonization has also been based on the denial of the South and the propagation of a Hanoi-centered vision of history. Still, there has never been a monolithic view. Official histories presented conflicted images of authority, variously identifying "the people," the government, the party, or

"Uncle Ho" as the focal point of political allegiance and the object of affective ties.

In writing this book, I have been cognizant of the many paths I might have followed and the number of ways in which postcolonial culture (and especially historical narrative) could be approached. For instance, I rarely go beyond the official texts at the center of my study, even though in some cases they are simply wrong and in others they are grossly misleading. Indeed, these texts are tendentious and combative, and they often skew well-known evidence to satisfy their particular needs—as did the French, the Chinese, and the Americans. The appeal and even necessity of challenging them and offering a corrective is clear, but this is not the project I have in mind. Instead of ascertaining truth, I am more interested in how postcolonial historians responded to the often false and tendentious claims made about Vietnamese.

I could have approached postcolonial historiography by taking a more comprehensive view and analyzing the major works produced by the Research Committee, the Institute of History, the Department of History at the University of Hanoi, as well as the works of individual authors, including Trần Huy Liệu, Minh Tranh, Văn Tân, Đào Duy Anh, Trần Quốc Vượng, Hà Văn Tấn, and Phan Huy Lê. The possibilities of this sort of approach are unlimited, but two come immediately to mind: a comparison based on institutional affiliations (the committee and the institute in contrast to the Department of History) or a more inclusive and diachronic reading focused on issues rather than specific texts or sets of texts. Or, to transcend political and ideological limitations, a reading of postcolonial historiography could and at some point obviously should include, if not focus on, the works of southern historians. Postcolonial culture could also be approached thematically: one could comb through various narratives to see how critical issues arise and how key problems are handled. Again, the possibilities are limitless, but some likely ones are national origins, feudalism, centralized government, relations between majority and minority populations, Nam Tiến (the Southern Advance, or Vietnamese colonialization of what are now the country's central and southern sections), and national reunification.

Although my own approach develops some of these possibilities, its point of departure and general trajectory are not the same. I am most interested in process—the process through which historiographical issues were constituted, how problems of interpretation and narration were resolved, and how

various elements of the national narrative became fixed and conventionalized. To engage this process I focus on the conversation that began in 1954
among historians in the North, specifically those allied with the Research
Committee and the Institute of History. This dialogue, which was published
on a monthly or bimonthly basis, was always aimed in the same direction—
toward a new canonical history of Vietnam—but there were frequent detours and pauses and many occasions when the steps were retraced.[10] Like
the postcolonial project I examine, my own work is also crisscrossed by a
variety of impulses, some easier to define than others, and it draws its inspiration from many sources. In addition to the official histories produced
by the committee and the institute, my research incorporates other kinds
of official literature: government directives, census reports, statistics, poetry
that was officially promoted, civic rituals, ethnographies, and museum displays. This combination of sources may seem indiscriminate, but it has contributed to my sense of how intellectual productions, especially official histories, resonated in a wider social setting. In some cases, in order to gain a
fuller understanding of postcolonial conversations, I juxtapose the sources,
in their heterogeneous splendor, with colonial texts, dynastic histories, or
the work of "reactionary" Vietnamese.

Chapter One | **Constructing History**

The Vietnamese have a rich historiographical tradition that can be traced to the thirteenth century. Court historians during the Trần and Lê dynasties (1225–1788) devoted significant resources to historiographical works. Once a new dynasty claimed the throne, it was obliged to write the history of the previous dynasty and to contribute scholarly works, including biographies of exemplary figures, geographical data, and compilations of folklore, reflective of the new era. Before the French occupation (1862–1945), historians of the Nguyễn dynasty (1802–1945) were extremely prolific. The distinguished scholar Phan Huy Chú composed two renowned works: *Annal of Imperial Orders through the Ages* and *Account of Things Seen Abroad*. By the 1860s, as the French were converting six southern provinces into the colony of Cochinchina, Nguyễn historians had finished more than half of the monumental *Veritable Records of Đại Nam,* which ultimately consisted of over five hundred books. As the French transformed the northern provinces of Vietnam into the protectorate of Tonkin, and as they created the protectorate of Annam out of the central provinces, Nguyễn historians continued working, and in 1890 concluded the final sections. Modeled on earlier historiographical patterns, the *Veritable Records* covered the period of the Nguyễn lords (1558–1777) and the Nguyễn dynasty from its origins in 1802 to the end of Đông Khánh's reign in 1889. Some years earlier, in 1884, Nguyễn historians published *The Comprehensive Mirror of Việt History*. This widely cited chronicle covers the entire pre-Nguyễn span of Vietnamese history, from the prehistoric kingdom of Văn Lang to the collapse of the Lê dynasty. During the reign of the Nguyễn emperor Tự Đức, court historians also completed *The Geography of United Đại Nam.* This gazetteer, which devotes one book to each of twenty-eight provinces, is divided into three sections, each of which represents the major regions: North, Center, and South. Because of its description of provincial resources and historical sites, as well as its attention to demography, this source is invaluable for research on nineteenth-century topics.[1]

Nguyễn scholarship is now considered indispensable, and even during Nguyễn times its importance was clear. And yet, because the Nguyễn emperors presided over Vietnam's loss of independence, postcolonial historians often viewed their accomplishments as compensatory devices that masked a state of disgrace; in other words, there appeared to be no correspondence between the Nguyễn court's intellectual interest in history and its political resignation vis-à-vis the French.

Like the Nguyễn historians, those associated with the occupation forces — including adventurers, administrators, merchants, scholars, and missionaries — were also enormously productive. Far more than their Nguyễn contemporaries, however, colonial authors spoke from a position of power. In addition to the scholars Léonard Aurousseau, Gustave Dumoutier, Maurice Durand, Pierre Huard, and Henri Maspero, a number of writers with missionary backgrounds (Léopold Cadière), commercial interests (Alfred Schreiner), or in military positions (Charles Gosselin) also presumed to speak authoritatively about the Vietnamese past. Institutions such as the French School of the Far East (École française d'Extrême-Orient) issued innumerable works that because of their distinguished imprimateur enjoyed quasi-official status.

Finally, a number of Vietnamese who allied themselves with the occupation also published extensively. Although some of these writers can be linked to specific institutions, such as schools, others were associated with journals or publishing houses in Hanoi, Haiphong, Hue, or Saigon. These writers probably had the greatest impact on how the Vietnamese thought about — or were supposed to think about — the past. In the 1870s, for example, the Catholic convert Trương Vĩnh Ký (a.k.a. Petrus Jean-Baptiste), a man characterized by postcolonial writers as the "exemplary lackey," published (in French) a two-volume history of Vietnam.[2] Colonial administrators promoted the use of his work in public schools, first in the colony of Cochinchina, then in the protectorates of Annam and Tonkin. Trương Vĩnh Ký's quasi-canonical status was further enhanced by colonial scholars who based much of their own research on what he had already written. Decades later, new pedagogical texts, such as those written by Trần Văn

Thược, Ngô Văn Minh, and Dương Quảng Hàm, were widely circulated in colonial schools.[3] In addition to viewing the occupation in a favorable light, some of these writers even thanked the French for having sparked their own interest in the history of Vietnam. In his preface to *Lessons in the History of Annam*, which was adopted by the Textbook Commission in 1930, high school teacher Dương Quảng Hàm declared:

> No one doubts the educational value of instruction in history, and national history must be considered among the most important of subjects taught in primary school. *This pedagogical truth, so evident all on its own, was nevertheless unknown to Annamites before the arrival of the French.* In the traditional Annamite curriculum, in fact, pupils only studied the Chinese chronicles: the history of Annam was not mentioned, neither in the program of study nor in the meetings at which the various programs were determined.[4]

For postcolonial writers, Dương Quảng Hàm's declaration was disturbing because of its essential truth. In precolonial times, the Vietnamese did indeed equate historical literacy to a knowledge of Chinese texts: the *Five Classics,* the *Four Books,* and chronicles of the Han, Tang, Song, Ming, and Qing dynasties. During the French occupation, when popular narratives of Vietnamese history were composed, the most influential ones were written by Trần Trọng Kim, whom postcolonial writers condemned as "feudal," "colonial," "petit bourgeois," "reactionary," "antinational," and "ahistorical," and Phạm Quỳnh, for whom they reserved still greater contempt.

In sum, one can justifiably state that during the French colonial period, histories of Vietnam were issued from three principal arenas: the Nguyễn court, the occupation forces, and Vietnamese who basically accepted the colonial mission. The published works of the latter group were often in French. After Vietnam's declaration of independence in 1945 and, more spectacularly, after 1954, historians in the DRV continued on the Việt-centric (as opposed to Sino-centric) path promoted by their "reactionary" predecessors. Similarly, they also sought to disseminate a basic understanding of the national past among "the people." To construct new interpretations, postcolonial writers relied on new kinds of evidence, used familiar data in unfamiliar ways, and approached the past according to new paradigms, even though traditional motifs often reemerged. Refining the techniques of their colonial predecessors, they also saturated public life with depictions of canonical figures and fragments of official narratives. Because the attempt to "build" or "construct" history (*xây dựng lịch sử*) constituted a key component of postcolonial recovery, this chapter examines how historians in the DRV gave voice to new visions of the past.

HISTORY AND THE PEOPLE, HISTORY AND THE STATE

In December 1953, with the Viet Minh victory over France nearly assured, the Communist Party's Central Committee issued a decree that formally established the Research Committee. Within this committee were three separate groups, one for each of the disciplinary divisions: history, geography, and literature. To historians appointed to the Research Committee—most of whom were still in the combat zone of Viet Bac—fell the task of composing a new general history of Vietnam. In June 1954, having returned to Hanoi, they began to publish the first issues of the *Journal of Literary Historical and Geographical Research*. In this journal, which appeared every month or so (until 1959), postcolonial scholars advanced tentative and experimental versions of "new history" (*lịch sử mới*). When the Research Committee was reorganized as the Institute of History (Viện Sử học) in 1959, official historians debated evidence, methods, and models in a new forum, the *Journal of Historical Research.*[5] Many of the scholars at the Institute of History had been affiliated with the original Research Committee, and they continued to work on its assignment: to compose a new, general history of Vietnam.

It should be noted here that committee and institute historians did not monopolize historical discourse. Historians in the Department of History at the University of Hanoi, the textbook division of the Ministry of Education, the Committee for Party History, the Museum of History, the Museum of the Revolution, the Ministry of Culture, and so forth all published extensively on a wide range of topics. And yet, even though a great number of scholars devoted themselves to the task of constructing history in the aftermath of colonial rule, because of their direct (or occasionally indirect) link to the party, the work of committee and institute historians was more clearly accorded canonical status. For this reason, they also played an essential role in establishing a new collective memory of the past; more critically, their research provided the foundation for new rituals of state.

At any given moment, the mechanisms of state involvement in historiographical projects were more or less opaque, and they also varied over time. Nevertheless, certain dynamics are clear. When the Central Commit-

tee founded the Research Committee in 1953, official historians were supposed to answer directly to the party. Committee historians acknowledged
this hierarchy in a number of ways. Trần Huy Liệu, the leading figure in
the postcolonial historiographical project, summarized the relationship this
way: "The Research Committee, belonging to the Central Committee, has
the good fortune to be guided, criticized, and assisted in essential ways by
the Central Committee." Expressing a positive view of this arrangement, he
used the form of the passive voice (được) that suggests good fortune (as
opposed to bị, which hints at misfortune). Historians also addressed their
self-criticisms to the Central Committee.[6] In a curious aside that alludes to
a more open conception of historical work, Trần Huy Liệu also mentioned
that the Research Committee consisted of historians who were members of
the Labor Party and of nonparty members as well. At the same time, however, that he tried to minimize the party's control over intellectual life, he
also noted that the composition of the Research Committee was itself a result of a Central Committee decree.[7] At the end of 1956, when the Research
Committee was redefined as a part of the government (the Ministry of Education to be precise), a similar strategy seemed to be in place because the
political structure of the DRV was doubled. Next to, and ultimately above,
the institutions of government were the institutions of the party (identified
in more recent sources as the state). Thus, as the party appeared to loosen
its grip over historiographical production in 1956, it actually maintained it,
but through a different bureaucratic web. Control over the Research Committee, which was never really removed from the party, officially reverted to
it in 1958, just as plans were announced to dissolve the Research Committee
and create in its place a number of successor institutes. At this point, the
new Institute of History was classified as a component of the State Committee for Science and Technology, which was redefined in the following year
as the State Science Committee.

Although the Institute of History has functioned continuously since 1959,
the wider institutional context has been revised a number of times: subsequent restructurations resulted in the Institute of Social Sciences in 1965,
the Committee for Social Sciences in 1967, and the Academy of Sciences
in later years.[8] Whether they were institutionally linked to the government
as opposed to the party, most committee and institute historians viewed
themselves as faithful executors of the state's will. Year after year, they compiled month-by-month progress reports that they forwarded to the Central
Committee, directly or indirectly (through the Ministry of Education), de-

pending on the institutional structure in place at that point. Underscoring their proximity and obligations to the center of state power, committee and institute historians often lauded the "wise leadership" of the government, the party, and Chairman Ho Chi Minh. Other historians, Phan Khôi most notably, claimed greater autonomy for themselves and played more adversarial roles.

Overall, though, the state-centered ethos of the Research Committee was evident in the many connections it had to other state institutions, both domestic and foreign. A survey of its activities in 1955, for example, reveals collaborative projects with the Ministry of the Interior, Ministry of Foreign Affairs, Office of Foreign News and Propaganda, the Association of Vietnamese Writers and Artists, and Teachers for Popular Education.[9] In 1959 and 1960, while they prepared to commemorate the 950th anniversary of the founding of the national capital at Hanoi, institute historians worked with the city's Administrative Council and the Ministry of Culture.[10] The journals published by the committee and the institute were peppered with excerpts from official decrees, accounts of national gatherings, and references to annual reports submitted to the government or party. Moreover, the specific projects to which committee and institute historians devoted their attention were not determined by the historians themselves; instead, triennial (in 1958) and quinquennial (beginning in 1961) plans established the research agendas, which were also subject to revision by party and government decree. Committee and institute historians attended study retreats at state-sponsored regional schools (khu học xá trung ương). At national congresses, Trần Huy Liệu and other luminaries were advised how to organize their research and urged to stress particular themes. At the congress held in 1955, for example, historians were formally instructed to emphasize "the fighting spirit" of the Vietnamese.[11]

Committee historians, responding to official cues, initially rejected what they viewed as the elitism of dynastic texts and proposed in their place more populist and inclusive renditions of the past. And yet, like the court historians of earlier times, committee historians tried to construct histories that promoted the interests of the state. Although the "new" historians in many ways shared the state-centered vision of their dynastic predecessors, they tended to present the state as a popular entity: thus, they reasoned, in serving the state they necessarily served the people. While they reaffirmed the pedagogical importance of their work, they also remarked that their reports, when issued in a timely manner, enabled the state to set plans for production. Their research confirmed the correctness of the revolutionary path by proving the legitimacy of the "historical laws" on which government and party policies were based. Or, it contributed to the establishment of a "new ideology" and a "new culture," and thus, by demonstrating the great fortitude of the nation, it encouraged the people to think and behave in more nationalistic ways.[12] Moreover, history was essential to warfare: it was a "weapon" (*vũ khí*), it elucidated the "laws of combat" (*qui luật tác chiến*), and it clarified the "principles of revolution" (*nguyên tắc cách mạng*). At the fourteenth conference of the Executive Committee of the party's Central Committee (held in 1959), the "grave responsibilities" of historians were reaffirmed: in addition to contributing to socialist education by producing, in the long term, a new national history, they would, in the short term, also participate in the struggle to reunify the land. Transformed into warriors and stationed on the cultural front, historians launched against the enemy innumerable assaults.[13] In a rousing statement, Trần Huy Liệu declared:

> History is a combative work, always active; it is not reserved for elderly people who, having ceased being active, sit at home doing research; historian cadres must not sit in the "ivory tower," or, more correctly, shut inside a room of the library to do research; they must dive into each area of social life in order to live, to discover things; they must not live only with the history of the past, they need to live right in the middle of the history of the present; they must not only write history, but contribute to its construction.[14]

While committee and institute historians conducted their research according to the demands of the party, and as they set out to reconstruct the canon, they were supposed to transform the manner in which canonical knowledge was formed. Specifically, historians were supposed to transcend the "solitary habits" (*thái độ cô độc*) of scholars and instead develop a more collective spirit.[15] At the center of postcolonial historiography was the committee or the institute, structures that in their very nature challenged bourgeois notions of authorship and ownership. The majority of articles published in the *Journal of Literary, Historical, and Geographical Research* and in the *Journal of Historical Research* were signed by specific authors, but the editorials were generally not. Moreover, hundreds of monographs and translations were attributed not to individuals but to collectivities such as the committee or the institute or to groups of scholars. Collective authorship was sometimes akin to anonymous authorship, and it also functioned as a consensus-making device.

Official historians developed additional strategies that underscored the collective and ultimately consensual as opposed to independent nature of historical research. By regularly including the insights of historians who operated outside the committee and the institute and of readers who lacked professional training, they transformed historiographical debate into a broadly inclusive adventure. At its inception, for example, the Research Committee began its own extensive debate about historical periodization by conducting a survey: How did Vietnamese from a wide range of backgrounds understand the divisions and general trajectory of the past? Trần Huy Liệu concluded an article on the cultural and political life of the 1920s by appealing directly to his readers: "These are only opinions I write in a letter. These issues still must be investigated further. I want to hear your ideas."[16] Committee historians never indicated precisely how many responses they received or their criteria for deciding which ones to publish. On one occasion, however, Trần Huy Liệu noted that they favored the contributions of those who disagreed with arguments that had already been expressed. In any case, from 1954 to 1959 the *Journal of Literary, Historical, and Geographical Research* published nearly one hundred letters from more than seventy writers.

When the Institute of History was established in 1959, the editorial board of its journal described the task of "constructing" history as the "common work of the people."[17] To this end, institute historians continued the committee's efforts to cultivate a personal rapport with readers. They encouraged readers to respond to the material published in the journal and to suggest new possibilities for historical research and method. Some of the most striking results of this approach appeared in a report on a poll of over one hundred readers. Because the respondents came from different groups (*tập đoàn*) and collectives (*tập thể*), the institute regarded them as representative of what it estimated to be thousands of readers. Expressing the journal's vital role in their daily lives, readers likened it to "food" (*món ăn*), "spiritual sustenance" (*món ăn tinh thần*), "tonic" (*thứ thuốc bổ máu*), and "necessity" (*nhu cầu*). For others, the journal functioned as a "teacher" (*người thầy*). Depicting the bond between journal and reader in more affective terms, one respondent replied: "Each month I wait for [the journal] as I wait for Mother to return from the market."[18] No doubt, the historiographer's office of dynastic times never received such praise; nor did it seek it.

This broader, more collective vision of history was realized, in part, through the cultivation of "historian cadres" (*cán bộ sử học*) — those with working-class backgrounds who received historical training while they continued their regular work. The genesis of this program is unclear because it was first mentioned only in passing. In the mid-1950s, Nguyễn Lương Bích, one of the institute's more prominent figures, translated excerpts from a Russian-language speech delivered in 1950 to Chinese academics. On this occasion, Soviet historian Kisselev discussed how historian cadres were trained in the Soviet Union.[19] Years later Vietnamese historians begin to address this topic in their own (pseudonymous) voices. Trần Huy Liệu, writing under the pen name of Hải Khách, presented one of the first descriptions of how historical cadres could be trained. To underscore the importance of this effort, he emphasized that historiographical work depended on the "collective strength" of the people.[20] As official historians contemplated the role of historian cadres, they also began to explore the possibilities of branch histories (*lịch sử của các ngành*) and local histories (*lịch sử của các địa phương*); soon they cast the historiographical net more widely still to include factories and mines.[21]

Historians from the institute tended to present these initiatives as evidence of an intellectual and political commitment to popular (rather than elite) conceptions of the past. This impression seems partially justified, at least as far as sources are concerned. As Trần Huy Liệu once noted, the years of colonial occupation and numerous wars had destroyed traditional kinds of documents and artifacts. Therefore, less conventional sources, such as family records (*gia phả*), lineage records (*tộc phả*), village records (*hương phả*), and poems and folktales as well would become the "bricks and stones" for "constructing" national history.[22] Historian cadres, one gathers, were simply to uncover local and personal archives and transmit them to a more official arena. It was also clear that local experiences were supposed to mesh with a broader, supra-local agenda, and thus they needed to be managed and shaped. Local histories, especially provincial ones, would dwell on local ties to the Viet Minh Front, local struggles that nurtured the revolutionary uprising of August 1945, and local devotion to the right side in the Resistance War. To capture, and in the process create, this new sense of how local histories converged with national ones, cadres in provinces such as Hà Đông were "mobilized" (*động viên*) to write personal memoirs. Similarly, histories of local communist cells (*chi bộ*) were incorporated into a more monolithic history of the party. But this process was uneven. Having criticized the "guerrilla" (*du kích*) methods of historian cadres, historians at the institute searched for new ways to broaden the historiographical mission. To ensure that local experiences intersected with new visions of the national past, the Local History Unit (Tổ lịch sử địa phương) was established in 1962. To support the work of the unit, historical associations (*hội*) were also formed.[23]

By aiming for consensus, new institutions and new habits undermined colonial and bourgeois ideas of authorship. Rather than emphasize the contrary claims of individual authors, and rather than present divergent views of the past as an intrinsic part of the historiographical process, collective authorship tended to bury the disagreements and to "recover" the past as a mute and static entity, an object, a block. This was most notably the case with the two-volume *History of Vietnam*.[24] In a more subtle way, the quest for a smooth and seamless narrative also suppressed conflicts in historical analysis and interpretation. In other words, discussion, disagreement, and debate were essential—but only *preliminary*—parts of the historiographical process. Rather than approach the past as a collection of potentially discordant voices, official narratives were supposed to harmonize them. Historical writing was no longer limited to the cloistered few; instead, it was a public enterprise whose political and social consequences were vast.

The academic conference may have a generic ring and appear as an entirely unremarkable part of scholarly life, but in postcolonial Vietnam it played a distinctive role. Consequently, the nomenclature of academic exchanges was highly refined. While the preliminary stages of research and investigation developed in "roundtables" (*tọa đàm*), "debates" (*thảo luận*), and "meetings" (*cuộc họp*), the final—that is, conclusive—stages were formalized in "conferences" (*hội nghị*) and "symposia" (*hội nghị thảo luận*). Because they marked the initial phases of historical investigation, the debates and discussions were often open-ended and sometimes extended over a period of months or even years. Some of them pinpointed specific historical problems, such as national origins, the status of Vietnamese literature written in Chinese, the slave mode of production, or the emergence of the Vietnamese working class.[25] Other debates and discussions focused on specific historical figures, such as Hồ Quý Ly, Nguyễn Trường Tộ, Phan Thanh Giản, Trương Vĩnh Ký, Phan Chu Trinh, Phan Bội Châu, or Lưu Vĩnh Phúc.[26] Despite the varied circumstances in which they emerged and the great heterogeneity in their historical roles, these figures had one thing in common: they were ambiguous and could not be characterized with ease. In traditional and postcolonial sources, for example, Hồ Quý Ly suffered the ignoble appellation of "usurper." For having displaced the legitimate Trần emperor in the early fifteenth century, he was typically blamed for the disastrous invasion of the Ming. At the same time, however, postcolonial historians (but not their precolonial progenitors or "reactionary" rivals) also viewed him as a visionary whose notions of politics were much in advance of his time. Depending on the issue at hand, debates and discussions sometimes culminated in more formal sessions—conferences—at which each of the participants enunciated his view and, by adducing pertinent data, attempted to convince others of its merit. On these occasions, the expectation was that the issue would be definitively resolved when one side finally succeeded in "knocking out" the other.[27] Conferences also were supposed to conclude the broader questions that had been raised in debates and discussions. One such conference, held in January 1961, surveyed the accomplishments of official historians and their research program for the coming years; the topics of other conferences included local, branch, and industry histories and historical methodology.

In one of a series of lectures that he delivered at Cornell University in fall 1983, archaeologist and poet Phạm Huy Thông was asked by Southeast Asianist Oliver Wolters why Vietnamese historians attended so many conferences. Phạm Huy Thông responded by explaining that shortages of paper prevented the publication and circulation of important research: because they could not discuss their work in print, scholars presented their research at conferences. This explanation is certainly corroborated by references to the rationing of paper in both the *Journal of Literary, Historical, and Geographical Research* and the *Journal of Historical Research*. In fact, the shortage of paper became so severe that in 1960 the Institute of History held a conference in order to assess its lack.[28] This claim is further confirmed by the state's emphasis on building pulp mills to increase supplies of paper.

But it would be a mistake, I believe, to appreciate the significance of the debates, discussions, conferences, and symposia in purely logistical or material terms. First, the presence of leading political and military figures such as Pham Van Dong and Vo Nguyen Giap made clear the state's role in monitoring historiographical work.[29] Second, committee and institute historians were not only allowed to debate certain issues; they were *obliged* to do so because the debates served as critical steps in the process of creating unanimous views: having articulated the differences in their interpretations of the national past, historians were also supposed to reconcile them. This search for unanimity was expressed in a wide range of contexts. For example, in a preface to an article on historical periodization written by Nguyễn Đổng Chi, the journal's editorial board remarked: "We should look at all of the various perspectives, but we should decide issues definitively."[30] Similarly, Minh Tranh observed that despite the volumes on Vietnamese history the question of slavery still had not been decided; "Now," he declared, "we must settle it once and for all" (dứt khoát).[31] Trần Huy Liệu shared Minh Tranh's sense that historians should quickly resolve the question of slavery; moreover, he urged them to settle as well the problem of hero worship and the cult of personality.[32] Trần Minh Thư insisted on the necessity of reaching a unanimous view of Phan Chu Trinh and the Tonkin Free School.[33]

By emphasizing historians' stress on unanimity, I do not mean to suggest that they always "achieved" it. In fact, on those occasions when they were supposed to announce their unanimous views, with their decisions reached "once and for all," historians often confessed their "failure" to have done so. Minh Tranh, for instance, mentioned that history professors had attended two study retreats in July 1954 to "unify their views" on historical periodization; but because a consensus had eluded them, they decided to continue the debate.[34] But the *quest* for consensus, whether or not it was actually reached, depended on the suppression of individual differences and the production of a synthetic view. Thus, even though the great number of conferences may have been linked to the shortage of paper, the logistical details should not obscure the basic assumptions that governed postcolonial productions: historical research, like historical narrative, had a beginning, a middle, and an end. While disagreements inevitably arose, just as inevitably they were resolved. Differences of opinion could be animating in the beginning because they led to the discernment of historical truth. And at that moment the differences dissolved. These examples attest to the ways in which the idea of authorship was broadened in the postcolonial DRV; they also illuminate the simultaneous push toward homogeneity.

HISTORY AS DIALOGUE

Dynastic Histories

Because "new history" set out to strip away the privileged status of the existing canon, the issues of interlocutors and intertextual dimensions are essential. When the Research Committee was established in 1953, committee historians condemned, as a matter of course, the elitism of dynastic texts: "History," they declared, "must focus on those who produce, not on mandarins and kings."[35] Some writers, including Phan Khôi, took an even harsher view of traditional sources, asserting that because they merely chronicled dynastic concerns they were "no longer of any use."[36] If initially there was an inclination to devalue dynastic sources, that tendency soon subsided, and within a short while official historians began to reimagine them in the most fantastic way. Instead of hallmarks of elitism and hierarchy—or signs, one might add, of Vietnam's cultural indebtedness to China—dynastic histories were reinterpreted as the textual equivalents of the One-Pillared Pagoda (Chùa Một cột): just as this pagoda architecturally expressed the uniqueness and genius of the Vietnamese, so, too, the dynastic histories communicated what was truly authentic.[37]

In 1958, just as the Research Committee was being reorganized into separate institutes of history and literature, Minh Tranh made absolutely clear the shift in the status of dynastic texts: no longer "feudal remnants" that should be destroyed, dynastic sources now figured as venerable traces of a heroic past.[38] On this same occasion, Minh Tranh also editorialized about the need for postcolonial writers to specialize in terms both of period and theme, and he identified Phan Gia Bền's work on the development of handicrafts, Nguyễn Công Bình's detailed analysis of how the Vietnamese bourgeoisie was formed, and Trần Văn Giàu's study of the Vietnamese working class as exemplars of this more focused approach to the past. Remarkably, and evidently without a hint of irony, Minh Tranh attributed the possibility, and necessity, even, of such specialized works to the fact that excellent general histories had already been written, and he specifically cited Lê Văn Hưu's *History of Đại Việt* from the thirteenth century and Ngô Sĩ Liên's *Complete History of Đại Việt* from the fifteenth.[39] In other words, although postcolonial writers initially distanced themselves from their "feudal" predecessors, they gradually sought to establish a new chain of succession that would directly link them together. Instead of insisting on a rupture with the dynastic past, they reinterpreted Lê Văn Hưu and Ngô Sĩ Liên as ancestors to be revered and repositioned themselves as grateful heirs. To celebrate "seven hundred years of historiographical tradition," to honor Lê Văn Hưu as the first historian of Vietnam, and to abide by a government and party decree, institute historians announced a spate of commemorative events.[40] This intellectual lineage is striking in a number of ways, but most dramatically because the work written by Lê Văn Hưu covered what in the thirteenth century counted as the whole of Vietnamese history: from the reign of Triệu Đà, beginning in 208 B.C.E., to the end of the Lý dynasty in 1225.[41] Ultimately, of course, historians at the institute managed to trace the origins of Vietnam not to the third century but to the third *millennium* B.C.E.

The commemorative attention devoted to Lê Văn Hưu may at first appear anomalous — other historians, after all, were not similarly feted; but because it reflects a new intellectual and even emotional attachment to traditional artifacts, it is part of a bigger pattern. Even before the commemorative event formally rehabilitated "feudal" scholars, postcolonial historians had already begun to cite their work as transparent and authoritative sources of essential data. Most often they relied on the Lê chronicle and the Nguyễn history written during the reign of Tự Đức, but they included other sources as well. To substantiate his astonishing claim that the Vietnamese nation (*dân tộc Việt Nam*) was first formed in the eighteenth century, Trần Huy Liệu adduced evidence from the Nguyễn gazetteer; in a commemorative piece on the Hùng kings, he turned to earlier sources that predated the work of Lê Văn Hưu.[42] When Lâm Hà studied feudal landholding patterns, he cited a wide range of traditional texts.[43] For his research on the origins of primogeniture, Nguyễn Đổng Chi drew material from Chu Cát Thi's eighteenth-century revision of a fourteenth-century text; for his work on the Tây Sơn uprising, he consulted the Lê dynasty gazetteer in addition to the Nguyễn chronicle.[44]

The point of these details is to confirm that even though the traditional texts were initially stigmatized they soon emerged as indispensable materials for "constructing" or "building" a new history of the nation. In recognition of this fact, institute historians dedicated themselves to the task of transmitting the sources, which originally had been redacted in Chinese or in the demotic script known as *nôm,* to a new generation of Vietnamese whose familiarity with the earlier scripts could not be assumed. On the contrary, *quốc ngữ,* the romanized version of Vietnamese, had become the most widely known script. Relying on scholars with the necessary expertise, they were able to make foundational texts accessible again. Beginning with their vaunted forebear Phan Bội Châu, who was active in the early twentieth century, translators moved to the fifteenth-century works of Nguyễn Trãi. Next came translations of the works of the prolific Lê Quý Đôn, the Lê official whose *Frontier Chronicles* provides a unique glimpse of southern Vietnam in the late eighteenth century. More surprising in a political sense, the institute also supervised the translation of Nguyễn dynasty sources.[45]

One assumes that the inclination to restore and perpetuate the connections between "new history" and the traditional texts responded, first of all, to practical concerns: simply, it was not possible to write Vietnamese history without them. But the translations registered in a more symbolic sense as well. Reviewing the circumstances in which the Research Committee was first established, Minh Tranh remarked that "some people" (whom he did not identify) had been skeptical about devoting so many resources to the historiography of Vietnam.[46] Knowledgeable as they were about the great epic histories of the ancient Greeks and Romans, as well as familiar with the history of France, he explained, these people viewed the prospect of a journal focused entirely on the history of Vietnam with extreme skepticism: "What was there in Vietnamese history," they asked, "that one could investigate at length?" In a few brief publications, they believed, all that could be said would have been said. In this way, by taking stock of Vietnam's historiographical canon and in making it intelligible to new generations of Vietnamese, postcolonial historians undermined the received impression that their national history was insignificant and mean. In its range and richness of detail, the traditional canon attested to the splendor of the national past. At the same time, for scholars determined to desinicize the past, the translation of dynastic texts into romanized Vietnamese reinforced the rupture: twentieth-century Vietnamese could engage the historiographical past even if they lacked the traditional tools.[47]

Finally, the act of translating the classics into modern Vietnamese also provided postcolonial historians with the chance to control the meaning of the past. For this reason, I assume, Nguyễn sources were among the first to be reproduced in *quốc ngữ*. These sources narrated the national past from a southern perspective: they emphasized the autonomy of the Nguyễn lords, their authority to both initiate and execute policy, and their brilliance in annexing and settling lands that were once inhabited by the Cham and Khmer. In celebrating the wit and cunning of Nguyễn Hoàng, who figured so seminally in the history of the South, southern sources reduced the Lê court in Thăng Long (Hanoi) to a distant entity whose power had been eclipsed by members of the Trịnh family. For historians with the committee and the institute, who were obliged to construct a national history that emanated from and revolved around Hanoi, such interpretations, with their claims and suggestions of southern autonomy, had to be carefully managed. As evidence of this impulse to control, one could refer to the publication of an excerpt from Phan Huy Chú's *Annal of Imperial Orders*.[48] To prevent a "misinterpretation" of the Nguyễn text, the extract was introduced by the editorial board, which urged readers to examine the chronicle "from the perspective of new history" (*quan điểm sử học mới*). This perspective, it was hoped, would allow readers to regard the text in a more critical spirit. To set readers on the right path, the board asked them to look in particular at Phan Huy Chú's representation of Lê dynasty landholding patterns and his description of fifteenth- and sixteenth-century social patterns. Readers understood, of course, that they were to believe that Phan Huy Chú had misconstrued the evidence and that, basing his argument on this misapprehension, he had wrongly attributed the momentum for the Southern Advance (Nam Tiến) to the Nguyễn lords. In committing this error, readers were to understand, Phan Huy Chú had occluded the more essential contributions of the Lê court in Hanoi. In addition to making important texts accessible to readers more at ease with *quốc ngữ* than with Chinese ideograms or *nôm,* the translations allowed committee historians to critique pro-Nguyễn (i.e., southern) points of view.

Colonial Interlocutors
In a historiographical tradition lasting more than seven hundred years, the near-century of colonial scholarship might have mattered little. But the pervasiveness of colonial texts — the extent to which they circulated within Vietnam and internationally as well — far surpassed the limited reach of traditional works. And, despite the brevity of colonial rule, the impact of these texts was enormous. For example, they fostered the idea that Vietnamese civilization was derivative and that, although they sought to replicate Chinese patterns, the Vietnamese had managed to produce only a poor copy. Inevitably, colonial writers reasoned, Vietnamese existed in a self-alienated state. Through the peculiar looking glass that is part of imperial domination, the French appeared to themselves as a salvational force. Only in becoming subjects of France, they insisted, could the Vietnamese be restored to themselves. Thus, in reciting mantras such as "our ancestors the Gauls" (*nos ancêtres les Gaulois*) and in shifting their emotional ties to Mother France, the Vietnamese could defend themselves against what the French perceived as China's inauthenticating and alienating lure.

It is not surprising, therefore, that immediately following the defeat of the French at Dien Bien Phu, the most renowned scholars were often the object of particular scorn. While colonial scholars had insisted on the derivative status of Vietnam's culture, postcolonial historians interpreted the artifacts unearthed in sites such as Cổ Nhuế as signs of its generative power. Rejecting the colonial impression that Vietnamese civilization had developed on the basis of imported technologies, the distinguished scholar Đào Duy Anh, for one, railed against Louis Finot and Victor Goloubew, archaeologists who had attributed Vietnam's bronze-age culture to the Han Chinese. Arguing against the diffusionists, he pointed to the instrumentality of what he assumed were the indigenous Việt. Similarly, Văn Tân criticized the archaeologists—he identified Léonard Aurousseau and E. Chavannes as the "chief culprits"—who, from his perspective, had misrepresented the prehistoric past, arguing that they had done so in order to promote the occupation. Commenting on the archaeologists' deceit, Nguyễn Lương Bích urged his contemporaries to criticize colonial sources rather than "worship" them. In each of these cases the issue is clear: postcolonial writers blamed colonial writers for having sinified their national past. To sustain this critique of French scholarship, they had to marginalize the aspects of Vietnamese history that substantiated the colonial view: for example, the role of Confucian theory and practice, the importance of Chinese historiography to the dynastic histories of Vietnam, and many dimensions of the literary canon. Trần Huy Liệu pointed in an opprobrious way to the volumes by Charles Robequain and Pierre Gourou.[49] In more collective and institutional terms, committee and institute historians imagined the French School of the Far East and the journal it produced as their most obvious interlocutors, not only because the journal had so influenced Western representations of Vietnam, but because it had also caused many Vietnamese to misinterpret their past. Similarly, committee and institute historians also struggled against the Association for the Intellectual and Moral Formation of Annamites, the brainchild of Phạm Quỳnh, and what they regarded as its vulgar collaborationist stance.

Despite the vituperation against the colonial agendas overall and against specific scholars, the colonial corpus was essential. Postcolonial scholars who worked on late-nineteenth and early-twentieth-century history, especially those who specialized in economic topics, found colonial sources impossible to avoid, and in these cases they tended to invoke them unpolemically. Trần Huy Liệu's objections not withstanding, the work of Charles Robequain and Pierre Gourou was particularly open to this more documentary appropriation. In their research on the Vietnamese working class, for instance, Văn Tạo and Đặng Việt Thanh relied extensively on Robequain's data; when Lê Xuân Phương theorized about the environmental determinants of social life, he, too, turned to Robequain and Gourou for "scientific" assessments of Vietnam's demography, geography, and climate. In his survey of the Vietnamese bourgeoisie, Nguyễn Công Bình consulted the work of Henri Bouchot and André Masson. While most topics in economic history concerned developments in the nineteenth and twentieth centuries, earlier periods were also discussed. For his research on seventeenth-century trade, for instance, Thành Thế Vỹ found the work of Pierre Huard indispensable. In conducting research on the Haiphong-Kunming railway, Phan Gia Bền and Nguyễn Khắc Đạm relied extensively on the works of Gaston Dupouy and Paul Ducret. Likewise, for such diverse topics as the effects of French capitalism in Vietnam or landholding patterns during feudal times, colonial journals (*Agricultural Economy, Indochinese Review,* and *Economic Bulletin of Indochina*), colonial reports on navigation and commerce, and publications from the Ministry of Colonies were essential.[50]

Contemporary Interlocutors

Until 1959, official historians condemned the political repugnance — meaning the elitism and exclusiveness — of traditional sources; after that they dwelled more on the chronicles' cultural and intellectual worth. Although postcolonial scholars viewed colonial sources with loathing, they also relied on them extensively owing to their wealth of statistical data. Toward their contemporaries and immediate predecessors who had allied with the French, promoted nonrevolutionary modes of decolonization, or supported the RVN, postcolonial historians took an invariably critical stance.

But even toward their allies — those who had fought against the French on behalf of the revolution — their attitude was often polemical. To prevent France from reconquering its former territories in the aftermath of World War II, the revolutionaries had united in common cause. Following their dramatic victory at Dien Bien Phu, however, they increasingly struggled among themselves to redefine the past and to interpret the recent history that all of them shared. In addition to celebrating the revolution's success, it was essential to define it, to sort out precisely how it had come about, and to determine what exactly it had altered. Because conflicting views about how to represent the revolution signaled new kinds of conflict in the present, the attempt to establish its origins, its trajectory, and its overall meaning was not just for the record. This effort was imbued with great social and political import. Similarly, the question of how to present the history of the Indochinese Communist Party, the Viet Minh, and the Lao Dong Party was also laden with conflict. Moreover, not only recent history but the most remote reaches of prehistory were also the focus of bitter disputes. As postcolonial historians gained the power to narrate the past, they disagreed among themselves about how such narratives should be structured. How could the past, they asked, best be broken down into meaningful parts? After the military conflict subsided, after the French were defeated and the agreements were signed, intellectual and cultural conflicts like these moved to the fore. Historiographical battles mattered. The interpretation of folklore, the identification of national heroes, claims about historical geography—in short, virtually anything that could be uttered about the past was open to contestation.

Relations between historians in Hanoi and their southern counterparts, whom they labeled "bourgeois," were also complex and not merely hostile. In spite of the political rift between the DRV and the RVN, despite the vitriol leveled against Ngo Dinh Diem and his "lackey collaborators," committee and institute historians on occasion also tried to establish closer ties to scholars in the South. In July 1958, the Research Committee sent a letter to the Textbook Preparation Center in Saigon. "Friends," the letter begins, "Allow us to introduce ourselves. We are the Research Committee established in 1953. Our responsibility is to study the development of Vietnamese literature and to bring the national genius and consciousness into play." Once the committee was formed, the letter explains, historians first turned their attention to modern Vietnamese history and then to national history from its origins to contemporary times "so that all could clearly see the nation's glorious past . . . , the greatness of the ancestral land [tổ quốc], and the heroism of the people." As for Vietnam's "beautiful landscapes," the letter explains, the committee sought to introduce them to readers so that their love of country would deepen.[51]

This letter is surprising in a number of ways, not least because the usual epithets have been completely suppressed. Instead, the tone is friendly but formal, and the rhetorical flourishes—references to "rotten imperialists" and "southern thugs"—have completely vanished. Having whitewashed, eviscerated, and generally defanged cultural life in the DRV—there were no references to Marx, Lenin, Stalin, Ho Chi Minh, or Mao and no references to socialism or communism—the letter focuses on what the committee imagines to be the shared experience of historians North and South. Because the country was "temporarily divided," they noted, historians in the North could not conduct research on southern patriots such as Trương Công Định,

Đỗ Trình Thoại, and Hồ Huấn Nghiệp; they had no materials for studies of Nguyễn Đình Chiểu, Huỳnh Mẫn Đạt, Bùi Hữu Nghĩa, and other southern writers. Similarly, historians in the South, they suspected, lacked sources for Đề Thám, the Scholar Movement, and the Tonkin Free School; they probably had few documents on Hồ Xuân Hương, Nguyễn Khuyến, and Trần Tế Xương. Five years later, the other notable exception to the break in intellectual ties occurred when Văn Tân in Hanoi and Nguyễn Phương in Saigon debated the origins of national reunification. Whereas the mood in the earlier letter had been conciliatory and restrained, the participants in this discussion adopted a combative and vituperative tone.[52]

As they struggled with and against their contemporaries to define the trajectory and meaning of the national past, postcolonial writers also returned to earlier disagreements that had first taken shape in the 1920s, developed further in the 1930s and 1940s, only to be submerged during the Japanese occupation (1940–1945) and the Resistance War (1946–1954). Historians from the committee and the institute were animated, at least in part, by issues that had arisen earlier in journals such as *Indochinese Review, Modern Learning, Women's News,* and, above all, *Southern Review.*[53] From the wide array of recent predecessors and near-contemporaries, two figures in particular stood out: Phạm Quỳnh, editor of *Southern Review* who was assassinated by the Viet Minh in August 1945, and Trần Trọng Kim (1887–1953), historian and administrator for both the French and the Japanese.

Postcolonial historians were often polemical, even with their political and intellectual allies, and they treated their political and intellectual foes severely. In a context in which conflict and acrimony often erupted, the bile aimed at Trần Trọng Kim and his landmark text *Summary of Vietnamese History* was still impressive.[54] Setting the attack in motion, Trần Đức Thảo criticized his "idealist" perspective (*quan điểm duy tâm*).[55] Trần Huy Liệu elaborated a far more scathing assessment. Through his "uncritical reliance" on the French scholars Robequain and Gourou, he argued, Trần Trọng Kim had revealed his "feudal" and "colonial" perspective; moreover, his approach to the Vietnamese past was also "antinational" (*phản dân tộc*) and "ahistorical" (*phi lịch sử*). "This perspective," Trần Huy Liệu wrote, "must be gotten rid of once and for all" (*phải bài trừ cho hết*).[56] Minh Tranh acidly remarked that of all the books written during the period of "feudal colonialism," Trần Trọng Kim's was the most representative.[57] Because he had "feudalized" (*phong kiến hóa*) the entire past, Trần Trọng Kim believed that Vietnamese society had been feudal since the moment that it first emerged.

In addition to having feudal, bourgeois, colonialist, antinational, and ahistorical perspectives, Trần Trọng Kim was guilty of other offenses as well.

Minh Tranh, for one, criticized Trần Trọng Kim's treatment of the ambiguous fifteenth-century figure Hồ Quý Ly.[58] Like other feudal historians, he charged, Trần Trọng Kim regarded the period of the late fourteenth and early fifteenth centuries as a "time of darkness." He saw Hồ Quý Ly as a simple usurper, mistook him as the "chief culprit" in the Ming dynasty's temporary occupation of Vietnam, and wrongly considered his reign illegitimate. But other historians, according to Minh Tranh, were interested in the "progressive" aspects of Hồ Quý Ly's reign. Rather than denounce him as a usurper, these historians sought to determine why his "enlightened" view had garnered such limited support. What they discovered was that Hồ Quý Ly's very brief reign had ended in disaster because "reactionaries" had deceived the people.

But it was over the Tây Sơn Rebellion in the 1770s, the record of dynastic successions, and the reunification of Vietnam that postcolonial historians clashed most fiercely with Trần Trọng Kim, despite the fact that they began with some shared assumptions. Conventional chronologies took note of this late-eighteenth-century rebellion, but still listed the Lê as the dynasty that ruled from 1428 to 1802. When traditional sources acknowledged the Tây Sơn dynasty, it was only to dismiss it as a usurper. Historians from the committee and the institute, however, *and* Trần Trọng Kim emphasized the legitimacy of the Tây Sơn Rebellion and the legitimacy of Tây Sơn claims to the throne. They believed that Lê dynastic rule lasted only until 1788, when Emperor Chiêu Thống and the empress fled to China to seek military assistance. According to their shared interpretation of these events, the imperial family's flight from Vietnam and the emperor's request for support from foreign troops left the country open to invaders. Therefore, when Nguyễn Huệ, one of the leaders of the rebellion, proclaimed himself emperor in 1788, official historians *and* Trần Trọng Kim argued that there was no other legitimate sovereign from whom he could have usurped the throne.[59] Trần Trọng Kim also depicted Nguyễn Huệ as a great diplomat and military strategist. He praised the leaders of the Tây Sơn Rebellion as "heroic individuals" who emerged during a time of "chaos" (*biến loạn*) and who observed the traditional standards of dynastic rule and succession. From Trần Trọng Kim's perspective, the Tây Sơn ended years of social unrest — turmoil for which they themselves bore no blame — and restabilized the realm. In other words, he believed them to be worthy of praise because they had *sup-*

pressed social disorder. Although Trần Trọng Kim stressed the legitimacy of the Tây Sơn, he traced the reunification of Vietnam to the first Nguyễn emperor, Gia Long, who ascended the throne in 1802.

For postcolonial historians in Hanoi, however, the Tây Sơn dynasty brought a corrupt and decrepit dynasty to its knees by *orchestrating* a rebellion. According to the new telos they proposed, the August Revolution of 1945 marked the completion of what the Tây Sơn had begun some 150 years before. In this configuration, the Tây Sơn were reincarnated as the inspiration for and the progenitors of the events of 1945.

These historiographical disputes were genuine, and their significance extended beyond academic circles into social and political ones. Still, the antipathy that revolutionary writers felt for Trần Trọng Kim cannot be wholly explained by their disparate views of fifteenth- and eighteenth-century events. It would also be a gross oversimplification to say that postcolonial writers reviled Trần Trọng Kim simply because they were on opposite sides of the political divide: the political landscape was far more variegated than mere dualisms could convey. Still, political differences did explain some of their contempt. During the later years of the French occupation, Trần Trọng Kim served as an inspector of primary schools, composed morality texts, assembled pedagogical guides, and generally promoted conservative and even Confucian ideals of social order. Like many of his contemporaries, he also believed that the colonial system of education needed to be reformed. Unlike more radical thinkers, however, he envisioned a bifurcated model in which the "roots" of the student body, meaning those with lesser ability, would devote their time to morality texts while the "branches," the more gifted students, would study technology, industry, and science.[60] After the coup of March 1945 toppled the French regime, Trần Trọng Kim collaborated with the new government established by the Japanese.[61] For these reasons, Trần Trọng Kim appeared to anticolonial activists as an apologist for French and Japanese colonization and as an advocate of even more social stratifications in a social system already riven with divisions. His frequent contributions to *Southern Review* intensified the gravity of his errors.

Historians in Hanoi rejected Trần Trọng Kim's views of Hồ Quý Ly and the Tây Sơn; they condemned his collaboration with the French and Japanese. Still, these specific objections do not fully explain the insistent, even obsessive quality of their attacks. Ultimately, I suspect, postcolonial historians were less troubled by the differences between themselves and Trần Trọng Kim than by the convergence between what he had already accomplished and what postcolonial writers still hoped to achieve: a highly regarded "modern" history of Vietnam.

In the 1920s through 1940s, Trần Trọng Kim was the most visible historian in Vietnam, and he was renowned for his pathbreaking synthesis of history. Throughout the 1950s, 1960s, and 1970s, southern intellectuals accepted his *Summary of Vietnamese History,* which was originally published in 1920, as the single most authoritative source. Indeed, until April 1975 the *Summary* and his study of Confucianism were standard fare in Saigon schools.[62] In 1958, as committee historians in Hanoi debated the potential structure and themes of a new general history, publishers in Saigon were reissuing the work of Trần Trọng Kim. In 1971, when institute historians in Hanoi finally published the first volume of their survey, publishers in Saigon reissued Trần Trọng Kim's *Summary* once again. Unlike scholars in the DRV, who attributed innovations in historical writing to themselves and to politically palatable figures such as Phan Bội Châu, southerners remained convinced that Trần Trọng Kim had written the first and most important modern history of Vietnam. While northern officials celebrated the "tradition of resistance against foreign aggression" and the "the spirit of unity" shared by all Vietnamese, southerners stubbornly continued on a divergent path. Although DRV elites saw regional identities as the noxious product of French and American meddling, southerners proudly traced their own political origins to the sixteenth century, when Nguyễn Hoàng was posted in the South. By countering northern representations, southerners affirmed the autonomy of culture and politics in the South. The spectral presence of Trần Trọng Kim, one could say, thwarted the DRV's dreams of total control.

Finally, I would argue that scholars in the DRV felt a special enmity for Trần Trọng Kim and Phạm Quỳnh because they had published in *quốc ngữ,* the romanized script whose origins are widely known. In the seventeenth century, Catholic missionaries in Vietnam devised the script in order to facilitate their evangelical work. Traditionally, Vietnamese who had not converted dismissed this script as a sign of cultural betrayal, but in the twentieth century, as radical anticolonialists began to regard it as a revolutionary tool, they sought to suppress its tainted past. To rehabilitate what had once been scorned as the medium of collaborators and traitors, they renamed it "Uncle Ho's script" and devoted enormous energy to its dissemination, especially among rural Vietnamese. What must have been painful to acknowledge, however, was the fact that the richness and viability of *quốc ngữ* were undeniably linked to loathsome figures such as Trương Vĩnh Ký, Phạm Quỳnh, and Trần Trọng Kim, who had promoted Catholicism and collaborated with the French and the Japanese.

Ultimately, because many aspects of "new history" were not new, the term began to function as a coded abbreviation that marked what was supposed to be a political as well as intellectual break with the past. Less than it bore a discrete significance of its own, the designation "new history" underscored the differences between texts written by historians with the committee and institute and the historiographical traditions that preceded and surrounded them. Paradoxically, however, in distancing their own work from "feudal," "colonial," and "reactionary" texts, historians in the DRV communicated its connections to them. That is, the very act of denouncing what was not "new" required some sort of engagement. Because no historian was more vilified by postcolonial writers than Trần Trọng Kim, he strangely metamorphosed into their most frequent companion. Only in opposition to him — and therefore connected to him as well — could postcolonial historians articulate their own positions.

THE "LIGHT" OF MARXISM-LENINISM

Charged with the responsibility of producing a new general history of Vietnam, historians from the committee, first, and the institute, later, responded to their mission with considerable zeal. Among their many accomplishments — in addition to the two journals — were a twelve-volume history of Vietnam's modern revolution, a comprehensive three-volume history of the anticolonial movement, two two-volume studies of the August Revolution, and a commemorative history of Hanoi.[63] From 1954 to 1975, literally hundreds of monographs were published on subjects ranging from historical geography to folktales, the bronze age, national heroes, national character, colonial rubber plantations, the Vietnamese bourgeoisie, and the American invasion of the South. In the 1970s and 1980s — after decades of debate — official historians published *History of Vietnam,* the two-volume survey intended as the standard text. Volume 1, which took nearly twenty years to complete (it was published in 1971), begins with the prehistoric kingdom of Văn Lang and concludes in 1854 with the Locust Revolt led by Cao Bá Quát against the Nguyễn emperor Tự Đức. Volume 2, which was over thirty years in the making (it was published in 1985), continues the narrative from the mid-nineteenth century to the August Revolution. In this instance, postcolonial historians implied that the founding of the DRV in 1945 concluded the historical process. However, that same decision, to conclude the narrative with the events of 1945, can be taken as a sign of continuity with precolonial traditions, according to which each new dynasty represented the history of the previous one.

Those who interpret official pronouncements in a literal way and focus on *completed* works—but neglect the contexts and processes from which these works emerged—tend to label them "Marxist," "orthodox," "communist," and so forth. Official historians have reinforced the habit of looking at the product rather than the process by characterizing their own effort in similarly reductive terms. Whatever their source, these characterizations wrongly suggest a high degree of coherence in postcolonial intellectual life and, therefore, miss the unevenness and fluidity that the pursuit of orthodoxy left in its wake. Indeed, the polyphonic, multivocal, and layered quality of official texts is precisely what makes them so intriguing. Despite the authoritative claims, in other words, the path to an orthodox reading of the past was not laid out according to any map; it was an exploratory adventure, filled with detours and impasses and guided by contradictory demands. In dwelling on the finished product, especially the two-volume survey, one risks overlooking the intellectual swerves and reversals that were so much a part of intellectual life in the DRV. In examining the delays and the deferrals, on the other hand, we gain a sense of which issues were difficult to resolve, generated debate, and thus obstructed the consolidated vision.

The early publications of the committee and institute—the journals as well as the monographs—were saturated with the rhetoric of novelty and innovation. Although expressions such as "according to new history" (*theo sử học mới*) and "according to the new historical perspective" proliferated in official texts, there was no attempt to say what, precisely, the term "new history" was supposed to mean. In some contexts, new history conveyed an oppositional relation to dynastic sources, which official historians often criticized as instruments and expressions of elite power. In those sources, they maintained, the world beyond the imperial court figured principally as a vast backdrop, a mere arena in which the court carried out its own agendas.[64] As Phan Khôi put it, the dynastic annals represented the activities of a small and reclusive elite; in their relentless fixation on the court, they neglected the common people.[65] He further argued that because the two main chronicles were merely the records of dynasties rather than genuine histories of the people, they were no longer of any use: historians were thus obliged to "write new history."[66] Reacting against the elitism of dynastic texts, new history would be popular and inclusive: unlike dynastic texts, which dutifully chronicled events, new history would convey the texture of daily life and chronicle the lives of ordinary people.

Other historians imagined new history as the inevitable consequence of the August Revolution: necessarily, the rupture in politics generated new renditions of the past. The lineage of this view is, in its own right, instructive. In 1956, an article on the Twentieth Party Congress of the Communist Party of the Soviet Union (CPSU), which had appeared originally in the Soviet journal of history *Voprosi istorii,* was translated into French and published in *La Nouvelle critique.* The French translation of the Russian original was then retranslated into Vietnamese and published in the *Journal of Literary, Historical, and Geographical Research.* This article remarked that "new history" in the Soviet Union derived specifically from the communists' seizure of power in 1917.[67] This sense of new history as the offspring of the revolutionary ascent to power was also manifested in Chinese texts—both in analyses of the new history of China and in Chinese discussions of new history in Vietnam.[68] In his discussion of Vietnamese historical works, for example, Chen Yulong (Trần Ngọc Long), a professor of history at Beijing University, commented that during the feudal period the history of Vietnam had been too narrowly focused on the "gang" (*bọn*) of emperors and kings; during the colonial period, he continued, history had been twisted and distorted. Only in the ten years since the August Revolution had progressive historians begun to reconquer the country's legitimate history (*lịch sử chân chính*). In this configuration, new history appeared as a product of political conditions; it did not result from specific institutions (such as the Research Committee) or from intellectual volition. Accordingly, Chen Yulong identified the works of the Research Committee as distinguished examples of new history, but he diffused the committee's implicit monopoly on historical discourse by citing individual writers who were not tied to the committee, as well as other centers of scholarship.[69]

The term "new history," in other words, was heavily burdened: it referred to a popular as opposed to elite historiography. It also implied an interpretive position that was hostile to the Nguyễn: emerging ineluctably from the rise of revolutionary power, new history straightened out the distortions of dynastic and colonial texts. Leading and lesser luminaries also characterized it as an interpretive approach based on the "principles of Marxism." In a collectively signed editorial piece, committee historians announced their commitment to such principles; but rather than analyzing or even describing *which* Marxist principles they had in mind, they simply cautioned against a "mechanical application" of those principles to the Vietnamese past.[70] Given the complexity of Marx's own writings and the layers of commentary and elaboration that surround them, the meaning of Marxism in any context must be established and not simply assumed. In addition to wrestling with the opacities of Marx's own work, Vietnamese Marxists further complicated the brew by mixing in fragments of texts from Hegel, Engels, Morgan, Lenin, Bukharin, Stalin, and Mao. To a fascinating degree, the Marxism of Vietnamese writers was also heavily indebted to Romantic nationalists like Herder and Renan. This strange amalgam greatly expanded—and ultimately collapsed—the meaning of Marxism. By excavating some of its layers, we gain a clearer sense of why references to the "Marxist historiography of Vietnam" shed so little light on postcolonial efforts to reconceptualize the past.

Official historians claimed that Marxism made it possible for them to approach the past in a "scientific" way and to produce a "scientific" history. This term, as multivocal as the one it was supposed to define, had a rich resonance in the framework of colonial rule. For example, in his conclusion to *Lessons in the History of Annam*, Dương Quảng Hàm reflected: "In a difficult period of its history, Annam had the good fortune to encounter France, a noble and generous nation. Under her tutelage, our country will be protected by *force* and introduced to *science;* it will adapt to the conditions of modern life and will become increasingly rich and prosperous. Let us thus intertwine in the same love our original homeland, Annam, and our adopted homeland, France."[71]

Like colonial officials and scholars, as well as Vietnamese collaborators, those who resisted colonial rule were in awe of science; and like their predecessors, they, too, tended to equate science with political and intellectual authority. Thus, when anticolonial activists maintained that Marxist historiography was grounded in science, they assumed for themselves the authoritative voice in which colonial officials and scholars had once spoken. In addition to signaling a position of power, the idea of "science" lent itself to the revolutionary project in other ways. The "scientific" qualities of Marxism made it possible to codify the "laws of historical development" (*qui luật phát triển lịch sử*); these "laws" in turn illuminated the "laws" of combat.[72] Because Marxist historiography was "scientific," official historians reasoned, it was disinterested, objective, impartial: Marxist histories were thus able to account for the broad social and economic processes that were relevant to society as a whole, unlike the "feudal" versions of the past—dynastic chronicles and the work of Trần Trọng Kim—which were "elitist" and narrowly centered on events.[73] Other writers further expanded the already overly broad range of meanings attributed to Marxism and science. According to the Chinese historian Men Qun (Minh Cương), who was cited by members of the committee, historical materialism formed the basis of historical science.[74] Historical science, Minh Tranh claimed, was essentially synonymous with the science of social evolution (tiến triển).[75] The idea of Marxist historiography as neutral, scientific, evolutionary, and omniscient was occluded by additional meanings. In his survey of Vietnamese historiography, for example, Jian Bozan (Tiễn Bá Tán) asserted that new history was distinctive because it was written from the "workers' perspective."[76] Instead of describing how that perspective had altered understandings of the past, he simply characterized it as a product of historical materialism. In sum, in the 1950s official historians esteemed historical materialism because of its detached and neutral universality and celebrated, at the same time, its fiercely partisan stance.

New history was variously categorized as progressive, Marxist, scientific, politically neutral, or politically engaged; it was based on historical science or historical materialism, on Marxism, Marxism-Leninism, or Marxism-Engelism. Given the tremendous burden that these terms were forced to bear, they were ultimately deprived of any precise conceptual content. And when aspects of new history were defined in affective or emotional terms, the hope of any clear referential value was completely eclipsed. Trần Huy Liệu, for one, traced historical science to the "light of Marxism-Leninism" (ánh sáng của chủ nghĩa Mác-Lê-nin).[77] Chinese professor Chen Yulong stressed this affective dimension when he praised the "ardor" (sự nhiệt tâm) of Vietnamese historians who were guided by the "light of Marxism-Leninism."[78] The task of Marxist historiography, official historians later affirmed, was to increase one's love of country and of labor; it was supposed to enhance one's love for the people, for socialism, and for communism; it would heighten one's belief in the revolution, faith in enlightened leaders, and esteem for the party.[79] While these emotional appeals multiplied, fundamental aspects of Marxism, as it is conventionally identified, disappeared. At some level, traditional Marxists see class conflict as the force that generates historical change, but many Vietnamese who identified themselves as Marxists were not particularly interested in class conflict; indeed, they were more fully devoted to a history of broad social unity and to the "tradition of resistance against foreign aggression."[80]

THE PAST REPERIODIZED

Throughout the 1950s and 1960s, committee and institute historians were obsessed with the problem of historical periodization.[81] Only in discerning the stages or parts of the past, they reasoned, could they move on to the next step of narrating it in a coherent and comprehensive way. This meant that until the problem of periodization was resolved the general history could not be composed. Therefore, in annual reports, year after year, official historians vowed to decide unequivocally (*dứt khoát*), once and for all, how the Vietnamese past should be divided. At the same time, in spite of—or because of—the enormous pressure they faced, they also confessed, year after year, their inability to do so.

At the beginning of 1954, as the People's Army of Vietnam was preparing its assault on French forces at Dien Bien Phu, the Research Committee distributed a questionnaire asking how the major periods of the past should be defined.[82] Once the French surrendered in May, and as the participants in the Geneva Conference turned their attention to Indochina, the party's Central Committee scheduled a study retreat so that the range of responses could be discussed.[83] Skipping past important details—regarding who had been queried, for example, and how they had replied—Minh Tranh, in a brief account of the retreat, simply noted that the participants had failed to reach a "unity of ideas" (*sự nhất trí ý kiến*). Urging historians to resolve the matter, he noted that historical science was the science of social progress, development, and evolution. He dismissed the "purely historical" work of French historians who divided the past into four static phases: ancient, medieval, modern, and contemporary. Citing *The Dictionary of Dialectical Materialism,* he praised Soviet historians who favored a "social evolutionary" approach to the past.[84]

In the process of gaining the power to represent the past, postcolonial historians abandoned traditional narrative forms. Because they depended entirely on imperial reigns and dynastic chronologies, and privileged a tiny coterie of elites, these narrative patterns no longer sufficed. The traditional patterns were also problematic because they were based on cyclical repetitions; they could not, therefore, accommodate the idea of progress or the idea of dynamic—and linear—transitions from one stage of historical development to the next. Because of their insistence on cycles, traditional techniques of narration also obscured the sources or agents of historical change.

The Five-Stage Model of History

Guided by the party, historians turned to Stalin's five-stage model of history. This model posited that all societies could be defined by their principal mode of production and that all societies progressed from an original state of primitive communism to slavery, from slavery to feudalism, from feudalism to capitalism, and finally from capitalism to communism. According to this framework, every civilization moved through these five stages.[85] Although official historians may have seen this model as a reasonable basis for reconfiguring the national past, they could not agree on how, precisely, to impose it. With complete ease, they could pinpoint the origins of the fifth of Stalin's stages: the socialist mode of production obviously began in 1945. But the earlier stages were more difficult to decipher. After all, who could locate the period of primitive communism? Who really knew when, or even if, slavery began? At what point did the feudal mode of production prevail? When did the dominance of the capitalist mode become clear? In the midst of this intellectual dilemma, historians also grappled with the fact that, internationally if not domestically, Stalin himself was becoming marginalized and even openly despised. This was especially the case once Khrushchev formally denounced him in fall 1956. As Stalin fell into disrepute in other parts of the world, other narrative frameworks—the three-stage model proposed by Marx, the Asiatic Mode of Production (also traced to Marx), and "bourgeois" models as well—seemed to warrant more attention. And yet, because Stalin was still revered by party elites, official historians had to define the past in the terms he had proposed.

The point of these observations is to stress that the work of historians was politically charged. Their attempts to periodize the past reveal not only historiographical problems, but the complex relations between intellectual endeavors and politics—domestic and international—as well. Official historians who rushed to commit themselves to one narrative framework or another (and even those who were only tentatively aligned with this perspective or another) ran serious risks; thus they prolonged the debates about how to periodize the past. By examining how official historians presented and revised their arguments, we gain a greater sense of the politics of culture in the aftermath of colonial rule.

For one, we can observe how the Stalinist model of historical development persisted, despite the fact that it was stunningly unproductive. Indeed, for more than fifteen years members of the committee and the institute seemed to agonize over the problem of periodization. Ultimately, they abandoned the Stalinist model and its alternatives and began to structure the national past according to two dynamics that, in their estimation, ultimately became intertwined: the succession of resistance movements, rebellions, and revolutions, on the one hand, and formations of the state—beginning with the kingdom of Văn Lang in 2879 B.C.E. and concluding with the establishment of the DRV in 1945—on the other. Because the role of historiographical models was ultimately so limited, one might be inclined to dismiss them as the intellectual debris of a society fragmented by social, cultural, and political strife. Furthermore, from the perspective of the twenty-first century, the debates on historical periodization seem stale at best. What is worse, because they were so clearly encoded in Stalinist terms, they can be misconstrued by contemporary readers as a simple sign of pro-Stalinist affinities. And in this case, "Stalin" stands as an abbreviation for totalitarianism and savagery.

For the Vietnamese in the 1950s and 1960s, however, the reconstruction of national history was an essential part of postcolonial recovery. Therefore, despite the Stalinist idioms, and despite the fact that historians at the institute later rejected the four-stage model of history, the five-stage model of history, and the Asiatic Mode of Production as well, contemporary readers should still try to grasp the significance of the debates during the years when they actually unfolded. In a fundamental sense, the problem of periodization was critical to the extrication of Vietnamese history from colonialist paradigms. Colonial archaeologists, for example, often assumed that the artifacts they unearthed in Vietnam, especially the impressive works in bronze, were of foreign derivation; they assumed that the principal dynamics in Vietnamese prehistory were determined not by the Vietnamese but by Chinese, mainly, and by Tai and Malayo-Polynesian peoples to a lesser degree. Thus, in their attempt to "set the record straight," postcolonial historians felt compelled to reinterpret Vietnamese history in its entirety. In order to identify the trajectory and meaning of the past, they directed their attention to the problem of prehistory and to the patterns that developed *internally,* within the region of the Red River delta.

And yet, in attempting to read the evidence from prehistory in authoritative terms, official historians turned instinctively to Marx—even though Marxist historiography was not especially concerned with prehistory.[86] Where Marx was silent or incomplete, Engels was more discursive. Drawing on Lewis Henry Morgan's *Ancient Society,* Engels, in *Origin of the Family, Private Property, and the State,* added two prefeudal and possibly prehistoric phases—primitive communism and slavery—to the Marxist categories of feudalism, capitalism, and socialism. Codifying the work of Engels, Stalin schematized the five-stage model of historical development, and, further distilling Stalin's condensation of Engels, *The Dictionary of Dialectical Materialism* canonized the five-stage model of history. In short, Soviet texts from the Stalinist period played an important role in postcolonial historiography because they provided, superficially, at least, new possibilities for looking at the prehistoric past. As Stalin's legacy was quietly or clamorously repudiated in other parts of the world, in Vietnam the Stalinist model of history ascended to a more venerated position, not because Vietnamese writers nurtured Stalinist proclivities, but because the Stalinist model recognized the importance of prehistory. Because they were aware of Stalin's dethronement, Vietnamese writers sometimes attributed Stalinist orthodoxy to Marx and Engels. In 1960, for example, when Trần Huy Liệu enjoined his colleagues to scrutinize any evidence of slavery in Vietnam, he urged them to do so in the "light of Marxism-Engelism" (*dưới ánh sáng của chủ nghĩa Mác-Ang-ghên*); but like his colleagues, he specifically cited the works of Stalin.[87]

In delineating the period of primitive communism, Minh Tranh initially argued that it had prevailed as the dominant mode of production for nearly three thousand years—throughout, in other words, the entire reign of the Hùng kings of the Hồng Bàng dynasty.[88] In a commemorative essay that celebrated them as the ancestors of the Vietnamese, Trần Huy Liệu similarly noted that the Hùng kings had flourished during the period of primitive communism, a period, he added, that all peoples or nations (*dân tộc*) necessarily passed through.[89] As historians struggled to define the development of the Vietnamese past after the period of primitive communism, however, even this initial certainty collapsed.

The slave mode of production, the second stage in the Stalinist model, generated an extensive "pen war" (*bút chiến*) that began in 1951 when Đào Duy Anh asserted that slavery had been the dominant mode of production in the kingdom of Âu Lạc (257–208 B.C.E.).[90] In his *Draft Summary of Vietnamese History,* Minh Tranh agreed with Đào Duy Anh's claim that the slave mode of production coincided with the founding of the kingdom of Âu Lạc in 257 B.C.E. But, he argued, one should trace its supercession by the feudal mode of production not to 208 B.C.E., but to 40 C.E., when the Trưng sisters launched a revolt against Han dynasty officials (see chapter 4).[91] At the same time, Nguyễn Đổng Chi questioned not so much the chronology of the slave mode of production but its relevance altogether. Citing the lack of conclusive data, he maintained that it was impossible to know if the kingdom of Âu Lạc had depended principally on one mode of production as opposed to another. Instead, inspired by the work of Soviet historians Anna Pankratova and Mikhail Pokrovsky (who was formally rehabilitated only in 1961), he proposed the idea of "clan society" as a category more pertinent to the Vietnamese past.[92] At this point, Đào Duy Anh retracted his earlier comments and argued that Vietnam had *not,* in fact, experienced a period of slavery but had passed directly from primitive communism to feudalism.[93] Rejecting the arguments of all his interlocutors, in 1956 Trần Văn Giáp proposed that slavery was the dominant mode of production during a considerably earlier period—throughout the Hồng Bàng dynasty, from 2879 to 258 B.C.E.![94] Although Minh Tranh and others urged historians to resolve the question of slavery—once and for all—this issue became increasingly contested.

In 1957, in an attempt to explain why this question so vexed Vietnamese writers, Nguyễn Lương Bích described the emergence of slavery as a historiographical concern, both in Vietnam and in other Asian countries.[95] Throughout the feudal and colonial periods, he said, no one had spoken of the slave mode of production because scholars were unfamiliar with historical materialism; with the disintegration of colonial power, however, revolutionary writers were able to investigate new theories of history. At the same time, Vietnamese writers became aware of similar debates in Korea, China, and Japan.[96] Referring to the debates then taking place, Nguyễn Lương Bích remarked that slavery, if it were to serve as an effective analytical tool, had to be further refined. Proposing a distinction between slavery based on the patriarchal family (*chế độ chiếm hữu nô lệ gia trưởng*) and an incipient kind of slavery (*chế độ nô lệ tảo kỳ*), he asserted that the slave mode of production had dominated from the time of the Trưng sisters' revolt in 40 C.E. to the revolt of Lý Bôn and the establishment of the kingdom of Vạn Xuân in 542.[97] But this argument also was deflated when, in the following year, the Soviet Asianist D. V. Deopik insisted that slavery had been widely practiced in earlier times.[98]

Years later, returning to this discussion, Văn Tân explained that, just as the Vietnamese had begun to explore the potential relevance of the slave mode of production to the historiography of Vietnam, the topic was declared taboo.[99] Only in 1960, when the restrictions against intellectual dissidence had eased, were writers able to explore the problem more fully. Historians from the institute, who appealed to the authority of Engels and Stalin, argued that slavery had indeed played a critical role in the history of Vietnam.[100] Historians from the University of Hanoi, who relied more on the work of Lenin—most notably Trần Quốc Vượng, Hà Văn Tấn, and Phan Huy Lê—published two pathbreaking studies, *Primitive Communism* and *The History of Feudalism,* from which they conspicuously omitted the concept of slavery.[101] Trần Quốc Vượng explained that although Lenin believed that most of the civilized societies of Europe had passed through a period of slavery, as had the majority of non-European societies, he had also noted some exceptions. The Slavic civilizations of Russia, Czechoslovakia, and Romania, he maintained, had bypassed the period of slavery, proceeding instead directly from primitive communism to feudalism. Inspired by Lenin's assertions regarding the Slavic countries, historians at the university insisted that beginning with the Hùng kings and the legendary kingdom of Văn Lang, during the reign of An Dương Vương, who ruled the legendary kingdom of Âu Lạc, and through the early stages of the Chinese occupation (from 2879 B.C.E. to 43 C.E., in other words) Vietnamese society was based on primitive communism. Because of the Chinese invasion of 43 C.E., they claimed, Vietnam could not have developed into a slave-owning society because it was integrated into an already feudalized China. The affront to Stalinist orthodoxy was clear, and even though such challenges had become commonplace in other parts of the world, in Vietnam these criticisms still mattered. Historians at the institute issued scathing reviews of both works. The debate between institute and university historians further unfolded in the following months.

In 1960, responding to the tumult over the problem of periodization and the question of slavery specifically, the Institute of History organized two informal discussions. Held on April 19 and May 21, these discussions were attended by more than 130 representatives from the Institute of History, the Department of History at the University of Hanoi, the Museum of History, and a number of other institutions. Even Prime Minister Pham Van Dong had, with "endless enthusiasm," joined in.[102] Among the first to speak was Văn Tân, who began by situating the debate on slavery in a broader international arena. In the Soviet Union, he explained, after more than forty years of debate, historians finally concluded that Slavic peoples had progressed directly from the period of primitive communism to feudalism *without* passing through an intermediate period of slavery. In China, however, where historians had been debating these questions for thirty years, they had not yet resolved them. Repeating the by-now familiar refrain, Văn Tân urged Vietnamese historians to consider all the relevant perspectives and to resolve, definitively and once and for all, the problem of periodization. Paving the way for an extensive delay, however, he also remarked that the Vietnamese had been working on this problem for only ten years.[103]

Far from generating "unity in thought and will," the 1960 discussions on slavery served as the occasion for scholars from apparently rival institutions to reiterate antithetical views. In articulating the conviction of his colleagues at the institute, Văn Tân bluntly asserted: "Basing our argument on the principles of Marxism-Leninism, we can state that Vietnam passed through a period of slavery." Rather than trace the roots of his argument to a specific text either by Marx or Lenin, however, he identified instead the work of Engels, and *Origin of the Family, Private Property, and the State* in particular. In this work, Văn Tân continued, Engels had asserted that all human societies passed through three oppressive phases: slavery, serfism, and wage labor.[104] Evaluating their national past on the basis of this claim, scholars from the institute, the Museum of History, and some without institutional affiliations (who came to express *ý kiến tự do,* or "free ideas") therefore agreed that slavery had once been the dominant mode of production in Vietnam.[105] Retracting his earlier retraction, Đào Duy Anh conceded that Vietnam had *possibly* passed through a period of slavery. Historians from the university, on the other hand, argued that Vietnam had progressed directly from the stage of primitive communism to feudalism.

If one looks at the conclusions of the 1960 discussions on slavery, the positions appear neatly divided: historians from the institute lined up on one side of the divide and those from the university were stationed on the other. If one looks at the details of each argument, however, the disagreements proliferate to a dizzying degree. No longer are there merely two or three approaches to the problem of slavery, but rather literally dozens. Historians from the institute — those who agreed that the slave mode of production explained parts of the past — had vastly different impressions. One of them argued that the slave mode of production had dominated for a period of roughly three thousand years, from the third millennium to the third century B.C.E. Another, who thought this view too restrictive, proposed a still more totalizing scheme. Others argued that the period of slavery had begun much later and identified the fifth century B.C.E., the third century B.C.E., and the first century C.E. as likely starting points.[106] Surveying the discrepant claims, Trần Huy Liệu remarked that some historians, frustrated by the lack of conclusive evidence, were on the verge of abandoning the question of slavery. He urged them, instead, to continue their research, to gather new data, and to investigate more fully the evidence that archaeology and folklore studies could provide. Surely, if examined in the "light of Marxism-Engelism," he said, the existing evidence would reveal new truths about the period of slavery.[107] This, after all, was their most critical goal: to reveal historical truth. Depicting historical debate as a competition, he remarked that everyone who helped construct national history would "win" the debate, regardless of whether or not they held the "correct" view. Although the discussions on slavery were intended to synthesize views, they clarified, instead, the unbridgeable gaps.[108] And in subsequent years, the differences became still more glaring. Slavery was the dominant mode of production for a short period in the late tenth and early twelfth centuries, some scholars argued; or it had prevailed only later, from the eleventh through fourteenth centuries, others claimed. These wildly divergent views make it clear that the evidentiary basis for the debate was thin; and whatever evidence one could muster could be adduced in contradictory ways.[109]

When they postponed the debates on the models of historical change proposed by Morgan, Marx, Engels, Lenin, and Stalin, most revolutionary writers initially agreed that Vietnam had emerged from prehistory as a feudal society and had remained that way for two thousand years. In judging the national past this way, these writers, either deliberately or unwittingly—we cannot know—reproduced the orientalist views of colonial writers: Vietnam was essentially stagnant and unchanging. Some scholars undermined such totalizing views by locating feudalism more specifically. Trần Đức Thảo, for one, limited its scope to Trần and Lê dynastic rule (1225–1788).[110] As the discussions of feudalism evolved, minor disagreements emerged, but the basic premise stayed in place. Moreover, it became clear that instead of looking at social conditions as the key to identifying one mode of production or another, official historians turned to political events.

Two of the committee's main contributors, Minh Tranh and Nguyễn Đổng Chi, for example, agreed that feudalism began in 40 C.E., with the uprising initiated by the Trưng sisters, and that it ended with the August Revolution in 1945. Minh Tranh divided feudalism into three stages and precisely dated the duration of each: the feudal foreign protectorate (40–939), national feudalism (939–1862), and the feudal colonialist system (1862–1945). Nguyễn Đổng Chi, on the other hand, claimed to see only two stages of feudalism, but he, too, supplied specific dates: the preliminary phase (*phong kiến sơ kỳ*), in which political power was relatively decentered (40–939), and a subsequent, more centralized phase (*phong kiến tập quyền*) (939–1883). Rejecting the term "feudal colonialist system," he described the French occupation (beginning in 1883, in his view) as a semifeudal and semicolonial state (*bán phong kiến và thuộc địa*).[111] During the early years of this debate, a brief hiatus occurred. When it resumed, L. V. Cherepnin indirectly joined in because his study of feudalism in Russia stressed the degree of political centralization as the crucial issue, not the details of politics nor the distinction between domestic and foreign control.[112] Still, most historians at the institute continued to see the past as essentially feudal and to regard political events as the key.[113]

This approach to the study of feudalism brought recent history into high relief. Compared to the shapeless and stagnant quality of the past, mid-twentieth-century events had a distinctive luster: "The August Revolution was not only a question of toppling the gang of invaders. It was also a social upheaval to break the feudal system which our people had endured for two thousand years."[114]

Stepping back from the stuff of the debates on feudalism and looking instead at their overall tenor, Nguyễn Hồng Phong examined the "confusion" on which they were based.[115] Their inconclusiveness, he believed, stemmed from the fact that sources for agrarian history were extremely rare. This lament points to a genuine problem, but it also neglects a critical concern: one should also emphasize the lack of congruity between the historiographical models and the empirical realities they were supposed to describe. But above all, the debates were stymied by the extreme plasticity of the essential term. In short, the term "feudalism" was applied to an astonishing range of situations. Describing the "national feudal" context in which Lê Văn Hưu had written *History of Đại Việt*, some historians tied "fully developed" feudalism to the prominence of Confucian bureaucracy.[116] In other cases, feudalism referred to the problem of widespread illiteracy or simply stood in opposition to modernism, a term that was also applied in totalizing and indiscriminate ways. Or, feudalism represented everything in the colonies that the colonial powers had condemned, and it accounted for the weakness of Asian countries vis-à-vis a predatory West.[117] By expanding the meaning of feudalism, official historians ultimately nullified its referential potential. This process was most apparent in the habit of using "feudal" as mere pejorative. In his criticisms of Trần Trọng Kim, who was in every sense his contemporary, Minh Tranh characterized him as a "feudal" historian guilty of having "feudalized" the past.[118]

As was the case with Cherepnin's study of feudalism, N. M. Druzinin's work on capitalism in Russia was supposed to focus the debates on specific conditions. Like the discussions of feudalism, however, those devoted to capitalism were similarly hindered.[119] Still, the question of capitalism generated a far more meaningful debate, partly because the principal issue, whether openly acknowledged or not, was the question of historical agency. Some historians discerned the embryonic stages of capitalism *within* Vietnamese feudalism, thereby pointing to capitalism's indigenous roots and to the contributions of Vietnamese to the "evolutionary process." Other historians envisioned the Vietnamese as essentially passive and attributed historical change to violent interventions. Both Vương Hoàng Tuyên and Chiêm Tế, for example, insisted on the fundamental rupture between (Vietnamese) feudalism and (colonial) capitalism and implied that were it not for the French colonialists feudalism would have indefinitely endured.[120]

The Asiatic Mode of Production
In an illuminating study, Brendan O'Leary identifies the Asiatic Mode of Production (AMP) as the "Loch Ness Monster of historical materialism, rarely sighted and much disbelieved." He also notes: "Whether the AMP existed in Marx's writings (at all, merely intermittently or continuously) has been constantly doubted."[121] Like Perry Anderson, Stephen Dunn, and a number of others, O'Leary traces the concept of the AMP to Marx's preface to *A Contribution to the Critique of Political Economy*. While his reference to a specifically "Asiatic" mode of production has generated and continues to generate an extensive debate, Marx himself never used this term again. Nor did Engels, his closest collaborator. Both critics and disciples of Marx have periodically returned to the idea of the Asiatic Mode of Production in order to define in more substantive terms what Marx himself mentioned only in passing. At the turn of the century, for instance, as the Bolsheviks were developing revolutionary strategies for the countryside, Georgy Plekhanov suggested that the conventional Marxist reading of social evolution fit only imperfectly with actual conditions in the rural part of Russia. Arguing that the success of the revolutionary movement overall would depend

on a viable strategy in the countryside, Plekhanov reintroduced the idea of the AMP. Because Lenin rejected the idea that the Russian countryside was somehow anomalous, this line of inquiry temporarily subsided. In the 1920s, however, after Lenin's death, the topic of the AMP reemerged and was avidly discussed by Ludwig Madyar and Eugene Varga and other specialists on China, India, and the Middle East. Again, the implication that Marxism, as it was conventionally understood, was relevant only to Europe was resisted. In 1929, Soviet historian S. M. Dubrovsky began to attack the theory of the AMP; and at the Leningrad Conference in 1931, Stalin specifically rejected it. His *Dialectical and Historical Materialism,* published in 1938 — a work that O'Leary has wryly characterized as Stalin's "party catechism" — did not include the AMP as one of the five modes of production.[122] Until the de-Stalinization of the late 1950s, the topic of the AMP was mostly avoided.

In 1957 and 1958, however, an East German historian, Elisabeth Charlotte Welskopf, and a Hungarian sinologist, Ferenc Tökei, revived the discussion of the AMP. That European Marxists once again addressed this problem was linked to Karl Wittfogel's staunchly anticommunist publications on "oriental despotism."[123] As it was conceived by its principal theorists (Madyar and Varga), the Asiatic Mode of Production accounted for the period between the primitive communal and capitalist formations and functioned as an Asian counterpart to slavery and feudalism in Europe.[124] In their view, Asian history was distinct because of the state's domination of society; moreover, they understood Asian society as a collection of villages, each one essentially the same as the next. Because villages were atomized, self-sufficient, and self-contained, their reasoning continued, neither the economic or social conditions for class consciousness could develop. Therefore, while European history was propelled from one stage of evolutionary development to the next — via the dynamism of class struggle — Asian history was singularly static. In seeking an objective explanation for the static and statist dimensions of Asian society, Plekhanov (initially) and Wittfogel (subsequently) determined that the geographical conditions supposedly specific to Asia gave rise to the despotism of the "hydraulic state."

Historians in the DRV were certainly aware of this broader discussion. In 1955, for instance, Minh Tranh remarked that Russian, Chinese, and Japanese historians had recently written a great deal about the AMP. So that his readers would grasp the significance of this apparently strange locution (*phương thức sản xuất Á Châu*), he provided them with a more familiar French gloss: *mode de production asiatique.*[125] For European Marxists, Stalin's death and de-Stalinization presented new intellectual and political possibilities, but in the DRV the constraints were more apparent, and members of the committee and the institute continued to work with the Stalinist model. Only in fall 1963 did their interest in the AMP resurface when, somewhat wearily, Nguyễn Lương Bích reintroduced it. "This [question of the Asiatic Mode of Production] is already an old issue," he recounted, "that has been discussed many times during the past half-century. Every so often," he continued, "it is treated as something new that needs to be discussed all over again, but the more it is talked about the more disagreement there is. So much is this the case," he said, "that to this day, Marxist historians all over the world still do not agree." Nevertheless, Nguyễn Lương Bích explained, as Vietnamese historians continued to struggle with the problem of historical periodization, they would be obliged to address the question of the AMP, and for this reason alone, he concluded, indulging in the double negative, they "could not *not* seek to understand it" (*không thể không tìm hiểu*).[126] The lineage that Nguyễn Lương Bích traced for the AMP intersected with some of the standard genealogies, but it also revealed some intriguing anomalies.

In a narrative ploy that seemed to reveal his own commitment to Stalin's five-stage model of history, Nguyễn Lương Bích outlined what he believed were the five stages of the debate on the Asiatic Mode of Production. He began by quoting Marx, as most do, and turned next to Plekhanov, observing that his analysis of the AMP, flawed though it may have been, had greatly influenced the work of Varga, Wittfogel, Karl Radek, and David Riazanov.[127] He moved on to Madyar, who, having synthesized the work of Plekhanov and Wittfogel, argued that the categories of slavery and feudalism did not fully explain what happened in China after the period of primitive communism and before the nineteenth-century invasion of Western capitalism. Only on the basis of the AMP, he claimed, could this period in Chinese history be adequately grasped. Although he named other historians who supported Madyar's view, Nguyễn Lương Bích also noted that many Soviet scholars opposed it. Demonstrating how an ambiguous concept had become even more opaque, he mentioned that Georgy Safarov saw the AMP as a hybrid in which the slave and feudal modes of production coexisted. Blurring the potential distinctiveness of the AMP further, he cited the Chinese historian Guo Moruo, who proposed that the Asiatic Mode of Production was essentially another name for primitive communism.[128] In closing his discussion of the first stage of the debate, Nguyễn Lương Bích referred to a conference held in Japan in 1928, where distinguished historians from around the world determined that the theory of the AMP was relevant indeed to studies of the Japanese and Chinese pasts.[129]

The second stage of the debate began in 1931, Nguyễn Lương Bích believed, when Yevgeny S. Iolk denounced Madyar's definition of the AMP and proposed Safarov's hybrid concoction in its place. At the Leningrad Conference that same year, however, all the existing interpretations were rejected and a new one was proposed. According to the new view, which was initially accepted in the Soviet Union, China, and Japan, the AMP was the special form that feudalism took in the countries of Asia. At another conference that soon followed, Japanese scholars reaffirmed their support for Iolk's interpretation of the AMP: it was a hybrid combination of the slave and feudal modes of production.[130] The third stage of the debate began in 1934 when Soviet historian Sergei I. Kovalev hypothesized that the AMP was an Asian variant of the slave mode of production. This new interpretation, Nguyễn Lương Bích remarked, was received with enthusiasm by Marxist historians all over the world. For nearly two decades, Soviet specialists on Asia, V. V. Strouve and V. I. Avdiyev most notably, and Chinese scholars such as Fan Wenlan, Hou Wailu, and Lu Zhenyu all based their analyses of ancient history on the theory that Kovalev had advanced. But Kovalev's interpretation was not universally acclaimed: historians in the Soviet Union, Japan (including some who had earlier supported it), and China—Guo Moruo specifically—challenged his view. These critics claimed that the AMP figured as a transitional phase between primitive communism and slavery.[131]

For Nguyễn Lương Bích, the fourth stage began in 1952 when Soviet scholars at the Academy of Sciences undertook their monumental ten-volume *History of the World*. In organizing this gargantuan project, they decided to abandon the category of the AMP altogether because it was "imprecise and too old" (*không chính xác và đã cũ lắm rồi*) and, many suspected, because it perpetuated mistaken views of Western historians who could only envision the East as the antithesis of the West (*lấy Đông phương đối lập với Tây phương*). Despite their initial support for the new Soviet stance, some Chinese, professor Dong Shuye for one, argued that the AMP was still a relevant concern because it accounted for specifically Asian experiences of feudalism. In 1962, when Soviet Asianist A. A. Guber visited Vietnam to attend a meeting on historical periodization, he echoed Dong Shuye: the Asiatic Mode of Production, he affirmed, was essential to discussions of feudalism in Asia.[132] Positioning himself on the cusp of the fifth stage, Nguyễn Lương Bích summed up the situation: after a century of debate the problem of the

AMP had not been resolved. As though the fivefold structure of his narrative had not already made his own attitude clear, he expressed it directly. The theory of the AMP, he argued, should be interred again, once and for all, because Marxism-Leninism (i.e., Stalin) had unambiguously established that all societies passed through five stages of history: primitive communal, slave-owning, feudal, capitalist, and communist.[133]

Making his case against the AMP, Nguyễn Lương Bích cited a passage written by Engels in *Anti-Dühring* and, more intriguingly, he quoted from a lecture Lenin had given at the University of Sverdlovsk:

> Throughout the past several thousand years, the development of every society, without exception, has shown that we experience the same laws. . . . In the beginning society is classless; next is the primitive communal phase and the disappearance of clans; next comes the society based on a system of slavery, the slave-owning phase. All of the countries in Europe today passed through that period. Furthermore, for the vast majority of nations in other regions of the world it was the same.[134]

In a dismissive and cynical tone, Nguyễn Lương Bích described the Asiatic Mode of Production as mere "speculation" (*ức đoán*) that was periodically revived according to time and place.[135] Indeed, in this time and place — in the early 1960s, as *two* states took shape and as the divisions *within* Vietnam tragically intensified — official historians increasingly turned to the AMP as the basis for interpreting the national past. The inspiration for this new emphasis must be traced to a multiplicity of sources, but, from the perspective of the state, its essential appeal is not hard to decipher. At a time when the DRV prepared to face a new crisis that promised to be more destructive than any it had already endured, the AMP breathed life into a fictive past. It stressed, above all, the power and centrality of the state and made the idea of class conflict irrelevant. The AMP embodied what was then the official ideal: a state-centered society unperturbed by internal divisions and unmarked by the passage of time.

THE MEANING OF THE MODEL

There is no evidence that the role of official historian disagreed with those who performed it. On the contrary, historians at the committee and the institute seemed to welcome the mission with which they were charged: to produce a new general history of Vietnam, from prehistoric to contemporary times. Nevertheless, their failure (or reluctance or inability) to complete the project is striking. Year after year they were instructed to resolve the problem of periodization, but just as routinely they announced that they had failed to reach any definitive conclusions. They often spoke contritely about the unfinished history, and yet they conducted their work in ways that were bound to prolong the debate. In 1961, for instance, official historians again expressed their regret that the volume was still not finished: after years of debate it was still unclear how the past should be periodized. They also recognized that the newly announced and much celebrated First Five-Year Plan reemphasized their original obligation. Thus, of the projects scheduled for the coming year, the problem of periodization was by far the most critical: finally, once and for all, they would resolve it. To overcome all difficulties and to realize the Five-Year Plan, they would approach their work with "revolutionary ardor" *(nhiệt tình cách mạng)*; that ardor, above all, was the crucial element.[136] But what began as an expression of regret metamorphosed into a warning: because new interpretive frameworks—in this case the categories of "bourgeois historiography"—were being reconsidered, the possibility of concluding the debate and bringing the project to fruition was more remote than ever. In 1962, Văn Tân urged his colleagues to resolve the problem of periodization; the following year, Cao Xuân Phổ repeated that plea; and years later, calling attention to the book that was still unwritten, Trương Hữu Quýnh recited the same lamentations.[137] But the increasing demands for a conclusion to the debates resulted in the insistence on still greater uncertainty about how the past should be periodized.

The meaning of this equivocation is impossible to discern. One can speculate that the foot-dragging tactics served as immunization against potential upheavals: as political fortunes changed, those who had once been favored could be easily denounced. Official historians were certainly aware of intellectuals such as Phan Khôi and Trần Đức Thảo whose candor had cost them dearly—despite the fact that politically they had aligned themselves *with* the revolution. Whether or not they agreed with his theories or tactics, official scholars must have also been alarmed by the abruptness of Trường Chinh's demotion. In this sense, the insistence on unanimity and the collective nature of historical scholarship tended to diffuse the question of liability: authorship could be traced to collective entities—the committee or the the institute—but not to specific individuals. It is also possible that the stalling functioned as an oblique form of protest—a protest against the intrusiveness of the state—and a comment on the pointlessness of scholarship that is driven by decrees.

The reluctance to conclude the debates may have also signaled profound reservations about progressive notions of history. An evolutionary conception of history rests, fundamentally, on the idea of history as a developmental process. History, from the evolutionary perspective, is a tale of teleological unfolding: ineluctably civilizations proceed from one stage of development to a higher, more advanced stage until—triumphantly—the goal has been reached. Because the evolutionary model of history is progressive and rejects the possibility of retrogression and regression, it required Vietnamese historians to evaluate as positive what they normally regarded as the most negative aspects of the national past—the Chinese occupation, French colonization, and American neocolonialism. Because foreign occupations and interventions intensified class antagonisms, the evolutionary model claimed, they generated new historical momentum. The wars and occupations, therefore, had hastened the process of history's progressive unfolding. Vietnamese historians who had survived the French and were then facing the Americans may have found it difficult to embrace this salutary view of foreign occupations. When official historians commented on the material poverty of the Vietnamese, they sometimes contrasted it with the prosperity of Japan—and they did not attribute Japan's industrial success to the combination of the Pacific War, the American occupation, and the cold war. On such occasions, they attributed the diminished condition of their own society to the damage caused by foreign occupations. Evolutionary ideas of history also subverted cyclical frameworks—the cycles of royal and dynastic succession and the cyclical reenactment of the original drama: Vietnamese fighting against foreign aggressors. Confronted with insurmountable differences, postcolonial Vietnamese fixated on the idea of social unity. Assertions that the Vietnamese were socially, spiritually, and politically united functioned as an incantation or charm; they conferred invulnerability. In this sense, the insistence on class conflict as the engine of historical change interrupted more talismanic notions of history as transcendence and overcoming.

In 1971, when the Institute of History published the first of its two-volume general history, it was clear that neither the four- nor the five-stage model had survived. Indeed, the survey handled the pre-Chinese period of the past by focusing on the Neolithic Revolution—the emergence of farming in fixed settlements—and metallurgy, especially the sophistication of Vietnamese bronzeworking techniques. Although the general survey referred to servants (*tôi tớ*), it made no mention of slaves (*nô lệ*). Twelve years later, when their counterparts in the Department of History at the University of Hanoi published the first of their two-volume survey, the models had similarly vanished.[138] Because the debates on historical periodization ultimately played such a minuscule role in new narratives of the national past, some critical questions necessarily arise. Why, for example, did Marxism (or Marxism-Leninism or Marxism-Engelism) nominally enjoy such preeminence when, in the end, the conceptual benefits were so slight? Because the debates on historical periodization apparently left so few traces, one may be tempted to dismiss them as the detours and ephemera stemming from the party's efforts to control intellectual production. My own inclination is to recognize that on the surface the debates exerted only a negligible effect on official renditions of the past, but also to argue that at other levels the consequences of the debates were enormous.

First, by working with evolutionary models of history, postcolonial historians situated Vietnam within a global community. The allegiance to Marxism and to Marxist historiography produced a highly coded vocabulary, a vocabulary whose referential value mattered far less than its power to signal or mark. In other words, what we can call a "marxish" framework announced Vietnam's escape from a cultural and political arena dominated by imperial France and called attention to the fundamentally new political and intellectual community to which it now belonged. No longer a small cog in the mighty French empire, Vietnam had emerged as an actor, an agent, in a powerful community extending across much of the globe. This new community included countries as distant as Cuba; as remote as Hungary, Bulgaria, and Romania; and as exotic as Poland, Czechoslovakia, and East Germany. From the more familiar terrain of Asia, it encompassed Mongolia, North Korea, and the PRC; and above all this new community included the Soviet Union. In the obsessive bipolarity of the cold war, the political and cultural elites of the DRV realized that Vietnam was obliged to choose: unambiguously, it had to position itself on one side or another of the principal divide. Even though it cultivated ties with the nonaligned movement (India, for instance), Vietnam's connections to the Third World were minimal. Instead, having disengaged itself from the First World, the DRV located itself as a vital part of the Second World dominated by the Soviet Union.

Although the work of revolutionary historians appears remarkably paro-chial—their hundreds of monographs and thousands of articles were de-voted almost exclusively to Vietnam—their range of interlocutors was much more vast. "Day by day," Trần Huy Liệu once remarked, "the work of the committee becomes more important, both in and outside the country."[139] Emphasizing the international importance of their scholarship, committee and the institute historians for a time published brief summaries of their work in French, which was still the only "international" language at their disposal; later, they translated the journal's table of contents into French, Russian, and Chinese.[140] Stressing the importance of Vietnam in a new inter-national arena, committee and the institute historians also reported on their contact with foreign journalists, diplomats, and scholars; they recounted the details of institutional links to the embassies of China and the Soviet Union, the Soviet Academy of Sciences, China's Ministry of Education, and the Soviet Committee on History and Economics.[141] They also traveled abroad: in 1954 Trần Huy Liệu visited the Soviet Union, where he met with Guber and toured the Soviet Archives; in 1955 Minh Tranh represented the Re-search Committee at the Asia Institute in Moscow.[142] The intertextual di-mensions of official histories also underscored the wider discursive commu-nity to which postcolonial writers belonged. In one issue of the *Journal of Literary, Historical, and Geographical Research,* for example, a translation of a Russian-language piece on the duties of Soviet historians appeared. Echo-ing the Soviet statement, an article in the next issue outlined the responsi-bilities of historians in Vietnam.[143] News of conferences in Moscow and of Soviet scholars' trips to China also emphasized the wider world to which the Vietnamese now belonged.

Colonial writers had often insisted on the exotic insignificance of Viet-nam, its obscurity and its distance from more vital and dynamic parts of the world. The tutelage of Mother France, they promised, would rescue it from oblivion: through the civilizing presence of the French, Vietnam would be "opened up" to the light of modernity and introduced into the world. Postcolonial writers obviously contested colonialist assumptions. In narrating the national past according to universal paradigms—Stalin's five-stage model of history (first) and the Asiatic Mode of Production (second) —historians in the DRV pointed to its global significance. "Vietnamese his-tory," they argued, was "an integral part of universal history." Even more, it was a "shining example" of world revolutionary history: of all the colonized countries, Phan Gia Bền claimed, only Vietnam had defeated the colonial power and established socialism through revolutionary means.[144]

Furthermore, as they adhered, even if only nominally, to the conventions of Stalinist historiography, postcolonial Vietnamese underscored their links to new centers of political power and intellectual authority. When Nguyễn Lương Bích outlined the century of debate on the Asiatic Mode of Production he did so within the context of the debate on historical periodization, but his analysis pointed in another direction as well: it called attention to the depth and continuity of the new community that, in the post-French era, included Vietnam. While they presented Vietnamese history as an essential part of world history to what they imagined was a worldwide audience, committee and institute historians also incorporated the icons of world revolutionary history into national narratives. They helped organize commemorative events devoted to the birthday of Lenin, the Russian Revolution, and the establishment of the People's Republic of China. With the intensification of the war in the 1960s, the DRV's impressive international connections resonated in new ways. Historians in the DRV regarded "the world" as a witness to the war and believed that the judgment was in their favor: the "progressive countries of the world" and "opinion in the world" recognized the righteousness of their cause.[145]

Second, through the historiographical debates of the 1950s and 1960s, official historians symbolically reworked the intellectual relationship between Vietnam and China. To demonstrate the validity of this claim, I would begin by remarking that the search for meaningful precedents and models is probably manifested in all societies, but in Vietnam this search has been conducted in particularly poignant ways. Vietnamese emperors, historians, poets, reformers, and revolutionaries have often looked to the authority of nonindigenous, especially Chinese, patterns in order to present their decisions and methods in an authoritative wrap. In the twelfth century, for example, the ailing Lý emperor Nhân Tôn sought to ensure the continuity of the dynasty in the period after his demise. Departing from Vietnamese practices, which left succession a matter for survivors to decide, he named his own successor. To justify his unorthodox method, he appealed to the unassailable authority of Mencius and of the Han emperor Wendi, who, more than a millennium before, had recited a Mencian edict on his own death bed.[146] In the late nineteenth century, the Nguyễn emperor Hàm Nghi fled the court in Hue as a sign of protest against the French. So that his flight

would signify as he intended — as a sign of resistance and not capitulation —
he issued an edict that cited the appropriate examples from Zhou, Qin, and
Tang times.[147]

The empiricist approach to Marxist historiography is concerned with veracity: with what degree of accuracy does it portray the past? But such an
approach misses the broader symbolic function of Marxism in postcolonial
Vietnam. In the 1940s, 1950s, and 1960s, Vietnamese intellectuals rejected
the historiographical models of dynastic times, based on Chinese exemplars, but they retained the traditional belief that idioms of authority originated *outside* of Vietnam. In this sense "new" historians resembled their
(feudal) predecessors. Moreover, postcolonial Vietnamese struggled against
a profound ambivalence. When they recognized the authority — and therefore allure — of foreign (in this case Soviet) models of history, they also cri-
tiqued them. Thus, as they appropriated these models, official historians also
modified them and applied them in innovative ways. The practice of borrowing particular models or idioms from another culture did not occur in
a transparent, mechanical way. One could even argue that, on the contrary,
Vietnamese appropriations involved a complex, critical process of transformation and that, in some cases, as in the ultimate rejection of the Stalinist
five-stage model of history, the authoritative model quietly disappeared as
an object of unspoken but unmistakable ridicule.

Although certain dynamics of traditional scholarship, such as the simultaneous incorporation and rejection of foreign authority, were present in
postcolonial debates on periodization, they appeared in a different guise.
For instance, postcolonial historians in the DRV often noted the importance
of Chinese interlocutors, but none of the texts they found essential had been
written by Chinese.[148] On the contrary, no matter how marginalized they
were in other intellectual settings, Soviet scholars occupied a more critical
place in their realm of scholarship.[149] But, it must be remarked, the Vietnamese often gained access to their works through Chinese translations and,
to a lesser degree, through French. Thus, even though they rejected Sinitic
culture, postcolonial Vietnamese relied on Chinese texts, but as *intermedi-
ary* devices. While Chinese contemporaries such as Guo Moruo and Fan
Wenlan enjoyed a certain prominence, they did so mainly as translators and
interpreters.

Third, even though the debates failed to generate new conclusions about
how to divide the past into meaningful segments, they made it possible to
reconfigure its scope. When the problem of periodization arose in the 1950s,

the conventional view was that the history of Vietnam went back some two thousand years, to the time of the Han dynasty occupation. In the course of the debates, however, a radically new chronology emerged: national history should be traced back at least four thousand and possibly even five thousand years.

Because committee and institute historians were obliged to periodize the past according to the Stalinist model, they concentrated on establishing the pace of the five stages. Every society, they were supposed to agree, began in a state of primitive communism and then, by necessity, passed through periods of slavery and feudalism. In the case of Vietnam, therefore, official historians had to determine whether the Hồng Bàng dynasty marked the period of primitive communism or the period of slavery. In trying to locate the various stages, postcolonial Vietnamese avoided more complicated issues. On what basis could myths of origins be intermingled with material traces, the physical evidence the archaeologists unearthed, to prove that the Hùng kings, the kingdom of Văn Lang, and the Hồng Bàng dynasty were genuinely historical? To be sure, postcolonial historians were not the first to say that Vietnamese history began with the Hùng kings; nor were they the first to pinpoint 2879 B.C.E. as the year in which their kingdom of Văn Lang emerged. Indeed, to support their own analyses, twentieth-century historians relied on the fifteenth-century chronicler Ngô Sĩ Liên. When Ngô Sĩ Liên identified that date as the origins of national history, he probably saw it as a way of alluding to the *longevity* of Vietnamese civilization rather than a literal point of departure. This speculation seems to be warranted by the fact that Ngô Sĩ Liên reconfigured many aspects of the Vietnamese past, especially those related to government, bureaucracy, and the civil service exams, so that in the period after the trauma of the Ming occupation the history of Vietnam would appear "normal."

In precolonial Vietnam, and in the premodern world more generally, what we now consider the separate realms of history and myth-history were richly intertwined. Armed with nineteenth-century European ideas about the definition of history as well as its purpose and meaning, however, colonial historians insisted on the distinction between genuinely historical as opposed to mythological renditions of the past. Colonial historians quickly categorized the kingdom of Văn Lang, the Hùng kings, the Hồng Bàng dynasty, and the idea of 2879 B.C.E. as an originary moment as examples of myth-history. As merely legendary explanations of origins, colonial scholars believed, they could not be considered as part of the historical record.

In postcolonial times, Vietnamese historians wanted literally to impose the figurative fifteenth-century ideas of origins, and they were able to do so, thanks in part, to the dogmatism of the Stalinist model. Thus, in the 1970s, as postcolonial scholars began to publish monographic studies of the Hùng kings, the five-stage model of history had disappeared from their intellectual horizon but the chronology that resulted from the debates on periodization remained in place.[150] In sum, relying at least nominally on Stalinist notions of history, postcolonial historians authenticated the symbolic propositions of fifteenth-century texts.

Along these same lines, it should be remarked that in new narratives of the national past the Hồng Bàng dynasty of Vietnam predated by far China's once-legendary Xia dynasty. By insisting on the historical authenticity of the Hùng kings and the kingdom of Văn Lang, postcolonial historians could dwell on a part of the past that predated the Chinese occupation by at least two thousand and perhaps even three thousand years! Although they acknowledged that the independence of Vietnamese civilization was ultimately eroded by *episodes* (not ten centuries) of Chinese occupation, its original and authentic essence was always recuperable. Paradoxically, as postcolonial historians struggled to divide the past into meaningful segments, they established instead a seamless narrative, a narrative in which the conditions of the third millennium B.C.E. produced the true telos of history: the August Revolution of 1945.

Finally, scanning through the debates on historical periodization, some have wondered why men who endured miserable lives in the jungle, who took tremendous risks fighting against the French, ended up writing such "boring" stuff. When I first encountered these debates, I regarded them as merely mechanical attempts to assign various parts of the past to particular slots: primitive communist here, slavery there, and so forth. Combing through the minutiae, however, I was struck by the sheer tortuousness and inconclusiveness of the debates. I also began to appreciate the elaborate hybridity of Marxism in Vietnam, and the fact that of all the Marxist scholars cited Marx himself enjoyed no real prominence. Marxism in Vietnam also had a richly affective dimension in that class ascription depended on emotional, political, and intellectual decisions—not merely the objective conditions of one's life. Thus, someone from the bourgeoisie could become "proletarianized."[151] Although the rich hybridity of the colonial occupations has been discussed, the fantastic creolity of postcolonial times has been rather neglected. To generalize that committee and institute historians were "Marxist," it seems to me, diminishes their inventiveness. In describing the revolutionaries' efforts to preserve the material traces of the past, Phạm Huy Thông also expressed the rich heterodoxy of Marxism in Vietnam:

> As early as November 23, 1945, just after the people's government took over the country, President Ho Chi Minh signed decree number 65, ordering the setting up of an Institute of Archaeology. And one of the decisions taken by our government following Dien Bien Phu and the Geneva Agreements . . . concerned the immediate reconstruction of the One-Pillared Pagoda, an artistic gem almost one thousand years old, which had been mined by enemy troops just before they withdrew from our capital. This initial step proved how seriously our leaders took history and the theses of historical materialism, how earnestly they understood and took to heart the aspirations of the people who, from time immemorial, have been deeply attached to things of the past.[152]

| **The Land of the Việt
and Việt Nam**

When the Committee for Literary, Historical, and Geographical Research was established in 1953, its principal obligation was to produce a new general history of Vietnam. Six years later, when the committee's historical section was reorganized as the Institute of History, the apparently simple feat of composing a basic history still had not been accomplished. Indeed, only decades later, in the 1970s and 1980s, did official historians finally publish a two-volume text. Whereas in the previous chapter I explored the historiographical dimensions of that delay, in this chapter I examine how debates on ethnic identities and on the history of interethnic ties prevented scholars from completing a new standard narrative of the national past.

In the nineteenth century, as the French military consolidated its conquest of Vietnam, colonial administrators changed its name to Annam, a term that originated with the Tang dynasty and literally means "Pacified (*an*) South (*nam*)." They also combined the three parts of Annam (Tonkin, Annam, and Cochinchina) with Cambodia and Laos to form the fundamentally new entity of Indochina.[1] In 1945, when revolutionaries reclaimed the power to name, they chose to revive the precolonial term "Việt Nam." Many scholars understood, however, that its traditional allusions to ethnic exclusiveness would have to be undone: no longer could it refer only to the ethnic Vietnamese. For more than thirty years, therefore, ethnographers, linguists, and specialists in other fields gathered evidence so that the new vision of Vietnam as an ethnically inclusive society could be refined. This process was formally concluded in 1979 when the government of the Socialist Republic of Vietnam (SRV) issued Decision 121, which declared Vietnam to be a multiethnic state composed of fifty-four ethnic groups.[2]

At the same time, the rhetorical insistence on diversity coincided with clear attempts to reshape and suppress it. To homogenize the social domain, DRV officials and their SRV successors sought to transform the details as well as the overarching structures of daily life. Ethnographic work, which was essential to new characterizations of Vietnam, also provided the means to alter existing conditions. In addition to simply recording what they saw, ethnographers introduced "standard" practices. With their "superstitions" abolished, "wasteful" rituals contained, and "feudal" family patterns dismantled, ethnic minorities were progressively disengaged from their autonomous, and therefore (from the perspective of the state) necessarily alienated pasts. The state also created new communities in which ethnic Vietnamese transplanted from the delta coexisted with ethnic minorities plucked from the mountains and midlands. To stabilize these new relations, ethnographers encouraged new modes of thought. Minorities were to abandon their sense of the Vietnamese as aggressive and imperialistic and the Vietnamese were to relinquish their habitual contempt for those whom they viewed as uncivilized. In fact, minorities and ethnic Vietnamese alike were urged to see each other as siblings (yet ones that were hierarchically ranked, to be sure).

Compelled to find precolonial precedents for what was entirely new — the idea that ethnic Vietnamese had always been bound to ethnic others by affective, familial ties — official historians had to reimagine the past. By obscuring the historicity of frontiers, they could present regions and peoples once considered remote as part of something much more transparent. By erasing the social and intellectual barriers between the Red River delta and the midlands and mountains, they were able to diminish the gaps between majority and minority groups. Or, they could read the system of tributary ties in distinctively asymmetrical ways. For instance, some historians claimed that in sending tribute missions to the Chinese emperor the Vietnamese emperor (in this context demoted to the status of king) affirmed the sovereignty of Vietnam. Others argued that Thai and Nung kings who paid tribute to the emperor of Vietnam did so to acknowledge their *lack* of sovereign status. And unlike southern historians who have traditionally devoted much attention to the topic of Nam Tiến (the Southern Advance), the centuries-long process through which ethnic Vietnamese settled and annexed what are now the country's central and southern parts, historians in the DRV more or less ignored it.

As historians excavated the precolonial past to find precedents for the present, ethnographers looked more closely at the French occupation. Although their work bore an uncanny resemblance to that of their colonial predecessors, postcolonial ethnographers emphasized the great chasm between their own enlightened tactics and the oppressive strategies of the French. For one, they regularly condemned the French for having stirred up interethnic tensions.[3] And, despite the homogenizing and centralizing project of which they themselves were a part, postcolonial ethnographers also criticized them for having restricted the power and authority of minority leaders. Making this argument on behalf of the Thai, the distinguished anthropologist Đặng Nghiêm Vạn opened with an astonishing claim: the Thai began to settle on "Vietnamese soil" at the beginning of the common era. Having moved into the northwest, which he described as an "integral part . . . of a stable and already centralized state," the Thai chiefs demonstrated their allegiance to the Vietnamese. He implied that because the Vietnamese received the proper signs of loyalty and submission, they did not interfere in Thai affairs. But the French, he complained, reduced the Thai chiefs to mere bureaucrats.[4] Although Đặng Nghiêm Vạn tried to contrast the subjugation of ethnic minorities under the French with the freedom and autonomy granted to them by the precolonial court and, by extension, the postcolonial state, other authors conveyed a different view. According to them, the French perpetuated rather than disrupted the patterns of precolonial times. Invoking an unusual understanding of feudalism, and on the basis of little evidence, ethnographer Lã Văn Lô, who was probably Tay, wrote that during feudal dynastic times the central government treated ethnic minorities as it treated all other subjects: it required them to abide by the same laws, perform the same corveé labor, and pay the same taxes. "This system," he declared, "was maintained unchanged by the French."[5]

A more reasonable approach to the French occupation would have emphasized the contradictions. In purely physical terms, the French dramatically decreased the distance between ethnic Vietnamese (as well as Chinese, Cham, and Khmer) in the delta and other ethnic groups in the midlands and mountains. In this sense, what postcolonial writers sometimes imagined as the interethnic intimacy of precolonial times became objectively possible. And yet, the colonial government, armed with the ethnographer's tools and insisting that each ethnic group be precisely defined, also established an elaborate taxonomy. The French, that is to say, lessened the *physical* distance between lowland and highland peoples and intensified the sense of *cultural* difference. The colonial government also elevated the economic power of some groups, such as the Chinese, increased the political status of other groups, including some of the Thai, and minimized the prominence of others.

Progressively, as French Indochina began to take shape, colonial officials developed new strategies for integrating the lowlands and highlands. The *mise en valeur* of the protectorates and colony — the process of converting them into potential sources of profit — required, first of all, vast infrastructural changes. French entrepreneurs opened mines, exploited forest resources, and established plantations for growing coffee, oil palms, rubber, and tea. So that natural and agricultural resources could be more easily extracted, the colonial government built railways and roads. Within a fifteen-year period (1912–1927), for instance, the surface of roads quintupled to around twenty-five thousand kilometers.[6] An elaborate network of highways and train tracks soon linked the wealth of the highlands to the new port facilities in Hanoi, Haiphong, and Qui Nhơn. Although the main highway extended from the Chinese to Siamese borders — following the trajectory traced originally by the imperial highway — and traversed the cities of Hanoi, Hue, Saigon, and Phnom Penh, two new lines went beyond the deltas and penetrated the highlands. According to French administrators who championed these sorts of improvements, trains and automobiles now connected regions that had once been "naturally detached."[7]

Although these infrastructural changes were economically motivated, they produced collateral results. Increasingly wearied by the heat and humidity of the lowlands — alerted to their epidemiological problems by physicians such as Alexandre Yersin — and inspired by Dutch journeys to the mountains of Sumatra and Java and British pilgrimages to Simla in the foothills of the Himalayas (the British colonization of the Cameron Highlands in Malaya occurred only later), the French also began to regard the mountains as a place for healthful retreat. Thus, they constructed a resort in the mountain town of Dalat. The increasing domestication of the highlands also occurred through colonial methods of policing and, in particular, the practice of exiling criminals and dissidents to the highlands. By constructing a detention center in Sơn La in the middle of Thai country, the French hoped to prevent collusion between prisoners, who were typically ethnic Vietnamese, and the population outside the prison.[8] Once the mountains and the plains were infrastructurally linked, ethnic Vietnamese began to migrate into the highlands. One administrator, identified only as "Saint Pouloff," predicted that the new road linking the Red River delta to the highlands would greatly accelerate the economic development of Thai territories; he also added that, to the "detriment of the Thai," it would also "unfortunately . . . favor the immigration of Kinh [ethnic Vietnamese]."[9] His remark is significant in that it alludes to the elements of social engineering so central to colonial ambitions. Like other colonial powers, the French also saw as their prerogative — and presented as a political and moral obligation — the possibility of reshuffling Indochinese peoples. In order to establish plantations, for example, French capitalists regularly evicted the "savage" mọi.[10] As an inspiration for these sorts of displacements, one official, Henri Brenier, cited what he believed to be a "remarkable and yet little-known accomplishment" of the League of Nations, which had succeeded in shifting a million and a half Greeks from Asia Minor to Greece.[11]

Christian evangelists and colonial entrepreneurs who built mountain retreats, plantations, hospitals, and roads irrevocably altered the physical and material relations between the people of the mountains and the people of the plains. At least as dramatically, the scholarly dimension of colonial rule also transformed those ties. French colonial officials in Indochina, like their counterparts in Africa and the Caribbean, and like Dutch and British officials as well, staked their claims to authority on their mastery of modern science; they viewed the ethnographic ordering of the human race as a signpost of that expertise. Thus, an entire army of colonial ethnographers set out to measure heads, examine teeth, and describe marriage patterns and wedding feasts; they redacted dipthongs, drew pictures of dwellings, and offered sketches of tribal dress; they observed the techniques of hunting and farming and recorded death dances and burials. In the process, colonial ethnographers compiled massive collections of empirical data. The result of this vast archive was a stunning portrait of the ethnic complexity of Tonkin, Annam, Cochinchina, Cambodia, and Laos. Not only colonial politics but also colonial scholarship dissolved the idea of Vietnam as the land of the Việt by promoting the idea of an Indochina that was ethnically mixed, and joined, through the process of adoption, to Mother France.

From the perspective of the ethnic Vietnamese, the French ethnographic endeavor introduced a new set of political and intellectual problems. Fully accustomed to the cultural arrogance of the Chinese, the Việt now had to endure a new layer of contempt. In the words of E. Chassigneux, one of the great synthesizers of colonial thought, "All of the inhabitants of Indochina were, without exception, primitive." However, he added, some groups, "benefiting from a civilizing influence from outside," were able to overcome their primitive state.[12] Pierre Huard agreed with this assessment and, to advance it a step further, he cited the Vietnamese custom of teeth-blackening as an "unmistakable sign of primitivity." Like Chassigneux, Huard also noted the "civilizing effect" of foreigners; he claimed that because of their extensive interactions with Chinese immigrants, southern Vietnamese, much more than their northern compatriots, had abandoned that "loathsome habit" (of blackening their teeth).[13] Thus in some ways the practices of the French reinforced the traditional hierarchy that privileged things Chinese: according to the French, the Chinese presence had allowed the Vietnamese (particularly in the South) to take the first tentative steps toward civilization. But colonial practices also created a new hierarchy that privileged the French and denigrated China as a once great civilization that had become stagnant and moribund. Because China was so clearly in decline it could no longer bear the burden of civilizing barbarian others, and thus it was the task of France to civilize the Vietnamese. Paul Doumer, governor general of Indochina from 1897 to 1902, best expressed this view when he characterized the Indochinese as "the race called upon to benefit from French civilization."[14]

French ethnographers also created a new sense of hierarchy that was much more comprehensive than either the Việt-centric or Sino-centric hierarchies had been. Chassigneux articulated this new notion of hierarchical relations when he observed that the ethnic groups of Indochina were naturally of unequal importance. "The Annamites, Cambodians, and Thai," he wrote, "are the most important peoples of French Indochina. But how many other groups must be at least briefly mentioned!"[15] The profusion of ethnic categories and the construction of dozens upon dozens of identities totally overwhelmed the tripartite distinctions of precolonial times: civilized (Việt), savage (mọi or mán), and people of foreign culture. Therefore, even though French ethnographers maintained a keen sense of hierarchy, their ethnographic method had a distinctly leveling effect: all ethnic groups, whether "primitive" or "advanced," could be taxonomized according to the same criteria, typically kinship, material life, rituals, and religion. Zealously, French scholars and officials began to transform the traditional methods of conceptualizing and politically structuring similarity and difference. As colonial ethnographers produced an inventory of ethnic groups, colonial administrators sought explicitly to preserve—which often meant to create—the boundaries between them. Recognizing the strategic importance of the Thai, the French granted them an autonomous state; in a gesture of reciprocity, some of the Thai fought on behalf of the French against the Viet Minh.

OVERTURES

Postcolonial writers usually identified the emergence of the Indochinese Communist Party (ICP) in 1930 as the turning point in majority-minority relations. Although they criticized the feudal dynasties, the French, and reactionary Vietnamese for having seen non-Việt peoples as barbarians, they praised the "enlightened perspective" of the ICP and Viet Minh. Explaining more fully what this perspective entailed, postcolonial writers invariably stressed that one of the ICP's principal goals was to unite all nationalities on the basis of equality. Because this utterance contains the word "equality," it was adduced as evidence of the ICP's egalitarian attitude toward *all* Vietnamese, in the broadly political as opposed to narrowly ethnic sense. In the 1930s, however, and in later decades as well, the Vietnamese often viewed themselves as the normative group; "nationalities," therefore, initially referred to non-Việt peoples. With ethnic Vietnamese excluded from this egalitarian equation, the ICP statement really meant that all non-Việt peoples were equal in status. While the ICP challenged traditional hierarchies that allowed one minority group to dominate another, it did not question the hierarchy that placed ethnic Vietnamese at the top. The evidence for this claim is abundant. Việt Chung, for one, mentioned that the Tay, Nung, and Thai minorities had been controlled by the Vietnamese monarchy through the tributary system. In addition to this hierarchy, which he saw as completely legitimate, illegitimate ones had also arisen. The Thai had dominated the Xá, Hà Nhì, and Cò Sung, he noted, and the Tay had preyed on the Nung.[16] Because the statement from 1930 has been so frequently misconstrued as proof of the party's commitment to the equality of all Vietnamese, later declarations have been similarly misread. Once the ambiguity of the original statement is restored, however, the ambiguity of subsequent revisions and clarifications becomes apparent. And because the ICP was obsessed with the "nationalities question," the statements quickly multiplied. The original statement issued in 1930 was revised in 1932, 1935, 1938, 1939,

1941, and again in 1945, at the end of World War II, on the eve of the ICP's disbanding.[17]

Policies announced in 1932 and 1935 emphasized the autonomy of nationalities and their right to self-determination: "After the overthrow of the imperialist yoke . . . each nationality will have the right to self-determination, i.e. to choose between adhering to the Union of Indochinese Soviet Republics and proclaiming itself a separate state."[18] But this statement, often taken at face value, requires a critical reading because official documents from that same period also emphasized the unity of ethnic Vietnamese and "national minorities" against the French. That some nationalities might choose to disengage themselves from the anti-French resistance, or, indeed, fight on behalf of France, as did some of the Thai, was not considered. What is most dramatic, however, is that from one moment to the next, *nationalities* were transformed into *national minorities*. Despite the insistence that nationalities would be free to determine their own political status, the unspoken assumption was already in place: nationalities would be converted into *ethnic minorities* within a centralized state governed from Hanoi.

In 1941, the ICP began to relocate the bases of the revolutionary movement in Southern China, Hanoi, and Haiphong to the highlands of northern Vietnam. In May, members of the Executive Committee met in the mountain province of Cao Bằng and formally established the Viet Minh Front as a way to focus popular resentment against the French and Japanese and to minimize the ICP's earlier emphasis on class.[19] Because the Viet Minh were far removed from the lowland cities and towns, which were controlled by the Japanese and French, they enjoyed a measure of safety and a degree of vulnerability at the same time. To gain essential support for the resistance, cadres carefully recruited among the ethnic groups in the highlands, relying on such key figures as Chu Văn Tấn, who was Nung, and Hoàng Văn Thụ, who was Tay, to establish links between highland peoples and the Viet Minh. Looking back on that early stage of the revolutionary movement, Đặng Nghiêm Vạn recollected that there had been no signs of tension when the "militants" arrived; on the contrary, he recalled, they had been welcomed affectionately, with a "boundless solicitude."[20] In his memoirs of the Viet Minh, whom he remembered through a soft-focus lens, Lê Quảng Ba, who was Tay, recollected that some of the cadres learned local languages and took "ethnic" names; Ho Chi Minh, he noted, was known to dress in Nung style and to speak some Nung words.[21] To facilitate the recruitment of highland peoples in the 1940s, Viet Minh cadres assured them that a greater Việt imperium was not in the making. But, as the physical boundaries became more porous, the cultural distance also declined, and the likelihood of an expanded, Việt-centered state loomed ever larger.

In August 1945, only days after Japan's surrender, the Viet Minh formally seized power. As the former revolutionaries' goals shifted from subverting the colonial government to stabilizing their own, the impracticality of their earlier positions became clear.[22] In short, those who had once risked their lives sowing disorder were determined to combat it. And their sense of urgency quickly intensified. In September, acting on behalf of the Allies, British troops began to arrive in the southern part of Vietnam. Instead of carrying out the mission with which they had been charged—to disarm the Japanese—the British, aware that France intended to reconquer Indochina, allowed some Japanese troops to retain their weapons so that they could keep the revolutionaries in check.[23] In the South, the revolution began to unravel; in the following year it was derailed in the North. In November 1946, the French shelled the port of Haiphong, killing thousands of Vietnamese, and in December they attacked the power station in Hanoi. The Resistance War, known outside of Vietnam as the First Indochina War, officially commenced.

Throughout the war (1946–1954), as the French tried to regain control of the former colonies, the DRV and a new front organization known as the Liên Việt rededicated themselves to the always ambiguous policy of national self-determination—because, skeptics assume, revolutionaries had to rely once again on the hospitality of highland peoples.[24] In 1951 the Vietnamese Labor Party was formed to continue the work of the ICP.[25] At the Second Party Congress convened in February, it was agreed that "the nationalities . . . must unite and assist each other in waging the resistance and building the country. We shall resolutely combat chauvinistic nationalism."[26] Although the prerevolutionary promise that nationalities would determine their own political futures was not overtly rescinded, it was clear that it no longer applied; even the much more limited idea of autonomy—within a framework dominated by the ethnic Vietnamese—had disappeared. Instead, the party began to make great displays of cultural concessions. For example, in 1952, when the Liên Việt seized control of the Northwest Autonomous Zone, it declared that any nationality having its own written script could continue to use it.[27] This statement, offered as an assurance, simply underscored the degree to which more meaningful guarantees were no longer valid. When the DRV declared that Vietnamese was the official language and the medium of instruction in public schools, the potential significance of this provision also vanished.

Without a doubt, the revolutionary movement and the Resistance War established a fundamentally new paradigm for international relations within Vietnam. However, rather than regard the new patterns as a shift from relations of inequality to those of equality, I would stress the ambiguity of the party's original position and focus on the emergence of new idioms for organizing relations of dominance and subordination. During the early stages of the anti-imperialist struggle, as they cultivated ties with non-Việt peoples, Viet Minh cadres acknowledged the purely instrumental aspect of those ties and recognized the potentially divergent paths that various nationalities might follow in postrevolutionary times. Before the revolution was settled, however, warfare broke out, and earlier references to autonomy and national self-determination were eclipsed by an insistence on the inviolable integrity of Vietnam. In this context, new kinds of hierarchical imagery emerged: acting as older brother (*anh*), the ethnic Vietnamese would lead the other national groups now recast as *ethnic minorities in Vietnam* and assigned the role of younger sibling (*em*).

THE ETHNOGRAPHIC IMPULSE

Decolonization depends, first, on the establishment of political independence.[28] To decolonize in a vaster sense, however, is to establish a new culture, a new history, new notions of politics and new political institutions, new economic structures and economic relations, and new notions of community. When the French surrendered at Dien Bien Phu in spring 1954, DRV leaders were free to relaunch the program of postcolonial transformation. To carry out these economic, cultural, and political changes, both the physical landscape and the conceptual framework for imagining Vietnam had to be revised. As the French had done before them, administrative elites in the DRV proceeded to reduce the distance between the delta and the highlands.

By improving the existing roads and constructing new ones, by establishing schools, by transforming swidden agriculturalists into cooperativized rice farmers, and, most critically, by transferring ethnic Vietnamese from the delta to the midlands and highlands, the DRV further eroded traditional boundaries. Those borders were intellectually undermined as well by the Research Committee, which functioned as a postcolonial antidote to the French School of the Far East, where colonial scholars had assumed for themselves the power and authority to represent the history and culture of Vietnam. Central to the postcolonial process of reimagining Vietnam was the issue of ethnicity. How could the idea of Vietnam be broadened beyond its original meaning of "the land of the Việt"? There is no need to comprehensively survey postcolonial ethnographies, but their significance, I should note, derives in part from their sheer cumulative effect. By examining them in some detail, we can see the tremendous flux and confusion that surrounded the question of ethnicity after 1954.

In the early issues of the *Journal of Literary, Historical, and Geographical Research,* their official organ, members of the Research Committee often talked about the social complexity of Vietnam. Phan Khôi, for one, urged his colleagues to oppose the elitism of traditional histories because they had merely chronicled the records and actions of mandarins and kings. Instead, he argued, "new history," because it was a history of the Vietnamese people as a whole, would speak the parts of the past that had previously been silenced. Almost as a postscript, and reflecting the confusion about questions of ethnicity, Phan Khôi noted that the expression "Vietnamese people" (*người Việt Nam*) included "racial minorities" (*chủng tộc thiểu số*) in the highlands.[29] Evidently anticipating some resistance to this claim, he added that even when racial distinctions were not made explicit they were clearly implied. Tactfully avoiding the more usual connotations of *kinh* — civilized and urbane — he observed that the term, which literally means "city" or "capital," was traditionally used to distinguish ethnic Vietnamese from Tho, just as the expression *người Huế* (the people of Hue), he noted, referred to the ethnic Vietnamese residents of that city but not to the indigenous Cham. Elaborating more fully on the heterogeneity of the "Vietnamese people," Phan Khôi specifically identified six "racial minorities," the Tôi, Mọi, Thày, Đầy, Tay, and Thai, as the relevant groups.[30]

To contemporary readers, Phan Khôi's clarification of the term "Vietnamese people" is offensive and, more to the point, simply wrong. First, from a contemporary perspective, the country's heterogeneity stems from ethnic differences rather than racial ones, although it must be pointed out that in the 1950s the two terms were used interchangeably. Second, although the term "Tho" is still used today, it no longer figures in the generic sense (meaning highlander) that Phan Khôi intended; it refers to a specific ethnic group. Third, "Tôi" and "Mọi" are both generic and pejorative terms: "Tôi" conveys the idea of people who are of lesser status and "Mọi" signals "savage." Fourth, the names of the groups Phan Khôi identifies as "savage" are no longer in use, at least not officially; the "Đá-vách Savages" (Mọi Đá-vách), for instance, seem to have been reclassified as Hrê. Fifth, the last four names in his list are simply variants of "Thai" and "Tay."[31] Finally, although the habit of designating ethnic Vietnamese as Kinh is now officially encouraged, during the 1950s and 1960s revolutionaries condemned it as "feudal." In place of Kinh, they proposed less arrogant and chauvinistic terms, such as Việt or Lạc Việt. In 1979, however, Decision 121, which listed the fifty-four ethnic groups officially recognized today, rehabilitated the term Kinh in order to diminish—I assume—the sense of Vietnam as the land of the Việt. Looking back on Phan Khôi's statement, today's readers easily point out his errors. But his explanation is instructive because it alerts us to how in the 1950s educated Vietnamese imagined Vietnam.

Among postcolonial scholars, Phan Khôi was not the first to emphasize the ethnic heterogeneity of Vietnam, but it was he who most clearly discerned its importance to historical narrative and analysis, and other historians soon followed suit. In one of his early articles on how to periodize the national past, for example, Nguyễn Đổng Chi divided Vietnamese history into four discrete eras: clan society, early feudalism, centralized feudalism, and the semifeudal and semicolonial stage. Although his discussion of the first two phases stressed the salience of specific racial or ethnic groups, his analysis of the two more recent periods omitted them altogether. The implication of his argument is that history itself is a process through which "tribal" differences are continually overcome.[32] Trần Huy Liệu also raised the question of ethnic or racial differences when he observed that there were many different kinds or species of people (*giống người*) in Vietnam. Whereas contemporary narratives often emphasize the warmth and familial quality of interethnic ties, Trần Huy Liệu underscored the sense of remoteness. Because the differences among the more important groups were so great, he noted, "we easily mistake each other for foreigners."[33]

Although scholars such as Phan Khôi, Nguyễn Đổng Chi, and Trần Huy Liệu recognized and even emphasized the ethnic complexity of Vietnam, other writers believed that these discussions were subversive and undermined the possibility of a cohesive national community. In response to these thoughts, a statement signed collectively by the Research Committee retorted that although the "colonialists had tried for a hundred years to destroy its unity" Vietnam from North to South was permanently "fixed" (*ổn định*). It was a single "unified bloc [*khối thống nhất*] characterized by a common language, territory, economy, and culture."[34]

The motivations behind this utterance can be understood in at least three ways. First, the political circumstances of the mid-1950s were truly alarming. Despite the provisions of the Geneva Accords, which emphasized that the seventeenth parallel did *not* mark a political boundary between North and South, and despite the DRV's claims to represent all of Vietnam, the "unified bloc" was split in the middle. The Republic of Vietnam in the South also presented itself as a sovereign and independent state in command of all of Vietnam. Once the French were defeated, the problem of the South became especially glaring; and the divergent meanings of the Southern Advance (Nam Tiến) resurfaced. Southerners were inclined to view it as the social, economic, and political processes that resulted in a new society and a new state in the South, whereas northerners tended to see Nam Tiến as a project orchestrated by the northern court and as an extension — rather than repudiation — of northern authority. In the DRV, the uneasiness that surrounded the idea of a separate state in the South was transformed into a more totalizing fear (and denial) of differences and divisions. In other words, the denial of differences and the assertions of unity and homogeneity functioned *pre*scriptively: Vietnam *should* have been "permanently fixed" when it was, in fact, genuinely divided.

Second, this insistence also reflected the deeply rooted conviction that Vietnam was, by definition, the land of the Việt. If Vietnam was now to be understood in an *inclusive* sense, how could the government in Hanoi manage the potentially centrifugal forces that ethnic diversity seemed to imply? In an effort to allay that fear, Trần Huy Liệu tried to clarify the relation between ethnic diversity, on the one hand, and national unity, on the other. In his own research, he explained, as he explored the origins of the Vietnamese nation (*dân tộc Việt Nam*), he had not only ethnic Vietnamese in mind; rather, he was interested in the formation of that broader community that linked various ethnic groups together in a new social, political, and cultural collective. Much of the confusion of contemporary debates, he claimed, must be attributed to the varied registers of the expression *dân tộc*. This term, which was composed of two roots, "people" (*dân*) and "ethnos" (*tộc*), could simply convey the notion of "country." In this case, he explained, it would be synonymous with *nước* (meaning water, literally) or *đất nước* (earth and water, literally). But *dân tộc*, he argued, could also mean "people" and be comparable to *giống người* (species or race). To illustrate the ambiguity generated by the term *dân tộc*, Trần Huy Liệu offered this example: "Việt Nam là một dân tộc có nhiều dân tộc," which means

(1) Vietnam is one country with many nations; (2) Vietnam is one nation with many nationalities; and (3) Vietnam is one nation with many peoples. To avoid this confusion, Trần Huy Liệu recommended that historians deploy less equivocal terms: "ethnic Vietnamese" should be referred to as *dân tộc Việt;* and "ethnic minorities" as *thiểu số dân tộc.* Any reference to "Vietnamese people" (*dân tộc Việt Nam*), he said, should be understood in its inclusive sense, as a reference to the entire community of ethnic Vietnamese and ethnic minorities in Vietnam.[35]

Third, the baleful effect of Stalin's *Marxism and the National Question* should not be overlooked.[36] As Eric Hobsbawm has wryly pointed out, although the intellectual merit of this essay is "modest, but not negligible — if somewhat derivative," it enjoyed great international influence among communists, generally, and in the dependent world particularly.[37] In Vietnam this text acquired a nearly sacred glow, and it routinely overwhelmed more reasoned discussions of ethnic differences, on the one hand, and broader collectivities, on the other. In *Marxism and the National Question,* Stalin insisted on this formulation: "A nation is an historically evolved, stable community of people, formed on the basis of a common language, territory, economic life, and psychological make-up manifested in a common culture."[38] Stalin defined the nation in order to censure it; he linked nationalism with counterrevolutionary agendas and condemned the "obfuscation" and "lying propaganda" carried out on its behalf. Vietnamese revolutionaries, on the other hand, celebrated the idea of the nation, but because they were also obliged to demonstrate the proper reverence for Stalin, they converted his condemnation of nationalism into a value-neutral set of conditions that, Vietnam, "unified in language, territory, economy, and culture," happily satisfied. Therefore, when Trần Huy Liệu sought to open up the debate on national unity and approach it from an ethnically *inclusive* perspective, he succeeded only in eliciting a more categorical denial of ethnic differences within Vietnam. A statement signed collectively by the Research Committee sternly reproached those (unnamed) authors who believed that Vietnam was one country with many nations. Vietnam, the committee countered, "is one nation; it is not several states, nor is it several nations. . . . Vietnam is one nation and that is the undeniable truth. . . . Everyone has already acknowledged that Vietnam is a single unified bloc." Offering no evidence for this claim, the committee merely repeated the magical passage from Stalin's key text. Promising to dispel any misconceptions about the true nature of Vietnam, the committee proposed to publish additional research proving that "in language, territory, economy, and culture, Vietnam is a single unified bloc."[39]

On the basis of these details, one could conclude that the problem in grappling with the ethnic diversity of Vietnam was principally linguistic because the Vietnamese use the same term (*dân tộc*) for nation and ethnicity. Despite this linguistic confusion, one could argue that the Vietnamese were fully aware and fully accepting of ethnic differences in Vietnam, but were reluctant, understandably, to link them to a separate administrative or political status. My own sense is that the linguistic confusion heightened the tension of the debates without, however, having directly produced it. In my view, the difficulty in discussing ethnic differences, on the one hand, and national unity, on the other, was essentially extra-lexical and stemmed from a genuine uneasiness about ethnic others. Historians like Trần Huy Liệu were supposed to map out the open, unmediated, transparent quality of social relations in Vietnam, yet at the same time they viewed the non-Việt part as essentially foreign.

Finally, although revolutionary writers cited Stalin in order to reinforce their claims, my guess is that they actually had French interlocutors in mind. If we recollect the basic historiographical framework for colonial scholars, the postcolonial insistence on the nineteenth-century ideal of the nation makes more sense. Postcolonial historians worked with a kind of urgency to undo the colonial appellations "Indochina" and "Annam" and to naturalize, legitimate, or simply make conventional, the idea of Vietnam. Whereas Ernest Renan's *What Is a Nation?* was one of the animating texts of the colonial regime, Stalin's *Marxism and the National Question* became the principal source in postcolonial times; it functioned as a Marxist reworking of the nationalist ideal. Although Stalin's (negative) ideal of the nation was entirely incompatible with the hyper-nationalism of the Vietnamese, scholars in the DRV still invoked it to support their own ideals.

The Research Committee, having sternly rejected the idea of a multinational state, must have been surprised when the government announced the establishment of the Thai-Meo and Viet Bac autonomous zones.[40] In a study of the Thai written in the 1960s, Nguyễn Đức Hợp characterized the creation of the autonomous zone as part of the DRV's attempt to "dispel misgivings among the Thai," who "longed for genuine autonomy."[41] In a similar survey published at the same time, however, Việt Chung claimed that the origins of the autonomous zones should be traced to the malevolent practices of the French: "The colonial policy of division and deception found its most perfidious expression during the last Indochina war. In the occupied territories, the French colonialists tried to set up so-called 'autonomous states.' "[42] Covering more than one-fifth of DRV territory, the Thai-Meo Autonomous Zone had a population of around half a million and included somewhere between twelve and nineteen ethnic groups.[43] The name of this autonomous zone was later changed to Tay Bac (Northwest). This modification may have signaled an attempt to move away from patterns established in China, where the names of autonomous zones reflected their ethnic composition. Or, it may have derived from the effort to diminish—rhetorically, that is—the dominance of the two main groups, the Thai and the Meo (who were eventually reclassified as Hmong), but it could have also reflected political concerns, since the Black and White Thai were on opposite sides of the revolutionary divide. In any case, by translating what was originally an ethnic appellation into cartographic terms, the new designation reinforced the idea of Vietnam as a territorial state; by fixing on the geographical relation between the national capital and the autonomous zone, this change of name also underscored the ideal of centralized government based in Hanoi.

A number of scholars (the work of Hanna Pitkin in particular) have written about the essential ambivalence of autonomy: an entity can claim to be autonomous only insofar as it is connected to another.[44] Autonomy, in other words, does not describe a state of utter self-containment; on the contrary, it stresses the fundamental connectedness between one entity and another. Recognizing that the idea of autonomy is indeed ambivalent, that it indicates both separation and connection, one can still argue that the DRV manipulated it in order to suppress the emergence of competing centers of power. To substantiate this claim, I would point to Decision 229-SL. If read very selectively, this document can be adduced as evidence of the DRV's progressive approach to divergent visions of politics. It proposes that "the nationalities living on the territory [of Vietnam] are absolutely equal. They enjoy all democratic liberties." If read at greater length, however, it naturalizes the annexationist process by which ethnic Vietnamese took control of what was once an ill-defined frontier. Furthermore, this document wipes out the potential autonomy of autonomous zones by declaring that "all nationalities . . . must unite and assist one another in the struggle for peace, reunification, independence and democracy for the whole country! All acts of contempt, oppression or division, of great national chauvinism and of narrow nationalism are strictly forbidden."[45] Before Decisions 230-SL and 268-SL formally established the autonomous zones, in other words, Decision 229-SL had already rendered them impotent. Nguyễn Đức Hợp summarized the situation precisely: "To guarantee the right to autonomy . . . is only one side of the problem. Another, more important, consists in insuring the smooth running of this autonomous power so that it may become a strong lever in carrying out socialist transformations, developing economy and culture."[46] The real meaning of autonomy was considerably less than initially suggested; what it meant in practice was that the pretense of autonomy could be temporarily maintained, pending reunification of the country and the absorption of autonomous zones into a new national framework governed from Hanoi.

Nevertheless, in recognition of the fact that the mere presence of autonomous zones attested to linguistic, cultural, territorial, and economic divisions within Vietnam, scholars cautiously began to pursue a more heterogeneous vision of the national community. At the end of 1955, for example, Nguyễn Lương Bích cited the usual passage from *Marxism and the National Question*. Instead of declaiming, as others had, that Vietnam was a "single, unified bloc," he observed that some *states* had many nations. Trần Huy Liệu had once been reproached for making a similar claim, but Nguyễn Lương Bích couched this same formulation in more legalistic and Sinitic terms: "Vietnam is one state [*quốc gia*] with many nations" (*dân tộc*).[47] As he set out to discuss the multiplicity of nations within Vietnam, he observed that of the criteria proposed by Stalin, he believed that language was the most important. In this sense, he said, it was impossible to consider Vietnam a single nation because the language of the ethnic Vietnamese (he used the "feudal" expression *tiếng Kinh*) was not the language spoken throughout Vietnam. Although the state had tried to propagate its use throughout the land, he noted, for many it still remained a foreign tongue. Similarly, he argued, although the Thai and Meo shared the same territory and economic life, they lacked a common language and could not, therefore, be considered a single nation. But the politics of autonomous zones and the intellectual pursuit of a multivocal rendition of the past still met with fundamental resistance. In February 1956, months after the founding of Tay Bac, Trần Huy Liệu recited a more embellished version of the usual incantation: from the Five Passes in the North to the Cà Mâu Peninsula in the South, Vietnam was a single unified bloc.[48]

Besides their obvious manifestations in policy, the politics of the postcolonial period surfaced in historical narrative as well, and, as the idea of ethnic inclusion increasingly took shape, ethnic Vietnamese were encouraged to develop new attitudes toward the people and places that had become part of Vietnam. Whereas the Vietnamese had traditionally regarded the mountains as strange places teeming with malevolent spirits and ridden with disease, postcolonial writers domesticated and aestheticized them by proposing a new sense of topography and borders. Tố Hữu's *Viet Bac,* for example, which won the national prize for poetry in 1956, looks back nostalgically at the days and months after the French were defeated at Dien Bien Phu. As the narrator prepares to leave the mountains and return to Hanoi, he reflects sentimentally on the beauty of the landscape and the people—indeed, the two are conflated—and, in a gesture that would have startled earlier generations of Vietnamese, he meditates on the emotional attachments he has formed:

> I'm going back, will you remember me?
> I'm going back, but I'll remember the flowers and the people,
> The green of the jungle, the fresh red of banana blooms.
> In the mountain peaks, sun shimmered on the knife at my side.
> On a spring day, apricot blossoms turned the jungle white.
> I remember hat makers whittling bamboo,
> Cicadas calling, the jungle's golden hues.
> I remember a young girl, alone, gathering shoots of bamboo.
> In the autumn, moonlight fell peacefully.
> I remember someone singing love songs with loyalty and grace.[49]

This landscape, now familiar and appealing, bears no sign of insalubrity nor, for that matter, any trace of the violence that has engulfed it—the knife at the narrator's side serves only to reflect the sun. In this new configuration, the mountains and the river deltas together form a cohesive whole; bonds of affection tie ethnic Vietnamese to minorities.

After the victory of 1954, postcolonial scholars devoted considerable energy to ethnographic work so that the new general history could be written. And yet, out of a strange deference to Stalin—strange because the Vietnamese revered what he had most vigorously condemned—the words "ethnology," "ethnography," and "ethnic minority" were seldom pronounced. In March 1957, however, Nguyễn Lương Bích translated an announcement from the journal *Soviet Ethnology* that noted that the Fifth International Conference on Ethnic Minorities and Ethnology had been recently convened in Moscow.[50] For scholars and political elites in Vietnam, the fact that the conference was held in Moscow fully transformed ethnographic studies into a wholesome, ideologically legitimate pursuit; the event also made it possible to rewrite the history of the discipline itself and to disengage ethnographic research from colonial paradigms. By the end of the following year, the ethnographic endeavor was officially recognized when the party dissolved the Research Committee and created in its place a series of institutes, including the Institute of History, within which were three smaller units (*bộ*) for history, archaeology, and ethnology. At the same time, control over the State Science Committee was shifted from the party to the government.[51] Thus, by the time the Institute of History was founded, the idea of ethnic and linguistic diversity had been consolidated as an unremarkable part of the intellectual terrain.

Even though the term for ethnology (*dân tộc học*) was neologistic, the field of ethnology was quickly declared an organic (*hữu cơ*) part of historical science, and Nguyễn Lương Bích set out to trace its ancient lineage.[52] The field of ethnology first emerged, he explained, in pre-Christian times: just as Herodotus was the father of history, so, too, was he the father of ethnology. Marxist ethnology shared these Herodotean roots, but in the mid-nineteenth century, he observed, through the work of Marx, Engels, and Georgy Plekhanov, ethnology developed in a new direction. In the twentieth century, thanks to the contributions of Lenin and Stalin, the discipline of ethnology had further evolved.[53] What is striking about this trajectory is the scrupulousness with which Nguyễn Lương Bích avoided any direct reference to the colonial origins and imperialist dimensions of ethnology, even though French scholars had composed all the existing ethnographies of ethnic Vietnamese (recast as Annamites) and of ethnic minorities (often under the rubric *montagnards*). In fact, his own account of ethnology was more openly indebted to Eugène Pittard's *Race and History* than to Marx's *Ethnological Notebooks* or Engels's *Origin of the Family, Private Property, and the State*.[54] Despite his impressive attempt to transcend the colonial origins of ethnographic studies, Nguyễn Lương Bích was also compelled to recall them. Later, to clarify the meaning of ethnology further, he included the French expression *études ethnographiques* (in parenthesis), hoping that this gloss would eliminate any lingering confusion.[55]

Once ethnology was institutionally recognized, state scholars reported with greater frequency on ethnographic studies outside of Vietnam. The new *Journal of Historical Research*, in fact, specifically earmarked a section for reviews of foreign scholarship. Two of the frequent contributors were Nguyễn Khắc Đạm, who translated a number of articles from Chinese sources such as *Contemporary China Biweekly* and *Historical Research,* and Trương Như Ngân, who regularly translated pieces from Russian sources, including *Soviet Ethnology* and *Historical Studies.* In this way Vietnamese readers not only kept abreast of ethnological work in China and the Soviet Union but in other countries such as North Korea, Czechoslovakia, and East Germany as well.[56] Not incidentally, this section also reveals the complex path of mediation that allowed Vietnamese readers to be apprised of events in other countries. One of the leading ethnographers in Korea, for example, became familiar to readers in the DRV through a Vietnamese translation of a Russian translation of a Korean-language original. Similarly, news of the Sixth International Conference on Ethnology, held in 1960 in Paris, was based on Soviet reports.[57]

The new journal also organized an ongoing discussion of ethnographic research in Vietnam, and a profusion of ethnographic works began to appear. Nguyễn Văn Khoa, for one, wrote on domestic servants in early Thai history; Nguyễn Tuấn Liêu investigated the *quảng* system of the Tay; and Nông Trung analyzed the relations among various branches of the Nung.[58] Instead of researching a particular ethnic group, Đỗ Thiện compiled a history of Lai Châu, one of the northwestern provinces with a high concentration of minorities; and Đặng Nghiêm Vạn recounted the history of various Thai migrations to that region.[59] Lâm Tâm compared marriage patterns and family systems and wrote about the history of Meo migrations as well as their practices of naming.[60] Whereas these scholars all approached ethnography in descriptive terms, some writers—Nguyễn Lương Bích, for example—began to address more theoretical issues relating to ethnicity and to the formation of ethnic groups.[61]

Between the time that the section on ethnology was established in 1958 and the end of the First Five-Year Plan in 1965, the Institute of History published numerous monographs, including a collection of Thai chronicles, a compilation of Soviet studies of ethnological theory and method, and a survey of ethnic minorities in northern-central Vietnam.[62] Although dozens joined in the ethnographic enterprise, the work of two writers, Lã Văn Lô and Mạc Đường, demands particular attention because their attitudes and, to a lesser degree, their empirical data, anchored ethnographic research.

Lã Văn Lô made substantial contributions to the field. In a series of articles published in the early 1960s, he investigated the historical origins and religious cosmologies of the Cao Lan, Nung, and Thai. He also wrote detailed accounts of the Tay, discussing their origins and early history, their religious beliefs and practices, the forms of their residential dwellings, and their folksongs and poetry.[63] But Lã Văn Lô is best remembered for his survey of Communist Party policy on nationalities in which he likened the development of some ethnic groups—the Tay, Nung, Cham, and Khmer—to that of the Việt because these groups had all experienced feudalism. But some minorities in the northern-central highlands, he explained, did not develop along the same lines; the cultural level of these group, therefore, was still very low (*thấp*).[64]

Mạc Đường, author of the pathbreaking survey of minorities in northern-central Vietnam, was then known for his research on the Zao (Dao in Vietnamese), but he also published detailed pieces on the Muong and on the Rục, one of the smaller minority groups of Quảng Bình. What made his work so distinctive was his willingness to cast ethnic studies in a wider political and social context; he looked comparatively at the economies of various ethnic groups, for instance, and investigated the history of interethnic relations in prerevolutionary times.[65] More to the point, it was Mạc Đường who inaugurated the series on ethnographic research by examining the historical origins of the Mán and the reason they were known by this name, which literally means "savage."[66] Because the Mán had immigrated to Vietnam relatively recently, he explained, they were forced into the more difficult terrain of the higher elevations—areas that earlier immigrants had been able to avoid. This explanation, it should be noted, was based on a highly tendentious chronology and a skewed sense of causality. In many cases, peoples who normally dwelled in the lowlands were pushed into higher elevations by the arrival of ethnic Vietnamese. Mạc Đường's matter-of-fact tone confirmed what was not directly stated but clearly implied: there *were* legitimate reasons to refer to the highland peoples as savage, and the rationale, while not explicitly stated, was apparent: civilization could be gauged by geography and, more specifically, by elevation. The people in the lowlands (i.e., ethnic Vietnamese) were fully civilized; those dwelling in the midlands were partially civilized; but highlanders were still savage, and the higher the elevation the greater the degree of savagery. The point is this: from the moment that ethnology and ethnographic studies were recognized as legitimate pursuits, the sense that ethnic Vietnamese were civilizationally superior to other groups was clear. And, because they were civilized, they were obliged to civilize those who were less advanced. Of all the minority groups in Vietnam, Mạc Đường explained, the Meo—whom he explicitly characterized as uncivilized—were the most numerous, but next came the also uncivilized Mán.

In an aside, it is worth remarking that when Decision 121 formally abolished "feudal" nomenclature in 1979, the category "Rục" had disappeared from official rosters, the category "Meo" was replaced by "Hmong," and the classification "Mán" was superceded by at least nine different names.[67]

As they grappled with complex political and methodological questions, postcolonial scholars were influenced by what they learned from Chinese and Soviet sources. In their attempt to write the histories of ethnic groups who had oral as opposed to written traditions, for example, they relied on Soviet expertise.[68] As Vietnamese scholars sought to "improve" the Thai script and invent systems of writing for other groups, they studied the example of "friendly countries"—China in particular—so that they could oppose "incorrect ideologies" and wipe out "local conservatism" (*tư tưởng bảo thủ địa phương*).[69]

Although postcolonial writers made a concerted effort to detach ethnographic studies from their colonialist forebears, the colonial antecedents quietly reemerged. In the first place, colonial ethnographies quite unavoidably functioned as the interpretive foil against which postcolonial scholars aimed. Lã Văn Lô, for example, recalling the ethnographies of the "imperialist lackey" Yves Bonifacy (he mentioned Alexandre de Rhodes as well), urged ethnologists to displace the colonialist texts by helping ethnic minorities compose their own histories.[70] Besides providing a vast range of (negative) interlocutors, colonial works also supplied the unacknowledged and probably unintended model of ethnography. Specifically, the judgments expressed by postcolonial writers bore a striking resemblance to the assessments earlier expressed in colonial texts. Whereas colonial ethnographers believed in the normative status of French culture and sought to establish the extent to which other cultures approximated or fell short of the goal, their successors assumed the normative value of Việt culture. The ethnic Vietnamese, in other words, were not merely one ethnic group among many others; they provided the norms according to which other groups could be measured: proximity to them signaled a higher level of civilization whereas distance indicated a level that was lower. In his research on the languages and written scripts of the Tay Bac and Viet Bac autonomous zones, Nông Ích Thùy (who was probably Tay or Nung) classified the ethnic groups of Vietnam—then assumed to be more than sixty—into several broad categories. The Tay, Muong, and Thai, in his estimation, were advanced (*tiến bộ*), unlike the Meo and Mán, whom he deemed decidedly backward (*lạc hậu*).[71]

The parallels with colonial practices are clear: E. Chassigneux, some thirty years before, had characterized groups such the Stieng, Chema, Sedang, Bahnar, Jarai, and Rhade as "savages of a traditional type."[72] When the Vietnamese (as an *inclusive* category) succeeded in getting rid of the French, the Việt (*exclusively*) positioned themselves as acting subject rather than colonial object. It thus became the obligation of the ethnic Vietnamese to count, label, evaluate, taxonomize, and tutor other ethnic groups in an attempt to determine their distance from or proximity to the civilizing center. With the French definitively ousted, the ethnic Vietnamese claimed the normative status and set out on their own mission to civilize unenlightened others.

In addition to measuring the cultural level of each ethnic group in relation to the ethnic Vietnamese, postcolonial scholars also ranked them in relation to each other. These hierarchizing tendencies were especially evident in discussions about writing and the necessity of developing written scripts (*đặt chữ*). One writer observed that the culture of the Tay, when compared with that of other groups, was clearly "advanced," but the Tay, too, lacked a written script.[73] In his effort to contrast the enlightened stance of the DRV with the wicked ways of the French—"colonial night" versus "Marxist day"—one of the specialists in Thai studies inadvertently called attention to their convergence. Demonstrating his own facility with civilizational judgments, Nguyễn Thành argued that the culture, economy, and politics of the Thai were far more elevated than those of other groups in Tay Bac. Making a claim that no empirical research would support, he argued that the Thai were the only minority in all of Vietnam to have their own written language. According to Thai intellectuals as well as to French ethnographers, he remarked, their script had existed for more than a thousand years. Whereas French colonizers, who "considered only themselves to be civilized and held the people over whom they ruled in contempt," had forced the Thai to abandon it, the DRV would "improve" (i.e., romanize) their script and encourage them to use it.[74]

As scholars in the DRV set out to improve the systems of writing that were currently in use and to create scripts for languages that lacked them, they also began to look in a standardizing way at the language that most of them shared. Nguyễn Lân asserted, "If we exclude the languages of our minority compatriots [*đồng bào thiểu số*], we Vietnamese have only one language, from North to South."[75] The hierarchizing of ethnic groups in Vietnam extended to the ethnic Vietnamese community as well in the sense that northern patterns were regarded as the normative ones. For example, those who are familiar with spoken Vietnamese know that distinctive regional patterns remain to this day, but not because either the DRV or the SRV regarded these variations with indifference. What *has* changed in the past forty years is that the Vietnamese who speak in what used to be called the northern dialect refer to it today as "standard Vietnamese."

As they began to integrate ethnic minorities into new narratives of the national past, postcolonial scholars often did so on the basis of an aggressively domesticating stance. Ethnic minorities assumed significance to the extent that their totems, dwellings, agricultural practices, languages, and literatures illuminated the origins and development of the ethnic Vietnamese. The inclination to mine minority histories and cultures in this way was especially pronounced in studies of the Muong, who were popularly regarded (and are still regarded today) as the pre-Sinitic version of the Việt. As Nguyễn Thế Phương explained it, he was inspired to do linguistic studies because "as the precursor of modern Vietnamese, the Muong language provides important evidence about our origins."[76] The *exclusive* and purely autobiographical intent of this project is rhetorically intensified by the manner in which the "our" of "our origins" is expressed. Because the term *chúng ta* includes the audience (whereas *chúng tôi* excludes it), the assumption is that his readers all shared ethnic Vietnamese roots. In a similar vein, Lâm Tâm researched the intertwined relationship between the Muong and the Việt, and, engaging in an earlier debate, Chân Thành studied Muong myths in order to clarify whether the early Vietnamese had depended on slave labor.[77] In what turns out to have been a prescient move — the historical links between the Việt and Tay are still being explored today — Lã Văn Lô asked if Tay legends yielded any information on the kingdom of Âu Lạc.[78] Implicitly, the significance of Tay systems of belief lay not in what they revealed about the Tay but in the light they might shed on the political history of the early Việt.

This practice of looking at minority languages, literatures, and histories for information on the ethnic Vietnamese can be read in antithetical ways. From a cynical perspective, it can be interpreted as an assimilationist habit (I would leave it at the unconscious level) that ultimately suppresses the specificity of non-Việt groups. A more generous reading would stress that these tendencies reflect a genuinely new attempt to see the historical interconnectedness of various ethnic groups and undermine, rather than strengthen, the potential chauvinism of the ethnic Vietnamese.

At the Fourth National Congress on Science, held in spring 1955—before the ethnographic enterprise had fully taken shape—members of the Research Committee were urged to put greater emphasis on the "fighting spirit" of the Vietnamese.[79] This insistence on the "fighting spirit" encouraged postcolonial historians to neutralize the potentially oppositional histories of ethnic minorities and to domesticate them in narratives of a homogeneous national past. These new narratives were centered on the idea of a totalizing unity inside the borders and an aggressive heterogeneity beyond. Superimposing on minority histories a highly stylized version of the Vietnamese national past, postcolonial writers devoted themselves to the histories of ethnic minorities who had opposed foreign invaders.[80] As ethnographic research became a commonplace, Đỗ Thiện and Văn Khôi studied minority groups in the northwest who, early in the twentieth century, had struggled against the French. Hoài Nam wrote about a Muong uprising against French rule. Lã Văn Lô pursued this theme by conducting research on the resistance of the Tay, Nung, and Thai to the French occupation. Mạc Đường examined how the ethnic minorities of the central highlands also fought against the French.[81] What these writers necessarily neglected to mention was that, from the perspective of certain minorities, the "foreign invaders" were sometimes ethnic Vietnamese; similarly, they assumed that the struggles of ethnic minorities against the French signaled solidarity with the Việt. In these new narratives of the national past, ethnic minorities were present to the extent that they manifested the "national character" in a story of struggle and overcoming. In 1965, summing up the thrust of more than a decade of ethnic studies, Nguyễn Đổng Chi remarked: "Our compatriots in the highlands have an indomitable spirit."[82]

This vision of the past, which was codified in official texts, civic rituals, commemorative events, and, more generally, in the iconography of everyday life, implies a seamless homogeneity inside Vietnam. By externalizing difference and dissent, it suggested that heterogeneous forces always originated outside the system.[83] The "tradition of resistance against foreign aggression" glossed over a different history, one of ethnic antagonisms *within* Vietnam and the sense among some minorities that the imperialist aims of the Việt— and not only the imperialist ventures of Chinese, Thai, French, or Americans—had disrupted more desirable norms. After 1945, for instance, some minorities allied themselves with the French. Moreover, those who fought against the French may have done so in an attempt to reestablish their own sovereignty, not to restore the social, political, and territorial integrity of a Việt-centered state. For the Thai in particular this reading of the resistance war is tempting. The "tradition of resistance against foreign aggression" invariably overwhelmed dissident histories and, just as critically, skipped over the process through which Thai, Nung, Muong, Cham, Jarai, or Khmer were incorporated into a territorial state dominated by the ethnic Vietnamese, even though it was this process, historical through and through, that accounted for their status as ethnic *minorities* in Vietnam.

Ethnographic research was often communicated in a managerial tone. In his survey of thirty years of Communist Party policies on minorities, Lã Văn Lô meant to stress the importance of ethnic minorities to the revolution of 1945; at the same time, however, and not inadvertently, one assumes, he underscored their subordination to the party: "Under the party's banner the nationalities of Vietnam led the August Revolution to success."[84] For him the history of the ethnic Vietnamese and the history of the party didn't simply intersect with minority histories; they generated them and gave them meaning: "The question of nationalities cannot be separated from the revolution." Ethnographic studies were invariably linked to the revolutionary process. When Nguyễn Khắc Đạm, for example, discussed the task of inventing (*sáng chế*) and improving (*cải tiến*) the written scripts of minority languages, he also mentioned how ethnographers were helping the government to develop minorities "in a socialist way."[85] Reviewing the recent developments in ethnographic studies, Nguyễn Lương Bích remarked: "The present marks the shift to socialism and all of our [ethnographic] work must contribute to building a socialist country."[86] Frequently reiterated were the notion of ethnographic research as a socializing tool and the idea of ethnic Vietnamese as the managers of a multinational state. Việt Chung, for one, once wrote: "If genuine equality among the nationalities is to be achieved, the minority peoples should overcome their age-old economic, cultural and social backwardness." The main concerns in the postcolonial period consisted of "helping the uplands catch up with the lowlands, the border regions with the central regions, the minority peoples with the Kinh (majority) people, and urging all nationalities to further develop their revolutionary spirit and great capacities and to unite closely so as to advance towards socialism."[87]

In 1963, when Phạm Ngọc Liễn proposed to narrate Vietnamese history from a multiethnic perspective (*quan điểm đa dân tộc*), and when Quang Chính echoed his suggestion, they appeared only to formalize a position which had for several years been in the making.[88] Even though the multiethnic vision of the past strangely resembled the monoethnic one, official scholars celebrated it as the centerpiece of a new community, one that was far more inclusively defined. In 1968, when the newly constituted Social Sciences Committee of Vietnam elevated the ethnology unit to the status of a separate institute, it clarified the political and intellectual legitimacy of ethnic studies and the importance of ethnographic work to the state.[89] Indeed, although the tenor of postcolonial ethnographies resembled the colonial one, a crucial difference remained. Whereas the work of "bourgeois" ethnographers was merely descriptive, the ethnological work of revolutionaries was instrumental; it set the wheels of socialist change in motion.

SOCIALIST TRANSFORMATIONS

Beginning in 1954, the DRV set out to transform both the global structures of social life and the day-to-day minutiae through, in part, the propagation of *quốc ngữ*, the romanized script. At one level, it is possible to see the postcolonial effort to disseminate it as a new twist in a well-established tradition that began centuries earlier with Catholic missionaries who, seeking to teach the catechism, transcribed spoken Vietnamese into an alphabetic language based on Italian and continental Portuguese. In the 1920s and 1930s, intellectuals from a wide range of political backgrounds—"reactionaries" (Phạm Quỳnh most spectacularly), "petit bourgeois" (writers linked to the group of poets known as Tự lực Văn đoàn), and "revolutionaries" (Phan Bội Châu is the exemplar of this group)—*and* French officials all advocated the use of the romanized script. In 1938, the colonial government generated still more momentum by establishing the Association for the Propagation of Quốc Ngữ.[90] After 1945, Ho Chi Minh urged the Vietnamese to "fight hunger, fight ignorance, and fight foreign invaders." Revolutionaries, who depicted themselves as the key propagators of *quốc ngữ*, regarded it as a powerful weapon, so the script that was once considered a sign of cultural betrayal was reconceived as the medium of socialist transformation.[91] The effort to promote the use of Vietnamese—as a spoken language written in the romanized script—was also part of the program to make the non-Việt part of Vietnam more Vietnamese.[92]

From a purely statistical perspective, this arrangement may not be surprising: given that the ethnic Vietnamese constituted an overwhelming majority (more than 85 percent) of the population, the dominance of that language had a logical appeal. One could also argue that even though the eradication of minority languages was lamentable, it resulted naturally from the encounter between majority and minority populations within the borders of a modern, centralized state. One could claim, in other words, that this dynamic was not specific to Vietnam. But the aggression with which the DRV dissolved existing communities, created new ones, and, in the process, introduced Vietnamese as the new lingua franca attests to something much more determined. The first and most crucial step was principally a logistical one: resettlement. By transplanting highland *and* lowland peoples to the midlands, the DRV created new, ethnically mixed communities and integrated them into an administrative framework centered in Hanoi. In fact, so extensively have the highlands been colonized by ethnic Vietnamese that the traditional distinction between the mountains and the plains has essentially disappeared.

In this regard, the case of the group currently identified as the Zao (Dao) is instructive. Traditionally, the Zao occupied the borderlands of Vietnam, China, Burma, Thailand, and Laos. Because the presence of the Zao antedated the fanciful maps of contemporary states, the boundaries appeared meaningless to them, and as a matter of course they routinely traversed them. As ethnographer An Thu observed, the Zao of Vietnam and China "all worship Ban Vuong and are linked together by family and tribal ties. Families often leave one country to settle in the other."[93] For the government in Hanoi, the proximity of the Zao to sensitive borders and, more to the point, their inclination to ignore them was obviously troubling. To absolutize what was in fact a very porous border, the DRV initiated in 1954 the Campaign to Sedentarize the Nomads.[94] To explain the necessity of sedentarization, officials disingenuously cited environmental problems (while neglecting to mention security concerns): by characterizing the Zao as swidden agriculturalists (practitioners of "slash and burn" techniques) and arguing that such techniques caused irreparable ecological harm, the Zao would have to be resettled at lower levels in the interior and, skeptics would add, away from the borders! According to this rationale, once the "nomads" were transplanted to lower elevations they would gradually abandon their old ways and give the forests a chance to recover from decades and even centuries of depredation. Similarly, the Campaign for Fixed Cultivation and Fixed Residence—a program that wrongly suggested that all swidden agriculturalists were, in fact, nomadic—persuaded other "high-perched" peoples to come down to the valleys where they were initiated into the intricacies of wet-rice agriculture.[95] As Đặng Nghiêm Vạn summarized it, the people's administration did its best to help groups of "slash-and-burn farmers settle down."[96]

Because this practice of "sedentarizing nomads" continues even today, the Vietnamese government, like the governments of Laos, Burma, Thailand, and Malaysia, maintains that it is the tribal peoples themselves who, by practicing swidden agriculture, have destroyed the habitats on which they have historically depended. Plenty of ecological research, however, has shown that the practices of the swidden agriculturalists, combined with their traditionally low population densities, have not irreparably harmed the forests. On the other hand, a great deal of damage, much of it irreversible, was caused by the American bombing campaigns and the use of chemical defoliants in the 1970s. More critically still, the disastrous effects of commercial logging should not be overlooked.[97]

But the point is this: rather than present themselves as the agents of sedentarization, DRV officials depicted highland peoples, specifically their agricultural practices, as the real impetus behind the campaigns. Once they were underway, these campaigns resulted in a dramatic erosion of the cultural, linguistic, political, and economic autonomy of non-Việt peoples. Instead of reconstituting the original but now displaced communities, DRV officials carefully engineered new communities that were ethnically mixed and economically linked through the process of cooperativization. An Thu, for one, chronicled the "progress" of some two thousand Zao who, from 1954 to 1968, were removed from their homeland near the Lao and Chinese borders and transplanted to the Đồng Vàng Cooperative in the province of Tuyên Quảng, an area that had earlier been ruled by a French settler as his own private fiefdom.[98] Within a short while, the Zao were joined by other minorities, specifically Tay, and by ethnic Vietnamese transferred from crowded villages in the lowlands. When he reported on the Đồng Vàng Cooperative in 1968, An Thu noted that it consisted of forty-eight households: eight Việt, six Tay, and thirty-four Zao. He explained that despite the traditional Zao saying "a Kinh [Việt] is like a panther at your throat, a Tay is like a tiger on your back," the Việt, Tay, and Zao were living in "fraternal harmony" and had begun to participate in the cultural life of a "multinational country."[99]

In Vietnam, as in other parts of Asia, kinship terms are hierarchically coded. Thus, as "fraternal relations" developed in the new cooperative, the ethnic Vietnamese implicitly assumed the role of *anh,* authoritative elder brother. The familial role of the Tay presumably varied: in relation to ethnic Vietnamese, they figured as *em* (younger siblings); but because they were culturally closer to the Vietnamese they functioned as older brothers (*anh*) vis-à-vis the "backward" Zao. This group, thoroughly lacking in authority, invariably appeared as younger siblings (*em*) of both the Tay and the Vietnamese. Learning from Việt and Tay peasants, An Thu remarked, the Zao "soon made innovations [in irrigation] of their own." Việt Chung shared this same impression: the introduction of "delta people" had served as a "catalyst" in the transformation of the highlands.[100]

Although the Đồng Vàng Cooperative was physically distant from the capital, it was enmeshed in a complex administrative web that linked it to district and provincial offices and to the center of government in Hanoi. It was also connected in multitudinous ways to the party; and frequently cadres came "to visit and to offer advice."[101] In this way the officially sanctioned aim of sedentarizing nomadic peoples metamorphosed into a much more comprehensive attempt to dissolve traditional communities and to rewrite the social geography of Vietnam. While it still made sense to see the Red River delta as the place of origin of the ethnic Vietnamese, the traditional notion that they lived *only* in the delta had been thoroughly revised. Once the ethnic Vietnamese became dispersed throughout the country, new policies and practices helped to universalize their language and culture. Socialist transformations also undermined the twin demons of economic autarky and isolation. According to Việt Chung, infrastructural changes, especially the extension of national, regional, and local communication lines at an "unprecedented tempo," made it increasingly possible to eradicate the self-sufficient economies of the feudal and colonial regimes. According to Đặng Nghiêm Vạn, new social and economic policies—and even the war—helped "nomads" (in this case the Khmu) transcend the limits of their traditional autarky.[102] As the members of Đồng Vàng increasingly organized their lives around the cooperativized cultivation of rice, former economies based on swidden agriculture and weaving dissolved.

But the economic allure of the highlands was not limited to wet-rice agriculture. The hill country, in fact, was famous for its wealth in timber, coal, and metals, resources that had been inexpertly exploited under the "colonial yoke." After the French were expelled, DRV officials introduced forestry on a grand scale, encouraged animal husbandry, expanded the size of plantations, and broadened the range of plantation crops. They developed a comprehensive industrial plan for Viet Bac, which included steel plants, coal, tin, and iron-ore mines, and a center for hydroelectric power. The old market town of Thái Nguyên, once the site of "straw huts and indistinguishable streets," was transformed into an industrial city; in fact, it became the region's political, cultural, and economic hub.[103] The mountains of the north and northwest, once the picture of remoteness, were now crisscrossed with railways and roads; the new industrial plants and administrative centers sparkled with electric lights.

As administrators wrote glowing accounts of how economic development had wiped out "feudal" hierarchies, they created new ones in their place. Although the most spectacular campaigns—Land Reform (1953–1956); the Campaign for the Correction of Errors (1956–1958), which functioned as a strange postscript to land reform's reversals of fortune; and the Plan for the Economic and Cultural Development of the Highlands (1960)—occurred in a clamorous and sometimes violent way, other campaigns, far more discreet, powerfully transformed both the economy and the culture of daily life. In the Storm the Hills Campaign, ethnic Vietnamese from the delta were recruited to plant rows of eucalyptus trees across the barren hillsides. When this effort failed, a new program, Clear the Hills by Torchlight, took its place. Inaugurated in 1963, this project arranged ethnic Vietnamese villagers in "settlement points" and supervised the planting of cassava.[104] Whereas these plants were lushly abundant at lower elevations, in the mountains they produced only mediocre results. Once the failure of the cassava campaign was apparent, a new movement to cover the hillside with industrial crops was decreed.[105]

Accompanying this *mise en valeur*, as the French used to put it, were dramatic changes in the built environment. As new administrative centers, public schools, cooperative stores, medical clinics, maternity wards, sports clubs, community centers, rice mills, mines, factories, warehouses, and water stations increasingly dotted the hillsides and valleys, the highlands began to mirror the lowlands more clearly. The domestication of a once-foreign landscape also generated new toponyms and imposed new meanings on traditional sites. The region around Dien Bien Phu, for example, once the heart of the Thai polity of Muong Thanh, became the place for civic rituals commemorating the victory over France in 1954. Similarly, ancient Thai citadels were transformed into DRV militia posts.[106]

Campaigns to transform the highlands extended into private domains as well. In the 1920s, when Lê Quảng Ba recruited among the Hmong (then referred to as Meo), he was stunned by the dilapidation of their houses, the pitiful lack of furnishings, and the prominence of opium smoking, gambling, drinking, and crime.[107] In his studies of the Khmu, Đặng Nghiêm Vạn echoed some of the same views: "What gives all Khmu houses a common appearance is, perhaps, the unfinished look about them and a certain slovenliness which reigns inside every house without exception." Their living conditions were "atrocious," he added, and included the burdens of corveé labor and crushing taxes. Articulating what must have been an odd criticism for a socialist, he explained that because the Khmu had not been allowed to own their own land many had lived in permanent serfdom and had suffered from famine and disease: malaria, cholera, smallpox, tuberculosis, leprosy, syphilis, pneumonia, intestinal diseases, alcoholism, and opium addiction. The rate of infant mortality was high. The Khmu, having never developed a written script, suffered from ignorance as well and their languages remained "rudimentary, primitive, like their way of life."[108]

When DRV officials launched the New Life Movement, they had these deficiencies in mind. In addition to constructing new public buildings and supplying them with electric lights, the New Life Movement replaced decrepit dwellings and settlements with hamlets that were "rationally built . . . with houses geometrically lined up along a carriageable road."[109] The Rural Hygiene Movement outlawed the construction of houses on stilts and the practice of placing them above animal pens. Such customs, cadres warned, contributed to disease and wasted a dwindling supply of wood. Movements and campaigns also emphasized the "triptych" of rural hygiene: the double septic tank, a bathroom, and curbed well.[110] In his studies of the improvements brought by the revolution to the Khmu, Đặng Nghiêm Vạn remarked, "While still waiting for deeper transformations, many Khmu hamlets, although not yet transferred to the lower lands, have gradually begun to take on the appearance of fixed settlements." The new-style homes of the new-style villages were equipped and adorned with new kinds of furnishings and gadgets: "If we cast an eye inside each house what strikes us first of all, in comparison with the situation of former times, will be the great variety of household objects: pots and cauldrons, pans and saucepans, jars and dishes, paraffin lamps, even thermos flasks, and sometimes a transistor radio, or, if one is near a main road, bicycles. The Khmu are settling down."[111] Other visitors impressed by the improvements in material life added wristwatches and alarm clocks to the list.[112]

As political cadres, health workers, technicians, and teachers introduced the material life of the lowlands into the midlands and mountains, they also monitored the structures and habits of daily life. The Free the Shoulder Movement, for example, tried to eradicate the use of the carrying pole; other campaigns eliminated traditional styles of dress and encouraged new patterns of consumption. In a record that chronicled the success of the Hmong (then Meo) in responding to government directives, ethnographer Lâm Tâm remarked, "A great change in clothing is taking place. Now they are buying much of their fabric at state shops. . . . Young people in particular have begun to wear modern clothes."[113]

The DRV also targeted life-cycle rituals. "Thanks to efforts by the new regime," An Thu pointed out, "such harmful customs as exorbitant wedding presents and expensive funerals, as well as numerous superstitions, have disappeared." Illustrating the salutary effects of official initiatives, he added:

> During my stay at Đồng Vàng, I had occasion to attend a wedding. To please their folks, the bride and groom had consulted a former witch doctor, who was now a member of the co-op. The bridegroom's family had given to that of the bride only twenty silver piasters, instead of one hundred, as formerly required. . . . After the wedding feast, the guests took home only a small parcel of food each instead of the traditional twelve kilos of pork. At the wedding, the co-op cultural groups alternated between traditional folk music and revolutionary songs.[114]

Although he was particularly struck by the changes in material culture, Đặng Nghiêm Vạn also was concerned with rituals and ceremonies, and he particularly admired the sense of community that was perpetuated by traditional rites. If they were "emptied of their feudal content" and "replenished with new meaning," he believed, their communal qualities could be absorbed by the national celebrations held annually on September 2. The "horizon of the ethnic minority" would expand "until it merged with that of the nation."[115] Other events, such as circuses and plays, provided additional occasions for instilling new norms and ideals. In a performance cited by Lê Quảng Ba, the actors tried to dispel superstitions by tossing incense burners into the river.[116] "With the progress made by medical science," Việt Chung remarked, "superstitions have receded considerably. Almost all quacks, charlatans, and sorcerers, who pullulated under the former regime, have renounced their practices, which they themselves now regard as a sham."[117]

In ways eerily reminiscent of the French, revolutionary writers were obviously transfixed by the idea of "the new." Lâm Tâm wrote of groups who had apprehended and engaged what was new: "Even the Meo no longer recognize themselves. The structure of their society has changed. Their way of living has been completely renewed."[118] Đặng Nghiêm Vạn expressed this sentiment best when he wrote: "Beyond the visible things such as cooperatives, infirmaries, schools, and collective forest exploitations, which could not have been imagined only fifteen years ago, the chief transformations are those in man: in his understanding, in his mental universe, in his receptivity to the newness of things." On the basis of his field research, he was able to conclude: "Nowadays the young generation of Khmu read newspapers and familiarize themselves with new techniques, especially in agriculture. They know that their present life as well as their immediate fate depend above all on their ability to adapt to the novelty of things."[119]

In praising the party's policy on nationalities, scholars in the DRV invariably identified the Constitution of 1959. In particular, they referred to article 3, which states that "all the nationalities living on Vietnamese territory are equal in rights and duties. All acts of discrimination against, or oppression of any nationality . . . are strictly prohibited." Or, to prove that the party's policies were enlightened, they noted that article 3 also provided for autonomous zones to be established. This is a selective reading, however, which omitted article 3's many counterimpulses. Although it states that autonomous zones may be created, it adds that they are inalienable parts of the DRV. Expressing the kind of cultural arrogance that the revolutionaries attributed to the French, article 3 also affirms that the state will help minorities "keep pace" with the economic and cultural advance. In article 25 the Constitution also declares that citizens of the DRV are entitled to freedom of speech, freedom of the press, freedom of assembly, freedom of association, and freedom of demonstration. Undermining these provisions, however, article 38 stipulates that the state forbids any person to "use democratic freedoms to the detriment of the interests of the state and of the people." According to article 7, the state also strictly prohibits opposition to the unification of Vietnam. The apparent exception to the politics of assimilation is articulated in article 102: "The People's Courts ensure that all . . . minorities may use their own spoken and written languages in court proceedings."[120] In fact, both the DRV and the SRV were committed to developing written scripts for languages that lacked them, and both governments published newspapers and textbooks in minority languages, especially Tay, Nung, Thai, and Hmong; broadcast radio programs in minority languages; and produced bilingual dictionaries. But these attempts grew out of a clearly statist ambition; the inclusion of minority languages in public life was intended as a temporary measure that was expected to diminish social and cultural differences—not perpetuate them.

In 1968, looking over the contradictions and reversals of the previous decades, Việt Chung managed to say: "The nationality policy of the Communist Party, inspired by Marxism-Leninism and applied in a most consistent manner, has brought the traditions of national unity into full play and caused them to prevail over antagonism." In this remarkable rendition of the past, he also synthesized the meaning of the present. Vietnam, he remarked, is a nation composed of more than sixty ethnic groups, and each ethnic group has its own culture. But, he continued: "On top of this extreme ethnic diversity is, however, a fundamental and ever closer unity, the fruit of centuries-old cooperation."[121] Other writers, including Lê Văn Hảo, alluded to the historical *lack* of contact between ethnic Vietnamese and ethnic others: "One of the most precious achievements of northern ethnologists is their discovery and study of . . . certain ethnic minorities hitherto little known or unknown and living in the remotest corners of the national territory." Providing a more accurate explanation for the "ever closer unity," he added that ethnologists studied the formation and development of ethnic groups and their material and cultural life in order to bring out their best traditions and reveal their backward legacies "so as to liquidate them step by step."[122] As Đặng Nghiêm Vạn eloquently expressed it: "Any human community, regardless of its . . . primitivity . . . has every possibility of freeing itself from the most cumbersome fetters of the past in order to engage directly in the construction of socialism."[123]

THE CONSOLIDATED VISION

With the reunification of the North and South in 1976, the question of ethnic identities emerged with a new urgency. In March 1979, as part of the preparations for the decennial census, the General Department of Statistics, in consultation with the Committee of Social Sciences and the Central Committee of Nationalities, issued Decision 121 on the "nomenclature of Vietnamese ethnic groups."[124] Decision 121, which enumerated the ethnic groups that are still officially recognized today, formally brought decades of debate to a close. In the 1950s, some scholars had reacted with uneasiness when Vietnam was described as a multiethnic state. Implicitly clinging to the idea of

Vietnam as the land of the Việt, and explicitly referring to Stalin, they rejected the idea of ethnic differences within Vietnam. In 1979, however, Decision 121 meticulously spelled out those differences and tried to permanently fix what experience had shown to be fluid. That contemporary assessments of ethnicity differ substantially from colonial accounts is not a surprise—nor is it remarkable that the DRV in the North and the RVN in the South categorized ethnic groups in dissimilar ways—but the fluidity *within* postrevolutionary, postcolonial, and postwar classifications is intriguing.

Before delving into the details of specific cases, it is useful to begin with some general observations. First, although Decision 121 was supposed merely to rationalize the system for identifying the ethnic groups, what it accomplished is much more complex. Decision 121 determined that Vietnam is composed of precisely fifty-four ethnic groups, no fewer, no more. At the same time, it ranked them according to the unassailable logic of numbers. With a population of nearly fifty-six million, the ethnic Vietnamese, officially recategorized as Kinh, were naturally on top. The smaller groups, the Brâu, Ơ Đu, and Rơ Măm, for example, with only a few hundred members each, were just as naturally at the bottom. In fact, the very existence of such small groups was supposed to attest to the DRV's heroic success in rescuing marginal groups on the verge of extinction.[125] This method of articulating the ethnic composition of Vietnam suggests that the Việt, because of their sheer numerical strength, naturally dominate other ethnic groups, and the habit of casting ethnic relations in kinship terms further underscored the natural, organic roots of unequal status. Although Decision 121 accorded greater status to some of the groups that were previously marginalized, it also eliminated—in nominal and administrative terms—ethnic minorities of much greater size and historical prominence. In this case the Cao Lan come to mind. Even though postcolonial writers themselves had conducted studies of the Cao Lan, by 1979 this group had administratively disappeared.

Second, Decision 121 obviously abolished the generic and pejorative terms *Mọi* (savage) and *Mán* (barbarian). But because changes in signifier often coincided with a new conception of the signified, it would be wrong to dismiss these changes as mere lexical variations. On the basis of official publications, it is possible to discern that those who were earlier categorized as *Mọi* were determined to belong to one of at least twelve different groups; *Mán* were reassigned to one of nine.[126] To abolish pejorative names and names that were assigned to one group by another, Decision 121 often (but not always) gave priority to names that were internally generated. In 1979, for instance, most of the group identified in 1978 as "Meo" became "Hmong." For Mèo Lài, however, the question of dual descent apparently came into play—the term literally means "cross-breed Meo"—and this group was administratively separated from the Hmong and classified as Pà Thẻn.[127] Because the Pà Thẻn, like the Hmong, are also considered a member of the Hmong-Zao language group (within the Austro-Asian family), the change was not, in linguistic terms, especially drastic, but the transfer does raise fundamental questions about the criteria for fixing ethnic identities, on the one hand, and for recognizing their fluidity, on the other. Given that exogamous marriages were not uncommon, the arbitrariness of static classifications is especially striking.

Third, Decision 121 dramatically restructured the composition of specific ethnic groups. Scores of categories nominally disappeared, dozens of new ones nominally appeared, and, although some classifications remained the same, their "content" radically shifted. For example, in 1978, just a year before the number of ethnic groups was set at fifty-four, official sources had routinely referred to the "more than sixty" ethnic groups in Vietnam. From one year to the next, around a dozen ethnic groups nominally disappeared.[128] Even more glaring irregularities arise when one compares census categories of 1979 with the categories of the necessarily partial census conducted in 1960. On the basis of this census, the DRV was described as a multinational state composed of thirty ethnic groups, but from the thirty groups that were listed in 1960 nearly half of them were missing, nominally, from the official inventory of 1979.[129]

Finally, Decision 121 also fundamentally reconfigured the linguistic portrait of Vietnam. Whereas colonial scholars and even scholars in the DRV considered some of the major languages, such as Tay, Thai, Hmong, and Zao, as critical components of the Sino-Tibetan family, in 1979 they were recast as part of the Austro-Asian family.[130] To fully convey the "state of flux" that surrounds Southeast Asian linguistics, I should note that non-Vietnamese scholars have also removed these languages from the Sino-Tibetan family and reclassified them either in the Austronesian or Austro-Asian family. Regardless of the linguistic evidence that supports (or challenges) the recategorization of languages, these reclassifications contributed to the postcolonial goal of extricating Vietnam from a framework dominated by China. By emphasizing its connections to mainland and insular

Southeast Asia, the new readings of language and ethnicity diminished the colonial conviction that Vietnam, a.k.a. the "Little Dragon," was simply a smaller and less brilliant version of China.

In any setting, the process of determining ethnicity is riven with politics and imprecision. Although a number of works have examined colonial—especially Spanish, British, and Dutch—manipulations, the material on postcolonial reconfigurations is more limited. In the case of Vietnam, the DRV presented Decision 121 as a rational, straightforward assessment of ethnic identities, but an investigation of specific groups reveals that something more complicated occurred. In 1978 for example, the Xrê figured as one of the "more than sixty" ethnic groups in Vietnam, but in 1979 they were administratively or nominally integrated into the Kohu. Because both of these two groups were considered part of the Mon-Khmer group of the Austro-Asian family, one could, perhaps, on the basis of linguistic evidence, justify the administrative absorption of one group by the other. In 1978, however, when the Kohu were listed as one of the "more than sixty" ethnic groups, their territorial range was identified as the Gia Lai-Kon Tum region of the central highlands. When the reconstituted Kohu resurfaced in 1979, however, they were traced to a more southern locale. Judging from official depictions, it appears that other groups (such as the Hrê) who once lived in that part of the central highlands were also transplanted to new locations, while at least two groups (the Brâu and the Rơ-măm) were resettled there.[131] Thus, even though Decision 121 was presented as a systematization of ethnic categories based on new research in linguistics, extra-linguistic considerations were also apparently involved. In any case, changes in name frequently corresponded to changes in place.

The example of the Cao Lan reflects yet another twist in ethnic classifications. In 1978, and for decades prior to that, the Cao Lan were recognized as a distinct ethnic group within the Mon-Khmer part of the Austro-Asian family. By 1979, however, they had disappeared as a discrete ethnic entity; instead, they were amalgamated with the Sán Chỉ, a group missing from earlier reports, and reclassified as members of the Sán Chay, a group that *was* included in previous accounts. The decision to link the Cao Lan and Sán Chỉ administratively and incorporate them into the Sán Chay meant that the Cao Lan were removed from the Mon-Khmer and repositioned in the Tay-Thai group.[132] Conventional notions of ethnicity have normally included the criterion of a common language, but in this case postwar writers acknowledged that "the Sán Chỉ and the Cao Lan speak different languages, but they can understand one another to some extent. The language of the Cao Lan is close to that of the Tay-Thai linguistic group, but their love songs (*sình ca*) and prayers are in Sán Chỉ, a Cantonese dialect."[133] This explanation, which is intended to smooth over the irrationality of linking these two groups together, raises additional questions instead. Why is Sán Chỉ, a dialect of Cantonese, classified as an Austro-Asian rather than Sino-Tibetan language?

Of the groups identified in 1979, some, such as the Zao, appear to have a continuous lineage that extends back through colonial and precolonial times. In fact, the category "Zao," as it was redefined by Decision 121, differed significantly from the earlier Zao. In the first place, more than a dozen new groups were added to the original Zao. Second, some—but not all—of the members of "discontinued" groups, specifically the Mán, Trại, and Xá, were incorporated into the Zao.[134] In other words, a continuity in proper names did not necessarily coincide with a continuity in content: the community identified in 1979 as Zao was far more numerous *and* internally diverse than any of its antecedents. Other discontinuities in Zao history and language are evident as well. Ethnographers of the 1960s, for example, normally traced the Zao to Fujian, Guangdong, and Guangxi provinces in China and dated their emigration to what is now Vietnam to the thirteenth, fourteenth, and fifteenth centuries. According to the 1979 narrative, however, the Zao emigrated to Vietnam at a much later date—in the late eighteenth and early nineteenth centuries.[135] Prior to Decision 121, DRV ethnographers had reasoned that because the Zao spoke Mandarin, and because their written script was based on Chinese ideographs, their language should be grouped within the Sino-Tibetan family. According to the "rationalized" categories of 1979, however, the language of the Zao bore no relation to Chinese.[136] Similar to other examples of postcolonial culture, which aimed at desinifying the Vietnamese past, Decision 121, which was issued, after all, following the border war between Vietnam and China, sought to deemphasize the potentially Sinitic origins of conditions in the present.

It is not entirely clear why some groups—the Zao, for one—became more prominent (numerically) and why the status of other groups—for example, the Cao Lan—declined. The impulse to link these changes to politics may be unreasonable and difficult to prove, but it is irresistible just the same. The case of the Zao is striking because postcolonial ethnographers were in the habit of depicting them in politically favorable terms. Consequently, their history was easily absorbed into new national histories structured thematically by the "tradition of resistance to foreign aggression." More than once, it was reported, the Zao had risen up against foreign aggressors; and even though their insurrections had all been "drowned in blood . . . the indomitable Zao kept struggling . . . , shoulder to shoulder with the brother peoples of the great Vietnamese national family!"[137] By enlarging the scope of Zao ethnicity, Decision 121 granted to them greater (numerical) prominence and thus appeared to reward their revolutionary credentials. Because the consequences of Decision 121 resonated in conflicting ways, however, it would be wrong to assume a merely transparent link between an ethnic group's politics in the revolutionary period and during the wars and its administrative status in postwar times. By greatly expanding the group of people categorized as Zao, Decision 121 heightened their quantitative status—that is, their numerical rank—but it also defused and undermined their earlier sense of community. Before Decision 121, the Zao defined themselves by their belief in a common ancestor; by adding new groups to whom that ancestor meant nothing, Decision 121 caused a key element of Zao identity to be eclipsed.

As one combs through the ethnographies and the census reports of both the DRV and the SRV, scores of incongruities arise. The administrative disappearance of certain groups, the appearance of new ones, and the practice of physically resettling vast segments of the population all attest to tremendous political and intellectual turmoil. More precisely, these changes reflect a lingering ambivalence toward the non-Việt part of Vietnam and the difficulty of conceptualizing Vietnam as an ethnically *inclusive* as opposed to *exclusive* state. To contextualize Decision 121 in a broader legal and political framework, I will conclude with some excerpts from the SRV Constitution, which was promulgated in 1980. Article 5 reads as follows: "The Socialist Republic of Vietnam is a unified State of all the nationalities living on Vietnamese territory, with equality in rights and obligations. The State protects, strengthens, and consolidates the great unity of all nationalities; it strictly prohibits any act of racial prejudice and any attempt to sow discord among nationalities." Article 13 reiterates the emphasis on unity and warns against actions that would disrupt it: "Our socialist homeland, Vietnam, is sacred and inviolable. All schemes and actions prejudicial to the independence, sovereignty, unity and territorial integrity of the homeland . . . shall be severely punished." Appearing after decades of movements and campaigns to transform the lives of minorities, the Constitution also makes the astonishing claim that "all the nationalities have the right to use their own spoken languages and scripts, and to preserve and promote their fine customs, habits, traditions, and cultures."[138]

A BRIEF VISUAL POSTSCRIPT

On entering the Museum of Fine Arts in Hanoi, one is urged to proceed to room number 1 in order to read the museum's displays, as it were, from the beginning.[139] Implicitly, the meaning of the exhibits is generated by their sequence: order is important. Because the museum is organized in a narrative fashion, one expects, on reaching the first room, to find stone tools from paleolithic and neolithic times and bronze implements from the first millennium B.C.E. These materials, it turns out, are in the third room; the exhibit actually begins with two rooms devoted to "ethnic" art (*mỹ thuật các dân tộc*). One's first impression is this: although the museum has technically included the works of ethnic minorities, by restricting "ethnic" art to these two rooms (located on the top floor at the end of the hall), it has also marginalized them.

Included in these two rooms are ceremonial robes, delicately woven purses, sashes, shoes, combs, headdresses, baskets, a baby's bib, and musical instruments from various Austro-Asian (Thai, Lự, Hmong, Zao, Pu Péo) and Sino-Tibetan groups (Lô Lô). Austronesian groups from the central highlands tend to be represented more generally, in geographical terms rather than linguistic ones. There are also scale models of a longhouse and boat. Each of the artifacts is enclosed in an abstract, empty, decontextualized space: a case. The stark, "deracinated" effect of the display is only partially mitigated by explanatory notes.[140] As in other rooms of the museum, the texts (in *quốc ngữ*) that accompany the display are strangely laconic. They vacillate between bland description and tendentious assertion. For these materials to resonate in a meaningful way, at least some allusion should have been made to the special exigencies of highland living and to the fact that the material lives of swidden agriculturalists differ entirely from those who cultivate rice in irrigated fields. If the practitioners of wet-rice agriculture have esteemed monumental architecture and colossal works of art, groups that practice shifting agriculture tend to organize their aesthetic sensibilities in terms of metalwork and weaving, arts that blend aesthetic and symbolic concerns with utilitarian functions and that can easily be transported from one site to another.

Because "ethnic" art precedes the exhibit of stone and bronze-age cultures, it appears to emerge from a strange achronic space located beyond the movement of time. When, episodically, history does intervene, it is the history of twentieth-century Vietnamese nationalism and the triumphs of central government. A scroll painting from the central highlands is instructive. In the foreground, this painting depicts what one is supposed to imagine as the staples of "ethnic" celebration, such as dancing and the ritual sacrifice of a buffalo. But it also contains some incongruous details: specifically, the tribal elders' ceremonial robes are emblazoned with DRV flags. In the background, the landscape presumably reflects the clichés of daily life rather than the rupture of feast and celebration: there are tents, looms, lean-tos, bunches of corn, and baskets of potatoes. But again, the anachronistic touches take over: the woof of the looms has been rendered in red and gold and the landscape's empty spaces have been filled with clusters of DRV flags. For students of imperialist and colonial cultures, this theme — the (colonial) filling of empty (native) space — has a familiar ring.

The formal structure of the exhibits makes it clear that "ethnic" art cannot be historically approached: had the museum adhered more resolutely to its own chronological frame, the examples of "ethnic" art would have been included in the rooms devoted to the twentieth century. The structure of the displays also makes it clear that "ethnic" art is inhospitable to thematic concerns and issues of genre. For example, to emphasize the generic conventions of various media, such as metalwork, woodcarving, or weaving, "ethnic" art could have been included in the section devoted to folk art (*mỹ thuật dân gian*). But just as the ethnic Vietnamese do not produce "ethnic" art — obviously no Việt artifacts are included in these two rooms — ethnic minorities are not "folk."

The interesting exception to this pattern of exclusion is the Cham. Because of their sheer magnificence, I suspect, Cham artifacts — the splendid sculptures, the stunning monuments (photographed or reproduced in miniature) — have been unobtrusively subsumed in the visual narrative of the Vietnamese national past. Rather than relegate Cham artifacts to the display of "ethnic" art, and, conversely, rather than devote an entire section to the Cham, which would call attention to their conquest and decimation, the narrative includes them in the sections on the Lý and Trần dynasties. This arrangement is particularly awkward because it was during these two dynastic reigns that the Vietnamese most definitively eroded the territorial and material basis of Cham civilization (although the greatest blows were delivered during the Hồ and Lê dynasties). The textual glosses make no mention of the process by which the Cham were conquered and their territories annexed; on the contrary. The explanatory notes merely remark: "At this time, as Lý-Trần art was developing in the North, our Cham compatriots in the South were making important strides in architecture and sculpture."[141] Like other settler colonies, such as the United States, Vietnam tends to represent its own imperialist past as the realization of a preordained pattern, an entitlement, its fate; thus, in the Museum of Fine Arts, the substitution of Vietnamese toponyms for Cham names reinforces the "natural" quality of Vietnamese domination.

In an empirical and experiential way, it is evident that in the past several decades the social landscape of Vietnam has been aggressively transformed. Because ethnic Vietnamese constitute more than 85 percent of the population, and because more than others they have both conceived and carried out the transformative campaigns, it is tempting to see Vietnam's increasing homogeneity as an expression of ethnic Vietnamese hegemony. Succumbing to this temptation, one could establish an analogy between the traditional theme of Nam Tiến (the Southern Advance)—the process through which ethnic Vietnamese from the Red River delta annexed Cham and Khmer lands—and what we can neologistically refer to as Sơn Tiến, the Advance into the Mountains.[142] But this temptation should be at least partially resisted: although the ethnic Vietnamese have effectively colonized what used to be the non-Việt part of Vietnam, throughout the French colonial period, and, more to the point, since the August Revolution of 1945, they, too, and especially Vietnamese in the countryside, have been targeted in innumerable transformative campaigns. Surveying the postrevolutionary changes in the Hmong, Lâm Tâm once reflected that so thoroughly have they been transformed that they "no longer recognize themselves. The structure of their society has changed. Their way of living has been completely renewed."[143] One could, with equal validity, apply this same formulation to the ethnic Vietnamese.

Since the policy of renovation (*đổi mới*) was announced at the Sixth Party Congress in 1986, many of the methods, attitudes, and perspectives identified in this chapter have been criticized and officially rejected. Nevertheless, by exploring how contemporary ethnic identities took shape in the 1950s through 1970s, we gain a better sense of how the meaning of "Vietnam" today differs so dramatically from recent understandings. Although the traditional idea of the Red River delta as the Vietnamese *heartland* remains in place, the premodern notion of the (non-Việt) hinterland has vanished: the entire territory of Vietnam is now officially conceived as a homogeneous whole.

Chapter Three | **National Essence and the Family-State**

For much of the past fifty years, Western writers have privileged political and military topics in their research on Vietnam. In the period since 1975 and, even more dramatically, since the Sixth Party Congress of 1986, the focus has shifted to economic issues. Given the range of cataclysms that have taken place in Vietnam, these interests are logical. From scholars who specialize in comparative Marxisms as opposed to Vietnamese studies, we might have anticipated a wider range of topics and a more concerted effort to illuminate other aspects of the recent past. Instead of making a few fleeting references to the "Maoist-style guerrilla warfare" of the Vietnamese, these scholars could more carefully examine the cultural and ideological concerns of the Vietnamese who identified themselves as Marxists. Undoubtedly, the problem of sources, especially the lack of translations, has made it difficult for Marxist cultural theorists to examine the theoretical positions of the Vietnamese, but other factors—the impression that the Vietnamese were preoccupied only with military concerns—are also at play. In sum, because cultural and intellectual history in the period after 1945 has been so seriously neglected, our collective sense of contemporary Vietnam is partial in the extreme.

Vietnamese conversations, however, reveal a deep and abiding interest in cultural issues, both in a theoretical sense as well as in more substantive terms. Before the founding of the Democratic Republic in 1945 and in the years since, numerous scholars have delved into the origins of culture, not Vietnamese culture specifically but culture in a more global sense. Some writers, subscribing to a belief that was at one time prominent in the Soviet Union, have argued that the relation between the (economic) base and the (cultural) superstructure was essentially transparent. From this perspective it seemed that a revolutionary transformation of the mode of production necessarily generated a new (socialist realist) culture that typified and reflected the new economic reality. Other writers rejected this mechanical idea of causality. Instead, they inverted the usual pattern in order to assign to culture a more determinative role: certain cultural formations, in other words, produced particular kinds of economies. Referring to the "cultural revolution" in Vietnam, these scholars looked at the prescriptive and utilitarian dimensions of culture and devised strategies for creating and disseminating a new canon of culture that would contribute to the realization of revolutionary goals.

At the root of Vietnamese debates about the origins and consequences of culture lay divergent conceptions of the term "culture." In some cases, it implicitly referred to literature, whether written in classical Chinese, *nôm* (the demotic version of Chinese), or *quốc ngữ* (romanized Vietnamese). In other moments the scope of culture was broadened to include the rich oral traditions that had circulated widely but were not committed to writing. The idea of culture could be more encompassing still, including customs, costume and dress, life-cycle rituals, and, more diffusely, the texture of daily life. And at least occasionally, culture was defined in a way that referred to health, hygiene, physical fitness, literacy, and intellectual and affective sensibilities, such as confidence in science, enthusiasm for labor, and devotion to the party. The first chapter in this book examined how the problem of historical periodization prevented historians from completing the new general history; the second chapter explored how disagreements about the very meaning of Vietnam contributed further to the delay. This chapter looks at how the problems of culture—how it should be defined, how the relevant examples should be identified, and how its historical and revolutionary roles should be understood—rendered the goal of completing the new general text even more out of reach.

As one sorts through the material on what writers in the DRV described as the "cultural revolution" (*cách mạng văn hóa*), it becomes clear that, unlike cultural revolutions in other settings (China, for instance), the cultural revolution in Vietnam generally valued the traditional canon. Instead of denigrating prerevolutionary culture in a totalizing way, instead of destroying its material traces, postcolonial Vietnamese more often sought a synthesis and a means to assimilate prerevolutionary culture to a postrevolutionary setting. One can also observe that several topics generated an inordinate amount of debate. These topics—literature, folklore, national culture, national essence, and antiquity—form the focal points of this chapter. But, in order to illuminate the dynamic interplay between cultural theory and cultural practice, I must also provide a general sense of the conversations on culture. This chapter begins, therefore, by examining the institutional bases of the cultural revolution and investigates how divergent views of culture produced contrasting visions of the remote and recent pasts.

TRAJECTORIES: REVOLUTIONARY CULTURE
IN THEORY AND PRACTICE

In 1959, on the occasion of the fourteenth anniversary of the August Revolution, Trần Huy Liệu offered an overview of the party's commitment to cultural and ideological work. Noting that the "ideological current of socialism was like the rising sun, like tidal waters surging across the five continents and the four seas," he traced the "seeds" of Vietnam's new culture to the establishment of the Indochinese Communist Party (ICP) in 1930 and to the years just prior to the party's founding (1926–1930). He also commented on the cultural activities carried out by the Indochinese Popular Front Movement (1936–1939) and the importance of the Association for the Propagation of Romanized Vietnamese.[1] But he traced the origins of the cultural front (*mặt trận văn hóa*) to February 1943, when the Standing Committee of the party's Central Committee met to discuss the cultural dimensions of the revolution soon to take place.[2] By this point revolutionaries had began to anticipate Japan's surrender; to usher in a new era, they planned for the general uprising to coincide with the war's conclusion. To this end, they elaborated a more comprehensive strategy for revolutionary agitation, meaning that in addition to the existing focus on political and economic issues, a new emphasis on culture—and even cultural revolution—was announced.

In 1943, to clarify the new emphasis on culture, the ICP issued an outline of Vietnamese culture, which articulated the new tactics and identified the three bases of revolutionary culture: nationalism, science, and the masses.[3] Describing the kinds of culture that the revolution should oppose, the outline listed conservative (*bảo thủ*), eclectic (*chiết trung*), eccentric (*lập dị*), pessimistic (*bi quan*), mystical (*thần bí*), and idealist (*duy tâm*) forms of culture and specifically condemned classicism, romanticism, naturalism, and symbolism.[4] This document also explained that the cultural revolution would displace Asian and European philosophies that were irrelevant to contemporary Vietnam, including those of Confucius, Mencius, Descartes, Bergson, Kant, and Nietzsche. In order to implement what the outline proposed, the Cultural Association for National Salvation, which ultimately became a branch of the Viet Minh, was established in April 1943. Cadres recruited to the cultural association developed a new journal, *The Vanguard,* as their principal organ and published the first issue in July 1944. In November 1946, the party, even as it went underground, reaffirmed its concern with cultural matters by organizing the First National Congress on Culture; in July 1948 the Second National Conference on Culture was convened.[5]

At the 1948 conference, Trường Chinh presented his *Marxism and the Question of Vietnamese Culture,* which subsequently emerged as a key document in the party's attempt to rethink cultural issues and to create and transmit a new cultural canon.[6] Over the years this document has undergone a number of corrections and revisions. The preface to the edition published in 1974, on which the following comments are based, attributes these changes to the need to "advance the struggle on the cultural front." Because of changes in the political context, one cannot be certain how much of the original text has been preserved. In any case, Trường Chinh begins his analysis by locating the problem of culture within a familiar framework: while culture and economy were inextricably linked, he explains, the economic base (*nền tảng*) was anterior to the cultural superstructure (*kiến trúc thượng tầng*). But rather than assigning a merely reflective role to culture, he discusses the gaps between the base and superstructure. To illustrate this dynamic, he cites the "awkward" attempts of Vietnamese poets to imitate the work of French Romantics, despite the fact that there was no correspondence between the setting that produced the Romantic movement in France and circumstances in Vietnam. Rephrasing the fundamental question, he asks: If the economy determines culture, does it follow that a particular cultural formation will disappear once the (economic) conditions that produced and sustained it have collapsed? To this query he unambiguously responds: "Naturally not." This disparity between economic formations and cultural expressions, Trường Chinh maintains, is especially evident in societies with stratifications based on class. In Vietnam, he asserts, referring to the situation in 1948, there were actually two cultural orientations; and he offers a marvelous explanation of how this phenomenon arose. In the part of country that the revolutionaries controlled, the dominant culture issued from the working class; in the sections controlled by France, on the other hand, culture was essentially bourgeois. For political reasons, this assertion may not be surprising, but it is striking, nevertheless, because it conflicts so dramatically with what was actually taking place.

Because the party and government sought to play an instrumental role in the proscription of some cultural expressions and the encouragement of others, they multiplied the institutional means to censor and suppress. In an attempt to prescribe certain cultural forms, they also organized new sources of cultural production. Progressively, new newspapers such as *Truth*, *The People*, and *The People's Army* began to circulate, presenting cultural issues in a new light. In addition to the newspapers, a number of journals also appeared: publications such as *Study and Practice*, *The Ancestral Land*, and *Literature and the Arts* contributed to the theoretical discussion of culture and, at the same time, propagated new cultural norms. Determined to construct a new national culture that was "optimistic" and "healthy," that inspired productivity, "love of labor," "love of class," and that fostered patriotism and instilled "the will to strive" and a "commitment to the political struggle," the government established the Ministry of Culture, which superseded the Ministry of Propaganda, in September 1955.[7] To facilitate the Ministry of Culture's ability to "realize the plan," the government created at the same time a complex institutional apparatus that radiated from Hanoi to the provincial and district levels and from these mid-points down to the commune (*xã*). Parallel institutions, such as the cultural house (*nhà văn hóa*) in the countryside and cultural clubs (*câu lạc bộ*) in towns, functioned as transmitters of revolutionary culture. Five distinct but overlapping sections within the Ministry of Culture (Publications, Film, Arts, Mass Culture, and Cultural Liaison) were supposed to ensure that culturally appropriate materials were available in urban centers and rural areas alike. Intersecting with the structures of the government were those created by the party, such as the Committee for Literary, Historical, and Geographical Research (1953), the Institute of History (1959), and the Institute of Literature (1959).

In addition to the congresses on culture, congresses devoted specifically to literature and the arts were also convened.[8] Through other institutions as well, including schools, universities, institutes, libraries, and museums, the government and party set out to transform Vietnamese culture. Thanks to their crisscrossing webs of local, regional, and national structures, political parties also played a critical role. Although the various front organizations were principally concerned with political and military issues, they had a tremendous impact on the dissemination of new cultural norms—as did the succession of movements orchestrated by the government and party—to promote struggle, to promote peace, to promote hygiene, or to encourage "good studying and good teaching."[9] Although the sources on local militias are still lacking, it is certain that the military performed a crucial role. In the first place, it was able to impose new cultural norms to a degree that other institutions could not, and, more than any museum, journal, or school, military service homogenized the social domain.

But the most critical propagators and disseminators of new culture were the innumerable associations (*hội*) and unions (*hội liên hiệp* or *hội liên đoàn*) formed after the founding of the DRV in 1945. A very incomplete list of such organizations includes those devoted to peasants, workers, women, students, writers and artists (together and separately), journalists, medical personnel, youth, youth workers, thespians (each commune had a theatrical troupe), singers, specialists in traditional medicine, Buddhists, mathematicians, physicists, metallurgists, filmmakers, and the blind.[10] Associations were also formed on the basis of scholarly disciplines, such as history and popular culture. To "liberate" the South, comparable organizations—for students, women, Christians, Buddhists, peasants, workers, writers and artists, journalists, and youth—were created there as well.[11] With the unification of the DRV and the RVN in 1976, the parallel unions and associations in the North and South—those that were relevant to postwar times, that is—were consolidated into a national framework.

At an art exhibition in 1951, Ho Chi Minh set the tone for official discourses on culture by reminding writers and artists of their role as "combatants."[12] Over the years, cultural "workers" and "combatants" were enjoined to produce novels, paintings, plays, films, posters, and poems that were nationalistic, scientific, popular, and patriotic. They were obliged to inculcate socialist ideology and "satisfy the desires for leisure." In deference to the conventions of socialist realism, cultural workers were also supposed to glorify work. To portray the utilitarian value of labor and material abundance was not enough because peasants and factory workers could not be merely productive—they also had to rejoice in labor and in the sense of community that they gained through work. Generally, cultural combatants were supposed to adhere to the maxim "socialist content, nationalist framework."

One of the key moments in the cultural revolution occurred in 1956 when the Association of Literature and the Arts announced the literary prizes for 1954–1955. Nguyên Ngọc, who later wrote under the pseudonym Nguyễn Trung Thành, received the first prize for *The Country Rises,* a novel about the heroism of the Bahnar peoples in their struggle against the French; Nguyễn Huy Tưởng received the second prize for *The Story of Luc,* a novel that romanticized the accomplishments of land reform; and two memoirs, *The Beloved South,* by Hoài Thanh, and *To the Workfields,* by Hồng Hà, shared the third prize. Tô Hoài received a prize for *Stories of the Northwest,* a collection of stories based on the years he lived in the Northwest Autonomous Zone and fought against the French. Among the poets receiving awards were Tố Hữu for *Viet Bac* (Viet Bac was the other autonomous zone), Xuân Diệu for *The Star,* and Hồ Khải Đại for *The Fighter.*

What these varied works have in common is their didacticism; the messages are always clear. In different ways, each of them illustrates new habits and ideals, such as the newfound affection between the ethnic Việt and ethnic minorities, appreciation of community, optimism toward the future, a belief in progress, and a commitment to the revolutionary struggle. Moreover, by celebrating the heroism of the Resistance War and the salutary effects of land reform, they present one-dimensional readings of recent history. In fact, those aspects of contemporary life that had generated the most conflict, the greatest degree of resentment, limitless ill will, and the deaths of countless Vietnamese, were repackaged as purely harmonizing events. By valorizing the details of peasants' humble lives and by positioning ethnic minorities at the center of poetry, short stories, memoirs, and novels, these works emphasized the literary, and therefore social, value of people who had traditionally been ignored, marginalized, despised, or simply represented as pathetic.

Although the characters and themes of these award-winning works were genuinely novel, a cursory look at the biographies of their authors reveals a more traditional pattern. The fact that a number of the prize-winning writers had official positions seems to suggest the kind of cronyism that revolutionaries identified as "imperial" and "feudal." Nguyễn Huy Tưởng, for instance, had been a distinguished member of the Cultural Association for National Salvation; he was a founder of the Vietnamese Association of Writers and Artists and edited the association's journal. He also served on the committee that bestowed on him the prize. Hoài Thanh, too, was a member of the Association of Writers and Artists and, like Nguyễn Huy Tưởng, also served on the awards committee. Tô Hoài had been active in the Cultural Association for National Salvation and belonged to the Association of Writers and Artists. Xuân Diệu, who began his career with the "bourgeois" New Poetry Movement, joined the Association of Writers and Artists following his conversion to the revolutionary cause and was a member of the DRV's First National Assembly. When Tố Hữu received the poetry prize for *Viet Bac,* he was an alternate member of the Central Committee.[13]

In response to the pressure to teach new aesthetic norms, Vietnamese writers and artists occasionally protested, but, one could argue, it was only after the American War, when the repressive practices that were expected to subside actually intensified, did popular resentment become sustained and truly destabilizing. In the 1950s and 1960s, even those who objected to the DRV's methods of controlling cultural production often agreed with the goals. Because cultural traditions had so clearly privileged a literati elite while the vast majority of the people had remained illiterate, and because the "civilizing mission" arrogantly proclaimed by the French basically reproduced, with different details, this same dynamic, many people in the DRV sympathized with the need to break culturally as well as politically with the past. There was also a logistical concern. Because revolutionaries had earlier expressed their commitment to mass literacy, and because the literacy campaigns were generally a success, a vast new reading public had begun to emerge. Now, workers, villagers, fisherfolk, and soldiers were poised to read poetry, short stories, and novels that appealed directly to them.

Still, a few writers challenged the cultural policies of the DRV. The most dramatic example of resistance was manifested in the "Nhân văn–Giai phẩm Affair" in late summer and fall 1956.[14] At that time, two shortlived publications criticized the attempts of the party and the government to control cultural production. The journals *Giai phẩm* (Works of Beauty) and *Nhân văn* (Humanities)—whose titles lampooned key items from the revolutionary lexicon: "liberation" (*giải phóng*) and "the people" (*nhân dân*)—remonstrated against the way the literary awards had been handled and questioned the increasing politicization of culture. Rejecting the pressure to promote certain themes and suppress others, and speaking out against the minutiae of official decrees, artists and writers such as Trần Dần, Tử Phác, Hoàng Cầm, and Phan Khôi sought to reclaim their creative independence. This challenge was precipitously crushed and, at the Second National Congress of Writers and Artists, held in February 1957, officials proposed a means of resolving the problematic link between culture and politics. In a rhetorical style that echoed other official documents, the Constitution of 1946, for instance, stated that writers would enjoy creative freedom; but their creative freedom would be realized under the party's direction and within the framework of Marxism-Leninism and socialist realism![15]

Because the criticisms expressed in *Humanities* and *Works of Beauty* so alarmed DRV officials by demonstrating that the cultural struggle had not sufficiently advanced, the Back to Reality (*đi thực tế*) Campaign was launched in August 1958.[16] Conducted in two "waves" and lasting until June 1959, this campaign required writers and artists, who mostly lived in the relative comfort of cities, to endure the hardships of village life. From this experience they were expected to gain a clearer sense of how the majority of Vietnamese lived their daily lives; with their perspectives thus broadened, writers and artists were supposed to be creative in ways that were more attuned to the realities of rural life.

Surveying the struggle on the cultural front during the period 1955 to 1957, a report issued by the Ministry of Culture summarized the goals of the cultural revolution this way: to wipe out illiteracy, reorganize education, instill new socialist ideas and morals, and raise cultural standards, most evidently in the realm of public health.[17] It also cited the most serious mistakes of the cultural revolution thus far: the republication of "unwholesome" books, the performance of "obnoxious" plays, and the restoration of "feudal" customs. To avoid such problems in the future, the report emphasized that cultural and artistic workers had to be more fully instructed in the ideas of socialism. Mapping out the Ministry of Culture's projected itinerary, the report noted that because imperialist and feudal ideas had already been eliminated, implicitly through the mechanism of land reform, it was time to begin the criticism of bourgeois ideas. The report concluded: "Our educational, medical, and cultural work has contributed to the formation and development of a new cultural life and a new man, through the struggle against reactionary and backward ideas and through education in the advanced ideas of socialism." These themes, formally pronounced at the Congress of Cultural Workers in October 1958, were also articulated in Ho Chi Minh's *Essay on Culture, Literature, and the Arts.* Denouncing the "bourgeois" idea of art for art's sake, he affirmed that culture could function meaningfully only if it served workers, peasants, and soldiers.[18]

In 1960 Đặng Việt Thanh discussed the relation between the August Revolution of 1945 and the cultural revolution that had since taken place.[19] He explained the importance of the cultural revolution with an intriguing reversal of reflection theory. Without such a revolution, and the improvement in the ideological level that it would ensure, he explained, Vietnamese writers would be incapable of producing literary works "worthy of their time." Emphasizing the incommensurability between historical circumstances—and alerting us to the experimental ethos so characteristic of that time—he criticized the attempt to simply appropriate Soviet notions of aesthetics, and socialist realism above all. In a different setting, as he cautioned against attempts to legislate aesthetics (in this case according to Chinese norms), Tố Hữu reiterated some of these same themes. He expressed the view that because literary productions often "lagged behind" political and economic changes, and because no decree could mitigate this dynamic, Vietnamese writers should be free to experiment with new forms and, in an unfettered way, "bring to light the thought and poetry of the people." He clarified his vision of culture through the inspired use of metaphor: "Our writing is a slow circling about, a listening, an answering." Less opaquely he affirmed that although it was possible to "aim a canon somewhere between the sea and the mountains, [in the realm of culture] there was no long march."[20]

At the Communist Party's Fourth National Congress, held in December 1976, it was declared that the Vietnamese had created three revolutions: in the relations of production, in science and technology, and in ideology and culture.[21] Specifically, the cultural revolution had "contributed to the building of the new life and the molding of the new type of people." These people of a "new type," the new socialist Vietnamese, were devoted to the principle of collective mastery; they felt great zeal for labor; expressed their patriotism in a socialist way; and were committed to proletarian internationalism. The new culture of the new Vietnamese was "socialist in content and national in character." It was a "crystallization" and "sublime expression" of what was best in the four-thousand-year tradition of the Vietnamese. This new culture fostered judicious ideas, wholesome sentiments, and fine customs; it opposed bourgeois ideology and had swept away colonialist and feudal cultures. More than in the past, the party would assume leadership in every cultural sphere: in publishing, cinema, and photography. Through the party's guidance, these various media would make the party's viewpoint clear. The party would also promote socialist literature (with a "marked national character") to underscore the value of the new system and of the new morality, develop national traditions, and describe outstanding collectives. At the same time, with the party's guidance, new culture would also criticize vestiges of the old society, such as modernism, formalism, schematism, and naturalism. In sum, following the methods of socialist realism, new culture would expose the origins of evil and foster confidence in socialism.

Many English-language studies have emphasized the global context in which Vietnamese history has unfolded to the extent that events and circumstances in Vietnam seem to have stemmed entirely from decisions made by French, Americans, Soviets, or Chinese. Some of the best scholarship, on the other hand, has implicitly reacted against this habit by examining the history of Vietnam in a context that is sealed, hermetic, and closed in on itself. Without overestimating the significance of external events, I would like to identify those events that most clearly affected cultural developments, because theoretical discussions among Vietnamese, like the cultural policies of the DRV and SRV (as well as the ICP, the Viet Minh, the Labor Party, and the Communist Party of Vietnam) developed in a broad cultural and political arena, even when they arose from and responded to internal circumstances and events.

After August 1945, when the Vietnamese freed themselves from French and Japanese rule, revolutionary leaders sought to reposition Vietnam in relation to the rest of the world. But postcolonial dreams of independence and autonomy were interrupted by the increasing tensions between capitalist and communist countries, tensions that made it impossible for former colonies to detach themselves from superpower conflicts. In the mid-1950s, after the Vietnamese defeated the French, the cold war further undermined the potential potency of the Third World. Newly independent countries could not remain uncommitted, it turned out: they were obliged to align themselves on one side or the other of the capitalist-communist divide. As the North Vietnamese began to insert themselves into a new international community dominated by the Soviets and Chinese, they became aware of serious fissures within the socialist world. Evidence of these divisions emerged in the wake of Stalin's death in 1953.[22] First, Khrushchev recognized Tito's "national communism" in Yugoslavia in 1955 and, in a move that stunned the rest of the world, he formally denounced Stalin at the Twentieth Party Congress in February 1956. Emboldened by these events, communists in Poland and Hungary began to agitate for national independence, which lasted until the Soviets crushed the Hungarian uprising in November 1956. While these events made the limits of de-Stalinization clear, they also suggested the wider range of possibilities that socialist states could imagine, if not actually achieve, in a post-Stalinist world.

Complicating what, from the perspective of the North Vietnamese, was already difficult terrain, tensions also began to develop between the Soviet Union and the People's Republic of China.[23] When the Chinese Communist

Party proclaimed the Great Leap Forward in 1958, Khrushchev openly criticized the notion that a society could "leap past" the period of bourgeois industrialization directly to communism. Mao's representation of the Taiwan Straits crisis of 1958 as a purely domestic issue further alienated the Soviets because it could have easily involved the United States. Reacting to these events, in mid-1960 the Soviet Union suddenly withdrew all Soviet technicians from China, along with the blueprints for factories and civil engineering projects. In 1966, when the Chinese Communist Party issued the manifesto of the Cultural Revolution, the rift widened further; and during the Sino-Soviet border clashes of 1969 the rupture was absolute. Thus, from the late 1950s through the 1980s—until Mikhail Gorbachev visited China in 1989—relations between China and the Soviet Union were either strained or openly hostile. Because of the DRV's vulnerability, North Vietnamese leaders needed to maintain working relations with socialist countries all over the world. The notion of "peaceful coexistence" between the Soviet Union and the United States rendered diplomatic questions even more complex and exceedingly strange, given that the American interest in Vietnam originated in fear of and opposition to the Soviets. Repeating this pattern on a more dramatic scale, Chinese and Americans began to work toward rapprochement in the early 1970s. By the end of the American War Vietnam's relations with China had begun to deteriorate, and in 1978–1979 war erupted on their common border.

The Vietnamese debates on culture did not reflect diplomatic alliances in a transparent way, but they were not independent of them either. In 1981, for example, at a time when the break between Vietnam and China was clear, Văn Tạo, one of the leading historians in the DRV and SRV, managed to survey Vietnamese culture in the period since the August Revolution of 1945 without once mentioning "cultural revolution," even though the Vietnamese had discussed and even anguished over the cultural revolution for nearly thirty years and at least a decade before the Cultural Revolution in China was launched.[24] Avoiding terminology that implicitly linked Vietnam to China, he simply described the "new culture." To sever their political and ideological links even further, he traced the origins of Vietnam's "new culture" to the Soviet Union of the early 1920s. In Moscow during that time, he explained, Ho Chi Minh had spoken extensively with the Soviet writer Osip Mandelstam, and from this dialogue sprang forth new ideas about socialist culture, which Ho, in turn, imparted to the ICP, the Viet Minh, the Labor Party, and the DRV. Only a decade before, Vietnamese writers had hailed the work of the Chinese writer Lu Xun as a model for the socialist transformation of culture. But in 1981, in addition to Mandelstam, the relevant interlocutors were Ricardo Molina, Romet Chandra, Constantine Simonov, Stakhanovitch, and Gaganova (but not Lu Xun!). When the importance of socialist realism, which was clearly a product of Soviet theorists, was affirmed at the Fifth Party Congress in March 1982, the links between culture, cultural theory, and international politics were not commented on, but the connections were apparent.[25]

THE GHOST OF CHINA

In the period after 1954, scholars in the DRV extensively debated the recent history of Vietnam and, particularly, the genesis and meaning of the most cataclysmic events. Some writers regarded the revolution as a modernist assault against feudalism; others viewed it as a class struggle between the peasants and workers, on one side, and the national bourgeoisie, on the other; and still others depicted it as a purely nationalist confrontation with colonialism. For those who described the Vietnamese revolution as an extended anticolonial conflict — that is, an "eighty-year resistance war" — the events of 1945 and 1954 represented the possibility (the necessity, really) of recovering culturally from the French occupation. In this case, cultural studies figured as a kind of retort to the French and, more specifically, to the aggrandizing claims of the civilizing mission: by concentrating on the brilliance of their own civilization, the Vietnamese could deflate colonial assertions of French superiority.

Some early examples of this strand of cultural studies were quasi celebrations of what one could, very anachronistically, call nationalist writers: Lý Thường Kiệt, Trần Hưng Đạo, Chu Văn An, and Lý Tế Xuyên. One of the most celebrated poets was Nguyễn Trãi, whose famous victory poem, poems addressed to military personnel, poems in classical Chinese, and, most critically, his poems in *nôm* were granted a place of special honor in the literary canon. The poet Đoàn Thị Điểm was also greatly esteemed for "Lament of a Soldier's Wife," a poem she wrote in classical Chinese. The considerable merit bestowed on Lê Quý Đôn stemmed from the astuteness of his work overall and his phenomenal productivity: he authored at least three chronicles, several volumes of poetry, two encyclopedic compilations, and numerous analyses of classical Confucian texts.[26] Continually searching for the pure and authentic, postcolonial writers heralded the development of the hybrid *nôm* script because it lent itself to the expression of genuinely Vietnamese (as opposed to Sino-Vietnamese) sensibilities. Although it can be dated to the fifteenth century and is linked specifically to the work of Nguyễn Trãi, it was in the eighteenth and nineteenth centuries that *nôm* literature truly flourished. One of the few women included in the postcolonial canon was Hồ Xuân Hương, the eighteenth-century poet whose works (in *nôm*) were suffused with the stuff of daily life, celebrating such ordinary things as a swing, a fan, and a loom. In addition to "furnishing" her poems in a familiar way, which was an unfamiliar practice, she also wrote obliquely of carnal love and pitilessly satirized monks and officials and others to whom others deferred. The sensuousness of her poems appealed less to postcolonial critics than did her irreverence toward "feudal" authority. More important still was the fact that she eschewed the usual (Sinitic) signs of erudition and aimed for something closer to home.

Many postcolonial critics who focused on the "masterpiece" of Vietnamese literature—Nguyễn Du's narrative poem *The Tale of Kiều*—were tempted to interpret it as a critical, allegorical reflection on the rise of the Nguyễn dynasty. So thoroughly did this become the standard reading that *The Tale of Kiều* was seen as a scathing indictment of those who had outmaneuvered the Tây Sơn, despite the fact that the poem had circulated centuries before the Nguyễn emperor Gia Long ascended the throne. Moreover, *The Tale of Kiều*, regarded by many as the national poem of Vietnam, was spawned by literary events in China; critics, in fact, often characterized it as an "adaptation" or "re-creation" of works from sixteenth- and seventeenth-century China.[27] While other *nôm* novels circulated anonymously and in the shadows cast by *The Tale of Kiều*, they were still revered as truly Vietnamese works even though many of them were translations or adaptations of Chinese originals.[28]

Because the Vietnamese literary heritage is rich and multifaceted, the attempt to commodify and package it was surely misguided. In any case, this endeavor also confronted many obstacles. First, postcolonial Vietnamese, who were more interested in the modernist or class dimensions of recent history rather than in nationalist statements against France, viewed literature—once it was committed to writing—as elitist. They saw it as the product of a society in which only a tiny number of men and virtually no women had the luxury of formal education. From this perspective, the celebration of literary achievements seemed to say that social disparities were normal and productive.

To preempt these kinds of criticisms, writers who were invested in the glory of the literary past tried to diminish its apparent elitism by arguing that all Vietnamese, regardless of social class, had helped to create the great works. To support this claim, they observed that even those who could not read—and until the postcolonial period that category included most Vietnamese—could recite long passages from the key texts of the literary canon. For skeptics, the argument that classical literature was popularly produced was difficult to sustain. In what sense was the ability to recite a classical text synonymous with its production? Were classical works simply codifications of oral traditions? Were peasants producers of classical texts thanks to the banal impression of literature as merely reflective? Did all literature represent the conditions of daily life in a mimetically faithful way? Or, without having put pen (or brush) to paper, were peasants the unwitting "authors" of the great works, because they constituted the dominant demographic force? What further detracted from the populist reading of the literary canon was the tremendous difficulty of individual works and of entire literary genres. The level of erudition that this literature required—the knowledge of Buddhism, Confucianism, Chinese political history, Chinese literary conventions, and specific works of Chinese literature—suggested that those lacking formal educations could not have authored it. Whether they recited such works was a different matter.

Analytically, the argument that peasants were producers of classical texts was not particularly compelling, but it is significant just the same because it underscores the desire of postcolonial critics to preserve rather than dismiss or demolish the cultural icons of the precolonial past. In other settings, some of these same critics ridiculed "feudal" institutions, but in this case they retrieved from them something of value: not only the literary works themselves but the manner in which they were disseminated as well. Specifically, they traced popular knowledge of classical literature to the Confucian examination system and to the fact that scholars who passed only the first or second, but not the third, level of exams were not eligible for positions in the capital. Thus, forced to remain in their native villages, these scholars taught at local schools, worked as private tutors, and gave readings of the great literary works at the village communal house (*đình*). Through this ritual of public reading, villagers who were themselves unable to read became familiar with written culture.[29] Popular knowledge of the classical tradition also stemmed from specific literary devices. The six-eight (*lục bát*) form, for example, created a rhythmic scheme by alternating between lines of six and eight syllables. This pattern played a mnemonic role that enabled auditors to memorize substantial segments of the major texts. In this way the most cherished examples of the scripted tradition passed into the realm of orality. By emphasizing the intermingling of the written and oral traditions, it was possible to perceive popular elements in the "high" culture of Vietnam. After all, many of the great literary works were redactions of oral traditions.

This account of how classical culture became meaningful to a vast non-reading public is also intriguing because it suppresses a crucial part of the mediation between elite and popular audiences. By dwelling on a remote past dominated by Confucian scholars, this group of postcolonial critics was able to neglect the principal intermediaries from more recent times. Playing a more crucial role than the examination candidates of an earlier era were nineteenth- and twentieth-century "reactionaries" who had introduced the classical texts to a popular audience. Working with phenomenal energy, the Catholic converts Trương Vĩnh Ký and Huỳnh Tịnh Của, for example, translated literary works written in classical Chinese and *nôm* into romanized Vietnamese.[30] This endeavor to make the classical tradition accessible to readers unschooled in classical Chinese or the high traditions of Buddhism and Confucianism was continued in the twentieth century by Phạm Quỳnh, who launched the journal *Southern Review*.[31] Anticolonial activists so despised Phạm Quỳnh that after the August Revolution of 1945 Viet Minh agents executed him. Making it clear that his death alone could not redeem him, postcolonial writers continued to revile him. One such author, expressing a sentiment that was widely shared, condemned his collaboration with the colonial regime *and* his reactionary approach to culture.[32] Still, no matter how much they vituperated against these "traitors" (*Việt gian*) and "lackeys" (*tay sai*), scholars in the DRV could not obscure the fact that it was the "reactionaries" who had transformed romanized Vietnamese from the stilted medium of catechisms into a rich and subtle language. Thus, as they tried to justify the inclusion of an elitist classical tradition in the revolutionary canon, they skipped past the pioneering efforts of Trương Vĩnh Ký, Huỳnh Tịnh Của, and Phạm Quỳnh and focused, incongruously, on the "progressive" elements of Confucian bureaucracy.

Seeking to cancel out the French tradition of disparagement, postcolonial writers set out to produce an inventory of Vietnam's great literary works. Having quieted the complaint that literature was intrinsically elite, they encountered a new obstacle: the great literary works of Vietnam were saturated with Sinitic traces. In spring 1955, just as this history of Vietnamese literature was beginning to take shape, Minh Tranh revived an old polemic by asking if "patriotic literature" (*bài văn yêu nước*) written in Chinese could be considered Vietnamese.[33] His question elicited a flurry of passionate and often combative responses, and within a short time the debate expanded further to consider Vietnamese translations and adaptations of Chinese works.[34] These debates had a tremendously destabilizing effect because they seemed to cast the centerpieces of the literary canon, works such as *The Tale of Kiều,* in a derivative light. Because the colonial occupation generated a nostalgic parochialism—a longing for an authentic past that had never existed—the question inevitably arose: How could postcolonial scholars agree to the reaffirmation of the traditional canon when it included works that were not "purely" Vietnamese?

At the end of 1956, Văn Tân announced that it was time to conclude the debate. He called for a resolution of the question that so vexed them: Could the poetry that the Vietnamese had written in Chinese be included in the canon? Văn Tân began his own exegesis by recalling the antecedents of the debate. The polemic over Vietnamese literature written in Chinese had first emerged, he said, in 1941 when Hoa Bằng published an article in *Modern Learning.* To his opening salvo, several writers replied. Only in the aftermath of the Resistance War, Văn Tân explained, did the issue reemerge. Still, after more than a decade of debate, neither side had succeeded in "knocking the other one out" (*đánh ngã được nhau*).[35] While Văn Tân believed that no one had cogently argued the case either way, he suggested that, provisionally at least, works that were written by Vietnamese in Chinese be included in the canon of national culture. Although he intended for this concession to conclude the debates, it reinvigorated them instead.[36]

Thus, the decolonization or reauthentication of culture was ineluctably transformed into a nativist adventure. Like nativists in Korea and Japan searching for pure, authentic, and indigenous traditions, nativists in Vietnam continually encountered the Sinitic dimensions of their own civilization. Histories of literature revealed the degree to which the cultural heritage of Vietnam intersected with that of China: many of the most cherished texts were originally redacted in Chinese or *nôm,* others were based on adaptations of Chinese classics, and some were apparently faithful translations of works written originally by Chinese. Whether these debates can be linked to a broader problematic of premodern versus modern, or specifically postcolonial, ideas of cultural patrimony is unclear. What is certainly the case, however, is that in their attempt to decolonize culture, the Vietnamese could not escape the presence of China.

Although the experiences of Japan and Korea are obviously more comparable to the situation in Vietnam, some examples from a European context are also illuminating. Like the medieval Europeans who wrote in Latin because it was the language of culture, the Vietnamese at one point wrote in classical Chinese because it was the language of civilization and learning. In premodern Vietnam, in other words, the very notion of culture and education was bound up with the civilization of China: to be cultivated meant that one was conversant with the cultural traditions of China. Vietnamese literati who wrote in *nôm* occupied a more ambiguous position, to be sure, because *nôm,* although different from Chinese, was still based on it, and those who wrote in *nôm* could do so only because they knew classical Chinese. Like Renaissance Europeans, whose work in vernacular languages was filled with quotations of Greek and Roman classics and whose frescoes and paintings were steeped in classical and biblical allusions, Vietnamese who wrote in *nôm* were still compelled to demonstrate their command of Chinese poetry and Confucian texts. In Europe, with the rise of vernacular scripts, the emergence of national states, and the attempts to delineate national cultures, Portuguese, Spaniards, French, Italians, and Romanians have not anguished over the fact that parts of their cultural heritage were originally redacted in Latin or alluded to Greek and Roman classics. Literary critics and historians of literature in France, for example, hardly regard the poetry of Théodolf d'Orléans as an exemplar of Roman or Italian literature. Even within Italy, the Tuscans are not about to view the Latin-language works of Florentine writers or the "Latinity" of Petrarch's (vernacular) sonnets as examples of Roman culture. Like all analogies, these are obviously flawed. The "death" of Latin may have made the vernacular appropriation of a Latinate past less problematic than the recognition that China was at the very core of what was supposed to be authentically Vietnamese.

Although Western scholars tend to see the transition from Chinese ideographs to the romanized script as having been complete by the twentieth century, there are some significant exceptions. Some of the revolution's most distinguished visionaries witnessed this process in their own lives. One of Ho Chi Minh's most famous poems, which recites the history of Vietnam from its origins in 2879 B.C.E. to the revolutionary present, was apparently written (in 1948) in classical Chinese. In the 1950s and 1960s, Trần Huy Liệu, one of the DRV's leading historians, often cited passages from his own journals, written in the 1920s and 1930s, in Chinese.

Postcolonial scholars undoubtedly agreed that the Vietnamese needed to disengage culturally from China and to establish new sources of cultural norms. To a degree that the colonial educator Paul Bourde could not have imagined, the Vietnamese, in fact, had begun to *se déchinoiser* ("dechinese") themselves.[37] And yet, at the level of the individual and of society as a whole, that disengagement was traumatic: to sever the cultural connection to China was, in many cases, akin to breaking the link to one's own past. What one expects in the decolonization of culture in Vietnam is a rejection of everything French, and to a certain degree this repudiation did take place. But French scholars and officials, in addition to insisting on the glory of their own civilizing mission, also characterized Vietnamese civilization as a poor reproduction of China's. Thus, as revolutionary writers attempted to mark the cultural boundaries between indigenous and foreign, they became more wary of the Sinitic patrimony than of the Gaulic one. Although revolutionary writers remained committed to the goal of systematizing the literary history of Vietnam, they no longer conceived of this project in its original terms. Rather than regard classical literature as the essential core of literary history, they came to view it as an important but limited part.[38] In order for cultural history to represent what was authentically Vietnamese and uncompromised by contact with China, the idea of culture had to be radically reconceived.

FOLK CULTURE

Although some of the great literary works were popularly known, thanks to the rituals of public readings, it was difficult to regard popular knowledge as a sign of popular authorship. Furthermore, whether it was written in classical Chinese or in *nôm*, Vietnamese literature "suffered" from Sinitic undercurrents and overtones. To transcend these problems, scholars in the DRV began to broaden the idea of culture, believing that beneath the veneer of Sinitic influences lay a powerful substratum of indigenous culture that was shared by all Vietnamese. Unlike the "high" cultural traditions, folk culture, they presumed, was unequivocally Vietnamese. The appeal of folk culture also stemmed from the demographic, and therefore political, fact that the majority of Vietnamese were villagers who spent much of their lives producing rice. Thus postcolonial writers began to look with greater interest at villagers and village traditions. In a schematization that contrasted the purity of rural traditions with the hybridity of urban ones, the village — not any village in particular but "the village" as a composite, ideal type — appeared as the hearth of authentic Vietnamese tradition. Villagers, far removed from the effects of the Chinese occupation and uncorrupted by a century of French colonial rule, figured as the custodians of authentic culture. Vũ Ngọc Phan articulated the new esteem for the village and for villagers by drawing on the work of Maxim Gorky, the Soviet theorist of culture. Peasants, he declared, were the very foundation of culture in general and of literature in particular.[39]

At one level, postcolonial historians sought to define culture in a way that could encompass rural traditions without excluding the erudition of the literati. At another level, because they were also responding to the biases and omissions of existing representations of the past, they planned to retrieve peasants from the margins of history and place them at the center. Although court chronicles often referred to villages and villagers, they did so in highly stylized ways. In dynastic sources, peasants were significant to the extent that they contributed to the well-being of the court: if they paid their taxes on time and performed corveé labor, their good conduct was duly noted. But comments on the good behavior of peasants were not really intended as references to rural people. Rather, such remarks signaled the skill and benevolence of rulers: order, peace, and prosperity in the countryside were signs of the emperor's virtue and competence; they indicated the legitimacy and breadth of imperial power. Dynastic histories also mentioned peasants when their actions were disruptive, when they withheld taxes, concealed parts of their harvests, or banded together in disorderly ways. In the mid- and late-fourteenth century, the *Complete Historical Record* reported, peasant families had broken apart and entire villages had been abandoned. To cure this epidemic of desertion and vagabondage, officials at the Trần court — "witnesses," Oliver Wolters has called them — recommended that schools be established in the countryside so that peasants could effectively be tamed.[40]

In the eyes of court chroniclers, comments on the behavior of peasants functioned as coded references to the imperial court; thus, the "appropriate" comportment of villagers underscored the merits of the court. Conversely, when peasants failed to carry out their normal duties, if they ceased to make salt, for example, or if they violated the sumptuary laws intended to indicate rank, their conduct confirmed the incompleteness of imperial control. When Lê Quý Đôn, the leading historian of the eighteenth century, traveled from Hanoi to the South, he was horrified to see that peasants in the region of Hội An rode about on horses, wore garments of silk, and used parasols to shield themselves from the sun.[41] He also noted that some peasants stored their betel in brightly colored boxes (despite the fact that they were legally permitted to use only black lacquerware), and that others had taken to wearing shoes. Just as references to peaceful rural scenes were encoded as favorable assessments of the emperor, examples of disorder appeared as oblique condemnations. Consequently, when Lê Quý Đôn chronicled the turmoil in the South, he blamed the Nguyễn lords—and certainly not the peasants whose behavior he abhorred. Critical references to peasants were also plentiful in Nguyễn dynastic records. In 1804–1805, Emperor Gia Long inaugurated a more comprehensive attempt to control villagers by issuing extensive regulations. Concerned with the wastefulness of rural life, Gia Long's court imposed sumptuary laws that limited consumption, especially of meat and wine, and restricted the amount of food and other forms of wealth that could be "squandered" on life-cycle rituals such as funerals and weddings. The sumptuary codes also curtailed the "wasteful" extravagance of pagodas and temples. The belief that government existed in order to keep the bad habits of peasants in check clearly motivated successive emperors as well. Officials at the court of Minh Mạng, for example, remarking on the theatrical traditions of villagers, characterized them as "undoubtedly evil."[42]

The traditional histories, in other words, had not entirely neglected villagers. But to Trần historians in the thirteenth century, Lê historians in the fifteenth and seventeenth, Lê Quý Đôn in the eighteenth, and Nguyễn historians in the nineteenth, a comment on the conduct of peasants, orderly or not, was indirectly an evaluation of the court. Whereas the good behavior of peasants underscored the efficacy of imperial rule and attested to the emperor's virtue, turmoil testified to the collapse of hierarchy and rank. This chaos of classes, in turn, was linked to the lack of imperial virtue. Villagers grew unruly when the court failed to inculcate in them a proper sense of obedience and order or when it ceased to display proper norms.

Postcolonial writers understood, of course, that Vietnam in the 1950s, despite some degree of urbanization, was still, at its core, an agricultural society and that daily life was unalterably based on the cultivation of rice. Day after day peasants worked in the fields, tilling the soil then planting and transplanting rice. Continuously they repaired the dikes so that their fields could be properly watered. At the end of the (ideal) season they harvested the rice, selling part of it to pay off debts, storing another part for consumption, and saving the rest as seed for the following year's crop. The daily life of villagers revolved always around the cyclical rhythm of planting and harvesting rice. Of this pattern revolutionary writers needed no reminder: the Viet Minh victory over France had depended to a great extent on the material support of peasants, and even urban Vietnamese maintained ties to their native villages. But the life of villagers, visible to all, so utterly ordinary and mundane, was also strangely elusive.[43] How could history in the "new perspective" apprehend it? Was it even possible to construct a history of ordinary people and everyday life? To grasp what was both apparent *and* inaccessible, revolutionary writers set out to survey the rich cultural traditions of villagers. Unlike the literati, who appreciated only the symbolic significance of villagers, postcolonial historians were determined to recognize the importance of peasants in their own right.

In the last stages of the Resistance War, revolutionaries in the Viet Bac Autonomous Zone began to gather material for anthologies of folktales, proverbs, and songs. In June 1954, when the first issue of the *Journal of Literary, Historical, and Geographical Research* was published, the discussion of folklore officially commenced with Trần Thanh Mại's article on *ca dao*, a genre of popular song composed in the six-eight form.[44] In the first decade of folklore studies, revolutionary writers addressed problems of interpretation and discussed more methodological concerns. What was the relation between folklore and history? What was the process by which oral traditions were popularly transmitted? To what extent did oral traditions influence classical texts?[45] Of the many writers who participated in these discussions, three in particular stand out: Văn Tân, Vũ Ngọc Phan, and Nguyễn Đổng Chi.[46]

In their efforts to anthologize Vietnam's rich tradition of folklore, scholars in the DRV followed in the steps of some illustrious predecessors. Early in the fourteenth century, for example, Lý Tế Xuyên compiled *Anthology of Vietnamese Palace Spirits,* a collection of biographies of emperors and literati and legends of guardian spirits. Late in the fifteenth century, Vũ Quỳnh and Kiều Phú completed *Collection of Strange Tales,* an anthology of folktales begun during the Trần dynasty (1225–1400) and to which subsequent authors added new material. In the sixteenth century, Nguyễn Dữ and other scholars compiled *Anthology of the Supernatural.* In the latter days of the Lê dynasty, two major works were composed. The anonymously authored

Annals of the Celestial South incorporated material from traditional histories but also included popular expressions. Around this same time, Chu Cát Thi revised the fourteenth-century work by Lý Tế Xuyên, presenting it as *Modern Anthology of Vietnamese Palace Spirits.*[47] To this impressive array of traditional anthologies, French colonial scholars contributed several more. In 1886, A. Landes published *Annamite Stories and Legends,* in 1887 Gustave Dumoutier published *Historical Tales of Annam and Tonkin,* and in 1890 Dumoutier published a second volume on Vietnamese folk culture: *The Songs and Popular Traditions of the Annamese.*[48] In addition to the classical anthologies produced by the Trần, Lê, and Trịnh-Lê courts and the translations of those texts provided by colonial scholars, a number of anthologies were also published by francophile Vietnamese. Here, again, the outstanding contributions were the work of the "exemplary lackeys" Trương Vĩnh Ký and Phạm Quỳnh. In terms of sheer productivity no one matched the industry of Trương Vĩnh Ký; but in the prerevolutionary part of this century, the most influential work in folklore was Phạm Quỳnh's *The Tonkinese Peasant through Popular Speech.*[49]

In the mid-1950s, in other words, as revolutionary writers set out to write a new history of the people, one that was based on the culture of villagers themselves and not on court chronicles or colonial dossiers, they were confronted not with a lack of sources but a rich abundance of them. In a sense, the postcolonial interest in folk culture, while it may have been prompted by genuine political and intellectual concerns, responded also to a fierce competition. In the period after 1954, scholars in the DRV, like their counterparts in the RVN, struggled to lay claim to the folk cultural canon: scholars from above the seventeenth parallel as well as those below it produced a flood of translations from classical Chinese and *nôm* into *quốc ngữ.* This was especially the case for scholars in the North. For them, what could be more antipathetic than leaving the names of the "traitorous reactionaries" Trương Vĩnh Ký and Phạm Quỳnh attached to the canon of folk culture? For scholars in the DRV the figure of Phạm Quỳnh was particularly troubling. Historically he was their most immediate predecessor—and nearly their contemporary—so the sheer proximity of his career was unsettling. For the generation of readers who came of age in the 1920s, and for whom the revolution and resistance were the formative experiences, Phạm Quỳnh was the instrumental figure who had translated classical culture into modern idioms; he was also the scholar most responsible for awakening modern readers to the richness of Vietnam's popular traditions. In the 1950s and

1960s, revolutionary writers had little need to argue the importance or the appeal of popular culture because Phạm Quỳnh had succeeded in doing so in the decades before. What is striking about the postcolonial anthologies produced by Văn Tân, Vũ Ngọc Phan, and Nguyễn Đổng Chi is the degree to which they assimilated the classical and colonial ones. During the Resistance War the Viet Minh and the Liên Việt fronts had clearly demonstrated their political and military prowess, but once they were in power they needed to articulate the intellectual and cultural basis of their rule. Until postcolonial scholars produced their own anthologies, the authority to canonize lay with their feudal and colonial predecessors and their reactionary cohorts.

As postcolonial writers struggled to systematize the links between the new state and the folk cultural tradition, they also, unavoidably, grappled with the actual substance of folk culture, especially its unassimilable aspects—its political corporatism, on the one hand, and hostility to the state, on the other. Village corporatism underscored the decentered as opposed to centralized arrangement of power, drawing attention to a multiplicity of centers rather than to a single omnipotent one. Folk traditions further subverted the idea of central government by representing it as a source of oppression. Undermining postcolonial attempts to homogenize the nation socially, politically, economically, and culturally, the cohesion of individual village communities suggested a highly atomized social domain made up of disconnected parts. Postcolonial attempts to idealize the village and to praise rural Vietnamese as the guardians of authentic culture could not fully cancel out the history of antagonism among villages or between villages and the state. Countless folktales celebrated the cunning of villagers and their ability to thwart the designs of officials, who were typically depicted as embodiments of arrogance in their encounters with social inferiors and as mere sycophants vis-à-vis their superiors. When these antistatist traditions applied to prerevolutionary contexts they earned the revolutionaries' esteem, but in a postrevolutionary and postcolonial setting they were denounced.

To diminish the subversiveness of *popular* culture (*văn hóa dân gian*), postcolonial writers began to dissolve it in a broader framework of *national* culture (*văn hóa dân tộc*). With this new notion in mind, they began to sort through the various examples of popular culture in order to decide which elements should be included in the canon.

In marking the transition from popular culture to national culture, the proposal of Nguyễn Đổng Chi stands out because of his intellectual prominence, first of all, but also because his proposal reveals the ambivalence of cultural studies in the postcolonial DRV. In the preface to his anthology, *The Treasure of Vietnamese Folktales,* he described his method for determining what to include and what to exclude. In general, he stated, he had included folktales that were "representative" of Vietnamese folk culture as a whole.[50] Although Nguyễn Đổng Chi did not define precisely what he meant by "representative," its meaning is not hard to decipher. Examples of "representative" folk culture were implicitly based on regional as well as ethnic exclusions: they originated in villages of ethnic Vietnamese, and villages of the Red River delta constituted the rural norm. One can also see that the richly oxymoronic idea of "official folk culture" was premised not on villagers and their splendid specificity, but on villagers as composite figures who reflected the appropriate blend of distinctiveness and conformity. Because postcolonial historians insisted that *all* of Vietnam was uniformly and justly governed from Hanoi, "representative" examples of folk culture demonstrated how villagers identified with the state as a source of political power, obviously, but also as the locus of affective ties. In sum, the collection of "representative" folktales revealed that the interests of rural people actually *coincided* with the interests of the state. "Representative" folk songs, it was suggested, "celebrated the indomitable spirit of the Vietnamese."[51]

Some of the work of Minh Tranh illustrates this point. In 1958, when he wrote about land reform (1953–1956), for instance, he glossed over the bungling and chaos that characterized the various "waves." Instead of recognizing that land reform laws were often arbitrary and had been arbitrarily applied, Minh Tranh remarked only that there were occasional mistakes in policy and occasional misapplications of policies that were basically correct. In the end, he observed, the peasants emerged from the experience of land reform with a heightened sense of commitment to the revolution and with greater affection for the party.[52]

As popular culture metamorphosed into national culture, it became clear that postcolonial intellectual life corresponded in important and unacknowledged ways with colonial and dynastic predecents. In dynastic histories, peasants might be represented as socially dissident, which reflected poorly on the imperial court; or they could play affirmative roles, in which case their behavior enhanced the court's prestige. In postcolonial historiography a similar pattern reemerged in that the behavior of peasants reflected not so much on the peasants themselves but on the state. And in some ways "revolutionary" histories were more conservative than dynastic ones. Whereas court chronicles at least recognized that villagers could act on interests that were at odds with those of the state, revolutionary histories were more likely to insist on their convergence. In postcolonial histories, peasants organized rebellions, they resisted, and they fought, but always on behalf of the just state still to come—realized, in 1945, with the establishment of the DRV. In exemplary fashion, Nguyễn Đổng Chi noted that peasant uprisings in the feudal period were patriotic and imbued with national consciousness.[53]

Once they converted peasant uprisings into expressions of nationalism and pro-state affinities, historians could identify them as determinative events.[54] Nevertheless, although official histories increasingly placed peasants and peasant movements at the center of history, they did so in a carefully managed way, always making one point clear: the success of the Tây Sơn, the Viet Minh, and the National Liberation Front depended not only on the contributions of peasants but on effective leadership as well. Peasant movements that lacked decisive leaders could never fulfill their aims.[55] Just as Nguyễn Huệ had commanded the army of peasants who defeated the Chinese and the Thai, so General Vo Nguyen Giap was leading the peasants who would ultimately prevail over the United States and the "traitors" in the South.

Postcolonial writers undermined the autonomy of folk culture in other ways. For one, they renounced the usual pretense of narrators who claimed simply to recount and they emphasized instead their authority to judge. In his essay on the famous folktale "The Catfish and the Toad," Văn Tân might have examined the ways in which this story illuminated the material or intellectual lives of peasants. Instead, what concerned him was whether the peasants depicted in this tale were politically reactionary or progressive. To make this determination, he called forth the authority of Maxim Gorky. Official historians also contained the potential disruptiveness of peasant culture by ignoring its purely local or contingent significance and by assimilating it, instead, to more universal frames of reference. In his approach to folktales, for instance, Nguyễn Đổng Chi sometimes relied on the Stalinist model of world evolutionary history. This approach encouraged him to compress individual moments of peasant unrest into an overarching "movement." Rather than explore the singularity of particular rebellions—the circumstances that caused peasants to rebel or what they hoped to accomplish—he superimposed on them the five-stage model of history. Could Muong legends demonstrate conclusively that Vietnam had at one point de-

pended on the slave mode of production? How did particular folktales clarify the transition from feudalism to capitalism?[56] Other historians, including
Nguyễn Hồng Phong, Trương Hoàng Châu, and Chu Lương Tiêu, operated
with similar notions: peasants and folktales were significant, they believed,
because they shed light on the evolutionary stages of the national past.[57]

Historians in the DRV very purposefully set out to study folk culture. By
composing an alternative view of the Vietnamese past based on folkways
and life in the village, they meant to make up for the biases and omissions
of dynastic chronicles. Because they labored with conflicted aims, however,
postcolonial historians who sought to bring folk traditions into relief often
caused them to become more fully submerged. As soon as official historians began to compose the counterhistory of Vietnam, the history based
on villagers and rural life rather than on the imperial court, folk culture
was called on to express the singular genius of the Vietnamese. This process fully eclipsed folk culture's potential autonomy and otherness, and it
was probably inevitable: as they tried to map out the history of popular culture, "historical workers" were also obliged to write history in the service
of the state.[58]

For this reason, the hierarchy that initially privileged peasants was far
from absolute. When it was reversed, peasants, once regarded as the life
blood of revolution, as the source of all that was pure and authentic, suddenly appeared ignorant, superstitious, and on the verge of political reaction. In short, they were responsible for the incompleteness of the (just)
state's control. Because of the "idiocy" of rural life, Minh Tranh explained,
quoting the famous and frequently misunderstood passage from Marx's *The
Eighteenth Brumaire of Louis Bonaparte,* peasants lived as homologous units:
like potatoes in a sack of potatoes, they existed side by side but still in
isolation.[59] Unable to conceptualize themselves in collective terms, peasants were bound to follow the initiative of those who were politically more
formed: only in these circumstances, Minh Tranh remarked, could peasants "have their own beliefs."[60] Only the guidance of the politically enlightened—Chairman Ho, the party, the government—could keep peasants' reactionary inclinations in check.[61] Even Vũ Ngọc Phan, who had once
championed peasants as the very basis of culture, articulated this view.[62]
When the hierarchy that privileged peasants was reversed, cities generally,
but especially Hanoi, figured as the estimable centers. Likewise urban dwell-
ers became civilized, open not to superstition but committed to science;
they were urbane and politically progressive rather than passive or reaction-

ary. The rehabilitation of urban culture was especially dramatic in the commemorative histories that appeared in 1960 in honor of the 950th anniversary of the founding of the national capital in Hanoi. What emerged, then, from the populist rhetoric of postcolonial texts was a keen ambivalence toward "the people."

Moreover, one could parenthetically remark, the interest in folklore, which was motivated by the desire to capture and to comprehend what was genuine and authentic, led in unanticipated ways to what was most inauthentic: the West. Despite the attempts of postcolonial scholars to coin a neologistic phrase, *phong tục học* ("customology," literally), the term "folklor" was retained.[63]

NATIONAL ESSENCE [64]

In the mid-1950s, members of the DRV's Research Committee sought to overcome the elitism of dynastic histories by writing a history of "those who produced," meaning peasants, and by celebrating folkways and village traditions. But because they were also supposed to highlight peasants' pro-state affinities, the history of "ordinary people and everyday lives" never really materialized. This same dynamic undermined attempts to survey popular culture: when only "representative" (i.e., state-affirming) examples were relevant, crucial elements of folk culture were necessarily suppressed. Complicating matters further, state scholars were also obliged to demonstrate the essential unity and homogeneity of Vietnam and the omnipotence of government centered in Hanoi at a time when leaders of the RVN insisted on the historical cohesion and separateness of the South. Consequently, as the war with the United States developed from a remote possibility into a current event, official historians became more distanced from the projects devoted to popular culture and even national culture. Instead, they seized on the idea of national essence (*quốc tuý*).

Early in the twentieth century, educated Vietnamese came into increasing contact with Japan. In some cases this encounter was direct; for example, the Eastern Movement (Đông Du) enabled a small number of Vietnamese to study in Japan. More usually, the contact occurred indirectly. Through the work of Phan Bội Châu and other anticolonial intellectuals, the Vietnamese became aware of Japan's astounding success in thwarting the imperialist ventures of the United States, Britain, and France and its military victories over China. What impressed Vietnamese activists was the idea of *kokutai,* the national essence that seemed to bind all Japanese together and to energize them. Japan's national essence was essentially a nineteenth-century invention: Meiji oligarchs exploited compulsory education, elaborate rituals of state, civic ceremonies, and so forth to drum into the minds of the Japanese that they *were* Japanese and that they shared a unique institution: the Japanese imperial line was unbroken and traced its origins to the sun goddess Amaterasu.[65] In the 1920s and 1930s, the Vietnamese began to explore the possible substance and potential significance of their own national essence.[66] In February 1940, when Japan "entered" Vietnam (with the cooperation of Vichy France), the Vietnamese were again reminded of the devotion and zeal that the idea of national essence seemed to encourage. As Japanese soldiers abruptly transformed the rice fields of Vietnam into crops of oil-producing peanuts, they also distributed pamphlets that defined the national essence of Japan and the Japanese national character.[67]

For the Vietnamese who survived World War II, the idea of national essence was inextricably linked with power and aggression. In the 1950s and 1960s, when the social, intellectual, and political heterogeneity *within* Vietnam caused the Vietnamese to destroy each other and to fall victim to an aggressive United States, the ideas of national essence, national character (*tính cách dân tộc*), national spirit (*tinh thần dân tộc*), and national soul (*quốc hồn*) were alluring.[68]

The new interest in national essence responded to the destructive differences of the 1950s and 1960s, but it emerged from another context as well. As we have seen, postcolonial Vietnamese were often receptive to the work of Stalin, not because they were essentially brutal or totalitarian (the only associations with Stalinism in the West) but because they found some of Stalin's ideas about history appealing. For instance, Stalin's five-stage model of historical evolution, the progression from primitive communism to slavery, from slavery to feudalism, from feudalism to capitalism, and finally capitalism to communism, made it possible for scholars to argue that Vietnamese history was "normal." For a society just emerging from nearly a century of colonial disparagement and from colonial charges of "backwardness," "savagery," "primitivity," and so on, the idea that *all* societies—Vietnam as well as France—passed through these five stages of development was seductive. In terms of postcolonial recovery, it was essential for the Vietnamese to cancel out colonial hierarchies, and the Stalinist model of history enabled them to do so. Incidentally, the idea of primitive communism and the tendency of socialist historians to link it to prehistory also encouraged postcolonial Vietnamese to historicize the prehistory of Vietnam—to convert the Hùng kings, the kingdom of Văn Lang, and the Hồng Bàng dynasty from the mythical to the genuinely historical.

Having argued that Vietnamese history was "normal" and could be assimilated to universal paradigms, however, postcolonial historians suspected that they had inadvertently overwhelmed what was uniquely Vietnamese. Thus, as they quoted Stalin, Lenin, Engels, and Marx, they also cited the German and French Romantics in order to resist the leveling and universalizing impulses of Marxist (or marxish) historiography. Just as Johann Gottfried von Herder, Heinrich von Treitschke, and Ernest Renan had identified the national spirit of Germany and France, intellectuals in Vietnam set out to define the national soul.[69] Miraculously, on the basis of what must have been a willful misreading of *Marxism and the National Question,* postcolonial historians managed to trace the idea of national essence not only to the Romantic nationalists, but to Stalin as well! In this instrumental text, Stalin harshly rejects any attempt to dehistoricize (i.e., essentialize) culture. On the contrary, he argues that a common national culture is historical through and through; it emerges, he insists, as an expression of a common language, common territory, and common economic life. Railing against the idea of national *character* (as opposed to culture), Stalin singles out Otto Bauer, who had insisted on the idea of national community based on shared spirit or *geist,* for special condemnation. How, he demanded, could one distinguish between Bauer's national character and the "mystical and self-contained 'national spirit' of the spiritualists?"[70]

In the 1920s and 1930s, and evidently in a Herderian mood, some Vietnamese intellectuals imagined the national soul in terms of language and literature. Because Vietnamese national essence, they argued, was inextricably bound up with the Vietnamese language, and because no literary work rivaled the virtuosity of *The Tale of Kiều,* this narrative poem was the consummate expression of Vietnamese soul. Other intellectuals, and Phạm Quỳnh most incongruously, argued that the Vietnamese national soul could be summed up as the "spirit of resistance to foreign aggression." Postcolonial Vietnamese who had fought in the Resistance War and were preparing to face the Americans may have admired the literary aspects of *The Tale of Kiều,* but politically they could not countenance its resigned and quietistic mood. Propelled by official decrees, they searched instead for a more activist and activating idea of national essence. At the Fourth National Assembly on Science held in February 1955, historians were actually instructed to emphasize the "fighting spirit of the Vietnamese" (*tinh thần tranh đấu*) in order to protect the country's peace and independence.[71] Because Phạm Quỳnh was probably the person whom the revolutionaries most despised, they could not allude to him or to other intellectuals of the 1920s and 1930s; nor, for that matter, were references to French and German Romantics appropriate. Thus, in a willfully misguided way, they relied on Stalin to legitimate the "spirit of resistance to foreign aggression." Whereas Stalin had paraphrased Bauer's position in order to denounce it, postcolonial historians cited that same passage in order to validate their insistence on the spirit of the nation. Occasionally they made cosmetic changes, referring to national spirit as "national tradition" (*truyền thống*), but official histories were still filled with the language of "spirit" and "soul." Thus, the original commitment to a history of ordinary people and everyday life, like the original interest in popular culture, metamorphosed into something very different. National culture overwhelmed popular culture, and national culture, in turn, was thoroughly submerged by national character and national essence.

Armed with this new paradigm, official historians discerned the "spirit of resistance against foreign aggression" all around them in the present and throughout the past. It was apparent, first of all, in the bravery and daring of anti-American acts; it was manifested in the heroic displays of Buddhists who demonstrated against Ngo Dinh Diem; when the people of the central highlands fought off the American invaders, they, too, contributed new chapters to the history of Vietnam's indomitable spirit.[72] Embedded within the "spirit of resistance against foreign aggression" was "the spirit of unity," which ran like a "red thread" throughout Vietnamese history.[73] The history of resistance—the American War, the Resistance War, the anti-Japanese campaigns in World War II, the eighty years of anticolonial resistance, the anti-Thai and anti-Qing offensives in the eighteenth century, the anti-Ming struggles in the fifteenth century, the anti-Cham and anti-Khmer campaigns, the anti-Mongol offensives in the thirteenth century, the anti-Song assaults in the eleventh century, the anti–Southern Han battles in the tenth century, and the anti-Han rebellion in the first century—revealed the essential unity of the Vietnamese.

For revolutionary writers, the first-century expulsion of the Han Chinese constituted what Mircea Eliade has called the prototype of exemplary action; the Trưng sisters who led that rebellion provided the archetype or the "transhistorical model."[74] Each successive hero and each successive struggle reenacted the "immortal spirit" that was passed, beginning with the Trưng sisters in 40 c.e., from one generation of Vietnamese to the next. As the "heroic tradition" and the "spirit of resistance to foreign aggression" were conjured up with ever greater vigor, they began to partake of a primordial essence; their genealogy, it seemed, extended back beyond antiquity to the prehistoric times of the Hùng kings. "As everyone knows," Trần Huy Liệu wrote, "our national history is, broadly speaking, the history of protracted struggle against invasions; and so, early on we became a heroic people."[75] Thus the twin pieties of postcolonial times — the tradition of resistance and the tradition of unity — came to life.

As they transformed historical events and historical figures into mythical ones, official historians ritualized military encounters so that each one represented the model expulsion of foreign aggressors from the sacred land of Vietnam. Here again, and again incongruously, official historians had recourse to Stalin. Although he had rejected essence and insisted on the diachrony of the historical process, and even though he had argued "it goes without saying that a nation, like every other historical phenomenon, is subject to the law of change, has its history, its beginning and end,"[76] official historians in the DRV called on him to substantiate this claim: "History has shown that once a nation emerges, nothing can divide it; nothing can eliminate it."[77] Once the "goal" of history was reached — in this case a unified Vietnam — the historical process was frozen. And even if it regained its capacity to move and transform, it could continue only along the same path: "The determined wheel of history is making our national entity ever more fixed."[78] Thus, in the face of its novelty and its fragile past, official historians proclaimed: "Vietnam was unified through a process of revolutionary struggle. . . . Because [that unity] was achieved in struggle, it has become a principle, an infinite power, which no ill-gotten strength can alter."[79]

The idea of national spirit made it possible to smooth over hints of antagonism between government and the governed; it overwhelmed ethnic heterogeneity, class tensions, regional identities; it transformed what was most profoundly historical into something immutable. In *Purity and Danger* anthropologist Mary Douglas analyzes notions of social pollution, proposing that certain kinds of pollution — danger pressing in from the outside — foster solidarity within.[80] Arguing along the lines suggested by Douglas, I would maintain that "pollution ideas" — the emphasis on external threats — flourished in postcolonial historiography because of the severity of internal tensions and contradictions. Although the "tradition of resistance against foreign aggression" may have resonated with Phạm Quỳnh's reactionary past, it was rehabilitated in the 1950s because the country was violently divided. By externalizing conflict, by locating all heterogeneity outside the system, the "tradition of resistance to foreign aggression" enabled postcolonial Vietnamese to overlook the extent to which they were at war *with themselves* and not only against aggressive others. The "tradition of resistance against foreign aggression" also established the fundamentally defensive posture of Vietnam, thereby sublimating its own imperial past. Because the idea of national essence was topographically expressed, it was linked to landscape and place. Thus the Vietnamese devoted themselves to the Sacred Land (*đất nước yêu quý*); they felt unlimited love for the Ancestral Land (*Tổ quốc*).[81]

By relying on the idea of spirit that transcends the contingencies of history, postcolonial historians paradoxically suppressed and even abolished what was genuinely historical. At the very moment in which their society was most open, most historical, and most indeterminate, they defended it against novelty, presenting it instead as immutable and impervious to change.[82] When official scholars narrated real historical events in a way that preserved almost nothing of the actual event, they re-created them as ritual prototypes or imitations of archetypal models. By evoking the mythicized memory of the Trưng sisters, for example, state historians endowed historical events with metahistorical meaning: twentieth-century Vietnamese who struggled against American aggression shared the eminence of first-century heroes who had resisted the Chinese.

In June 1965, just months after the Johnson administration initiated Flaming Dart (air raids against the North) and Operation Rolling Thunder (sustained bombing of the North), after two marine battalions landed in Danang, as eighteen combat battalions arrived in the South and as Westmoreland requested forty-four more,[83] Trần Huy Liệu countered by transforming the war into a sacred event (*chiến tranh thần thánh*):

> Since August 1964 . . . the American imperialists have widened the war in Indochina and used their navy and air force to invade the Democratic Republic of Vietnam, but the People's Army of the North has dealt them a decisive blow. From the South to the North more than thirty million Vietnamese are fighting in the salvation war against the Americans. . . . All the progressive countries in the world have voiced

support for our cause and day by day they watch our sacred war unfold. . . . At no other moment has the history of our Ancestral Land known such glory.[84]

Unavoidably the question arises: What kind of history suppresses the historical in favor of the mythical? What kind of history resurrects mythicized figures and mythicized events in order to narrate twentieth-century events? Eliade has suggested that only in heroic literature can suffering be normalized; only transcendent explanations of historical contingencies can justify it and make it bearable. Without recourse to archetypes, he maintained, the terror of history would be intolerable; historicism simply says: it happened that way.[85] By sublimating history and appealing to transcendent ideals such as the "tradition of resistance to foreign aggression," official historians provided what George Mosse has described as an "ideology for confronting mass death and destruction."[86] In glorifying the ideal of collective sacrifice, the history of spirit produced a unitary conception of culture that canceled out the divisive and subversive potential of folkways. It smoothed over more troubling conceptions of the past and assessments of the present. So that the idea of popular culture did not, for example, imply divisions between rural Vietnamese and governing elites, official historians redefined it and honed in on the "fighting spirit" as its essential core. What was supposed to be the history of ordinary people and everyday lives metamorphosed into a paean of praise for their collective spirit of sacrifice. When the Popular Culture Association was established in 1966, it was charged with spreading the word of the heroic tradition. As the rhetoric of resistance translated the violence of the war into a more glorified idiom, it created extraordinary people in the heroic mode; it kept them from mere ordinariness.[87]

In 1983, when the Institute of Folklore was founded, scholars began anew to regard village culture as a "national treasure." And since the policy of renovation (đổi mới) was announced in 1986, the village, as opposed to the cooperative, has been reinstituted as an administrative unit. Spurred on by the government in Hanoi, hundreds of northern villages have established a "covenant for a cultured village" (quy ước làng văn hóa) as a way of reviving traditional forms. But these "traditions" are of recent vintage. As Nguyễn Quang Ngọc from the National University in Hanoi has noted, current leaders regard as a mistake their predecessors' habit of dismantling traditional villages and creating cooperatives in their place. At the same time, as he clarifies the selectiveness with which previous patterns have been reintroduced, he also remarks that it would be a mistake to allow villages to revive their traditional features "at will."[88]

THE CULT OF ANTIQUITY [89]

In fall 1954, Nguyễn Đổng Chi first raised the issue of how the Vietnamese past should be periodized. Months later, Trần Huy Liệu posed the question that had to be settled before the problem of periodization could be resolved: To what point could one trace Vietnamese national origins? Chinese historians, he noted, were in the process of researching their own national origins.[90] Just as this discussion began, the Research Committee also received its instructions to emphasize the "fighting spirit of the Vietnamese."[91] In a curious way, these two endeavors—the quest for national origins and the historiographical emphasis on the "fighting spirit of the Vietnamese"—became linked. From this strange union emerged what I have called the cult of antiquity.

The question of national origins was first articulated by Trần Huy Liệu, but Nguyễn Lương Bích soon followed by reiterating the comment about historians in China and adding that Soviet historians were engaged in a similar debate.[92] He then went one step further and declared that even though Chinese and Soviet historians had been discussing the issue of national origins for many years they had not yet reached a conclusion. And this, he suspected, would be the case in Vietnam: only after an extended period of debate could historians hope to reach a unanimous view. Indeed, what they quickly observed was that for a number of reasons the origins of Vietnam were difficult to discern. By "nation" (*dân tộc*), what were they to understand: people, simply? a territorial state? Similarly, what exactly was meant by "Vietnamese"? Did it encompass only those of Việt ethnicity, or did it instead emphasize territory and politics?

Because of the critical ambiguity in the expression "Vietnamese nation" (*dân tộc Việt Nam*), a kaleidoscopic range of responses was offered. Trần Huy Liệu surveyed some of the possibilities.[93] One historian, he noted, had suggested that Vietnamese national origins dated only to 1930, when the ICP began to organize Vietnamese on a nationwide basis, from North, through Center, to South, and from the deltas into the highlands. Until this moment, this historian believed, no one had conceived of Vietnam in such a comprehensive and totalizing way. Trần Huy Liệu based his own interpretation on the impression that states were synonymous with nations and on the Marxist theory that states emerged in capitalist settings. Therefore, referring to the transforming effects of French capitalism, he suggested that the origins of the Vietnamese nation should be traced to the nineteenth century. In an attempt to legitimize this claim, he also adduced political and geographical data and maintained that the Vietnamese nation could not have possibly emerged before the late eighteenth century, because only at this point did the Tây Sơn emperor Nguyễn Huệ rule over what is currently, in territorial terms, defined as Vietnam. As he continued his survey, Trần Huy Liệu noted that Đào Duy Anh was at one point inclined to trace Vietnamese national origins to the founding of the Trần dynasty in 1225, or to 1010, which he characterized as the moment the Lý emperor Thái Tổ created a centralized state. Nguyễn Lương Bích, he observed, had argued that Vietnamese national origins should be located at a still earlier point: either in the tenth century, when Đinh Bộ Lĩnh inaugurated Vietnam's imperial tradition and the Early Lê dynasty began to centralize government, or in the eleventh century, when the Lý emperors continued the centralizing process. Trần Huy Liệu then remarked that Đào Duy Anh revised his earlier view and began to argue that Vietnamese national origins should be traced back to the tenth century to the reigns of the Đinh and Early Lý dynasties (rather than to the thirteenth century, as he had earlier claimed). As far as Văn Tân was concerned, however, national origins were still more remote: in his discussion of literary history, he linked them to the time around the common era.[94] A few years later, Minh Tranh indicated his agreement with what was becoming the conventional view: Vietnamese national origins emerged around the beginning of the common era.[95] For postcolonial Vietnamese, this discussion of national origins may have been partly illuminating, but it must have been disturbing as well. What, indeed, was the evidentiary basis for making any claim at all if talented and serious scholars located national origins at various points between the first and twentieth centuries?

Had the postcolonial Vietnamese turned exclusively to Chinese sources, the issue of national origins would have been obscured in additional ways. First, on the basis of the work of the Han historian Sima Qian, the entity now known as "Vietnam" did not exist. From the perspective of the Han Chinese, the region of the Red River delta became genuinely historical in the first century B.C.E. when the imperial court in Chang'an divided the region between the Yangzi and Red rivers into several administrative domains.[96] In other words, from the perspective of the Han emperors, the Vietnamese were not a distinct people; they were one of the "Hundred Barbarians" or

"Southern Barbarians" destined probably to fall under the civilizing spell of the Han. Postcolonial Vietnamese obviously could not accept this chauvinistic, Sino-centric view of Vietnam's past; it would be more appropriate to claim that the Han court had merely superimposed an administrative system on a state that already existed. In this way, the periods of Han and Tang domination could be redefined as interruptions of a pattern that was already in place and that reappeared with even greater clarity in the tenth century. Most antithetical to any nativistic quest, and the search for origins is precisely this kind of venture, is the idea that self-authentication should depend on external sources. Thus, in rejecting Chinese explanations of Vietnamese origins, postcolonial historians could overcome the impression, shared by Vietnamese and non-Vietnamese alike, that Chinese dynastic histories were essential to the early history of Vietnam.[97]

Once they removed the burden of proof from the usual Han dynasty sources, postcolonial historians were expected to come up with alternative explanations so that they could determine how to periodize the past. Only then could they proceed with their principal task, which was to write a general history of Vietnam. The issue of origins, however, intrigued them on another level as well.

French colonial scholars had written extensively on the national origins of the Vietnamese, basing their claims on Chinese sources and also on the physical evidence unearthed in excavations. In the late nineteenth and early twentieth century archaeological research in Vietnam, as in other parts of Asia, was dominated by European scholars. Prior to the excavations planned and executed by Europeans, the Vietnamese had not concerned themselves with the buried traces of the past. Among the Europeans' most exciting finds were the nearly two hundred bronze drums they unearthed in southern China, the Red River delta, and in other parts of Southeast Asia.[98] In 1924, responding to the efforts of Henri Parmentier and other Europeans to systematize the findings, the French School of the Far East organized a conference in Hanoi, and in the following years the principal figures published their thoughts on the bronze artifacts. Although European archaeologists marveled at the physical artifacts they had recovered, their sheer virtuosity, especially of the Đông Sơn bronze drums they found in Vietnam, caused them to reject the possibility that they had been locally produced. Such refined creations, they reasoned, represented the genius of a more refined people: Javanese, perhaps, or an "unknown Mediterranean race." In 1931, on the basis of evidence he had seen in the Swedish National Museum in Stockholm, Olov Janse argued for the European as opposed to Chinese origins of bronze culture in Vietnam, and he even identified the two main sources: the Hallstatt sites of western and central Europe and the region of the Caucasus. A few years later, when Janse began working at the Đông Sơn site, he converted to the Sino-centric view of bronze culture in Vietnam. In any case, even if the Europeans could not ascertain the provenance of the bronze drums with precision, they confidently ruled out the possibility that they had been locally produced. As for the chronology of the bronze age in Vietnam, European scholars argued for a relatively recent date. Whereas the bronze culture of Mesopotamia had flourished as early as 3000 or even 3500 B.C.E., they suspected that bronze culture developed in Vietnam millennia later. In 1929, Victor Goloubew succinctly expressed these views when he stated that the bronze age in Vietnam was inspired by China and that it began no earlier than the middle of the first century C.E.

Many Vietnamese rejected the idea that the clarification of national origins should depend on Chinese texts, on the one hand, and French, European, and North American misreadings of the prehistoric past, on the other. In November 1945, just months after the Viet Minh formally seized power, Ho Chi Minh signed Decree 65, which established the Archaeological Unit.[99] From that moment, often laboring under inauspicious and even dangerous conditions, revolutionary scholars began their intellectual assault on colonialist representations of Vietnamese prehistory. In 1953, with the French on the verge of surrendering, the Labor Party established the archaeological unit as part of the new Research Committee.

The reinterpretation of Vietnamese prehistory was based most obviously on its material traces: scholars in the DRV examined the tools from paleolithic and neolithic times and investigated the bronze artifacts that they determined had begun to appear around 2000 B.C.E. But the physical evidence was also linked to historiographical assertions. The earliest history of Vietnam was written by Lê Văn Hưu in the thirteenth century, but the earliest surviving texts were produced in the fourteenth century.[100] In his brilliant excavation of these fourteenth-century texts, Oliver Wolters has pointed out the symbolic function of antiquity, specifically the kingdom of Văn Lang, as a metaphor of good government. As the name for or repository of an idealized past, "Văn Lang" signified a golden age when Vietnam was ruled by sages and when order and tranquility reigned throughout the realm.[101] In the late fourteenth century, as Trần dynasty rulers observed the increasing chaos and disorder in the countryside and in the court, they longed for a restoration of the normative pattern represented by Văn Lang. In the fifteenth century, Wolters explains, the Lê dynasty historian Ngô Sĩ Liên produced a new comprehensive history, which incorporated the thirteenth-century text but also brought it up to date and framed it overall with a new set of concerns. Lê literati such as Ngô Sĩ Liên looked back at the Trần dynasty (1225–1400) and, with some trepidation, tried to reconstruct how things had gone so disastrously awry. The combination of the Trần court's incompetence and the treachery of Hồ Quý Ly, who first inserted himself in the royal family and then, in 1400, usurped the throne, provided the Ming Chinese with a pretext to invade. If the Vietnamese could not properly govern themselves, the Ming felt not only legitimate in seizing control but even obliged to do so.

For Trần rulers, "Văn Lang" was an ideal more than a specific time and place, and, to the extent that they thought of it in more literal terms, they located it in the seventh century B.C.E. Because of the destructiveness of the Ming invasion and occupation (1407–1427), however, fifteenth-century Vietnamese had new preoccupations. Specifically, they felt compelled to demonstrate that Vietnam had come to resemble Ming China more clearly. To lend greater dignity to the Vietnamese past, as they believed dignity was defined by the Ming, they transformed Vietnamese antiquity into a much more ancient tradition. Whereas Trần dynasty scholars had turned to the image of Văn Lang as a symbolic expression of excellence, Lê dynasty scholars began to regard it as a testament to the historical longevity, and therefore prestige, of Vietnam. The new function of Văn Lang required a new lineage, so Ngô Sĩ Liên located its origins in the year 2879 B.C.E.. As a result of this historiographical maneuver, the mythical antiquity of Vietnam actually predated the mythical antiquity of China: the Hồng Bàng dynasty (2879–258 B.C.E.) preceded the Xia dynasty (2205–1766 B.C.E.) by more than six hundred years.[102] But, it should be pointed out, in assigning a specific chronology to the Hùng kings, Ngô Sĩ Liên was not necessarily insisting on its historical veracity. The chronology he devised was supposed to function politically rather than mimetically.

Postcolonial historians, on the other hand, have progressively converted the Hùng kings, the Hồng Bàng dynasty, and the kingdom of Văn Lang into genuinely historical entities. These transformations have been based, first of all, on the conflation of significantly different kinds of evidence: material traces unearthed in archaeological digs, dynastic chronicles, collections of legends and spirit tales, and "The History of Vietnam from 2879 B.C.E. to 1945," the poem that has been attributed to Ho Chi Minh.[103] The suggestion that the patterns of contemporary Vietnam were established as far back as the third millennium B.C.E. rests on questionable assumptions, including the idea that the Vietnamese of today were the Vietnamese of millennia ago and that they have continuously occupied the Red River delta. By addressing himself to the question of chronology, the fifteenth-century writer Ngô Sĩ Liên remedied a historiographical point that had potentially great political ramifications. For postcolonial Vietnamese, the issue was again historiographical and the consequences were clearly political. By tracing national origins to 2879 B.C.E., historians were able to assert the antiquity and venerability of Vietnam. Because the antiquity of Vietnam predated the antiquity of China, Vietnam was recast as a truly generative power, and postcolonial scholars were able to affirm that Vietnam was not, as the French had claimed, a minor derivation of China. More critically, this new chronology, or, rather, the new insistence on the veracity of an old chronology, underscored the fact that Vietnam was originally autonomous, independent, and in command of its own fate. Thus the real anomalies in national history were the foreign occupations, not the periods of independence. The recent experience of division was brief and aberrational; national unity was declared to be the norm.

This conversion of antiquity from a textual device into a mimetic truth has emerged over time as a result of extensive discussions and de facto resolutions. In 1956, Trần Huy Liệu cited new legislation by the party's Central Committee and the local authorities of Phú Thọ that established the precise date on which the Vietnamese would commemorate the death anniversary of the Hùng kings: the tenth day of the third lunar month.[104] "The . . . words death anniversary" (giỗ tổ), Trần Huy Liệu noted, "recall for us warm feelings and profound thoughts about the roots [nguồn gốc] of our nation [dân tộc] and record our gratitude to our ancestors for having established our land" (xây dựng ra đất nước). Like their contemporary heirs, the Hùng kings had "struggled against invaders." "Without the Hùng kings," he remarked, "there would have been no Đinh, no Lê, Lý, Trần, Hồ, Lê, Nguyễn, no DRV." Although the death anniversary would be marked by special festivities in the Hùng Temple of Phú Thọ, he explained, it would be commemorated by all Vietnamese. Trần Huy Liệu then drew on recent archaeological research and fifteenth-century texts to fix the period of their rule: the reign of the Hồng Bàng dynasty, which was founded by the Hùng kings, extended from 2879 to 258 B.C.E.[105]

As the canonization of the Hùng kings began to take shape, it intersected with another conversation, the discussion among official historians on how to periodize the national past. Thus, superimposing the Stalinist model of history on the prehistory of Vietnam, Trần Huy Liệu described the time of the Hùng kings as the period of primitive communism—a stage, he affirmed, that every nation must pass through. Because the importance of Văn Lang in pre-twentieth-century texts lay in the norms it embodied and its longevity, there was no imperative to make its location precise; rather, the vague sense that it had flourished in the region of the Red River delta sufficed. Trần Huy Liệu's commemorative text, however, likened the location of Văn Lang to the entirety of contemporary Vietnam. Whereas the "beloved land" (*đất nước yêu quí*) had once been united, it was, in 1956, tragically divided. Trần Huy Liệu lamented: "Our compatriots [*đồng bào*] are oppressed by the fascist rule of Ngo Dinh Diem, the lackey of the American imperialists."[106]

In this commemorative account of the Hùng kings, Trần Huy Liệu constructed a history without ruptures or seams. Until the violence of the 1950s, he implied, the prehistoric past had been linked to the present in a continuous, uninterrupted way. In presenting the Hùng kings as the historical antecedents of contemporary Vietnamese, Trần Huy Liệu undermined what was then the conventional chronology: Vietnamese national origins, many agreed, could be traced back approximately to the beginning of the common era. The idea that the Hùng kings, the Hồng Bàng dynasty, and the kingdom of Văn Lang dated back to 2879 B.C.E., and that collectively they defined the origins of the Vietnamese, had to be more carefully cultivated before it could be fully integrated into the collective memory of the Vietnamese. For instance, directly following the commemorative piece by Trần Huy Liệu was an article on literary history by Văn Tân stating that the history of the Vietnamese went back some two thousand years.[107] In 1958 a poem by Nguyễn Thượng Hiền was published in Hanoi. Like his better-known contemporary Phan Bội Châu, Nguyễn Thượng Hiền had been forced into exile by the French. While living in China, he had written a poem that claimed that the Hồng Bàng dynasty was four thousand years old.[108] But only months later, Minh Tranh reiterated the conventional chronology: the origins of the Vietnamese went back some two thousand years.[109] Years later, in 1960, Văn Tân revised his earlier position, but he still claimed that the Hồng Bàng dynasty had ruled for a period of four hundred years, from the seventh to the third century B.C.E.[110] When the German playwright Peter Weiss traveled to Hanoi in 1969, at least two of the people he interviewed at the Institute of

Literature defined the Hùng kingdom of Văn Lang in this same restricted way: as a phenomenon that had lasted from the seventh through the third century B.C.E.[111]

When Trần Huy Liệu introduced the Hùng kings in 1956 as the "roots of the nation," he seemed to inscribe them in a framework of primitive religion. "As we already know," he wrote, "agricultural gods are symbolic figures in ancient China."[112] Further emphasizing the sacred role of nature gods, he remarked: "Every tribe worships a figure which for them has special value." In response to these comments, several historians began to discuss the totem of the ancient Vietnamese.[113] Which was more representative, they asked, the Lạc bird or the dragon? What was the place of snakes and crocodiles in the iconography of the early Việt? But before this conversation could further unfold, in fall 1959 it was abruptly halted. Although the reason for its termination was not made clear, my own speculation is that when he introduced the Hùng kings as the ancestors of the Vietnamese, Trần Huy Liệu had the ethnic Vietnamese in mind. When he raised the question of totemic devotion, he further clarified the exclusiveness of the category "Vietnamese." Indeed, in the mid-1950s most ethnic Vietnamese still thought of Vietnam as the land of the Việt. Although they were beginning to explore the possibility of "Vietnam" as an *inclusive* term, they could not yet fully imagine it. At the same time, even though the field of ethnology had begun to take shape, it was still problematic to speak about ethnic differences in Vietnam, whether in the present or in the prehistoric past. The point of commemorating the Hùng kings, after all, was to naturalize the idea that all Vietnamese (in the political as opposed to ethnic sense) shared a common source. But when Trần Huy Liệu linked the Hùng kings specifically to the Việt, he undermined their unifying and integrative potential.

Throughout the 1960s, the interest in the Hùng kings, the Hồng Bàng dynasty, and the kingdom of Văn Lang as historical entities as opposed to textual devices was increasingly expressed. In 1960, the Institute of History identified a number of scholars whose research would be focused on prehistory: Nguyễn Linh, Lê Văn Lan, and Hoàng Hưng. In 1961, citing the work of Soviet archaeologists, Diệp Đình Hoa asserted that the inhabitants of Văn Lang possessed the technology of the potter's wheel, that they were divided into classes, and that they were governed by a state that protected the interests of those who owned slaves.[114] In October 1966, "archaeologist cadres" and "ancient history cadres" put the subject of the Hùng kings on their research agendas. In November, cadres from the Institute of History, the Museum of History, and the Department of Linguistics at the University of Hanoi met to discuss how their research could benefit the Hùng Kings Museum, in accordance with the suggestion of "comrade" Lê Duẩn and the Provincial Committee of Phú Thọ. In February 1967, as a result of a meeting of representatives from the Ministry of Culture, the Institute of History, the Museum of History, and the Cultural Committee of Phú Thọ, and the participation of numerous "comrades," the focal points of the research on the Hùng kings were decided: archaeology and popular culture would be the main topics.[115] Throughout 1967, the interest in the Hùng kings and the Hồng Bàng dynasty developed at an unprecedented pace. In May, Văn Tân published an overview of the Hùng kings and reflected on their significance to Vietnamese history as a whole; in July, Nguyễn Linh outlined the issues in Hồng Bàng history that researchers needed to explore; in August Đào Tử Khai offered his ideas on the major advancements in Hồng Bàng society; in September Hoàng Thị Châu examined class relations during Hùng times; and in December Trương Hoàng Châu linked the first traces of bronze culture in Vietnam to the Hùng kings.[116] So that research on prehistory could be conducted in a more cohesive fashion, the Institute of Archaeology was founded in 1968.[117] From 1968 to 1970, the Institute of Archaeology, the Institute of History, the Museum of History, and the University of Hanoi organized four conferences on the Hùng kings.[118] After the American War, the intellectual and political interest in the Hùng kings increased. In one of the most influential expressions of the postwar period, the late Phạm Huy Thông described the "three times" the country was founded: Văn Lang in 2879 B.C.E. by the Hùng kings, Đại Cồ Việt in 939 C.E. by Ngô Quyền, and the Socialist Republic of Vietnam in 1975.[119]

This recitation helps to clarify the process through which new interests were constituted or created and how conclusions were reached in the period after 1954. For readers who imagine Vietnam during this time as merely a combat zone, these details suggest the multiplicity of concerns unrelated to military issues.

Since 1975, the cult of antiquity has become fully consolidated. The idea of the Hùng kings is firmly entrenched in the signs of daily life. The surprisingly stark Ho Chi Minh mausoleum, for example, was built on the tree-lined boulevard renamed after the Hùng kings. Because the Hùng kings have been enshrined as the ancestors of all Vietnamese, in the politically inclusive as opposed to ethnically exclusive sense, each year on March 10 (the lunar dates have been abandoned), elaborate commemorative ceremonies are conducted at the Hùng Temple in Vĩnh Phú. To more fully inscribe the Hùng kings in the festal life of Vietnamese, temples and shrines in their honor have appeared in delta villages and mountain towns. Although Vietnamese national origins were until recently wildly imprecise, varying from the seventh century B.C.E. to the tenth or twentieth century C.E., they have now become fixed—2879 B.C.E.—as a result of postcolonial debates.

The cult has also expanded beyond the Hùng kings themselves, the Hồng Bàng dynasty, and the kingdom of Văn Lang to include the most celebrated traces of bronze culture. Anyone who has traveled recently in Vietnam can attest to the ubiquity of (replicas of) the Đông Sơn bronze drum. The Museum of History, the Museum of the Revolution, and the Museum of Fine Arts in Hanoi all display them in an ostentatious and celebratory way. Undoubtedly, somewhere in or near Hanoi is a plaster factory where workers cast and paint reproductions. Because museums in Vietnam are conceived principally as didactic institutions, the replication of "unique" artifacts is viewed not simply as legitimate, but as an essential pedagogical tool. Thus, the "bronze drums" with the chipped paint and the expanses of white plaster do not cry out as fakes; they speak in proudly didactic tones. The *image* of the Đông Sơn bronze drum has also been extensively reproduced: both the Museum of History and Vietnamtourism have replicated the distinctive, stylized bird of the drum's tympanum so that it circulates on letterhead, bulletins, tour buses, T-shirts, baseball caps, ashtrays, and vases. The starburst pattern of the tympanum also adorns innumerable scholarly works, including the Vietnamese dictionary published in 1988 by the Institute of Linguistics and the journal *Vietnamese Studies*. In sum, it is fair to say that the visual culture of contemporary times is richly laced with references to the bronze-age culture of Vietnam. In terms of scholarship, one simply has to look at standard narratives of the Vietnamese past to see how deeply entrenched the fact of bronze-age culture has become.

The cult of antiquity provides a conceptual, visual, and ritual center for national identity. It rewrites Vietnamese history in a self-generating instead of derivative mode and establishes Vietnam as a focal point of Southeast Asia rather than an insignificant periphery of East Asia. While the cult of antiquity demolishes the key principles of colonial scholarship, it introduces, unintentionally one assumes, new problems that subsequent historians will have to resolve. For instance, by reorienting Vietnamese history toward the Eastern Sea (not the South China Sea!) and Southeast Asia, the cult of antiquity highlights aspects of the Vietnamese past that other narratives have kept in the shadows, especially Vietnam's own history of imperial conquest, territorial annexation, and cultural assimilation. Although the postcolonial reification of the "tradition of resistance to foreign aggression" often succeeded in reducing the complexity of the past to a simple defensive gesture, the cult of antiquity alludes to other dimensions. At the core of a Southeast Asian-ized Vietnam lies Champa, the essential—yet also suppressed—link to Vietnam's reconstructed past.

THE FAMILY-STATE

In their compelling discussions of Vietnam during the 1920s through 1940s, Hue-Tam Ho Tai and David Marr have commented on the attempts of communists to transform the family-centered habits of the Vietnamese.[120] This endeavor, by the way, never met with complete success, and the use of kinship pronouns among people not formally related flourishes even today. Instead of focusing their affective ties on their families, the Vietnamese were encouraged to think in less particularistic ways and to reorient their loyalties toward broader entities and ideally toward the nation. Activists of this generation were troubled by Vietnamese pronouns, which were invariably based on kinship, and especially by the absence of a fixed "I." As is the case in other Asian languages, the "I" in Vietnamese is not stable; rather, it changes in relation to the person being addressed. Thus the "I" as *em* ("younger sibling") in one conversation can become the "I" as *chị* ("older sister") in another. In cases of actual kinship, age and gender determine which pronouns are used, but the use of pronouns in public life, where social relations were expressed in terms of fictive rather than actual kinship ties, status first and then age were the key factors. In an attempt to stabilize the "I," activists of the 1920s and 1930s resurrected the "feudal" pronoun *tôi* (meaning "your subject"). They tried to approximate a more stable idea of "you" by redefining kinship pronouns such as *ông* ("grandfather") or *bà* ("grandmother") to mean "Mr." or "Mrs." Reflecting the attempt to defamilialize Vietnam, the term for socialism (*chủ nghĩa xã hội*) is lexically linked to the village (*xã*). Indeed, one of the principal goals of socialism, as it was defined from the 1920s to the 1980s, was to normalize new notions of community based on the village, the cooperative, the collective, the village (again), and above all, the multiethnic state—instead of, and in opposition to, the patrilineal clan.

This decentering of family ties became more pronounced after the August Revolution and the Resistance War, when land reform, cooperativization, and collectivization dismantled the physical basis of family and ancestral ties. Moreover, new terms, such as đồng chí ("comrade") gained wider currency in public life while the use of familiar pronouns was discouraged, except in cases of literal kinship.

But because terms such as "comrade" and even the "I" (as tôi) did not easily take, the centrality of the family, whether literal or fictive, was difficult to transcend. Ho Chi Minh, for one, was enormously resistant to the new nomenclature, and he very purposefully cultivated fictive kinship ties. In *Unforgettable Months and Years,* General Vo Nguyen Giap recalls the momentous events of 1945, when Ho appeared so resplendently in Ba Đình Square and recited the Declaration of Independence. From his account, what evoked even greater emotion than the declaration itself was the question he addressed to the hundreds of thousands of Vietnamese who had assembled in the square. "Can everyone hear?" he asked. "Yes," they hollered in reply, and in that moment, Vo Nguyen Giap explains, "Ho Chi Minh and the sea of people became one."[121] In both the Vietnamese original and the English translation the image of the people-as-one is clear; the "sea of people" undermines the idea of society as a pluralistic composite. But only from the original do we learn that the idea of the public was communicated in familial terms. When Ho Chi Minh addressed the audience, he referred to himself as "uncle" (bác) and to the people as "nephews" and "nieces" (cháu). Ho Chi Minh appeared to cherish the avuncular image that popular speech and even official publications bestowed on him. On occasion, when reporters asked why he had never married, he was known to reply that indeed he had—the name of his wife was Vietnam. (In fact, he married at least once and had children whom he did not publicly acknowledge.) When asked that same question, women, too, sometimes similarly replied: "I have a husband. His last name is Viet, his first name is Nam." Later, as Ho Chi Minh aged and became, therefore, more venerable, he was recast in a grandfatherly mode as Cụ Hồ (cụ means "father's father"). Despite terms such as "cadre" and "comrade," the practice of using kinship terms endured, at least until the death of Ho Chi Minh in 1969. With the rise of Lê Duẩn, who did not present himself as the charismatic uncle (bác) or grandfather (cụ), the practice was more effectively suppressed. Still, the degree to which ordinary (but unrelated) Vietnamese continued or ceased to use kinship terms from 1970 to the mid-1980s is unclear. Since the mid-1980s, however, they are again widely used. At the same time, it must be noted, the use of bạn or các bạn ("friend" or "friends") for "you" has become more widely practiced.

This assault on pronouns that allude to blood ties, however, whether they are literal or fictive, was carried out in an arena in which the idea of family was still a legitimating device.

In the 1950s and 1960s, the "tradition of resistance against foreign aggression" and the "spirit of unity" functioned as the organizing clichés for reconstructions of the past. From the third millennium B.C.E. to the present, historians habitually maintained, the Vietnamese had continually united to fend off foreign invaders. Trần Huy Liệu once observed that the burden of "our ancestors" (*tổ tiên ta*), meaning the Hùng kings, was that they struggled not only against nature but against invaders as well, and in this way they had protected the frontier (*bờ cõi*). Following the example of the Hùng kings, the Trưng sisters, Ngô Quyền, Trần Hưng Đạo, Nguyễn Trãi, Nguyễn Huệ, and finally the DRV had rallied the masses to drive out invaders and restore the land of the Hùng kings to its rightful heirs. In the 1970s, during the last stages of the American War, these clichés were supplemented by the "fighting spirit" and the "indomitable spirit" of the Vietnamese. When the American War ended, however, the utility of "the fighting spirit" obviously declined; objectively it was no longer necessary and, in fact, officials of the Socialist Republic may have worried that it wrongly emphasized action and even aggression at a time when the government was concerned with maintaining the status quo.

The metaphors of family and state have not been limited, of course, to postrevolutionary and postcolonial Vietnam. In other settings, too, the tendency to naturalize political power through appeals to the family is a practice of long standing. The family presents the "natural" model of a relationship that is clearly hierarchical, but one that is also based on reciprocal ties. According to this model, a political ruler is supposed to govern like a parent, with wisdom and benevolence; and subjects, like children, must be filial—they are constrained to obey. When Ho Chi Minh was construed as a grandfather or uncle, the unspoken meaning was clear: just as "Uncle Ho" conducted himself as a wise and benevolent leader, his nieces and nephews revered him and happily obeyed. But, it should be remarked, postcolonial invocations of the family-state also moved beyond the sense of hierarchical relations and of reciprocal ties to suggest affective bonds as well. One famous photograph, reproduced and sold in souvenir booths, showed Ho Chi Minh sitting cross-legged on a patch of grass, radiating warmth and revolutionary ardor as young children danced happily about him. The power of this image stems from the fact that it both calls on and transcends traditional images of the family-state. Whereas Vietnamese monarchs were supposed to be stern, reclusive, and concealed behind an elaborate series of enclosures and screens, "Uncle Ho" or "Grandfather Ho" is playful and open. Moreover, once ancestor worship was extricated from a Sinitic and Confucian framework and redefined as an indigenous practice, it provided the link between prerevolutionary habits and postcolonial designs. Rather than displaying ritualized signs of respect in a merely particularistic way, postcolonial Vietnamese were supposed to do so in a collective way by honoring national heroes and heads of state.

Finally, instead of emphasizing only the hierarchical relations and reciprocal obligations between parents and children, the image of the family and of the family-state has filtered into a new context to provide a model of ties between siblings. In the first scholarly works produced in the Democratic Republic, the Hùng kings and the idea of the family-state played an understated, but still significant, role. In his commemorative piece on the Hùng kings written in 1956, Trần Huy Liệu remarked that the Vietnamese commonly used the term *đồng bào,* which he defined as "children who had one father and the family one clan" to refer to people who lived together in the same country.[122] In other words, the term *đồng bào* usually translated as "compatriot" and literally meaning "from the same womb," presents a figurative way for acknowledging the ethnic diversity of Vietnam. Just as each sibling in a family invariably differs from another, each ethnic group is unlike any other. But, like siblings in a family, all of the peoples (*dân tộc*) of Vietnam are harmoniously united within the "great Vietnamese ancestral family" (*đại gia đình Tổ quốc Việt Nam*).[123] Thus, at a time when the question of ethnic heterogeneity seemed to suggest not only differences but also divisions, the Hùng kings were reconstructed as the progenitor of *all* Vietnamese.[124] The point is that while the DRV physically dismantled patrilines and encouraged the Vietnamese to use nonkinship terms of address, it also nurtured the idea of the family-state. The idea of siblings may seem to imply a horizontal leveling, as though all siblings are equally subordinate to their parents, but in Vietnamese kinship terms the relations between siblings are also construed in a hierarchical manner.

A standard tour guide declares that in the "arms of the Motherland," successive generations of the fifty-four ethnic groups — large and small, older brother and younger sibling — in the great Vietnamese national family "have always stood side by side with one another, sharing weal and woe, shedding sweat and blood to defend and build up their homeland."[125] Through its insistence on consanguinity, the cult of antiquity underscores the idea of the family-state as the model for politics. Just as elder brothers and sisters naturally watch over younger siblings, ethnic Vietnamese (again identified as "Kinh") naturally guide their younger siblings and teach them to comport themselves in a civilized way. And just as authority in a family resides "naturally" in the father, authority in postcolonial Vietnam is located naturally in a benevolent — and yet not exactly father-figured — state.

Chapter Four | **Chronotypes, Commemoration:**
A New Sense of Time

In the first three chapters of this book I examine the themes that prevented official historians from completing a new general history of Vietnam (or completing it in a timely fashion): historical periodization, the idea of "Vietnam," and the problem of culture. In each of these chapters I explore the genesis of what are now taken as incontrovertible facts: that Vietnamese national origins can be traced to 2879 B.C.E., for example, or that Vietnam is composed of fifty-four different ethnic groups. I also investigate how some of the basic elements of contemporary life — ethnic identities, the cult of antiquity, the emphasis on the family-state — were consolidated, if they did not originate, in the 1950s and 1960s. Like the earlier chapters, this one, too, is thematically structured, but in it I highlight the social and cultural consequences of historical debate.

CONFLICTING AESTHETICS OF SPACE AND TIME

Contemporary notions of collective memory are often associated with the pioneering work of Maurice Halbwachs.[1] Whereas earlier writers — Henri Bergson, for example — interested in the social role of memory regarded it as the genuine, organic recollection of those who had experienced a common past, Halbwachs was concerned with the constructedness of collective memory and its orientation toward the present rather than the past. He viewed collective memory as an "instrument of reconfiguration" rather than an act of mimesis: memories of the past were created and not merely retrieved.[2] To explain the function of collective memory, Halbwachs drew on the social theory of Émile Durkheim, proposing that the (constructed) memory of the past provided a tool for integrating the various parts of society into a cohesive whole.

In transferring Halbwach's line of argument to the context of postrevolutionary and postcolonial Vietnam, I suggest how political and intellectual elites sought to restructure and reshape collective memory through rituals of commemoration. Scholarly journals were saturated with commemorative texts, and commemorative occasions prompted conferences, special publications, and journeys to commemorative sites. More to the point, public life was also richly laden with commemorative occasions: against a backdrop of banners and flags, commemorative events were ostentatiously proclaimed; boulevards and public squares provided the stage for processions and parades. Each commemorative occasion instructed the Vietnamese to "recall" certain historical figures or events and to "remember" them in particular ways. In this sense, the rituals of commemoration functioned in the present-minded and integrative way that Halbwachs imagined. Although recognizing the importance of Halbwachs, I would go a step further and argue—partly on the basis of work by Victor Turner—that the rituals of commemoration also emphasized new concepts, new expressions, and new sources of authority.[3] These rituals registered, or were supposed to, in at least three different settings.

First, political power in dynastic times was communicated through concealment: the emperor was potent precisely because he could not be seen. The architectural design of the Nguyễn imperial city of Hue, for instance, conveyed this aesthetic very clearly. The Citadel enclosed the imperial city in its entirety, creating a clear sense of inside and out. Within the city walls, the Royal Palace, which was known colloquially as the "Great Inside" (Đại nội), instituted a still more restrictive notion of inside and out. The Forbidden City, accessible only to members of the royal family and selected servants and eunuchs, further emphasized the idea that political power manifested itself through inaccessibility, remoteness, and concealment.[4] Normally the emperor sequestered himself within this series of increasingly restricted enclosures. On the rare occasions when the emperor moved outside the imperial city, he was enclosed inside his palanquin, which was, in turn, surrounded (further enclosed) by an extensive retinue of attendants and officials. The sheer expanse of his entourage, and legal injunctions as well, prevented the curious or impertinent from stealing a glimpse. The aesthetic of enclosure operated at other, more ordinary levels as well: townspeople lived on narrow, winding streets with gates that were opened in the morning and closed each night; villagers, especially in the North, resided in hamlets that were enclosed by a wall of bamboo. For colonial officials, however, power was marked not through seclusion but in spectacle and display. Thus the colonial aesthetic favored monumental buildings, large public squares, and wide boulevards arranged in a grid pattern because they lent themselves to public gatherings and grand displays.

That revolutionaries appropriated colonial notions of political power and public space was dramatically made clear on September 2, 1945, when, positioned on a stage in Ba Đình Square, the botanical garden built by the French, and speaking into a microphone, Ho Chi Minh recited the Declaration of Independence to an audience of one million Vietnamese. This spectacle, so expressive of how ideas of power had been transformed, soon crystallized into one of the revolution's main clichés. In the context of daily life, the idea of politics as a public concern was diffused in ways that were obviously less momentous than the events of 1945 but that were more overwhelming in the end. Through the proliferation of commemorative festivals, the imperative to be political was clear: it was not possible to simply opt out. Lest the sense of politics as public display be construed as an endorsement of colonial norms, however, postcolonial commemorations celebrated a new set of figures and events.

Second, traditional festivals focused on events relevant to the family and the village. They were centered on life-cycle events: the birth of a son (which ensured the continuity of the patrilineal clan), betrothal, marriage, or death. They included agricultural rites to ensure prosperity and coincided with the tilling of the fields, the planting and maturation of crops, and the harvest. Traditional festivals honored local deities or tutelary spirits; they recognized local events, such as a villager's success in the Confucian exams. Whereas festivals in precolonial times were perceived principally as local events that responded to local concerns, the celebrations promoted by the French stemmed from different motivations. Colonial commemorations were intended to be broadly inclusive and to overwhelm what was local and particularistic. Through the Association for the Moral Instruction of Annamites (AFIMA), colonial and collaborator ideologues organized commemorative occasions to instill a greater awareness of French history: even a schematic understanding of the French past, they imagined, would heighten the Vietnamese sense of being emotionally attached to Mother France. To inculcate a fictive genealogy, and thereby instill a new notion of filiality among the Vietnamese, teachers in colonial schools urged children to express reverence for their great Gaulish ancestors. Colonial commemorations celebrated key figures and key events in the history of French imperialism: Pigneau de Béhaine, the Catholic bishop who in 1787 petitioned the court of Louis XVI on behalf of Nguyễn Phúc Ánh, the future Nguyễn emperor Gia Long; the Saigon Treaty of 1862, which was forced on the Nguyễn court by the Spaniards and French and which ceded three southern provinces to France; and the Patenôtre Treaty of 1884, which formalized the French protectorate over Vietnam. Colonial commemorations also honored figures and events in the history of Vietnam, but they did so very selectively, choosing only innocuous and anodyne types. In 1925, for instance, as Phạm Quỳnh, Nguyễn Văn Vĩnh, and other collaborator elites promoted the idea of *The Tale of Kiều* as the "soul" of Vietnam, colonial officials sponsored commemorative celebrations devoted to its author, Nguyễn Du.[5]

Much more ambitiously than colonial officials and with far greater success, postcolonial elites also sought to shift the focus of festivals and commemorations away from the village and the family and toward the state. Postcolonial commemorations attempted to displace more private celebrations of birth, courtship, marriage, and mourning; they interrupted private reflections on the extended clan and redirected devotional practices to figures of state—now recast in familial terms. How many altars and how many shrines were dominated by portraits of "Uncle Ho"? The state-centered ethos of commemoration was also apparent in the sacralization of September 2 as National Day and in the presentation of Hanoi as the historic center of politics and culture. Unlike private commemorations, which caused a cessation of labor and a tremendous consumption of wealth, postcolonial commemorations reaffirmed the commitment to labor—in the factories, in the fields, on the battlefront—and the conservation of resources, whether in the form of rice, chickens or pigs, cigarettes, quids of betel, or cloth. As postcolonial elites claimed for themselves the power to manipulate time in the present and the authority to clarify the links between present and past, they transformed the texture of daily life. Although the revolution was initially accomplished through political, diplomatic, and military means, the institution of revolutionary authority was carried out in a multiplicity of far more ordinary forms. New holidays and new celebrations overwhelmed the atomizing effect of merely local ones. Rather than fragment the social domain and decenter politics as traditional festivals had done, new commemorative events homogenized society and pointed to Hanoi as the center of power.

Third, postcolonial Vietnamese — specifically scholars and officials — internalized colonial notions of "universal" time. For court historians in dynastic times, days, months, and years did not simply succeed one another in a linear infinity. On the contrary, the Vietnamese kept historical records in a complicated way that combined linear *and* cyclical notions of time. In official records, a year was identified according to two sets of markers: one based on dynastic reigns and the other based on sixty-year cycles of the zodiac.[6] Thus, the year that Western sources identified simply as 1700 was identified by educated Vietnamese as *canh,* meaning the seventh heavenly stem, and *thìn,* meaning the fifth earthly branch (which is symbolized by the dragon); thus, within this particular cycle of sixty years, the year 1700 was the seventeenth. To pinpoint the relevant cycle of sixty years, the year was also identified as "Chính hòa 21," meaning that it was the twenty-first year in the reign of the Lê emperor Hy Tông. Moreover, according to dynastic texts, politics also was a cyclical phenomenon. Early in its cycle, a dynasty rose to power; progressively its power declined and ultimately it was superseded by a new dynasty. The succession of imperial reigns *within* a dynasty was also regarded as a manifestation of the essentially cyclical rhythms of politics and time. Indeed, like the cosmos itself, history and politics were governed by cyclical patterns of order, disorder, and the restoration of order.

While most Vietnamese understood the intricacies of the sixty-year cycles, only educated elites could provide the other coordinate, which was based on dynastic reigns. Without that understanding, one would have no way of placing a particular year in a broader temporal context. Thus, while the affairs of state were recorded with these two sets of coordinates, one based on astrology and the other on politics, the temporal dimensions of ordinary lives were figured in astrological terms.

Colonial officials ridiculed cyclical notions of time and sought to regulate colonial subjects by imposing a uniform sense of (linear) time. They were appalled by the complexity of Vietnamese dates and by the apparent indifference to linear notions of time based on the idea of a fixed originary moment. What they were looking for, but did not find, was a specific point from which one could calculate temporal remoteness or proximity in a precise and uniform way. From their perspective, a calendrical system that lacked such an event had no coherent way to structure the flow of time. In the case of Vietnam, historical events, inscribed as they were in cycles of sixty and in terms of dynastic reigns, had to be appreciated with a far greater degree of relativity. In particular, the French regarded the use of the zodiac as proof of primitivity and pressured the Vietnamese to convert dates of birth to numerical years. For children and middle-aged adults, such conversions were easy to determine. Knowing that their daughter had been born in the year of the horse, for instance, parents could easily identify her as a girl of ten and on that basis calculate the specific (numerical) year in which she had been born; surely her parents would not mistake her for a young woman of twenty-two or a mature woman of thirty-four, forty-six, or fifty-eight. When older people were obliged to convert the cycles of the zodiac to the linearity of numerical years, however, uncertainties arose. As they tried to translate the year of the horse, for example, into Gregorian time, some people could not be sure whether they had been born in 1870, 1882, or 1894. The point is that although colonial officials condemned the imprecision of indigenous measurements of time, most Vietnamese found them more than adequate. From their perspective, whether someone was born in one numerical year or another was irrelevant; what mattered were the characteristics associated with particular signs of the zodiac and the position of one's birth within the cycle of sixty. For ordinary Vietnamese, the linearity of "universal" time and the relentlessness of the clock had no special merit; they were content to regulate their lives according to the phenomena of sunrise, sunset, the stages of the moon, equinoxes and solstices, and seasons — the events by which preindustrial peoples traditionally demarcated time. Just as colonial administrators restructured personal archives by recording specific dates of birth or death, they also reshaped popular notions of history in a broader, collective sense. Dismissing traditional conceptions, they began to emplot the Vietnamese past in the framework of universal time; where dynastic chronicles recorded cycles of power and decay, colonial historians saw linear developments.

The Vietnamese who survived the French and Japanese occupations obviously inherited colonial conceptions of time as a discrete and always measurable entity that moved inexorably from one unrepeatable moment to the next. While ordinary people may have been reluctant to reperiodize their own lives according to a linear progression, postcolonial scholars and officials set out to present the national past in the framework of developmental, linear time. The instrumental moments of the past no longer took place in the years of the ox, hare, or dragon, or in the first year of one cycle or another. Instead, they were slotted into a specific point in a timeline that continuously unfolded, without the imprecision and repetition of cycles. Events that were more proximate to the present were encased in great temporal detail: not only were particular years cited but specific days were as well. And whereas traditional methods of honoring individual lives were based on death dates, birth dates increasingly provided the anchors for postcolonial rites. Like the great moments of world revolutionary history, crucial aspects of national history were now represented in world historical time.

And yet, the festal calendar of postcolonial times developed in a distinctly bifurcated way: most holidays were celebrated on dates fixed by the Gregorian calendar, but others were calculated according to the cycles of the moon, which still governed popular conceptions of time. Tet, the greatest celebration of the year, marks the beginning of the lunar cycle, and this cycle of lunations continued to provide the basis for agricultural rites and ceremonies to honor the Hùng kings, who were enshrined as the ancestors of the Vietnamese. Some events were figured in accordance with both the lunar calendar and the Gregorian one. The Vietnamese victory over Qing troops at Đống Đa was fixed in 1789, but its celebration—on the fifth day of the first lunar month—varied from year to year. By representing certain aspects of the past in world historical time, postcolonial commemorations emphasized Vietnam's new position in an international and global community; by insisting on the parts of the past that could only be rendered in "local time," commemorative texts also established a reserve, a gap between the inside and out, a private space that was accessible and meaningful only to the Vietnamese. It should be remarked that, despite official attempts to reconfigure time in universal terms, the traditional methods are still popularly used. Birth dates, for instance, are presented according to the cycle of heavenly stems and earthly branches. During festivals such as Tet, the Vietnamese commonly switch back and forth between lunar and solar time: *tháng tư*, in such cases, can refer to the solar month of April and to the fourth month of the lunar cycle.[7] New Year celebrations of a particular year are still identified according to the cycle of heavenly stems and earthly branches: thus Tet of 1968 is identified as Tết Mậu Thân, meaning Tet of the forty-fifth year, which is represented by the monkey. Moreover, many scholarly works parenthetically include modified versions of traditional dates.[8]

Despite the ostentation of their claim to write "new history" (*lịch sử mới*), postcolonial historians resembled their dynastic forebears in a number of ways. Echoing Trần historians from the fourteenth century, official historians of the 1950s and 1960s believed that government could induce citizens (subjects) to behave in proper ways by providing proper instruction.[9] Whereas their predecessors traced the origins of social order to the inculcation of proper norms, postcolonial historians stressed the pedagogical role of historical knowledge itself. Indeed, after the French surrender at Dien Bien Phu, official historians began to set the stage for the commemorative mania that was about to erupt. Echoing historians from dynastic times, who habitually appealed to Chinese exemplars, Trần Huy Liệu remarked: "Chairman Mao has said that China had national heroes during its feudal period, and the Vietnamese too must declare that during several thousand years of history, Vietnam too had heroes." Others turned to the Chinese historian Jian Bozan, who believed that national heroes and the patriotic feelings they instilled were essential to history's didactic mission. Soviet historian Alexander Guber clearly shared this view: history, he said, should make the people "proud of their country" and "encourage faith in the people's struggle."[10] Emphasizing that ordinary people had played the decisive historical role, postcolonial historians still vowed to acknowledge the role of leaders.[11] The didacticism of the 1950s and 1960s, in other words, was based on the belief that popular, meaning widespread, knowledge of the past would cause "the people" to behave in appropriate ways—that is, in ways that benefited the state.

As official historians set out to honor Ho Chi Minh, whom they viewed as the greatest luminary of their own time, some clouds appeared on the horizon. In March 1955, *The New China Daily* published the historian Sha Ying's indictment of the "reactionary" historian Hu Shi, who, like other scholars from the "oppressive classes," had incorrect views. "According to that gang of scholars," Sha Ying charged, "history is like a chunk of clay which the great towering figures shape to their will."[12] In February 1956, at the Twentieth Congress of the CPSU, Khrushchev further complicated the question when he denounced the cult of Stalin.

To these objections, DRV historians replied in a number of ways. Instead of singling out specific individuals, Trần Huy Liệu responded by venerating the Hùng kings as the ancestors of the Vietnamese.[13] Because these kings were part of a prehistoric and even legendary past, they were far removed from current debates; to honor them was hardly cultish in the contemporary sense. Minh Tranh much more directly replied:[14] when one looked at the vast sweep of history, he reasoned, it was clear that the decisive roles were played by masses of ordinary people. Still, he continued, without denigrating the role of the masses, one could distinguish between individual agency, collective endeavors, and impersonal forces. To illustrate the various sources of historical momentum, Minh Tranh cited the radiant and exemplary individual Chairman Ho, who, activated by impersonal forces ("the bright light of Marxism-Leninism") founded the Communist Party, envisioned by Minh Tranh as the consummate expression of a collective endeavor. When Trần Huy Liệu rejoined in the conversation, he announced some discouraging news: "The bright light of the decree of the Twentieth Party Congress of the Communist Party of the Soviet Union has denounced the cult of personality."[15] Still, like his colleague Minh Tranh, he sought to preserve the status of exemplars. In his view, it was possible to esteem great figures without creating a cult of personality. Expressing some impatience with the apparent impasse, Trần Huy Liệu encouraged the Research Committee to settle "once and for all" the questions of hero worship and the cult of personality. With new resolve, Minh Tranh articulated a sentiment that many of his colleagues shared: "The Vietnamese people, like the people of any other country, revere their national heroes, the figures who 'illuminate our past' " (*làm rạng rỡ lịch sử*).[16]

Due to the circuitous transmission of key texts from the Soviet Union to Vietnam, however, the debate on hero worship was prolonged. In October 1956, the Research Committee published a Vietnamese translation of a French translation (published in *La Nouvelle critique)* of a Russian-language essay. Filtered through this sequence of mediations, its meaning was essentially that although heroic figures "illuminated" the past and served as patriotic exemplars, the act of emphasizing their exemplary status tended to diminish the role of the party and the people.[17]

In any case, the hints of caution and restraint soon disappeared. Between December 1956, when the first commemorative piece appeared, and 1976, when the Socialist Republic subsumed the DRV and the RVN, the two journals of history published more than one hundred commemorative texts. Once the Research Committee was reorganized as the Institute of History in 1959, and the question of individual versus collective agency had been relegated to the realm of theoretical debate, historians collaborated with the

Ministry of Culture and other such entities so that celebrations could be more publicly staged.[18] History's pedagogical thrust became clear when a profusion of bright red banners appeared in Hanoi's boulevards and alley-ways. Ordinary folk who ventured into the street were continuously cued to remember the Trưng sisters' uprising in 40 C.E., the founding of the national capital in 1010, or Trần Hưng Đạo's victory over the Mongols in 1288. They were supposed to reflect in a gracious and filial way on the anniversary of Lê Quý Đôn's death. Commemorative fanfare also signaled the quasi-sacred nature of recent events: the founding of the Revolutionary Youth League in 1925, the establishment of the Indochinese Communist Party in 1930, the August Revolution of 1945, the Viet Minh victory at Dien Bien Phu in 1954, and the emergence of the National Front for the Liberation of the South in 1960.

The impressive numbers of commemorative essays and the festivals that accompanied them underscore the frequency with which the Vietnamese were urged to remember. Many commemorations celebrated military vic-tories and specific individuals whose heroic acts of armed rebellion had strengthened the state. Others highlighted key figures and events in the cul-tural history of Vietnam. Although the vast majority of commemorations were devoted to the Vietnamese and to events in Vietnam's national past, foreign exemplars were occasionally included. Figures such as Marx and Lenin, for example, are widely known but others, such as the anti-Habsburg, Transylvanian prince Ferenc Rákóczi; the anti-Ottoman, Hungarian activ-ist Khristo Botev; or the Bulgarian leader Georgi Dimitrov, are more ob-scure. Commemorations that focused on foreigners, whether familiar or un-known, appeared to remind the Vietnamese that they were connected to a much wider world.

Historical analysis is not normally based on simple serialization. With the impulse to commemorate (kỷ niệm), however, such an enumeration—a list—is essential because it establishes the intensity of postcolonial rituals of remembering. Although it is partial, the list that follows also clarifies the focal points and the sequence of commemoration; more critically, it alerts us to their cumulative effect, which far exceeded the substance of any particu-lar one.[19] The effusion of commemorative occasions may remind us of the crucial interplay between remembering and forgetting, and may recall for us that memory itself is "a substitute, surrogate, or consolation for something that is missing."[20]

1956:

— The Hùng kings (death anniversary)
— The August Revolution of 1945
— Nguyễn Trãi (fifteenth-century patriot)

1957:

— The Resistance War (1946–1954)

1958:

— Hoàng Hoa Thám and the Yên Thế uprising of 1913
— The victory at Đống Đa in 1789 (anniversary)
— The August Revolution (13th anniversary)
— Phan Đình Phùng and the Scholar Movement (1885–1889)

1959:

— Hoàng Hoa Thám (anniversary of his death)
— Lê Văn Hưu (thirteenth-century historian)
— The August Revolution (14th anniversary)
— The October Revolution in Russia (42nd anniversary)
— Vladimir Lenin's *Materialism and Empirio-Criticism* (50th anniversary of its publication)

1960:

— The Indochinese Communist Party (ICP) (30th anniversary of its founding)
— The Women's International (50th anniversary of its founding)
— Ho Chi Minh (70th birthday)
— The Democratic Republic of Vietnam (DRV) (15th anniversary of its founding)
— The August Revolution (15th anniversary)
— Hanoi (950th anniversary of its founding)
— Hanoi (6th anniversary of its liberation)

1961:

— The August Revolution (16th anniversary)

1962:

— The ICP (32nd anniversary of its founding)
— The Trưng sisters' rebellion (40–42 C.E.)
— Karl Marx (anniversary of his birth)
— Hoàng Diệu (80th anniversary of his death and the fall of Hanoi)
— Nguyễn Trãi (520th anniversary of his death)
— The Resistance War (16th anniversary of its outbreak)
— National Day in the Soviet Union

1963:

- Nguyễn Huệ and the battle of Đống Đa
- The ICP (33rd anniversary of its founding)
- The Cuban Revolution (4th anniversary)
- Phan Bội Châu (22nd anniversary of his death)
- The victory at Bạch Đằng (675th anniversary)
- International Workers' Day (33rd anniversary of a Vietnamese rebellion)
- Lê Lợi (founder of the Lê dynasty; 530th anniversary of his death)

1964:

- The *Journal of Literary Historical, and Geographical Research* (10th anniversary)
- Lê Quý Đôn (eighteenth-century scholar; 180th anniversary of his death)
- Nguyễn Huệ (180th anniversary of two important victories)
- Trương Định (anticolonial activist from the South; 100th anniversary of his death)
- The People's Republic of China (15th anniversary of its founding)
- The battle of Vụ Quang (70th anniversary)
- The Research Committee (11th anniversary of its founding)

1965:

- The National Liberation Front for the Liberation of the South (NFLS) (4th anniversary of its founding)
- The N'Trang Lớng Movement against France (50th anniversary)
- Trương Định (101st anniversary of his death)
- Nguyễn Trãi (his populist thought)
- The DRV (20th anniversary of its founding)

1966:

- The victory at Đống Đa (anniversary)
- Trần Huy Liệu

1967:

- The uprising in the South (26th anniversary)
- Nguyễn Trãi (525th anniversary of his death)
- Phan Bội Châu (100th anniversary of his birth)
- Marx's *Capital* (100th anniversary of its publication)
- The October Revolution (50th anniversary of its founding)
- The Cuban Revolution

1968:

- The uprising of Lam Sơn (550th anniversary)
- The battle of Bạch Đằng (680th anniversary)
- Phan Bội Châu
- Karl Marx (150th anniversary of his birth)
- The August Revolution (23rd anniversary)
- The Museum of History (10th anniversary of its founding)
- The NFLS (8th anniversary of its founding)

1969:

- The victory at Đống Đa (180th anniversary)
- Nguyễn Thiện Thuật (125th anniversary of his birth)
- Ngô Thì Nhậm (163rd anniversary of his death)
- The DRV (25th anniversary of its founding)
- The Lao Động Party (40th anniversary of its founding)
- The first victory at Bạch Đằng (1,030th anniversary)
- The NFLS (9th anniversary of its founding)

1970:

- The DRV (25th anniversary of its founding)
- The NFLS (10th anniversary of its founding)
- The victory at Đống Đa (181st anniversary)
- Văn Miếu (900th anniversary of its founding)
- Vladimir Lenin (100th anniversary of his birth)
- Ho Chi Minh (80th anniversary of his birth)
- The August Revolution (25th anniversary)
- Friedrich Engels (150th anniversary of his birth)
- Lê Hữu Trác (250th anniversary of his birth)

1971:

- The Tây Sơn Rebellion (200th anniversary)
- Sơn Tây Citadel (anniversary of its establishment)
- The Paris Commune (100th anniversary of its founding)
- The Nam Lào uprising (70th anniversary)
- The Women's Association (10th anniversary of its founding)
- Chu Văn An (600th anniversary of his death)
- The Viet Minh Front (30th anniversary of its founding)
- Lê Hoàn and the victory at Chi Lăng (990th anniversary)
- The DRV (26th anniversary of its founding)
- The Resistance War (25th anniversary)
- The uprising of Bà Triệu (anniversary)

1972:

— The Trưng sisters (1,030th anniversary of their deaths)
— Nguyễn Đình Chiểu (150th anniversary of his birth)
— Lenin (102nd anniversary of his birth)
— Ho Chi Minh (82nd anniversary of his birth)
— Nguyễn Trãi (530th anniversary of his death)
— Nguyễn Văn Cừ (60th anniversary of his birth)
— G. Dimitrov (90th anniversary of his birth)
— The Soviet Union (50th anniversary of its establishment)

1973:

— The NFLS (13th anniversary of its founding)
— Ho Chi Minh (83rd anniversary of his birth)
— The Trưng sisters
— Ngô Thì Nhậm (170th anniversary of his death)
— National Day
— The Research Committee (20th anniversary of its founding)

1974:

— Lenin (104th anniversary of his birth)
— Phạm Hồng Thái (50th anniversary of his death)

1975:

— The LDP (45th anniversary of its founding)
— Ho Chi Minh's *The French Colonial System on Trial* (50th anniversary of its publication)
— The insurrection in the South (15th anniversary)
— Ho Chi Minh (85th anniversary of his birth)
— The DRV (30th anniversary of its founding)

1976:

— The Soviet Academy of Sciences (250th anniversary of its founding)
— Khristo Botev (100th anniversary of his death)
— The October Revolution (59th anniversary)
— Lê Quý Đôn (250th anniversary of his birth)
— Ferenc Rákóczi (300th anniversary of his birth)

Commemorative texts and events, I have argued, always bore a didactic burden. In general, they were supposed to inculcate a history-minded perspective and, more specifically, they were supposed to normalize certain ways of "remembering" the past. In a superficial sense, the postcolonial canon of heroic figures resembled precolonial versions.[21] Of the many heroes it enshrined, a great number had enjoyed cultic status in the past. For instance, the first history of Vietnam, written in the thirteenth century by Lê Văn Hưu, recognized the importance of the Trưng sisters and Ngô Quyền. Subsequent texts, such as *Palace Spirits,* the popular compilation of the fourteenth century, and *Complete Historical Records of Đại Việt,* the fifteenth-century chronicle, praised the impact of additional figures, including Trần Hưng Đạo and Nguyễn Trãi. These traditional heroes, it should be noted, reappeared in the pantheon of postcolonial times. But surface signs of continuity need to be critically read because heroic figures were not simply plucked from the precolonial canon and deposited in a twentieth-century shrine. Because commemorations responded to the exigencies of the present, traditional heroes often lost their usual significance and acquired new layers of meaning that were more in tune with contemporary times. They were reintroduced, one could say, through a complex process of reconstruction and recodification.

For other reasons as well the emphasis on continuity should not be overstated: although some traditional heroes reappeared in the postcolonial canon, their status had clearly declined.[22] In his history of Vietnam, written in the thirteenth century, Lê Văn Hưu showed great reverence for Triệu Đà, whom he venerated as the founder of the nation. The fact that he was Chinese was irrelevant; what mattered was that Triệu Đà had declared the independence of Vietnam vis-à-vis China. Postcolonial writers, repelled by the idea of tracing Vietnamese independence to a person of Chinese descent, mentioned Triệu Đà only in passing. Because he was concerned with the establishment of imperial traditions, Lê Văn Hưu was not terribly interested in Ngô Quyền, a figure whom postcolonial writers highly esteemed. Instead, in his discussion of tenth-century events, he focused his attention on Đinh Bộ Lĩnh, who had proclaimed himself emperor (*đế*); Ngô Quyền, on the other hand, had identified himself only as king (*vương*). For postcolonial historians, who were indifferent to royal titles but obsessed with chronology, Ngô Quyền was the more critical figure: his kingship, proclaimed in 939, predated Đinh Bộ Lĩnh's emperorship by nearly thirty years. Like his postcolonial heirs, Lê Văn Hưu was fascinated by the Vietnamese defeat of Song dynasty troops; unlike his successors, however, who underscored the cunning and brilliance of the eleventh-century general Lý Thường Kiệt, he was more impressed by the conduct of Lê Hoàn the century before.

While the postcolonial canon demoted some of the traditional heroes, it essentially banished others. Although Phùng Hưng had a prominent place in *Palace Spirits,* he all but disappeared from the postcolonial pantheon.[23] Phạm Ngũ Lão, the poet and general from Trần times who was greatly admired by modernists of the 1910s and 1920s, was largely ignored in postcolonial times.[24] Lê Lợi, much praised by the fifteenth-century historian Ngô Sĩ Liên for his expulsion of Ming dynasty troops and officials, was eclipsed in twentieth-century texts by Nguyễn Trãi. The postcolonial pantheon also introduced new characters, principally Nguyễn Huệ. The fact that he flourished in the eighteenth century explains his omission from the thirteenth-, fourteenth-, and fifteenth-century works. His omission from nineteenth-century texts, however, was a question of politics. Because the court historians of the Nguyễn dynasty (1802–1945) generally reviled the Tây Sơn rebels and regarded Nguyễn Huệ in particular with contempt, they identified him as a problematic but certainly not heroic figure.

When postcolonial scholars indulged in their predecessors' habit of "blaming and praising," their veneration of some figures set the standards according to which others were classified as villains (Phạm Quỳnh and Trần Trọng Kim come to mind). Finally, the veneration of some figures and the vilification of others also left a kind of residue, a roster of ambiguous types who could neither be lauded as heroes nor simply scorned. In 1961, in fact, the Institute of History identified seven such figures whose value had yet to be assessed.[25] Each of these was subjected to a posthumous interrogation. Periodically, verdicts were presented, and when they were not, historians were urged to resolve, "once and for all," the crimes and contributions of the person on trial. These interrogations were also played out in a broader intellectual and political arena. In 1962, for example, Nguyễn Kim Anh translated an essay on the judgment of historical characters that had been written by the Chinese scholar Wu Han. That same year Trần Huy Liệu linked the problem of historical judgment to the question of commemoration.[26] These gestures and statements emphasize the degree to which postcolonial commemorations were *engaged* in the Sartrean sense or *involved* in reinterpreting the past.

To bring these "discontinuous continuities" into relief, we can examine how postcolonial scholars treated some of the "stars," specifically the Trưng sisters and Nguyễn Trãi, and how they approached a glorious event: the Vietnamese defeat of Mongol invasions.

The Trưng Sisters (Americans as Han Chinese)

In scholarly texts and in popular culture, the two Trưng sisters, who led a rebellion against the Han Chinese in 40 C.E., normally play a prominent role, but the reasons for their prominence have varied.[27] For the thirteenth-century historian Lê Văn Hưu, they were monumental exemplars of valor and strength. But as *female* exemplars they were also quite odd, and thus their resistance against the Chinese registered at two different levels. Lê Văn Hưu acknowledged that "in establishing the nation and in proclaiming themselves queens," the two sisters suggested a kind of parity between China and Vietnam: like the Chinese, the Vietnamese, too, could establish a "royal tradition." Because they were women, however, the Trưng sisters prompted Lê Văn Hưu to have negative thoughts. "What a pity," he reflected, "that for a thousand years after this, the men of our land bowed their heads, folded their arms, and served the [Chinese]; how shameful this is in comparison with the Two Trưng Sisters, who were women! Ah, it is enough to make one want to die!" With a similar mix of uneasiness and admiration, a fifteenth-century poem echoed this impression: "All the male heroes bowed their heads in submission / Only the Two Sisters proudly stood up to avenge the country." A popular seventeenth-century poem also lamented that the rebellion against Han rule was led by "mere girls."[28] While these texts convey different meanings, they share similar concerns. As *female* exemplars of heroic behavior, the Trưng sisters violated normative patterns; they represented not only heroism, but deformation and transgression as well, and their bravery led to indictments of men.

In other cases, the importance of the two Trưng sisters was greatly subdued because the consequences of their rebellion were so meager: within a few years it was crushed and the Han Chinese resumed the occupation. This seems to be the perspective of the fifteenth-century historian Ngô Sĩ Liên, who was, however, full of praise for the power of the posthumous cult. This particular cult, which focused not on the two sisters but on Trưng Trắc alone, transformed her into a spirit—a goddess of agriculture, to be more precise—who prevented natural disasters such as drought and floods. The posthumous cult recognized her potency—but disengaged her from the context in which she first arose. As the object of cultic adoration, Trưng Trắc no longer resonated as a historical actor rebelling against Chinese aggression. The early-eighteenth-century scholar Cao Huy Diệu, who also was uninterested in first-century events, was fascinated with the posthumous cult, which then included both Trưng Trắc and Trưng Nhị. Whereas Ngô Sĩ Liên linked the cult to agricultural rites and attributed both benevolence and efficacy to the spirit of Trưng Trắc, Cao Huy Diệu was more impressed by the images of order and prosperity associated with the cult. He recalled the splendid temple, the extravagant ceremonies, and the decorum of the cult's devotees: "The temple hall is majestic and well cared for. People enter with dignity and depart with reverence. On festival days for welcoming the spirits, the local people perform in battle array with elephants and horses."[29]

Although the Trưng sisters deserve a much more detailed discussion, my purpose here is to indicate, even if only schematically, the various values and burdens they have had to bear. As postcolonial historians tried to map out a new national past, they seized on the Trưng sisters to determine anew what they signified—or *should* signify—for mid-twentieth-century Vietnamese. In an essay on the Trưng sisters that he wrote in 1955, Nguyễn Minh omitted any reference to the "royal tradition" and neglected to stress that women rather than men had orchestrated a heroic rebellion. Deferring to intellectual and political currents of his own time, he celebrated the Trưng sisters as leaders of an *international* and *class-based* attack on feudalism. "Human history is the history of class struggle," he wrote. "Together the people of Vietnam and the people of China fought against the gang of Chinese feudalists."[30]

This class-based assessment of the two sisters did not long endure. In spring 1962, as official historians began to commemorate their heroic resistance against Chinese invaders, who ultimately crushed their revolt, the Trưng sisters metamorphosed yet again. Instead of uniting Chinese and Vietnamese in a class struggle against (Chinese) feudalists, the sisters now attested, and brilliantly so, to the "indomitable spirit of the Vietnamese." Accordingly, their significance was adjusted to reflect that they were the first Vietnamese to "chase away" the Han.[31] This commemoration also praised the Trưng sisters for demonstrating the "capacity of women" (*khả năng của phụ nữ*). Unlike precolonial accounts that remarked on the heroism of women in order to criticize the passivity of men, this commemoration celebrated their ability to unite all Vietnamese against an external foe. The analogy that was not made explicit was easily inferred: just as women in the first century inspired others to resist the Chinese, women in the twentieth would lead their compatriots against a new foe. Coincidentally, just months before, the Women's Association for the Liberation of the South had been formed and, a few years before, commemorative events celebrated "thirty years in the party's leadership in the struggle of women."[32] The 1962 commemoration also appeared just as Nguyễn Thị Định, one of the few women who attained a high level of authority during and after the American War, began to assume a more prominent role in the National Front for the Liberation of the South.[33] Finally, in addition to praising the Trưng sisters' success, this commemoration pointed to their eventual demise and to the fact that within a few years of the rebellion, the Han occupation resumed. And yet, the new emphasis on the failure of the revolt did not diminish what the Trưng sisters had achieved. On the contrary, it contrasted their heroism and bravery with the fecklessness of other Vietnamese. It also emphasized that in the contemporary struggle against the United States, revolutionary leaders benefited from what the Trưng sisters tragically lacked—popular support and a powerful military. Their struggle would surely succeed.

For the rest of the decade, interest in the Trưng sisters seemed to subside. But this decline stemmed, I believe, from the postcolonial logic of numbers. Just as it was "natural" to celebrate in 1962 an event that had culminated in 42 C.E., in 1972 it was "natural" to do so again.[34] The more critical point, though, is that historical commemoration is not simply a case of reproducing traditional glosses; and this is especially the case in postcolonial Vietnam, where the significance of the traditional pantheon was ostentatiously reconceived.

Borrowing from the work of Mircea Eliade, I would argue that the rebellion led by the Trưng sisters was reconfigured in postcolonial times as the "prototype of exemplary action."[35] In resisting the Han Chinese they rehearsed what later became the essential drama: the expulsion of aggressive foreigners from the sacred land of Vietnam. As that model was periodically restaged, successive heroes and successive struggles reenacted the "immortal spirit" that had passed, beginning with the Trưng sisters in 40 C.E., from one generation of Vietnamese to the next. In the twentieth century, thanks to the "bright light" of "Uncle Ho," the Communist Party, and the People's Army, the Vietnamese would bring to fruition what the two sisters had begun.

Celebrating the Trưng sisters' dates of birth was, of course, was out of the question because they were not known. But the celebration of their deaths, I would argue, had a positive appeal unrelated to practical or empirical concerns. In timing commemorations to correspond with the deaths, postcolonial writers proceeded along traditional lines to create a new sense of shared ancestry.[36] Whereas ancestors in the strict sense of sanguinary ties reified differences and particularisms, ancestors in a figurative sense supplied the basis for thinking about broader collectivities, contemplating a shared heritage, and working toward common goals. The postcolonial search for an integrative set of ancestors culminated in the canonization of the Hùng kings and allusions to the "primordial womb" from which sprang all Vietnamese. Because the Trưng sisters, like all Vietnamese, traced their ancestry to the Hùng kings, they provided a genuinely historical link between contemporary Vietnamese and legendary forebears. Unlike Nguyễn Minh, who presented their revolt as an antifeudal struggle, official commemorations avoided the question of class—because the Trưng sisters were part of the collaborator elite that worked on behalf of the Han Chinese. Instead, they created new genealogical fictions to drown out the colonial insistence that the Vietnamese had descended from the Gauls.

The Battles of Bạch Đằng (Americans as Mongol Hordes)

No less dramatic than the reconstruction of the Trưng sisters' first-century rebellion against the Chinese, the postcolonial refashioning of the two battles of Bạch Đằng is also equally intriguing. In historical memory today, the battles of 939 and of 1288 are seamlessly linked in a narrative of struggle and overcoming. Reminders of these battles, which are imprinted on postage stamps, inscribed in narrative, and stenciled on street signs, insert themselves into daily life. Just as every Vietnamese city and town has a boulevard or street named after the Trưng sisters, they also have toponyms honoring the heroes of Bạch Đằng: Ngô Quyền and Trần Hưng Đạo (a.k.a. Trần Quốc Tuấn). The village of Đường Lâm in Hà Tây also boasts of Ngô Quyền's mausoleum, and the village of Hải Hưng is home to Trần Hưng Đạo's temple. At the Museum of History in Hanoi, visitors can gaze upon a nearly life-sized replica of the battles—minus the Song and Mongol ships!

Given that Ngô Quyền and Trần Hưng Đạo are principally associated with military history today, the manner in which they first appeared in postcolonial texts is surprising. When official historians initially discussed Trần Hưng Đạo in the mid-1950s, they barely mentioned his success as a warrior. Instead, they scrutinized him as a scholar and admired his famous *Proclamation to Officers and Soldiers* (*Hịch tướng sĩ*). By convention, this proclamation was cited as an inspirational piece: compelled by his words, Vietnamese soldiers continued to fight until, against all odds, they defeated the Mongols for the third and final time. But in 1955, the question that perplexed them had little to do with either the Mongols or Trần Hưng Đạo's motivational powers. Rather, the much-beloved poem attributed to him was at the center of an extensive debate. The problem, specifically, was this: Could Trần Hưng Đạo's proclamation be considered a part of national culture? Because it was written in classical Chinese (*chữ Hán*), some had reasoned, it was not authentically Vietnamese and thus had to be excluded from the canon.[37]

When the subject of Trần Hưng Đạo next arose, scholars were no longer concerned with the problem of culture. Instead, they looked at him as an exemplary general who, unlike men of lesser fame, had perceived the importance of mass support for defensive campaigns. Trần Hưng Đạo was a visionary, in effect — a pioneer.[38] Repositioned in his new career, Trần Hưng Đạo became the precursor for General Vo Nguyen Giap, whose command of the People's Army had enabled the Vietnamese to triumph over the formidable French. In the mid-1950s, as the United States began to take the place of France, Americans appeared as the new Mongols against whom a popular Vietnamese army would have to fight. As American intentions and methods became more transparent, this analogy yielded a host of potent associations.

In 1962, the subject of Trần Hưng Đạo and the Mongols resurfaced. In their survey of recent research on the topic, Nguyễn Văn Dị and Văn Lang started out by making the familiar strange: they identified some of the important but virtually unknown battles that led up to the great victory at Bạch Đằng.[39] Returning to what everyone already knew, they noted why this victory was so important: for the third and final time, the Vietnamese defeated the Mongols and expelled them definitively from Vietnam. But the victory at Bạch Đằng was also meaningful, they wrote, because of what it revealed about Trần dynasty science and military arts. Criticizing major contemporary works that had misrepresented crucial points, the authors discussed four main themes.[40] First, they claimed, Trần Hưng Đạo's strategy of planting pikes at the mouth of the Bạch Đằng River demonstrated his strategic brilliance, not simply a cunning use of tricks. Second, because the size of the Mongol navy was considerable, with probably more than six hundred ships, the scope of Trần Hưng Đạo's strategy was tremendous. Third, they argued, the timing of the Mongol retreat was not serendipitous; it was according to Trần Hưng Đạo's plan. He forced them to retreat at low tide because he knew that only in these conditions would their ships be impaled on the pikes. This strategy demonstrated Trần Hưng Đạo's skill in using the natural environment against a far more powerful foe. Fourth, the authors concluded, Trần Hưng Đạo was knowledgeable about the size and strength of Mongol ships, but instead of being awed by their might he used their strength against them: their bulk made their impalement on the pikes that much more destructive.

Having identified the interpretive errors of their contemporaries, Nguyễn Văn Dị and Văn Lang linked them initially to the much demonized Trần Trọng Kim, who had, beginning in the 1910s and 1920s, "popularized erroneous views." Although they saw him as the purveyor of critical mistakes, they did not regard him as their inventor. The source of his errors, they believed, was the Nguyễn chronicle *Comprehensive Mirror,* which had reduced the great victory at Bạch Đằng to mere coincidence.

Whether Nguyễn historians were influenced by Japanese accounts of the Mongol invasions is impossible to say, but the parallels are striking. Japanese historiography consistently attributed Japan's "defeat" of the Mongols to the gods (*kami*), who simply forced the Mongol ships away from the coast and back out to sea. Japanese texts did not read the intervention of the gods as a response to human ineptitude; instead, they interpreted it as evidence of Japan's divinity. When the Nguyễn chronicle and Trần Trọng Kim presented the events of the thirteenth century as marvelous happenstance, they may have been motivated by a similar desire — to show that Vietnam was cosmically blessed. But postcolonial critics believed that such notions of causality belittled the idea of human initiative. Instead of recognizing Trần Hưng Đạo's talent for minute calculations and his overall strategic command, the Nguyễn chronicle and Trần Trọng Kim attributed his success to something whimsical and possibly even comic: the Mongol ships were miraculously impaled.

Given the political exigencies of the 1960s, the objections raised by Nguyễn Văn Dị and Văn Lang are not surprising, but the remedy they proposed seems strange. To gain a more accurate impression of thirteenth-century events, they maintained, contemporary scholars had to return to Ngô Sĩ Liên's fifteenth-century account.

In 1963, in recognition of the 675th anniversary of the victory at Bạch Đằng, the Institute of History, the Ministry of Culture, and the Executive Committee of Hồng Quảng organized a commemorative event. Underlying this commemoration were two temporal conversions: the traditional name for the year (Trùng Hưng 4) was converted into Gregorian terms (1288), and the lunar date (the eighth day of the third lunar month) became April 9.[41]

Because of changes in the physical landscape, the Bạch Đằng River does not appear on contemporary maps, so the commemorative event was held in Quảng Yên, the point where the Bạch Đằng River used to flow into the sea. Presiding over the commemorative ceremony, Trần Huy Liệu began: "Not only did the battle of Bạch Đằng conclude the third victory of the [Vietnamese] army against the Mongol invaders, it also brought all the Mongol invasions that took place between 1257 and 1288 to an end." Implicitly linking events of the thirteenth century to those of the twentieth, Trần Huy Liệu then recounted the reaction of a Korean historian with whom he had traveled to the commemorative site the year before. This historian was well aware of what the battle of 1288 meant to the Vietnamese, but he emphasized its regional and even global dimensions. Contemporary Vietnamese, therefore, should also realize its global significance; they should understand that the defeat of the Mongols at the battle of Bạch Đằng redefined the course of world history because it thwarted their expansionist aims.[42] Overall, Trần Huy Liệu declared, the battle demonstrated the power of the people to rise up and protect the ancestral land (*Tổ quốc*). After the failed attempts of the Mongols, the colonialist French and the fascist Japanese invaded Vietnam, but like the Mongols, they, too, were forced to retreat. Having defeated the Mongols, the French, and the Japanese, the Vietnamese would once again reorient the course of history, and again on a global scale. Making the analogy between the Mongols and the Americans explicit, Trần Huy Liệu wrote: "But during this time, as we commemorate the battle of Bạch Đằng, as we face the catastrophic invasion of the American imperialists and Ngo Dinh Diem's gang of lackeys, our compatriots in the South, under the leadership of the National Front for the Liberation of the South, have once again risen up to protect the country, the homeland, and life. The American-Diem gang in the twentieth century is far more cruel and barbarous than the Mongols were in the thirteenth."[43]

Progressively, the "Bạch Đằng tradition" assumed greater cohesion in the past and greater relevance to the present. In 1968 a new round of ceremonies for the battle of 1288 was planned, and in commemorative festivities the following year, the first battle of Bạch Đằng, the battle of 939, was the key event.[44]

Nguyễn Trãi (Americans as Ming Chinese)[45]
The fifteenth-century poet-strategist Nguyễn Trãi made his first appearance in official histories in August 1956. Like the heroes of other commemora-

tions, Nguyễn Trãi was celebrated for his skills at waging war, but initially he appeared as a patriot who symbolized the "peaceful intentions of the Vietnamese."[46] As Minh Tranh explained it, people who defended their country against foreign invaders, as had Nguyễn Trãi, could not be considered warlike (*hiếu chiến*).

In postcolonial commemoration, the logic of exemplarity insisted on the power of descent: Nguyễn Trãi, like so many venerated figures, was the progeny of a patriotic clan. During the Ming occupation (1414–1427), his father, Nguyễn Phi Khanh, was suspected of seditious plans, arrested, and imprisoned in Nanjing. In evaluating Nguyễn Trãi's historical role, dynastic chronicles and colonial texts stressed his filial piety: following his father's arrest, Nguyễn Trãi thought "day and night" of seeking vengeance against the Ming.[47] Postcolonial commemorations also recognized him as a filial son; but they were more concerned with the disturbing contrast between the purity of his lineage, the righteousness of his life, and the utter ignominy of his fate: unfairly suspected in the death of Lê emperor Thái Tông, Nguyễn Trãi was executed in 1442.[48] Before his humiliating demise, however, Nguyễn Trãi had distinguished himself as a great military adviser. Minh Tranh identified him as Lê Lợi's chief strategist and the person who, more than any other, contributed to the Vietnamese victory over Ming troops in 1427. From his perspective, Lê Lợi's ascendance to the throne as the emperor Thái Tổ in 1428 was the direct consequence of Nguyễn Trãi's brilliant advice.

But Nguyễn Trãi was not only a man of military prowess, Minh Tranh pointed out; he was also a man of deep learning. Once the Ming were thoroughly vanquished, he composed one of the more famous poems in the Vietnamese canon, *Proclamation of Victory over the Wu*.[49] He also turned to the texts of classical Confucianism in order to make certain precepts meaningful to a new age. Casting Confucian values in a new light, he pointed to the essential connection between benevolence and activism (*nhân giả là động*) and, to disseminate his views more widely, he wrote a manual on family morality.[50] Concluding his summary of Nguyễn Trãi's accomplishments, Minh Tranh remarked that because he was unsurpassed as a strategist and a great intellectual as well, Nguyễn Trãi should be known to people around the world.[51]

In September 1956, a month after Minh Tranh's essay appeared, the Ministry of Culture organized a commemorative assembly on Nguyễn Trãi.[52] As Trần Huy Liệu began to deliver his celebratory speech, he reiterated the idea that the accomplishments of Nguyễn Trãi should be internationally known: he should be remembered as a politician, military man, writer, and as a patriotic intellectual who resisted invaders and esteemed peace. To stimulate the memory of "comrades" and to facilitate his proper recognition among "foreign patriots" as well, Trần Huy Liệu explained, Nguyễn Trãi would be honored annually, in accordance with the solar calendar, on September 19.[53] As he elaborated on Nguyễn Trãi's achievements, Trần Huy Liệu repeated much of what Minh Tranh had already mentioned, but he also embellished the earlier description. Not only was his family patriotic, it was also poor. Poverty combined with patriotism, it should be noted, conferred even greater legitimacy than patriotism all on its own. The family history of Ho Chi Minh was ultimately portrayed in similar terms, despite the lack of evidence to confirm it. Like Minh Tranh, Trần Huy Liệu also praised Nguyễn Trãi's contributions to national culture. He then made a rather strange claim: by composing *Family Instructions* (*Gia huấn ca*) in *nôm,* the demotic version of Chinese, Nguyễn Trãi helped break the dependence of Vietnamese literati on classical Chinese.[54] In fact, the ability to read and write in *nôm* depended on a knowledge of Chinese. As was the case with Minh Tranh's account, in Trần Huy Liệu's depiction a tension arose between Nguyễn Trãi the defender of peace and Nguyễn Trãi the warrior: in fighting to protect his country and to preserve peace, he represented the "indomitable spirit of the Vietnamese." Trần Huy Liệu continued, "Because of that beautiful tradition, since the time of Nguyễn Trãi there have been a number of glorious battles: the Tây Sơn Rebellion, the eighty years of struggle against the French, and the August Revolution. That same beautiful tradition was again expressed in the sacred war of resistance nine years ago and in the present war to unify the country."[55]

It is striking that both Minh Tranh and Trần Huy Liệu represent the conflicts in which Nguyễn Trãi was involved as the inspiration for the "glorious battles" that came centuries later. According to dynastic histories and colonial texts, the role played by Nguyễn Trãi in the events of the 1420s was essentially secretarial; he drafted official reports, prepared diplomatic correspondence, and issued proclamations.[56] Evidently, the commemorative recollection in 1956 responded not only to the memory of Nguyễn Trãi but to the political circumstances of the day, and thus he was burdened with emotional and ideological baggage that resonated with contemporary concerns. The Geneva Accords, formalized in July 1954, specified that within a two-year period, nation-wide elections would be held in order to reunify the two temporary regroupment zones (not states!) in the North and South. Many revolutionaries feared that despite the provisions of the Geneva Accords the elections would never take place because they would legitimate Ho Chi Minh's ascent to power — a possibility most loathsome to the Americans and their allies in the South. As the July 1956 deadline approached and then passed without the elections taking place, supporters of Ho Chi Minh perceived the degree to which Americans and southern Vietnamese were opposed to reunification based on the power of the former Viet Minh. Into these circumstances the reconstituted Nguyễn Trãi was suddenly thrust. Like Nguyễn Trãi, who "fought against the Ming because he loved peace," peace-loving Vietnamese would have to wage war against the American invaders and their allies (always depicted as "puppets" and "lackeys") in the South.

Following the commemorative ceremony of September 1956, Nguyễn Trãi largely disappeared from official histories until September 1962, when, on the occasion of the 520th anniversary of his death, new commemorative events were held. The 1962 commemoration identified Nguyễn Trãi as a towering figure in the history of Vietnam and, in a more surprising move, honored him as a populist thinker. In place of the literatus who composed poetry in *nôm,* and substituting for the Confucian scholar, the new Nguyễn Trãi was renowned for his "ideology of the people" (*tư tưởng dân* or *tư tưởng nhân dân*). In this commemoration, Nguyễn Trãi also metamorphosed into the *leader* of the uprising at Lam Sơn.[57] Colonial histories and court chronicles recorded that Lê Lợi gathered troops in Lam Sơn in 1418–1419, but they presented the assembly of troops as a backdrop to the dramatic, diplomatic events on the main stage. The mixture of military skirmishes and diplomatic negotiation associated with Lam Sơn was not, in other words, traditionally construed as a battle. Beginning in 1962, however, official texts drummed in the link between Nguyễn Trãi and the "battle" of Lam Sơn. So successful was this gesture that in popular reflections on history today it is not possible to think of one without the other. In subsequent commemorations, Nguyễn Trãi the scholar and Nguyễn Trãi the lover of peace were more completely eclipsed by Nguyễn Trãi the warrior. As he was more fully enshrined as a military hero, his scholarly achievements slipped into the shadows. In 1967, the Institute of History and the Ministry of Culture organized a celebration to commemorate the 525th anniversary of Nguyễn Trãi's death.[58] Seeking to create popular indignity over fifteenth-century events, and to use that anger as a motivational device, a new round of commemorations — this one in honor of the 550th anniversary of the uprising Lam Sơn — was slated for the following year.[59]

Postcolonial writers reshaped the details and in some cases the contours of fifteenth-century events to establish what must have seemed a compelling analogy. From their vantage point in Beijing, Ming officials had looked out judgmentally at the rest of the world. Convinced that their own institutions were intrinsically superior to those of the "barbarians," and confident in their sense of China as the natural arbiter of world events, they were scandalized by the behavior of the Vietnamese. With unusual ferocity Ming troops invaded Vietnam. Then, believing that proper Ming institutions would flourish only in a sinified society, Ming officials set out to transform the Vietnamese. Determined to wipe out the traces of an inferior culture, they ransacked royal libraries in Hanoi; to eradicate evil customs, they forbade tattooing, the lacquering of teeth, and betel chewing. Just as the Vietnamese of the fifteenth century must have been stunned by the hubris and violence of the Ming, Vietnamese in the 1960s and 1970s were shocked and terrified by what the Americans did. So that they might master the tragic events of the present, the Vietnamese "remembered" the devastation of the Ming conquest more than five hundred years before. The reinvented persona of Nguyễn Trãi and the reconstructed "memory" of the Ming occupation functioned as mnemonic devices; they were the key elements in a more manageable vision of political humiliation, military terror, and cultural devastation.

In the aftermath of the American War, commemorative attention to Nguyễn Trãi became still more pronounced. In postwar commemorations, he was still celebrated as a brilliant strategist who undermined the Ming Chinese, but his scholarly accomplishments were restored to him, as was his fame as a literary figure.[60] And yet, the events of the fifteenth century complicated the "tradition of resistance against foreign aggression." After all, the Ming occupation endured, even if only briefly, because sufficient numbers of Vietnamese collaborated — in the etymological sense of working together and in the political sense as well — with Ming officials. In other words, the "memory" of the Ming was supposed to remind the Vietnamese of their great power and their ability to overcome more powerful foes, but it also underscored the degree to which the Vietnamese had been genuinely — and violently — divided.

The Eighteenth Century Revisited: Nguyễn Huệ and the Tây Sơn

From around 1600 until the late eighteenth century, political power in Vietnam issued nominally from the Lê dynasty court in Hanoi; in fact it was monopolized by two seigneurial clans, the Trịnh in the North and the Nguyễn in the South, who both presented themselves as loyal executors of the imperial will. In the 1770s, three brothers from the village of Tây Sơn in the province of Bình Định orchestrated what is celebrated today as the Tây Sơn Rebellion, which caused the temporary decline of the Nguyễn, the permanent demise of the Trịnh, and the total collapse of the Lê. Before delving into the postcolonial reconstruction of these events and the figure of Nguyễn Huệ, the brother who established the Tây Sơn dynasty, it is useful to look at interpretations of the late eighteenth century that were conventionalized by historians at the Nguyễn court and by colonial scholars.

Consulting *Lessons in Annamite History,* a popular work written by the literary critic Dương Quảng Hàm, one is reminded of the comment that historical narrative can be more cannibalizing than the real cannibalism. He describes the events of the 1760s, 1770s, and 1780s—the period of the Tây Sơn—in a clipped and vertiginous style that reproduces the worst possibilities of both political history and narration.[61] Historians in the DRV objected to this work on numerous grounds, but what most vexed them was its relentless attention to the political maneuvers of elites and its indifference to broader social contexts. By neglecting the social conditions in which the events of the 1770s took place, Dương Quảng Hàm and others easily misrepresented the motives of the Tây Sơn and the meaning of what they achieved. According to conventional readings of the late eighteenth century, political corruption in the South made it possible for the Tây Sơn brothers to convert personal misdeeds such as gambling and thievery into a social rebellion. Traditional sources also maintained that because the Lê emperor was still legitimately enthroned when Nguyễn Huệ proclaimed himself emperor in 1788, Nguyễn Huệ was only a usurper. The rightful heir to the Lê dynasty was the Nguyễn dynasty established in 1802.

The postcolonial refashioning of the Tây Sơn began to unfold in 1956.[62] What became apparent, first of all, was that two of the brothers, Nguyễn Nhạc and Nguyễn Lữ, had essentially disappeared whereas Nguyễn Huệ appeared larger than life. In their early publications, official historians were unsure how to characterize the movement led by the Tây Sơn. Was it a peasant uprising, a national movement, an insurgency, a rebellion, or revolution? Minh Trinh, for example, referred to the Tây Sơn *uprising* as a perfect example of the "fighting spirit" of the Vietnamese.[63] As historians continued to reshape the events of the 1770s and 1780s, they focused much more emphatically on place, specifically on the site of Đống Đa, where Nguyễn Huệ led his troops against the much more powerful Qing Chinese. This victory, Trần Huy Liệu declared, was another "glorious page" in the national history of fighting against foreign aggression.[64] Progressively, after many revisions, what Nguyễn historians had dismissed as the mischief of riffraff became the Tây Sơn Rebellion of 1789.[65] As postcolonial commemorations continued to evolve, however, the fact that the rebellion failed became its essential trait. In this way, postcolonial historians could construe the August Revolution of 1945 as the completion of what the Tây Sơn had begun.

According to the official narrative, which was finally published in 1971, the oppressiveness of the Nguyễn family in the South caused the people tremendous suffering and prompted them on many occasions to rise up and rebel.[66] But their rebellions were quickly suppressed. Moved by the misery that peasants had to endure, the Tây Sơn began to organize them. Gradually, the new survey continues, the rebels gained support and completely "liberated" (*giải phóng*) the South; in 1785 they repelled an invasion of the Thai. Having secured the South, Nguyễn Huệ and his army headed to the North to drive the Trịnh troops from Thuận Hóa. But instead of stopping there and returning to the South, Nguyễn Huệ continued the fight because he wanted to unify the whole country. The people of the North, who "warmly welcomed" Nguyễn Huệ, formed peasant armies to help him wage war against the Trịnh. Thus, the movement that had begun in Qui Nhơn came to engulf all of Vietnam. Once the Trịnh were defeated, Nguyễn Huệ headed back to the South. But when the Lê emperor Hiển Tông died in 1788, his successor, Chiêu Thống, allowed the Trịnh clan to resume its seigneurial role. Nguyễn Huệ had no choice; he had to go north once again. This time, fearing their final demise, officials at the "feudal" and "reactionary" Lê court requested the Qing dynasty to send in troops. When news of this treasonous act reached Nguyễn Huệ, he proclaimed himself emperor because no legitimate ruler was on the throne.

At one level, the newly reconstituted Tây Sơn Rebellion reproduced the "prototype of exemplary action." Like the revolt of the Trưng sisters, it succeeded in repelling foreign invaders, and like the sisters' successors—Ngô Quyền, Trần Hưng Đạo, and Nguyễn Trãi—the Tây Sơn Rebellion also transcended the original model. Applying the rhetoric of the twentieth century to the eighteenth, postcolonial writers described the Tây Sơn as the model of "people's war." Unlike the success of the Tây Sơn Rebellion and Nguyễn Huệ's imperial reign, which were only transitory, what the DRV was about to achieve would be permanent. Because the unity of Vietnam had been achieved through revolutionary struggle, Trần Huy Liệu once wrote, it was "a principle" that no "ill-gotten strength could change."[67] Or, as the Research Committee put it: "History has shown us that once a nation has emerged nothing can divide or eliminate it."[68]

Through a web of analogical links, contemporary Vietnamese who supported the revolution and fought the French and Americans were transformed into descendants of Nguyễn Huệ. Through this same process, Ngo Dinh Diem acquired a new genealogy as well: he became the embodiment of the corrupt and nefarious Chiêu Thống. Like his impotent predecessor, Diem also had called in foreign troops to occupy and divide Vietnam. Despite the allegorical power of linking Ngo Dinh Diem to the Lê emperor, the importance of Nguyễn Huệ and the Tây Sơn eventually receded. Because the Tây Sơn had temporarily weakened the Nguyễn lords, Southerners often saw them in an antipathetic light. As the end of the American War came more fully into view, leaders in the DRV became more concerned with the postwar integration of the North and South. More unifying visions of the past would have to be designed.

Revolutions

The commemorative impulse flourishes in settings where struggles to define the past are at the forefront of daily life. This impulse stems from many sources and expresses itself in many ways, but it always involves the stabilization of meaning. For these reasons, the commemorative process itself is inherently fluid. A single commemoration can distill the complexity of the past into a perfect kernel or condensation of truth, but a subsequent commemoration can just as easily revise or suppress that truth as reaffirm it.[69] To further grasp the interplay of commemoration's productive and censoring mechanisms, we can examine commemorative representations of Vietnam's recent revolutionary past. Rather than present the shifts in the revolution's meaning as simple progressions from one position to another, we can regard them as overlapping, often competing, voices in a prolonged conversation.

Many writers have commented on the richness and ambivalence of the term "revolution" but perhaps none so compellingly as Hannah Arendt.[70] In

"The Meaning of Revolution" she observes that revolution can signal transformation and rupture, but it may also mark a return to or a restoration of a previous form. Because the Vietnamese term for revolution (*cách mạng*) means literally "changing the mandate of Heaven," it signals *change within continuity*. Postcolonial representations of the revolution demonstrated a striking degree of divergent meanings. In official discourses of the North and in popular consciousness as well, the August Revolution of 1945 was, by the mid-1950s, permanently fixed; although the revolution had come to function as a landmark, at least in the North, its meaning was surprisingly unstable. At any given moment, the August Revolution had several sets of origins and significations, not all of them complementary, and over time its meaning varied.

Historians in the DRV basically posed the same set of questions. When did the revolution begin? How had it occurred and what exactly had it accomplished? Was the Vietnamese Revolution a bourgeois revolution that dislodged feudal society? Or was it a proletarian one that undermined the structures of capitalism? Was it a peasant revolution in which workers as well as bourgeois intellectuals played only a minor role? What was the role of economic forces? Did they have a momentum of their own or were emotional and affective dimensions—human agency—more crucial? If the role of human agency was more instrumental than objective economic conditions, which aspect of human agency should be stressed—an elite cadre of leaders or hundreds of thousands of peasants and soldiers? Did Vietnam's revolutionary momentum emerge spontaneously from the people or was it constructed at the top of society and essentially imposed on those below? Or, was the August Revolution essentially a nationalist revolution against colonial power? Although they raised the same sets of questions, historians responded in extremely dissonant ways.

First, the designations "Vietnamese Revolution" and "August Revolution" overlapped but were not always interchangeable; furthermore, the significance of the two terms changed from one reading to the next. In some cases, the "Vietnamese Revolution" implied or made explicit the connections between events in Vietnam and those in China. This revolution was perceived as a vast social transformation that took decades, or even centuries, to unfold. Peasants were at the forefront of this revolution and resentment stemming from landlessness and rural poverty propelled them. Conceptually, this notion of revolution was linked to Mao and his reversal of Marxist theory: rather than perceive peasants as political reactionaries and even counterrevolutionaries, Mao depicted them as the very fount of revolutionary fervor. Articulating this view, Trần Huy Liệu once wrote: "The Vietnamese Revolution, like the Chinese Revolution, was fundamentally a peasant revolution."[71] This revolution was internally generated and internally aimed against Vietnamese institutions and practices that prevented cultural, political, and economic modernization. Incidentally, this view of the revolution as a long-term social transformation also reduced the French occupation to epiphenomenal status: although colonization had exacerbated the existing tensions it certainly did not produce them. When peasants launched an assault against feudal power and the hierarchies on which it was based, the colonial occupation necessarily collapsed; but the French were not the principal target. In other words, by regarding the main antagonists as Vietnamese, this vision of revolutionary change casts the French colonialists in subordinate roles.

Initially, the Research Committee suggested a high degree of continuity between the Vietnamese Revolution and the August Revolution. For example, in an editorial piece published in 1955, the committee stated: "The August Revolution was not only a question of toppling the gang of invaders. It was also a social upheaval to break the feudal system which our people had endured for two thousand years."[72] The editorial further defined it as a national, democratic, and popular revolution, characteristics that easily overlapped with those of the Vietnamese Revolution. When the editorial addressed the question of agency, however, the ideological distinction between the Vietnamese Revolution and the August Revolution became clear: unlike the Vietnamese Revolution, which was attributed to the activism of peasants, the August Revolution was led by "the representatives of the proletarian class." In the 1920s and 1930s, there were surely urban workers (proletarians) in Vietnam, but they did not form a working class (proletariat). Therefore, when writers referred to the "representatives of the proletarian class," they meant the Indochinese Communist Party. Unlike the Vietnamese Revolution, which tried to dislodge social and economic patterns that had been in the making for hundreds and even thousands of years, the August Revolution was aimed principally against the French and culminated in the Viet Minh seizure of power in 1945. The August Revolution (with its unmistakable echoes of the October Revolution) was much more clearly linked to the history of the ICP; it also suggested a basic sympathy with the principles of Marxism-Leninism — meaning Stalin's codification of the Marxist canon. By insisting on the instrumental role of the party as the substitution for the missing proletariat, references to the August Revolution also hinted at the deficiencies that supposedly inhered in peasant populations: superstition, parochialism, and reactionary and counterrevolutionary politics.

In April 1956, underscoring this more Soviet-centric view, Ho Chi Minh declared to an audience assembled in Ba Đình Square: "The people of Vietnam and the people of the Soviet Union are like brothers in the great socialist and democratic family. For many years, our two peoples have been united, striving together under the victorious banner of Marxism-Leninism to establish national independence and democratic freedom, to build socialism, and to protect world peace." Representing the Soviet Union, Anastas Mikoyan replied: "The Soviet people clearly express their love and their warm friendship for you [các đồng chí và các bạn] and ardently wish you many successes in building a new life, developing industry and agriculture, and raising the material and cultural conditions of life."[73] Prompted by Mikoyan's visit, and recalling the joint Vietnamese-Soviet declaration of July 1955, the Research Committee began to narrate twentieth-century history—and thus the history of the August Revolution—in a way that placed communist parties and the Soviet Union at the center.

This particular narrative proceeded as follows. After the First World War, and through the establishment of the Communist International, revolutionary movements in the colonies became linked to working-class struggles in capitalist countries. The Vietnamese first learned of the "new working-class power" through Phan Bội Châu, who in 1920, while living in exile in China, came across a copy of *An Investigation into the Actual State of Russia*.[74] But the first Vietnamese to visit the Soviet Union and to learn of the Russian Revolution directly was Ho Chi Minh. Having participated in the founding of the French Communist Party, he was sent to the Soviet Union to attend the Comintern Congress scheduled for October 1923. The Vietnamese Revolution then came under the leadership of the Comintern (*bộ tham mưu quốc tế*, literally "international chief of staff"), and Vietnam and the Soviet Union became irrevocably linked. In 1926, during commemorative events devoted to the October Revolution, some leaflets introducing the October Revolution and the "new Russia" began to circulate in Saigon. From this moment, the Vietnamese Revolution was no longer an isolated event. It was part of the worldwide proletarian revolution, and the Vietnamese were fully oriented toward the Soviet Union.

Subsequently, the narrative continues, the Vietnamese Revolutionary

Youth Party, the precursor of the Indochinese Communist Party, was formed.[75] In November 1929, after the communist organizations had already taken shape, the Vietnamese people continued to commemorate the October Revolution and to use the red flag with its hammer and sickle. In 1930, when the ICP unified the communist parties, it became a cell of the Comintern (*chi bộ của quốc tế cộng sản*). In September 1930, the first Vietnamese soviet (in the village of Võ Liệt) was formed, and soon it encompassed the three provinces of Nghệ An, Hà Tĩnh, and Quảng Ngãi. By this point, a number of Vietnamese students were already attending the Stalin School in Moscow, and Vietnamese representatives had participated in international organizations. The years of the Popular Front government (1936–1939) allowed the Vietnamese greater opportunities to study Marxism-Leninism; and newspapers, which printed commemorative accounts of the October Revolution, introduced Vietnamese readers to the "victory of socialism." The success of the August Revolution of 1945 stemmed, first of all, from the combative strength of the Vietnamese and the leadership of the ICP, but the Soviet defeat of Japan's Kwantung army was also essential because it forced the Japanese to surrender. During the nine-year war of resistance against France, the Soviets continually expressed their solidarity with the Vietnamese and exposed the cruelty of the gang of American and French interventionists. At the end of 1949, when the Soviet Union and China both recognized the DRV, the Vietnamese people joined with the nine hundred million democratic people led by the Soviet Union.[76] "After peace was restored, while building up the North and fighting to unify the country," the Research Committee explained, "we received Soviet assistance in every respect, in material as well as moral terms, domestically and internationally. Through delegations to the Soviet Union, coming into contact with Soviet people, we could clearly see that the love between Vietnamese and Soviets was like the love between brothers from the same womb, living together in the great socialist family."[77]

Among this narrative's many striking elements, one of the more curious is that it identifies Phan Bội Châu as an almost unwitting receiver of new ideas; his knowledge of the "new Russia" appears to have come about fortuitously—by accident, it seems, he came across a certain book. Indeed, in his autobiography, Phan Bội Châu depicts this period in his life as generally lacking in purpose: "In the Seventh Month of the Year of the Sheep [July/August 1919], I left Hangchow for Peking, then went on to Japan. From this time on, during the four years from the Year of the Sheep to the Year of the Dog [1919–1922], whenever I felt at loose ends, I would set out on a trip, without any particular purpose." But he contrasts the aimlessness of his life at that time with the deliberate and purposeful quality of his encounter with socialism, communism, and news of the Soviet Union:

> In the Eleventh Month of the Year of the Monkey [December 1920/ January 1921], I heard that many people from the Socialist and Communist Parties of Soviet Russia had arrived in Peking and that the headquarters of the Soviets was at Peking University. My curiosity was aroused, and I wished to learn the truth about the Communist Party. So I got out a book that was an investigation of the actual state of Russia written by a Japanese, Fuse Katsuji. After going through it several times to work out its meaning, I translated it into Chinese in two volumes. This book treated in great detail the Soviet government's ideology and institutions. I rushed off to Peking taking the translation with me, wishing to use it to introduce myself to the members of the Chinese and Russian socialist parties.[78]

At no point in his life did Phan Bội Châu identify himself as a communist, and in his later years he even expressed great skepticism toward revolutionary upheaval. But he played a critical role, nonetheless, in introducing the Vietnamese to communism and to Soviet practices in particular. Because the politics of the present had to be motivated by the actions of the past, postcolonial historians minimized the importance of Phan Bội Châu and emphasized, instead, the instrumentality of Ho Chi Minh. Motivated by teleological concerns they focused on the activism of Ho Chi Minh, who had traveled directly to the Soviet Union and developed clear, unmediated ties to the revolutionary source.

On other occasions the August Revolution was presented not so much as a set of discrete, autonomous events as a subset of Communist Party history. This revolution was initiated at the top; the ICP was clearly in control; and the revolution itself could be linked to specific edicts and decrees. In some cases, this narrower view of the revolution became even further restricted. In July 1957, for instance, Trần Huy Liệu traced the origins of the revolution to May 1941, when the Eighth Conference of the ICP's Executive Committee issued a specific resolution. Describing the August Revolution as a national and democratic revolution aimed against imperialism and feudalism, he also credited its timing to a decision resulting from the party's National Conference held on August 15, 1945, in Tân Trào.[79] In other cases, this constricted view of the revolution could be considerably broadened. Months later, and in a commemorative mood — it was the occasion of the fiftieth anniversary of the October Revolution — Trần Huy Liệu again identified the ICP as the August Revolution's essential source. At the same time, however, he also located the ICP in a broader (Soviet-centric) context. Skipping past Phan Bội Châu and the mediation of Japan, Trần Huy Liệu wrote: "Our country received the seeds of the Russian Revolution through two principal routes, from Moscow to China to Vietnam, and from Moscow to France to Vietnam."[80] Whereas earlier analyses, including those offered by Trần Huy Liệu himself, had emphasized the direct, unmediated link between Vietnam and the Soviet Union, this one underscored the mediated and indirect quality of those ties: only through France, on the one hand, and China, on the other, did the Vietnamese gain access to a new world centered on the Soviet Union.

In stressing the worldwide context in which the August Revolution occurred, Trần Huy Liệu created an impressive pedigree: as the offspring of the great revolutionary progenitors the August Revolution was pure; it did not simply spring forth from a random concatenation of events, as some Western writers had claimed. On the basis of this broadened, more global view of the revolution, the two decades that preceded the events of August 1945 gained greater salience; but in the process, these decades had to be aggressively reshaped.

Many scholars outside the DRV have observed that during the 1920s and 1930s the political landscape of Vietnam was richly variegated; the sheer proliferation of political parties, the web of shifting alliances, the intensity of intellectual life — despite, or even because of, the severity of French censorship — all attested to the indeterminate and experimental ethos of the time.[81] One of the great dramas in the modern history of Vietnam is how that richness and variety were effectively wiped out, and how Ho Chi Minh and the ICP came to dominate what was once an extremely varied terrain. A number of historians have explained the ascendancy of the ICP and Ho Chi Minh by dwelling on the actions of the colonial government, whose repressive policies prevented more moderate groups, such as the Vietnamese Nationalist Party (Việt Nam Quốc dân Đảng), from seriously challenging the colonial status quo. In contrast, some of the leading scholars in the DRV presented the 1920s and 1930s as a period in which the commanding role of Ho Chi Minh and the ICP was already assured, as though only they could advance the legitimate interests of the Vietnamese.

The historiographical attempt to make the August Revolution of 1945 entirely dependent on the ICP surfaced in innumerable settings, but it was particularly striking in commemorative texts. Such was the case in 1960, on the occasion of the thirtieth anniversary of the party's founding.[82] The first step in this commemorative process was to disengage the ICP from the conflict in which it initially arose. Specifically, what was once referred to as the Revolutionary Youth Association or the Revolutionary Youth League was rhetorically transformed into a party (*đảng*). This slight lexical shift made it possible to establish more remote—and thus more venerable—origins for the ICP. Trần Huy Liệu observed: "The Vietnamese Revolutionary Youth Party was the precursor [or seed, *tiền thân*] of the ICP."[83] From the "seed stage" in 1925, one gathered, the party sprang to life in 1930, came of age in 1945, and reached maturity in 1951 with the reconstitution of the Labor Party.

Although commemorative texts treated Ho Chi Minh's ascendancy as preordained and predetermined, more empirical studies of the 1920s through 1940s have restored the earlier ambiguity. As Huỳnh Kim Khánh, Hue-Tam Ho Tai, and David Marr have made clear, Ho Chi Minh's dominance was by no means a given. So extensively was the Youth League riven with disputes that in 1929 it effectively dissolved. Communism's conflicted beginning was reinstitutionalized in the two groups that formed from its remnants: the Indochinese Communist Party and the Annamese Communist Federation. Recognizing that their rivalry weakened the revolutionary movement, these two groups agreed to set their differences aside, and in February 1930 they formed the Vietnamese Communist Party. By this point, however, yet another communist group had appeared. Whereas the Vietnamese Communist Party traced its own descent to the Youth League, the Federated Indochinese Communist Party identified the New Vietnam Revolutionary Party as its own progenitor. In an attempt to bring these disparate groups together, Ho Chi Minh presided over a "reunification" conference (now described as the ICP's first plenum) in October 1930, and on this occasion the Indochinese Communist Party—the ICP so celebrated in revolutionary texts—was officially founded.[84] In addition to smoothing over the Youth League's conflicted status and the conflicted origins of the ICP, revolutionary writers also sublimated the gap between 1945, when the ICP officially disbanded, and 1951, when it was reconstituted as the Labor Party. Rather than analyze the methodological, ideological, generational, regional, and dispositional differences that fragmented revolutionary groups, postcolonial scholars tended to suppress them.

With the conflicted elements of its own past submerged, the Indochinese

Communist Party appeared as the unambiguous center of a single revolutionary movement. Not merely one among a number of revolutionary groups, the ICP was elevated to the status of a totalizing, all-encompassing entity. The commemorative text declared:

> Our Party—formerly the ICP and the Labor Party today—which is the vanguard of the Vietnamese working class, led the glorious August Revolution and is now building socialism in the North and, at the same time, struggling to unite the Ancestral Land. Speaking of the party: the party is the faith and the source of enthusiasm of the working class and laboring people. However, knowing the party, cherishing the party, and being dedicated to the party, if they are only based on a limited understanding or on feelings, are not enough. To know the party, to cherish the party, to be dedicated to the party in a profound way require one to know the history of the party, to assess the party's work in a sound way, and to join the party's destiny to one's own and to the nation's, and to harmonize one's own future with the future of the party. Every breath, every thought, every action of every party member is for the party and the people. The party determines the destiny of the nation, the progress of the nation, and therefore, of all of us. Therefore, we see ever more clearly that the history of the party is for us one of endless devotion and that the history of the party is an effective educational tool for every party member and for the laboring masses struggling under the party's banner.[85]

As though the party described this way was not already monolithic and fully hegemonic, the commemorative text concluded by further denying the hints of internal dissent: "Therefore, not only did the Party win many victories along the road of revolutionary struggle, but it also protected the unity of the Party, prevented factionalism, bringing the Party's special characteristic into relief: from the past to the present, it has been a united Party."[86] The party's unity and its position as sole commander of the revolution were reaffirmed by other participants in the commemorative assembly. "From 1930 on," Nguyễn Hồng Phong remarked, "there was a single, undivided revolutionary movement, and that was the revolutionary, national, and democratic movement led by the Indochinese Communist Party."[87] At the same time, he also recognized some of the ICP's main precursors, but characterized them as essentially regional variations—northern, central, and southern—of a single impulse. As for the Nationalist Party: after it was wiped out in the debacle of Yên Bái in 1930, he explained, the remnants who fled to China became a "reactionary, counterrevolutionary" group. Similarly, although he acknowledged the reformists and the Trotskyists (with the negative pluralizer *bọn*, meaning "gang"), he also dismissed them: because they lacked popular support, he explained, they were not influential.[88]

At least one author explicitly linked the August Revolution to the colonial occupation. In spring 1954, the writer cryptically identified as "Chiến" (meaning "war") declared that the August Revolution of 1945 could not be separated from the eighty years that preceded it.[89] Although contradictions between peasants and feudalists were already pronounced before the arrival of the French in the 1860s, he explained, the colonial conquest intensified them to a new degree. Thus, the events of August 1945 brought decades of oppression and revolutionary ferment to fruition. According to this writer, the success of the August Revolution, which was aimed against the feudalists, the colonialists, and, he noted, the "gang of Trotskyists" as well, stemmed from a combination of party leadership and peasant support. What is intriguing in this statement is Chiến's insistence on the fissures *within* the revolutionary movement and his inclination to designate feudalists, colonialists, and Trotskyists alike as the targets of the revolutionary struggle. It is unclear whether Vietnamese "Trotskyists" had any real commitment to "permanent revolution" or whether they actually opposed the Stalinist idea of socialism in one country. What is clear is that in Vietnam, the term "Trotskyist" functioned as a kind of shorthand; it was a prefabricated label used to denigrate those revolutionaries who distanced themselves from what aspired to be the center of revolutionary power—the ICP.[90] Thus the revolution described by Chiến was not only preoccupied with the class struggle, it was also concerned with "illegitimate" revolutionaries whose presence threatened to complicate the arrangement of power in postrevolutionary times. In using the term "Trotskyist" as pure epithet rather than signifier of revolutionary doctrines and theories, Chiến (and others) simply made more clear their own adherence to Soviet and specifically Stalinist frames of reference.

The attempt to produce an orthodox, canonical reading of the past was characterized by great fluidity, and the very act of memorializing the past presented the chance to revise it. Commemorating the thirteenth anniversary of the August Revolution in 1958, the Research Committee remarked that thanks to the August Revolution and the war of resistance against France, feudalism had been completely eradicated—from the seventeenth parallel on up. There would be no more famines in the North because productive forces had been freed; illiteracy, too, was on the verge of being completely wiped out. By including the Resistance War (1946–1954) in this commemorative account, the Research Committee implicitly located historical agency in the Viet Minh and in subsequent fronts.[91] This inclination to shift attention away from the party and to focus instead on the front organizations was reiterated in another commemorative essay, written by Văn Tạo, who bluntly stated: "The Front led the revolution to victory."[92] Party-centric visions of the August Revolution portrayed the Viet Minh, and later the Liên Việt, fronts as tools devised, manipulated, and thoroughly controlled by the ICP, even after the party's "disappearance" in 1945 and despite the empirical evidence attesting to the discontinuities between the party and the fronts. Nevertheless, that Văn Tạo attributed the revolution's success specifically to the Viet Minh and not the party is striking because it emphasizes the importance of national unity as opposed to class struggle. Only months later, I should add, did Văn Tạo distance himself from this view. Rather than imply, as he had before, that class dynamics were essentially irrelevant and that national unity was the key, he stressed the role of the proletariat (meaning the party) in ensuring the revolution's success. In support of his new stance, he cited Stalin's *The Question of Leninism*.[93]

Reacting against Văn Tạo's and even the Research Committee's inclination to assign a minimalist role to the party, Minh Tranh depicted both the August Revolution and the Resistance War as a mass revolution "under the leadership" of the party.[94] As he stressed the mass quality of politics in the North, however, and insisted that the party played the central role, Minh Tranh also rendered politics in the South in purely personal terms, characterizing Ngo Dinh Diem as the "wretched thug" (*kẻ xấu xa*) who had sold the country to the imperialists. To critics of the Diem government, this characterization undoubtedly seems apt, but the fact remains that at that point (1958), Diem still had substantial support. By reducing the structure and tenor of politics in the South to the venality of a single figure, Minh Tranh could ignore the extent to which the Vietnamese themselves disagreed about how to organize their lives in the period after the French and Japanese occupations. His characterization of Diem also reminds us of the intermingling of "radical" historiography and more traditional kinds, where appellations such as "gang," "rascal," and "thug" guided the readers' impressions.

To approach the shifts in perspective from a new angle, it is useful to survey the work of particular writers, in this case Trần Huy Liệu, because he was so visibly at the center of official attempts to rethink the past. In summer 1954, in his first published assessment of recent events, Trần Huy Liệu likened the Vietnamese Revolution to the Chinese Revolution and described it as a peasant revolution aimed against feudal landholders.[95] That fall, in his second set of published remarks, he identified the revolution as a struggle aimed principally against French colonial power. This new conceptualization emerged from his attempt to locate historical agency and to distinguish the revolution's main stages. Trần Huy Liệu began by remarking that the revolution could be periodized in two different ways. According to Mao, the revolution consisted of three different phases; according to Lenin, it consisted of only two. Arguing that the three-stage model more accurately accounted for events in Vietnam, Trần Huy Liệu began to focus on the second, or bourgeois, stage of the revolutionary movement. He examined reformist movements from the turn of the century, all oriented toward Japan: the Eastern Movement, the Tonkin Free School, and the Modernity Movement. Underscoring the rich hybridity of revolutionary theory in Vietnam, he suggested that although the form of these movements was "feudal," their content was "bourgeois," and they constituted, therefore, the second of three revolutionary stages.[96]

These arcane references to revolution in two versus three stages encapsulate the range of signification attached to the Vietnamese Revolution and the August Revolution; and they remind us, once again, of the opaque and coded quality of postcolonial discourse. Although some writers became more or less associated with one position or the other—Trường Chinh argued the merits of the three-stage revolutionary model whereas Văn Tạo promoted the theory of the two-stage revolution—the positions of most writers were not fixed, and in many cases they implicitly rejected the idea that these frames of analysis had any relevance to events in Vietnam.[97]

Two years later, Trần Huy Liệu appeared to withdraw altogether from the discussion of revolutionary stages, even though he reiterated his earlier view that the revolution was principally aimed against the French.[98] On this occasion, he identified the death of the patriot Hoàng Diệu in 1882 and the fall of Hanoi to France as the watershed in the modern history of Vietnam. These two events made it clear that the problem of an aggressive, predatory West could no longer be considered a remote and marginal affair of the southern frontier because suddenly the French also had control of the North and Center. The Nguyễn court in Hue, which had speculated that territorial concessions in the South would discourage any further encroachment, was suddenly an instrument of (and not an obstacle to) colonial conquest.

Within a few months (in August 1956), Trần Huy Liệu again rejected the relevance of the two- and three-stage models when he characterized the August Revolution as a bourgeois and democratic revolution that aimed to abolish feudalism and imperialism and *to redistribute land to the cultivators.*[99] When he emphasized the importance of land reform, Trần Huy Liệu was undoubtedly responding to the turmoil that was then taking place within the DRV generally and within the Labor Party as well. To gain a clearer sense of why the Vietnamese Revolution and the August Revolution assumed so many different forms, we can look at the specific circumstances in which Trần Huy Liệu's proposed his new interpretation.

In December 1953, as the possibility of a Vietnamese victory over France began to appear likely, the party passed the land reform law.[100] The timing of this legislation is instructive because it emphasized or was intended to emphasize the party's retreat from the class-suppressing tactics of the Liên Việt Front and its new commitment to (the appearance of) politics based principally on class. Whereas the earlier stages of the Resistance War required the unity of all Vietnamese regardless of class background, the final defeat of France depended more critically on the cooperation of peasants. To gain greater support from the poorest of the poor, DRV leaders organized a mass mobilization for eight "waves" of rent reduction, which peasants, supervised by party cadres, were supposed to carry out. Rent reduction was then to be followed by one trial wave and five regular waves of land reform. Seeking to avoid the violence and disruption that land reform might unleash, DRV leaders identified the stratifications within the peasantry—landless, poor, middle, and rich—and defined the criteria for determining a peasant's rank. What this finely calibrated law did not adequately account for, however, was the generalized degree of rural poverty. Although the colonial occupation had produced enormous estates in the South, landholdings in the North were limited. What the land reform law imagined as glaring differences—between landlords and rich peasants, for example, or between rich peasants and poor—often turned out to be quite slight.

Because rural poverty was so extreme, it was not possible to simply confiscate the "wealth" of rich and middle peasants and redistribute it to poor and landless ones. In fact, the land reform law specified that both middle and rich peasants could retain their land, draught animals, farm implements, and other forms of property, and it even provided for middle peasants to receive additional land.[101] Further illuminating the precariousness of class identities in Vietnam, the land reform law also specified that not all of those who rented out land could be uniformly treated as landlords. Rather, the law required that a landlord's behavior and political sensibilities also be taken into account. Thus, when peasants and cadres set out to redistribute rural property, they were allowed to *confiscate* the property of landlords who were reactionary and despotic. The property of more progressive landlords could be *requisitioned,* but not confiscated; and the property of landlords who had openly supported the resistance had to be *purchased.*[102] Less than a year after the land reform law was promulgated, and in response to disastrous floods, it was amended (in September 1954) so that the importance of class recrimination further declined. At that point the DRV simply wanted to avoid the likelihood of famine by leaving the existing rural economy in place.

The fervor of the cold war, however, mitigated against a consistently moderate approach to the problem of rural poverty. In March 1955, the Seventh Party Plenum determined that the economic and political deterioration in the North could best be curtailed by accelerating the pace and broadening the scope of land reform and by more systematically suppressing counterrevolutionaries in the countryside.[103] But the situation continued to deteriorate. In July 1955, representatives from the DRV and the RVN were supposed to meet to discuss the terms of reunification, which was scheduled, according to the Geneva Accords, for the following year. When the Diem government refused to participate in these negotiations, the essential ambivalence of the revolutionary movement—whether to emphasize class struggle or national unity—came fully into view. At the Eighth Conference of the party's Executive Committee in August, the thoroughly conflicted impulses of the DRV were clear. It resolved to accelerate the pace of land reform and vowed to root out and destroy the landlord class (now viewed in its entirety as a reactionary class); but it also urged all patriotic Vietnamese, regardless of class, to unite against the "Mỹ-Diệm" (American-Diem) regime in the South.[104] Further complicating the situation, the Twentieth Party Congress of the CPSU, held in February 1956, alerted the Vietnamese to the nefariousness of "enemies within." At this point, many DRV elites believed, not only the "Mỹ-Diệm clique" in the South and the "reactionary landlord class" in the North, but enemies *within* the party threatened to derail the revolution.

In June 1956, as the final stages of land reform were taking place, an editorial in *The People,* the party's paper, criticized land reform cadres (meaning low-ranking members of the party and newly recruited peasants) for having failed to distinguish between ordinary (exploiting) landlords and patriotic ones who had fought against the French. In August, *The People* printed Ho Chi Minh's "Letter to the Peasants and Cadres on the Successful Completion of Land Reform in the North," which, despite the congratulatory tone of the title, further elaborated on the errors committed during land reform.[105] Specifically, he noted, some cadres had failed to grasp the land reform policy correctly and had failed to follow the "mass line." In an aside, one can add that land reform placed peasants in a position of power without providing, however, any means to maintain their new status. Once land reform cadres left a village, vengeful landlords could prey on those who had abused or criticized them and seized their wealth. Besides antagonizing landlords who opposed the revolution, land reform also alienated those who had loyally supported it, including members of the party, many of whom lost their land, were expelled from the party, were arrested, or even imprisoned. Within the party, there was also a great deal of conflict between more established cadres and new peasant recruits. In September 1956, at the Tenth Conference of the party's Executive Committee, the formal critique of land reform — the Campaign for the Correction of Errors — was officially launched. But whereas the pieces published in *The People* attributed the errors of land reform to cadres who had failed to understand and apply the land reform law properly, the Executive Committee found fault with the policy itself. Because the policy was based on the party's "mistaken view that class [was] the overwhelming determinant of all social relations," the party itself — and not the executors — was to blame.[106] The Campaign for the Correction of Errors, in other words, determined that class categories were not sufficient indicators of political and social status because they were arbitrarily assigned.

This momentary emphasis on land reform as the revolution's principal goal, expressed in this case by Trần Huy Liệu but reiterated by countless other authors as well, has been offered — and accepted — as proof of the revolution's essentially socialist goals. What many writers have described as the "Marxist orthodoxy" of the North Vietnamese, however, can also be perceived as a kind of ideological — and temporary — camouflage. Responding to internal circumstances and to developments in international politics, scholars and officials in the DRV in some cases stressed and in others minimized the importance of socialist transformation. In this instance, Trần Huy Liệu's insistence on land reform as the revolution's primary objective — and the implication, therefore, that class really was the key determinant of social relations — ironically coincided with the party's attempt to dismantle many of the changes that land reform had painstakingly brought about.

When postcolonial historians commemorated the revolution as a product of class conflict, they imagined the ICP, which they characterized as "the party of the working class," as the revolution's conductor. On other occasions, however, historians offered significantly different assessments of modern and contemporary history. In an extensive, three-volume study, Trần Huy Liệu treated most of the nineteenth century as a prolonged war of resistance against French imperialism.[107] In his memoirs, he again depicted recent history as an essentially anticolonial struggle, but with a new twist.[108] Because the emphasis on anticolonialism stressed national unity, the rhetoric of class was entirely lacking: he hardly mentioned the working class, the feudalists, or the bourgeoisie. In these personal and literary reflections on the recent past, Trần Huy Liệu also omitted theoretical concerns: it scarcely mattered whether there had been two revolutionary stages or three. The revolution he depicted related only in a subsidiary way to the events of August 1945 when the Viet Minh formally seized power. Far more crucial was the whole fabric of social and political change that had occurred during the past eighty years. This much vaster montage of initiatives was represented politically in the Restore the King Movement (Cần Vương) of the 1880s and, intellectually, in the Tonkin Free School at the turn of the century. This transformation of the thoughts and habits of ordinary Vietnamese was reflected in the explosion of print culture in the 1920s and 1930s, the founding of the Revolutionary Youth League in 1925, and the establishment of the Indochinese Communist Party in 1930. This larger revolution was manifested in the Nghệ Tĩnh Soviets of 1930–1931 and in the mass literacy campaigns of the 1930s which, in an unprecedented way, drew together rural and urban Vietnamese. This view of the revolution stressed the incalculably complex interplay of changes that unevenly, in fits and starts, utterly transformed the social, cultural, and political landscape of Vietnam. This long view of revolution was more concerned with broad social changes; it considered the reconception of politics and learning so that mass action, and not only the protests of a scholarly few, suddenly mattered. The origins of this revolution were diffuse and the revolution itself was decentered: it did not, in other words, simply burst forth in August 1945 on the basis of party decrees.

Indeed, in his memoirs Trần Huy Liệu presented the Indochinese Communist Party as only one among a number of other revolutionary groups—he himself had been a member of the Nationalist Party before he joined the ICP; and when he referred to his "struggle" to join the Communist Party he described an internal struggle, the conflict within himself—not against the French—about whether or not he should join.[109] In this long view of the revolution, the role of the ICP was diminished to the extent that it was seen as a product, rather than progenitor, of the revolutionary movement. Whether this revolution was conceived in terms of stark oppositions—the Vietnamese against the French—or more internally, as a transformation of the Vietnamese themselves, it was understood as a local—meaning national —concern. It was not necessarily a small part of a much bigger pattern, of international communism, for example, and the actors were all Vietnamese. From this tableau of revolutionary transformation, the towering and foreign figures of Lenin, Stalin, and Mao had vanished.[110] As for the villains in this revolution, they were, in some instances, unmistakably the French. When the antagonists were clearly delineated, so were the protagonists: these were the Vietnamese, depicted in a homogeneous and undifferentiated way. But this revolution was also aimed at the Vietnamese, at the oppressive institutions they themselves had created and the social and political practices that made them easy to conquer. If Trần Huy Liệu's memoirs depicted the revolution in its broadest, most monumental sense, they also conveyed its experiential dimensions in deeply personal terms. Revolution not only meant triumphant gatherings in Ba Đình Square; it also meant bleakness and suffering in the jungle and in colonial jails.

In the 1970s, a much more teleological view of the revolution started to surface. Historians began to argue that, far from issuing from the events of a few decades or even the past century, the August Revolution had begun to take shape in the most remote stages of prehistory.[111] In this narrative, the revolution appeared as both a reenactment and a completion of an originating drama in which the Vietnamese fought against foreign invaders. More than four thousand years before, the Hùng kings had "fought against foreign aggressors and protected the frontier." Like their prehistoric forebears, the Vietnamese had continued to expel foreign aggressors; in the first century C.E. they expelled the Han Chinese, in the tenth century the Southern Han, in the eleventh the Song, in the thirteenth the Mongols, in the fifteenth century the Ming Chinese, and in the eighteenth the Manchus. In bringing an end to the French and Japanese occupations, the August Revolution provided a new instantiation of a primordial pattern; this revolution recreated the essential ethos of the Vietnamese past. In the years immediately following the August Revolution, this interpretation did not widely circulate; after the Resistance War it still had limited appeal. Only in the 1970s, as the end of the American War and problems of reunification came to the fore, did this view gain much currency. Then, the American War was reconfigured as simply the latest in a long line of national struggles to repel foreign aggressors: with one last dramatic thrust, the Americans would be defeated and the goal of four thousand years of history would finally be reached. After political reunification in 1976, this view of the August Revolution remained—at least officially—in place. Living in what seemed to them an occupied land, many southerners regarded themselves as the victim of "foreign" aggressors.

Reading through postcolonial commemorations of the Vietnamese and August Revolutions, one is struck by the range of debate, the richness, the subtleties. And yet, one should not overlook the fact that despite these great differences postcolonial Vietnamese nevertheless shared fundamental assumptions. Specifically, they rejected a number of theories of how the Viet Minh came to power.[112] The distinguished sociologist Paul Mus, for one, attributed their success to the simple fact that no one opposed them. Japan's surrender, he claimed, created a "power vacuum" in which only the Viet Minh were organized to take action. Because his work was so influential, first in France and then in the United States, his interpretation became the bedrock on which other scholars built. In American circles, the once-standard works of Joseph Buttinger repeated the same clichés. Despite the disagreements among them, postcolonial writers also rejected orientalist explanations of the August Revolution: not one of them entertained the idea that "Heaven's Will" or the "Mandate of Heaven" lay at the base of Viet Minh success, a view popularized by Frances Fitzgerald in *Fire in the Lake*. While postcolonial writers emphasized dissimilar motives and divergent methods, they all believed in the social origins of revolution—human agents responded to cultural conditions and economic concerns, and, above all, to politics. Whether for four millennium or for forty years, the Vietnamese prepared; they organized in a multiplicity of ways: within the village, the district, the province, the region; according to age and occupation; and above all on the basis of politics. Whether they allied themselves with one group or another, the Vietnamese were politicized and acted to determine their own fate.

Since 1954, commemorative events—the speeches, the festivals, and banners—and a profusion of commemorative texts have shouted out: "History matters!" Without intending to, the commemorative approach to the past also underscored the elusiveness of what the text and the festival presumed to capture. Because the postcolonial effort to encapsulate meaning depended not only on reiteration, but erasure and new layering, it highlighted the malleability of what is supposed to be fixed.

In 1960, to commemorate the 950th anniversary of the founding of Hanoi, official historians published a number of articles and, more spectacularly, in collaboration with photographers, curators, archivists, and literary critics, produced a grand commemorative volume, *The History of the Capital of Hanoi.*[113] Accounting for the entire sweep of the city's nearly ten centuries of history, the volume is divided into three main sections. The first covers the feudal period (1010–1883); the second focuses on the French colonial era (1883–1945); and the third chronicles the history of Hanoi as the capital of the DRV. Each of these three sections includes a selection of photographs and maps. Finally, an extensive appendix is divided into two units: one is devoted to poetry and the other functions as a kind of gazetteer, describing the city's scenery, both natural landscape and the built environment. Emphasizing the richness of Vietnamese literary traditions, the selection of poems includes compositions from the eleventh through twentieth centuries written in classical Chinese, the demotic script, and romanized Vietnamese.

Because this commemorative volume is so impressive, and because it so poignantly reflects the postcolonial dilemma, it deserves a detailed discussion. First, it works as a counterhistory to French representations of Hanoi. Whereas colonial accounts celebrated the city's "refashioning," which consisted of razing many of the original structures and rebuilding them according to European desires, this volume indicts the French occupation. Paradoxically, while it covers the colonial period extensively, this commemorative history also manages to reduce the French occupation to the status of mere backdrop against which the revolutionary movement unfolded; it transforms the city from a site of political humiliation and cultural alienation into a sign of cultural integrity and political strength. In the decades following the 1960 commemoration, other writers continued this new style of urban history, publishing additional volumes, sentimental and adoring in tone, devoted to the "beloved capital" of Vietnam.[114]

Second, the commemorative volume seems to represent a shift in the rhetoric of nation. Before this point, nationalist images were rooted in the physical terrain and in an exaggerated awareness of borders—not the boundary between North and South, obviously, but the boundaries that encircled Vietnam as a whole. In 1960, because the vision of territorial integrity was impossible to sustain, the commemorative history appealed to the iconography of another time, when the capital cities of traditional Southeast Asian polities were presented as microcosms of the entire realm. At the same time, this more traditional idiom was enveloped in a new layer because the Vietnamese were also aware of the French—especially Parisian—sense of the capital as the culmination of all that was desirable and good: cultural norms, political power, and economic potency were concentrated in Paris, and from the center they radiated out into the provinces. Whereas France promoted the idea of Saigon as the "Pearl of the Orient," officials and scholars in the DRV countered with the image of Hanoi as the center of power, on the one hand, and refinement, on the other.

Third, through the power of prescriptive speech, the commemorative volume attempts to normalize new notions of authority. Here it is important to point out that although this history emerged initially as part of the larger commemorative ethos, its impact was far more enduring. Whereas other commemorations demonstrated the high degree of historiographical fluidity, this commemorative volume lays out a new canonical reading of the past and of Hanoi's place in national history, one that essentially, although awkwardly it must be said, remained in place for decades after the commemorative event. In this sense the 1960 history of Hanoi points in new ways to the power of commemoration.

Nguyễn Lương Bích offers some introductory comments in which he establishes the book's interpretive thrust.[115] The city first emerged as the national capital in 1010, he maintains, when the Lý emperor Thái Tổ identified Thăng Long (the precursor of Hanoi) as opposed to the existing capital of Hoa Lư as the center of dynastic power. Thăng Long, as many have noted, means the "rising dragon." This arresting image communicates strength in a totalizing sense: just as the dragon (*long*) commands the earthly realm, the idea of ascent (*thăng*), and implicitly flight, signals mastery of the heavens. The fifteenth-century history of Vietnam (*Toàn thư*) explains that the name "Thăng Long" stemmed from the fact that, as royal junks sailed up the Red River, the emperor saw a golden dragon rise up from the clouds and hover above the city.[116] In the commemorative volume, however, "Thăng Long," the ascending dragon, represents the "image of people rising up to defeat foreign aggressors."

In an effort to rewrite the city's origins, Nguyễn Lương Bích had to disagree with his peers who believed that the "birth" of Hanoi derived from Chinese initiatives.[117] Instead, by superimposing the rhetoric of twentieth-century politics on the remote past, he claimed that centuries before the city's official founding in 1010, Hanoi had already gained fame as an important fortification (cứ điểm) in the "national liberation movement" against China. In addition to supplying Hanoi with a more prestigious lineage, one that emphasizes Vietnamese initiatives as opposed to Chinese, Nguyễn Lương Bích also equates the founding of the capital with the emergence of centralized rule. Among many Vietnamese scholars, this assertion has by now assumed the status of truth, but a number of scholars outside of Vietnam, Keith Taylor most compellingly, have argued that centralized government developed gradually over the course of several centuries rather than springing forth all at once in the year 1010.[118] Still, Nguyễn Lương Bích declares that for 950 years, Hanoi functioned as the political, economic, and cultural center of the country; similarly, he claims that throughout its history the city has served as the "nerve center" (đầu não) of national liberation movements and of every effort to build the country. It is also Nguyễn Lương Bích who introduces the trope of Hanoi as the microcosm of the entire country. Thus, through the power of synecdoche, "the history of the capital provides a condensation [hình ảnh thu nhỏ lại] of the entire country's past ten centuries of history." Because the part (Hanoi) represents the whole (Vietnam), it follows that the reoccupation of the capital, which occurred on the fortuitous date of 10/10/1954, signaled that the entire country would soon be free.[119] Finally, alerting readers to the complex intertextuality of official histories, and underscoring the extent to which postcolonial Vietnamese identified with—and therefore sought to distance themselves from—colonial archetypes, Nguyễn Lương Bích thanks the Soviet Institute of History for having provided a copy of The History of Moscow. While the requirements of the two volumes and the conditions in which they were prepared varied considerably, he notes, the layout of The History of Moscow inspired and enriched the work of historians in Vietnam.

In the first chapter of the commemorative volume, Nguyễn Lương Bích carefully summarizes the history of the capital from the eleventh through the fourteenth centuries.[120] Noting that the toponym "Hanoi" was of recent vintage, having been assigned to the city by the Nguyễn emperor Minh Mạng in 1831, he surveys the names by which the capital was formerly known. Describing them as references to fortifications built by the "gang" of Chinese mandarins, he acknowledges that they indicated the city's defensive significance. But, he emphasizes, only when the Lý emperor designated Thăng Long as the site of central government in 1010 did the city emerge as the nation's undisputed center of culture, economy, and politics.

To bring Hanoi's singular status into sharper focus, Nguyễn Lương Bích discusses the previous capitals, beginning with Phong Châu, the capital of the prehistoric Hùng kings, and Cổ Loa, the capital of An Dương Vương. While both of these sites protected "kings and lords," he argues, there was no evidence that they functioned as political, economic, or cultural centers of the entire realm. Similarly, during the Chinese occupation, he notes, a number of new ramparts were established, but they were military fortresses rather than genuine cities. Although the Vietnamese had periodically revolted against Chinese rule and had established self-rule in centers such as Mê Linh, Long Biên, and Ô Diên, these places also lacked the stature of a true capital. After independence, he continues, Vietnamese kings and emperors sought the safety of cities that were easy to defend. Thus the Ngô dynasty retreated to Cổ Loa and the Đinh and Early Lê dynasties took refuge in Hoa Lư. When Lý Thái Tổ relocated the capital to Thăng Long in 1010, Nguyễn Lương Bích insists, he did so not because of his own desire, because of "special talents," or because the city was equipped with walls. On the contrary, he stresses, these walls, which had been built by the Chinese administrator Gao Pian (Cao Biền), had already been destroyed. The Lý emperor chose Thăng Long, he maintains, because the "social setting and the ways in which Vietnamese society was developing at that time allowed him to do so." Unlike earlier dynasties that protected themselves by remaining "isolated" and "aloof," he continues, the Lý dynasty saw itself as a part of social life. It was evident, Nguyễn Lương Bích argued, that the new capital responded much more to social dynamics—the desires of the people—than to court-centered imperial concerns.[121] Because the origins of the capital had to resonate with contemporary events in an appropriate way, in these explanations Nguyễn Lương Bích neatly suppresses the undecipherable and contingent factors that ultimately resulted in the identification of a new capital. Instead, he depicts the eleventh-century decision to locate the capital in Thăng Long as an event that was motivated, overdetermined, and foreordained.

Next, Nguyễn Lương Bích chronicles the construction of the two main parts of the capital, the Imperial City and the Citadel. Within the Imperial City, the first Lý emperor built a series of palaces and royal residences; the second emperor further embellished it by constructing the Forbidden City and expanding the existing residences and palaces. In addition to building temples, pagodas, gardens, and shrines, the Lý emperors also built four gates, each one facing one of the cardinal points, walled in the imperial compound, and dotted the perimeter with guard posts. Reflecting their belief in the sacred power of elevated spaces, the Lý also built a number of hills.[122] Like the Imperial City, the Citadel was blessed with a beautiful landscape, which Nguyễn Lương Bích discusses in detail. The natural beauty of the forests, rivers, and lakes was enhanced, he remarks, by numerous constructions: Buddhist, Confucian, and Daoist temples, shrines, pagodas, and towers; royal temples and pavilions where foreign diplomats were received; and a variety of markets that facilitated commercial exchange. Having described the various stages in which the Citadel was constructed, he moves next to the city's economy. He mentions agricultural production, commercial institutions, and trade, and provides especially lavish detail for the handicrafts: spinning and weaving; brick, tile, and plasterworks; porcelain production; bronze metallurgy; gold and silver smithery; printing; fan making; distilleries that produced wine from lotus blooms; and machine shops. He also provides a glimpse of the city's cultural life: its educational facilities; entertainment and the arts; and the religions people practiced, their superstitions, their beliefs, their customs and habits, and the festivals they staged. As for the political dimensions of Thăng Long, Nguyễn Lương Bích surveys them in a similarly methodical way. He addresses the question of administration and security, the court, foreign relations, and political upheavals such as conflicts within the feudal ruling class, dynastic changes, and peasant rebellions.

This painstakingly detailed portrait concludes in a surprising way—with the city's destruction. In fact, the process of rebuilding the capital, only to have it laid to waste once again, becomes the dominant theme. Early in the thirteenth century, Nguyễn Lương Bích explains, Trần feudalists, who sought to usurp the throne from the Lý, set the capital on fire. Once the Trần seized the throne in 1225, they began to rebuild the sections of the city that they had destroyed, but later that same century the capital was ravaged yet again, this time by the Mongols. Again it was rebuilt, but before long the Cham attacked and four times set the city ablaze. For years, Hồ Quý Ly had plotted to seize the throne, and when he finally did so in 1400 he designated Thanh Hóa as the new capital, which he built with lumber, bricks, and tile plundered from Thăng Long! Soon the Ming dynasty invaded and delivered the final blows. Because much of the Imperial City had already been destroyed, the Ming army demolished the temples, towers, pagodas, and shrines that lay beyond. They also confiscated precious objects, such as the bronze bell of Quy Palace and the tip of Báo Thiên Tower, and transformed them into weapons. Because of such devastation the original Imperial City was still (in 1960) mostly denuded and few traces of the pre-Ming structures remained. But the popular part of the civil city essentially survived, Nguyễn Lương Bích asserts, and as the rest of Vietnam developed culturally, economically, and socially, this part of the city was also transformed. For these reasons, Nguyễn Lương Bích maintains, despite all the destruction, and despite the fact that the capital was temporarily moved to Thanh Hóa, Thăng Long retained its role as the political, cultural, and economic center of Vietnam. That normative pattern was reaffirmed early in the fifteenth century, when, "relying on the strength of the people," Lê Lợi succeeded in expelling the Ming. Once he reclaimed the capital in 1428, he founded the Lê dynasty and set out to rebuild the city. Thanks to his efforts and to those of subsequent Lê emperors, Nguyễn Lương Bích concludes, Thăng Long became bigger, more beautiful, and more crowded and bustling than before.[123]

In the second chapter, which covers the early fifteenth through late nineteenth centuries, Nguyễn Lương Bích repeats the structure of the previous one, outlining how the city's two main components—the Imperial City and the Citadel—were progressively rebuilt.[124] Having discussed the reconstruction of the built environment, he veers toward the topic of politics, which he arranges thematically—political organization, security, the court, and mandarins—and chronologically: the Lê period (1428–1527), the Mạc seizure of the city (1527–1592), the Lê-Trịnh period (1593–1787), and the Tây Sơn (1788–1802). Compared with his treatment of economic issues in the earlier period, his handling of the Lê economy is surprisingly brief and unstructured. Despite the global and national transformations then taking shape—and despite his own reliance on the memoirs of European merchants and missionaries such as J. P. de Marini, Samuel Baron, and S. Richard, he claims that during this period no major economic changes occurred. He offers generic comments on the importance of agriculture, identifies landholding patterns, including private, communal, and state, and notes that Lê emperors, unlike the Lý and Trần, conducted the ritual tilling of the soil and planted the first grains of rice *inside* rather than outside the capital, each year on the same plot of land.[125] He sums up the status of Thăng Long's economy during Lê times by blandly asserting that with its vibrant commercial life the capital remained, as always, the country's economic hub; but because of "fettering restrictions" (*hạn chế trói buộc*), Thăng Long was unable to transcend its essentially feudal foundations.

What should be observed here is that during Lê times, the economy of Vietnam began to fragment in unprecedented ways. This fragmentation became more pronounced in the mid-sixteenth century when a distinctly bifurcated pattern of politics arose, with the Trịnh lords in the North and the Nguyễn lords in the South. Specifically, the economy of what is now considered the central coast (but was then viewed as the South) became much more integrated into new patterns of global maritime trade. The entrepôt of Hội An began to flourish as Chinese, Japanese, Javanese, Arab, Persian, Portuguese, Spanish, Italian, and Dutch merchants arrived to trade goods that were ultimately bound for more remote destinations.[126] Whereas maritime trade played a determining role in the southern economy, its role in the North was less dramatic. Foreigners, especially Japanese and Dutch, developed commercial ties with the Trịnh family in the North and often visited the entrepôt of Phố Hiến, but the economy of the region around Thăng Long remained agriculturally based. In this sense, Nguyễn Lương Bích's reluctance to discuss the details of Thăng Long's economy during Lê times can be read as a strategy of avoidance.

In a passage that would surprise Western readers who are aware of Catholic evangelism in Vietnam, Asia more generally, and indeed throughout the world, and in a way that seems to reproduce his laconic approach to the Lê economy, Nguyễn Lương Bích suggests that with regard to the religious traditions of Lê times, no major changes occurred. After asserting the basic continuity of Lý and Trần patterns, he offhandedly remarks that one new religion, Christianity (*đạo Gia-tô*), was introduced. Initially, he states, the Trịnh lords allowed missionaries to build a residential dwelling and a church, but as the number of churches continued to grow (by the seventeenth century within the city of Thăng Long alone there were already three) and as more and more missionaries arrived, the Lê-Trịnh court began to issue anti-Christian edicts.[127] This passage is intriguing in that it recognizes the presence of missionaries and the court's attempt to control them, but it turns a blind eye to the Vietnamese who adopted the Catholic faith. This omission seems to be part of a more generalized attempt to present Hanoi as the center of authentic, indigenous, and oppositional (i.e., anti-Chinese and anti-Western) culture. Still, the audience to whom the commemorative history was addressed was well aware of Ngo Dinh Diem's Catholic roots and the fact that his most ardent supporters had Catholic backgrounds, too.

The section on Thăng Long during the Lê period concludes with a metamorphosis. In 1802, when the Tây Sơn dynasty collapsed, the entire North—including the capital—came under Nguyễn rule. Nguyễn Lương Bích remarks that because the new dynastic capital in Phú Xuân (Hue) compared unfavorably with the grandeur of Thăng Long, the Nguyễn rulers began physically to diminish it. From that moment the city began to decline: first it was reduced to an administrative center (*trấn thành*) with jurisdiction over a number of provinces, and then it was further reduced to the status of a provincial town (*tỉnh thành*). Nevertheless, Nguyễn Lương Bích explains, because the new Nguyễn capital was such a novel creation—and because the dynasty lacked popular support—Thăng Long retained its status as the cultural, political, and economic center of all of Vietnam.[128] (Nguyễn narratives of these events probably ignore the purported grandeur of Thăng Long and depict it, instead, as the heart of "enemy" territory.)

Representing these centuries are images of earthenware towers and busts and boxes made of gold, and illustrations of the Lê court, Trịnh palaces, works of art, and military drills. Included also are drawings of major Buddhist pagodas and temples, pictures of Tortoise Tower, the Temple of Literature, Phùng Hưng Mausoleum, the flagpole, and some of the city's gates. Finally, photographs of Hanoi's many rivers and lakes also appear.

The Colonial Capital

In chapters three and four of the commemorative volume, Mai Hanh recounts the history of Hanoi during the colonial period.[129] Skimming through a narrative that is by now widely known, Mai Hanh explains the sequence of steps that resulted in the French conquest. Wrongly believing that territorial concessions would appease them and bring a halt to their military aggression, the Nguyễn court in Hue yielded first three and then three additional provinces in the South. Having gained control of the South, the French then proceeded to the North and ultimately to the central part of Vietnam. But the French, Mai Hanh claims, were not principally interested in Vietnam. What they sought was a route to China, which one French explorer described as the "greatest source of wealth in the world."[130] Because the British already controlled the major ports in China, France would have to gain access via alternate routes. So, the conquest of Vietnam was a necessary but also ancillary goal: by gaining control of the South, French merchants hoped to sail up the Mekong River and enter China through the "back door." To their great disappointment, however, the merchant-explorers soon learned that the Mekong, because of its frequent impasses, would not supply such a route; thus they began to plan a new operation. On the basis of a new set of cartographic misconceptions, Jean Dupuis and other adventurers imagined the Red River as the route to China's prodigious wealth. To gain access to China, Mai Hanh explains, French adventurers twice seized the city of Hanoi, once in 1873 and again in 1882. In 1888, the cities of Hanoi and Haiphong came under direct colonial rule, unlike other parts of the North, which were administered indirectly as a protectorate.[131] Subsequently, after the conquest was complete, and after the limitations of the Red River had become clear, French strategists decided on a new tactic: not through river routes would they slip into China, but rather via railways from northern Vietnam.

Mai Hanh first approaches the colonial transformation of Hanoi from the perspective of administrative policies and colonial methods of policing, but much more extensively he examines the physical aspects of French rule. When they first seized the city, he states, the French began to reshape it as the political and military center of the North; once the "pacification" was complete, they reconstructed it as the base for centralized rule over all of Indochina. Late in the nineteenth century, using prisoners as well as wage laborers, the French filled in lakes and ponds and planted trees; they built boulevards and streets, an electrical plant, a watermill, a match factory, a textile mill, a distillery, a hospital, and a church. Early in the twentieth century, the "gang of colonizers" built the headquarters for the *résident supérieur;* the post office, a treasury, a music hall, a garden, more streets and boulevards, and stables. The materials for these projects, he maintains—the bricks, lumber, and bamboo—were often pilfered from workers' homes.

To make the mechanics and the consequences of the occupation clear, and perhaps to poke fun at the colonial obsession with statistical data, Mai Hanh includes some fascinating tables.[132] One chart describes housing starts between 1897 and 1904; it specifies the types of building material (brick or thatch) and the identity of the builder (Vietnamese or European). This data, while not surprising, demonstrates the city's rapid growth: during this eight-year period alone, more than fifty thousand new homes were built. To amplify this sense of unrestrained expansion, Mai Hanh provides data attesting to the city's burgeoning population. Discussing other aspects of the colonial transformation, he introduces similar kinds of statistical data.

Although the third chapter tells a story of Rabelaisian growth and, in apparent mimicry of French sources, suggests that a gleaming city arose from an empty slate, the fourth chapter reads like a eulogy for what the French demolished. Of all the colonial powers, Mai Hanh observes, the French were the most "shamelessly destructive." In order to "civilize" a backward people, he explains, the French colonialists planned to transform Hanoi into the cultural center of French Indochina; but instead, he asserts, they "bumped up against" the indomitable spirit of the Vietnamese who, having exhausted military means of defending themselves, turned to the cultural front. The French, in a ferocious mood, soon destroyed the temples, towers, pagodas, citadels, and shrines that served as focal points for Vietnamese resistance. First the French wrecked Báo Thiên Pagoda, a treasured site constructed in the eleventh century, and built a cathedral in its place. On the ruins of Báo Ân Pagoda, which they systematically plundered (absconding with precious sculptures that they took to France), they constructed the post office and the palace of the *résident supérieur*. This process continued, Mai Hanh recounts, until the French colonialists had destroyed almost the entire city. At that point, in a rare but also meaningless expression of remorse, Governor General Doumer declared: "I came across but could not save some things of interest. Especially the gates and walls were worth keeping. They were distinctive and had a commemorative and historical value that merited our respect. Those things could have adorned some of the new districts and streets."[133]

While French administrators emphasized what the colonial occupation had accomplished in terms of education and instruction, Mai Hanh underscores how the French restricted access to education, beginning with the suppression of the Tonkin Free School in 1908. Although he recognizes the colonial attempts to improve primary and secondary education and introduce vocational instruction, as well as the decision to found the University of Hanoi, Mai Hanh suggests that those gestures responded to colonial needs for Vietnamese collaborators rather than the desires of the Vietnamese to have genuine access to modern knowledge. The fourth chapter closes with some comments on the Association for the Propagation of Romanized Vietnamese, which was established in 1938 by the Indochinese Communist Party. As with Mai Hanh's discussion of education, his coverage of the press begins with French suppression and censorship and concludes with examples of Vietnamese overcoming. In effect, the material in this chapter is presented as a tale of dialectical unfolding: as the political and economic aspects of the occupation became ever more exploitive and repressive, the revolutionary movement expanded and took shape. Step by step—from the French conquest through World War I, from 1918–1930, from the founding of the ICP in 1930 to the August Revolution of 1945—the revolutionary movement coalesced until it finally exploded.

Whereas the commemorative volume of Hanoi covers prehistory to the nineteenth century in fewer than one hundred pages, it devotes many more to the brief period of colonial rule. Mai Hanh's attention to Hanoi's reincarnation as a colonial city stemmed partly from the richness of the sources. French colonial bureaucrats, like their Dutch and British counterparts, kept highly detailed records of what they encountered. But the disproportionate coverage devoted to the colonial version of Hanoi may have also figured as a strategic device: by narrating the colonial transformation in such lavish detail, Mai Hanh perhaps sought to heighten the drama of the French defeat. Despite their aggression, their sense of entitlement, their awesome technology, and their tremendous resources and resolve, the French were forced, first by the Japanese (in March 1945) and then by the Vietnamese (in August 1945), to surrender. But the unintended effect of his narrative is this: when revolutionaries triumphantly seized control of the city in 1945 and again in 1954 after the Resistance War, the city that they "reclaimed" was substantially different from the one they (figuratively) had lost. At the level of rhetoric and representation rather than empirical truth, the power of postcolonial narratives emerges from the continuity between what was lost and what was recovered. But here the implication is clear: the capital reclaimed by the Vietnamese was in most ways a colonial concoction.

Colonial accounts of Hanoi, such as the one written by André Masson, typically depict the city's "transformation" with great systematicity and extraordinary pride. Echoing the attitudes of other colonial powers, French scholars and administrators admired the way that the city came to reflect the urban aesthetics of modern France.[134] But rather than lay out photographs of the train station, the opera house, the museum, and the resplendent boulevards with restaurants, villas, hotels, and department stores, as French surveys automatically did, the commemorative volume proceeds in a different way. The first image is a well-known one depicting nearly a dozen Vietnamese trapped at the neck and the feet by the *cangue;* the second shows the guillotine; and the third presents Hỏa Lò Prison, where French officials beheaded many Vietnamese. Subsequent photos show several houses: one on Hàm Long street where the first communist group was established; one that served as a liaison office near Hương Tuyết Pagoda; another, a dyehouse on Hàng Bông, in which the basement functioned as the headquarters of the party's Central Committee; one on Nhà Street where the party located its propaganda offices; and finally the thatched-roofed house of a woman named Hai Vẽ, which doubled as the seat of the Standing Committee of the party's Central Committee. There are also photographs of offices where the ICP's various newspapers were published during the period of the Popular Front. Another photograph portrays the emaciated victims of the 1945 famine, which is attributed exclusively to the French and Japanese and not at all to Allied bombing. The excitement of the postwar era is depicted in photos of rallies at the People's Opera House, the seizure of the *résident supérieur*'s palace, the liberation army marching into Hanoi, the house where Ho Chi Minh drafted the Declaration of Independence, and the podium on which he recited it on September 2. Except for two photographs, one of a pile of rubble in Bạch Mai and another depicting the flight of the People's Army from the capital, the images of the Resistance War communicate the strength and determination of the Vietnamese rather than the power and destructiveness of France and Japan.

The National Capital "Restored"

Like the chapters of the commemorative volume on the colonial occupation of Hanoi, those devoted to the city's history since 1945 are similarly rich in detail, in the realm of politics and military logistics above all but also in terms of culture and economy.[135] Nguyễn Việt begins this section by meticulously recording, often on a day-by-day or even hourly basis, the events of the August Revolution and the Resistance War. Reflecting the depths of the ICP's popular support, he points out, people filled the streets and waved the red flag with the yellow star; at rallies they shouted: "Overthrow the invaders!" "Complete independence!" "People's power!" To render this historic instant more palpable still, Nguyễn Việt chronicles the route of the revolutionary procession. From a meeting at the Opera House, people poured into the boulevards and streets: they crossed Tràng Tiền and walked along the lakeshore until they reached the post office. Soon torrential rains commenced, but the procession continued: to Hàng Đào and Hàng Ngang, up to the Northern Gate, and to the governor general's mansion. The author's inclusion of these details may seem gratuitous, but they are essential. Whereas chapters three and four mapped out the process through which the French took possession of Hanoi, this passage unveils the steps by which the Vietnamese reasserted their control of the city and conveys how the jewels of the colonial occupation were endowed with new meaning. By mentioning specific streets, Nguyễn Việt also reminds his readers of the revolutionaries' power to rename: the colonial toponyms entirely disappeared. Moreover, his reference to the initiative of the ICP is supposed to make agency clear: the rallies, the speeches, the waving of flags were testaments not only of popular zeal but also to the party's choreographical skill.[136] The objective as well as symbolic reconquest of Hanoi reached a climax on September 2, 1945, when, from the botanical gardens at the center of what was once a purely colonial milieu, Ho Chi Minh recited the Declaration of Independence.

Within days, however, a very different drama began to unfold. On September 9 the first contingent of Guomindang troops arrived to carry out their plot, which was backed by American imperialists. Accompanying them were collaborators from the Vietnamese Nationalist Party and the Vietnamese Revolutionary League who had been living in China.[137] As the Nationalist Chinese in the North stripped the Japanese of their weapons and turned them over to enemies of the Viet Minh, British troops in the South rearmed French soldiers and even Japanese so that they could suppress the revolutionary uprising. The country's independence, so magisterially proclaimed, was now in serious doubt.

Although Nguyễn Việt refers to the rounds of negotiations between the DRV and France, he focuses on the contemporaneous details of military history, commenting on each new installation of French weapons and troops. In November 1946, in a naval bombardment of Haiphong, the French killed thousands of Vietnamese. Soon they seized control of that city and of Lạng Sơn as well. But it was the assault on the power plant in the capital that pushed the Viet Minh to the brink. Determined to "protect the entire country," Nguyễn Việt declares, the residents of Hanoi held fast, their spirits buoyed by the passionate words of Ho Chi Minh: "Compatriots! We wish for peace and already achieved it. But . . . the French colonialists are encroaching and are determined to conquer our country once again. No! We would rather all be martyred than lose our country and be slaves."[138] Juxtaposing these valiant sentiments with Hanoi's reconquest, Nguyễn Việt recounts how French troops continued to advance. Moving street by street, building by building, they took control of the Southern Gate, the police station, the office of *National Salvation* newspaper, the National Assembly, city hall, the post office, the People's Opera House, Long Biên Bridge, and the region around the Grand Cathedral. Again, the details are essential because they structure the drama of resistance, which Nguyễn Việt divides into three periods. The first stage began in 1948, after the departure of the People's Army from Hanoi, and concluded in 1950 with the defeat of French troops near the Chinese border. The second period extended from 1951 to March 1954, when the party's Executive Committee laid plans for the assault on Gia Lâm airfield. The third phase opened with the siege of Dien Bien Phu in spring 1954 and concluded with the Geneva Conference in late summer and fall of that year.

For Americans, who often imagine a much later chronology for the Vietnam War, Nguyễn Việt's perspective is surprising. By 1950, he maintains, the U.S. Information Office began to "feed information" to newspapers in Hanoi; by 1951, because France had issued directives that restricted the press, newspapers in the capital basically functioned as mouthpieces of the Americans. Assessing the overall impact of these moves, Nguyễn Việt suggests that the cultural policies of the French and the Americans aimed to put the Vietnamese "to sleep":

> Into Hanoi came a flood of American books, newspapers, photographs, and films. Books and newspapers propagated the cold war and advertised American weapons; pornographic literature and detective novels were sold in Hanoi at very cheap prices and sometimes given away; photographs of American officials such as Truman, Arthur, and Ridgeway were sold, as were posters of naked women.
>
> Little by little, American films came to dominate in the theaters of Hanoi, always showing romantic love, robbery, assassination, killing, and lust; American actors were better than French ones, so American films drew bigger audiences than the French films.
>
> It must be recognized that, from the time the Americans began to intervene directly in Indochina, the French colonialists were helped by their American masters in terms of ideas, money, and means, and they were attentive to raising the techniques of propaganda, [making it] more tricky and deceitful, more subtly and cunningly poisoning the people.[139]

Similarly, Nguyễn Việt's discussion of the Geneva Conference emphasizes issues and perspectives that other narratives either overlook or actually reject. Describing international negotiations in a way that Americans and Europeans might find jarring, he observes that in April 1954, the governments of the American, British, and French imperialists had to meet with the Soviet Union, the People's Republic of China, and related countries to discuss the restoration of peace in Indochina. At that time, he reports, the siege of Dien Bien Phu was closing in, and on May 8 the French were forced to surrender. According to the Geneva Accords, Hanoi was to remain within the "enemy's regroupment zone" for a period of eighty days. Rather than use that time to prepare for their departure in legitimate ways, Nguyễn Việt explains, the French took advantage of it to plunder—removing machinery, building materials, important documents, and medicines. Overnight Hanoi became a city that lacked water and electricity, with no factories and all work at a standstill. The enemy also tried to depopulate the city by offering money to those who agreed to go south. To organize the exodus more fully, the Americans sent Admiral Sabin to Hanoi; soon many Vietnamese were loaded into American planes and flown to Saigon.

Unlike foreign descriptions of Vietnam in the period after the Geneva Conference, which tend to focus on geopolitics and the malfeasance of the DRV, Phan Gia Bền's narrative emphasizes ambiance and mood. Setting the stage, he remarks: "The liberation of Hanoi not only delights the people of Hanoi; it is also a historic event and a day of great significance for the entire country; it is a glorious victory of the army's and the people's nine years of arduous fighting and fortitude."[140] In passages that parallel the earlier narrative of the August Revolution, Phan Gia Bền comments that on October 8, units of the People's Army were positioned along the various roads leading into Hanoi. On October 9, the People's Army began to reenter the city through the five main gates and spread out into each zone. Even though the streets had been deserted only moments before—it was 6:00 A.M.—people quickly lined up on both sides, waving flags, throwing hats into the air, and clapping their hands. While these preliminary steps to secure the capital were carried out, more troops waited outside the city and prepared for their historic entrance on October 10, 1954. After years of living under the "iron heel" (*gót sắt*) of the aggressor, the people of the capital felt enthusiasm and joy. By the tens of thousands they poured forth into the streets, wearing their finest clothes and holding flags, photographs, and flowers. Stressing that the liberation of the capital was celebrated not only in Hanoi but throughout the country, Phan Gia Bền quotes from the Saigon edition of *The People,* citing letters of congratulation sent in by Vietnamese peasants and representatives of minority groups.[141] Newspapers in China, the Soviet Union, and in many other countries as well, he notes, were "spellbound" by Hanoi's liberation.

After this gush of sentiment, however, Phan Gia Bền discusses the reconstruction of Hanoi in a style and tone that are more bureaucratic than effusive. Providing readers with an overview of how cities function, he describes the restoration of public utilities (electricity and water), the resumption of public transportation (streetcars and rail), the delivery of mail, and the organization of banking. Schools at all levels were opened in order to wipe out the pervasive problem of illiteracy. But the most serious issue concerned food. During the colonial period, as much as 80 percent of the rice consumed in the capital was produced in the South. To encourage rice production, he comments, the Committee on Military and Political Affairs canceled the head tax, the security tax, the wares tax (imposed on merchants), and the tax on identification cards for overseas Chinese.[142] Through these measures and as a result of land reform, which dispossessed some landlords of their holdings, the production of food was gradually increased. In addition to discussing agricultural policy, Phan Gia Bền also clarifies the attempts of the party and government to encourage industrial development through state-run as well as private enterprise.[143]

Whereas Phan Gia Bền concerns himself with the material aspects of socialist reconstruction, Võ Văn Nhung dwells on its political, social, and cultural dimensions. Taking a broad view of culture, Võ Văn Nhung begins with the DRV's commitment to advanced learning, evident in the tremendous number and great variety of research facilities it established. He also spells out the various types of instruction, including the popular education classes (designed to improve adult literacy); primary, middle, and high school education for children and teens; and advanced professional studies, especially in medicine. He highlights the main elements of the press and of broadcast media, such as Voice of Vietnam, and, to demonstrate the great expansion of print culture, he compares the number of books published in colonial and postcolonial times. These details underscore the dramatic increase in textbooks, monographs, manuals, novels, magazines, and journals. Võ Văn Nhung's treatment of mass cultural production also includes a discussion of film, a medium of great power in any setting and particularly relevant to Vietnam, where one legacy of the colonial occupation was widespread illiteracy. In addition to mentioning the system of formal education, he cites the many museums, libraries, and exhibition halls that also raised the educational levels of the Vietnamese. In his summary of culture and the arts, Võ Văn Nhung sketches out the main developments in theater, music, and the visual arts, but he also includes events that have wider popular appeal, such as circuses and puppet shows.

Although each of these elements is interesting in its own right, the coverage of postliberation politics is especially striking. First, it is apparent that Võ Văn Nhung understands politics principally in administrative and managerial terms: the meticulousness with which he depicts the complex web of intersecting and overlapping institutions makes this clear. One consequence of his approach is that in addition to spelling out the multitudinous ways in which individuals were connected to society and to the state, it also (inadvertently, one assumes) calls attention to the unpredictability and unilateralism of state practice. In other words, these details convey how easily, but also how erratically and unevenly, the state manipulated individual lives.

Once the Committee on Military and Political Affairs had "tightly secured" the city, Võ Văn Nhung explains, the Administrative Committee of Hanoi was established. Initially, in fall 1954, the intramural city was divided into thirty-six zones (*khu phố*), which were jointly administered by the Administrative Committee and the Administrative Work Team. In 1955, after the population of the city soared, the intramural part was split into four districts (*quận*) monitored by the cadres' Commission on District Administration. Within each of the thirty-six zones, new administrative layers evolved: the Board for the Administration of the Zone, the People's Board, and the People's Protective Board. Although Võ Văn Nhung defines the People's Board as a popular organization, it is evident that its main functions were determined by the state. Therefore, in addition to conveying the thoughts and wishes of the people to higher levels, the People's Board was also supposed to mobilize them—to attend popular education classes, help one another, practice good hygiene, and maintain order. Võ Văn Nhung emphasizes that the People's Board and the People's Protective Board served as the mechanisms for mutual assistance and mutual defense, but readers may have understood that they also encouraged mutual surveillance. In 1957 the People's City Council was formed so that it could send representatives to the Administrative Committee. In 1958, because the Board for the Administration of the Zone had "matured," the intramural districts were abolished and the original thirty-six zones were consolidated into twelve zones. Each zone was then subdivided into sixteen to twenty-five blocks (*khối*); each block was further divided into five or six teams (*tổ*); and each team had between thirty and forty households (*hộ*). Võ Văn Nhung is careful to point out the inclusive and broadly representative quality of these institutions and to stress that ordinary citizens had the right to criticize policies as well as the behavior of officials and cadres, but readers can infer that these institutional and administrative structures, which are the stuff of bureaucratic dreams, also had a real bearing on how people conducted their day-to-day lives. They influenced access to health care, housing, and food, they had an impact on assignments for work and school, and they determined as well the microenvironment in which one spied on others and was spied upon.

For the most part, Võ Văn Nhung's attention is devoted to the intramural city, but he also provides a glimpse of extramural affairs. Initially, the part of the city that lay beyond the walls was separated into four districts, which were segmented into forty-six villages (*xã*), which were, in turn, further divided into many hamlets (*thôn*). The extramural city was administered by the Administrative Committee of Hanoi and the Board Representing the Committee on Military and Political Affairs. After the waves of land reform, however, these two committees were transformed into the District Administrative Committee. Each village also had a Village Administrative Committee and was divided into subhamlets (*xóm*), which were the responsibility of subhamlet heads (*trưởng xóm*). Once the hamlet associations were founded, the size of the village administrative committees expanded. Although Võ Văn Nhung's intent is clear—he wants to demonstrate how thoroughly the postcolonial state respected the will of the people—he clarifies, instead, how extensively the people were feared by the state.

Having described the nets and webs that progressively enmeshed the people of Hanoi, Võ Văn Nhung steps back from the city itself in order to gain a perspective on the capital's relation to the rest of Vietnam. To dispel any doubts about the city's centrality, he enumerates the many national entities that were headquartered there: the government ministries, the highest offices of state, the National Assembly, the prime minister's mansion, and the political councils representing the main administrative and institutional units—that is, the innumerable committees (*ủy ban*), departments (*cục*), and ministries (*bộ*). The party's Central Committee as well as the Executive Committee of Hanoi were also based in the capital. Finally, Hanoi was also home to the mass organizations: the General Labor Union, the United Trade Union of Hanoi, the Youth Union, the Women's Union, the Commerce and Industry Union, the Democratic Party, the Socialist Party, the Fatherland Front, the Central Fatherland Front, and the Fatherland Front of Hanoi, which was established, Võ Văn Nhung remarks, "to carry out the policies of the Party and the Government."[144] The sheer excess of these details illuminates at least one incontrovertible fact: in the postcolonial DRV there was no possibility of living one's life in a private, withdrawn, or apolitical way. Although the presence of "popular" associations may have hinted at popular forms of government, one was obliged, in fact, to join them. If the Vietnamese in the 1920s and 1930s found it difficult to conceive of "the public," by 1960 they had no way to escape it.

To appreciate the degree to which these administrative structures truly mattered, it is instructive to look at the origins and implementation of the programs to abolish "social evils" — superstitions, first of all, but other evils as well. Before the liberation, Võ Văn Nhung reminds us, when people felt ill they sought out the advice of the fortune-teller rather than the physician. To demonstrate the pervasiveness of the fortune-tellers and the degree to which they preyed on ignorant people, he reports that during the three days of Tet in 1957 more than twenty of them were stationed at Ngọc Sơn Temple and that the people of Hanoi paid them considerable sums. This display of the fortune-tellers' greed occurred despite the fact the party and municipal authorities had begun, only the year before, a didactic campaign against superstitious beliefs. In 1958, officials undertook new efforts: they controlled those people who spread superstition, dispersed the crowds of people at festivals, and removed books that were "no longer needed":

> Classes were organized for more than 375 mediums, sorcerers, and fortune-tellers from a number of districts. They were educated and their trades were changed. In all sincerity, they revealed their tricks for deceiving and harming the people and, at the same time, they spoke out their regret and promised to explain to others why they had renounced their old ways, why they now made their living in an appropriate way, and why people should not have believed them. After that some speeches were arranged so that tens of thousands of people in the villages, zones, and markets with fortune-tellers and sorcerers would learn of their wickedness.[145]

In 1959, Võ Văn Nhung also explains, campaigns to unmask the "magic" of sorcerers and fortune-tellers were launched. In the presence of officials they had to reveal their props and their tools; in a performance witnessed by tens of thousands of ordinary Vietnamese they submitted their tricks to scientific dissection. After that, no more fortune-tellers appeared on the streets; and at pagodas and temples the ritual of lighting joss sticks also declined.

The people were also instructed to oppose other social evils, such as rural festivities that went on for days, lavish funerals and death anniversaries, and weddings with expensive gifts of silk, gold, pork, and rice. The Marriage and Family Law of 1959 outlawed arranged marriages and the marriage of children. Before the liberation, Võ Văn Nhung recalls, there were over ten thousand prostitutes and more than two thousand drug addicts in Hanoi alone. After liberation, prostitutes learned new lifestyles and new occupations; by the end of 1959, drug addiction had completely disappeared. Likewise, he notes, the problems of begging and homelessness were also addressed. As for delinquents (*cao bồi*), those troublesome youth had vanished, thanks to the Three Goods and Two Bads Movement of the Executive Committee of the Youth Labor Group of Hanoi.

The structure of the photographic section of the volume encourages readers to reflect on the power of the state to incorporate and subsume. It begins with the juxtaposition of two photos shot on the same day (October 9, 1954) of the same street in Hanoi. In the first photo, which bears a caption that reads: "The Army of the French Federation controlled," the street is completely deserted; it is desolate, devoid of life. In the second shot the same street is packed with people; the mood is joyful and effusive. Here the caption reads: "The arrival of the People's Army." This section concludes with a photograph of a scale model of the National Assembly and is interspersed with images that attest to the state's popular appeal. In a rally held January 1, 1955, the people of the capital welcome the return of the party's Central Committee, the government, and Chairman Ho; in 1959, at a rally in Ba Đình Square, they celebrate National Day. Photographs of "Mỹ-Diệm" (the Americans and Ngo Dinh Diem), on the other hand, emphasize popular hatred for the regime.

Because a healthy state is self-sustaining and prosperous, a number of photos revel in farm labor and factory work. On what appears to be a cooperative farm, cultivators rally behind a tractor's inexorable advance. In the city, skilled laborers process rubber; they build machines (one photo features the Tự Lực, or Self-Reliance, brand); they produce textiles, bicycles, shoes, soap, and cigarettes or engage in the delicate crafts of making ivory sculpture or lacquer ware. To satisfy their material needs, the people of Hanoi shop at the state store or cooperative.

But life in a socialist state is not limited to production; it is also devoted to cultural activities and to pleasure. Thus socialist workers build Lenin Park; people visit the Army Museum or the Museum of the Revolution; they watch films and delight in dramatic performances; and children enjoy books in the

National Library's Young Readers' Room. The people of Hanoi join clubs; they exercise and swim. Expressing the revolutionary reclamation of colonial sites, one snapshot captures a gathering of Vietnamese artists at the People's Opera House. Suggesting that advanced medical care was available not only in cities but throughout the North, one photo shows doctors performing open-heart surgery in a rural clinic. Because socialist states value education, a series of photos depicts pedagogical scenes: a classroom of preschoolers, an elderly man preparing lessons for a popular education class, and a group of students filing into Nguyễn Ái Quốc Party School. Thanks to the transparency of social life in the DRV, the boundaries that once separated those who worked from those who studied have dissolved: in one photo a group of students builds a lavatory; in another, they have become factory workers. Just as advertisements in a capitalist society nag and harangue, urging citizens and subjects to buy and consume, billboards and broadcasts in socialist states continually remind and instruct. To convey the diversity of sources from which these instructions emanate, the commemorative volume includes photographs of the Progressive Printing House, a radio tower, and a megaphone mounted on bamboo poles.

The Symbolism of the Center
The 1960 commemorative history of Hanoi resonates at a number of levels. It is like other postcolonial texts in the sense that it subverts colonial depictions of Vietnam and the Vietnamese; it also derails colonial representations of France and the "civilizing mission." In the process of dismantling colonial self-portraits, these texts discredit those who mediated between the Vietnamese and the colonizers, such notables as the Catholic polyglot Trương Vĩnh Ký, the French and Japanese collaborator Trần Trọng Kim, and the right-wing scholar-entrepreneur Phạm Quỳnh, in addition to countless others.

In its capacity as counterhistory, the commemorative volume undermines colonial representations of Hanoi by aggrandizing it. Hanoi, from the perspective of the French, was of limited interest, unlike Saigon, the "Pearl of the Orient," which the French revered as their own creation, and unlike Hue, which they openly admired. As for aesthetics, colonial officials found Hanoi unappealing; intellectually they were not drawn to the city's rich history. When French administrators decided to base their headquarters there, they did so not out of any real attachment to the city, but because of its proximity to China. For colonialists, Hanoi became an object of interest only insofar as they destroyed it. In his study of the capital during the "heroic period," André Masson makes it clear that the colonial vision of architecture and urban space could not be realized in a piecemeal fashion and that only a close approximation of the clean slate would do. As he narrates how the original city was demolished, he provides an inventory of the pagodas, temples, monuments, and streets that were wrecked and cleared away. Then he describes the new streets, the new districts, the new quarters, the new monuments—in short, the testaments to the grandeur of France. Postcolonial histories, and the commemorative volume above all, esteem Hanoi and treat it with piety. "Brothers on the Cà Mâu Peninsula and sisters on Phú Quốc Island," Trần Huy Liệu once wrote, "all bow to Chairman Ho, the Party's Central Committee, the Government of the DRV, and the beloved capital of Hanoi."[146]

In Masson's history of Hanoi, and in colonial histories more generally, the Vietnamese appeared as incidental players whose marginality contrasted with the centrality of the French. The Vietnamese were allowed into colonial narratives to the extent that they figured in certain codified ways: as signs of defeat (Vietnamese who agreed to peace treaties and commercial pacts), as exemplars of collaboration (Vietnamese who served as translators), or as opponents who were tracked and hunted like beasts. In postcolonial histories, the Vietnamese are the sources of authority and the principal agents of historical change.

In another sense as well the postcolonial histories of the city function as counterhistory, but in a national as opposed to colonial setting. A number of Vietnam's revolutionary elites viewed Vietnamese cities as irrevocably tainted. For instance, in his analysis of Vietnamese women, which he published in the early 1940s, Nguyễn Lương Bích (who also contributed to the commemorative volume) argued that women who lived in cities had been corrupted by Western ways.[147] Writing in the late 1940s, Trường Chinh expressed this same prejudice but in nativist rather than gendered terms: while he idealized Vietnamese villages as bastions of purely indigenous traditions, he condemned the inauthenticity—meaning foreignness—of cities. These tensions are obviously not unique to Vietnam, but there the gravity of such debates has been more apparent. Implicitly arguing against these convictions, the commemorative volume presented Hanoi as a place of self-possession rather than self-alienation.

On this point, it should be made clear that the perspectives and attitudes proposed by the commemorative texts were probably not shared by most

Vietnamese. Although the commemorative celebrations sought to diminish the sense that Hanoi was a colonial creation, many Vietnamese viewed it as precisely that: because the French had destroyed so much of the original city and then rebuilt it according to their own sense of aesthetics and economic needs it was farfetched to imagine the capital as anything other than a colonial projection. In some circumstances, particularly during the American War, the popular impression of Hanoi as a French imposition overwhelmed even official depictions. For example, in 1966 the *New York Times* sent Harrison Salisbury to the DRV to investigate allegations that the United States had dropped bombs on the capital's civilian sections. As Salisbury surveyed the damage—the allegations were obviously true—he noted the reaction of his hosts. As for the future, they expected that the city of Hanoi would be completely wiped out. Salisbury observed that rather than mourn this anticipated loss, the North Vietnamese talked about architectural plans to build a new capital. Even when they contemplated the city's restoration once the war ended, they stressed that it would not serve as a seat of government. Hanoi, they believed, was a small, old, and ugly city that symbolized the French occupation.[148]

In addition to countering colonial discourses on Hanoi, Vietnam, and the Vietnamese, and besides responding to debates taking place within the DRV about the relative worth of villages and cities, the commemorative history reaffirms postcolonial claims that since 1010 Hanoi was the seat of centralized government. It insists that for 950 years Hanoi has been the only legitimate center of authority—because its power was based on popular support. To present the postcolonial state as the heir to that venerable past, the commemorative volume includes photos showing the jubilation of August 1945, when people rallied in the street, demonstrated, and sang, and the joyful pandemonium that greeted the People's Army on its return to Hanoi in fall 1954. These images suggest a reassuring transparency: society consists of "the people." There are no barriers, no divisions, no institutions to intervene or mediate. Like most complex texts, the commemorative history of Hanoi is also highly conflicted. In addition to portraying "the people" as the original source of political power and the principal agent of change, it also presents them as essentially passive but potentially dangerous. To shape "the people" in appropriate ways, the state must inculcate new norms.[149] And thus, despite its high-minded praise for "the people," the commemorative volume also stresses that the legitimacy and appeal of the state stem from its ability to combat evil—not only in the limited arena of "social evils" but in a much more global sense as well.

In contrast to the empirical evidence, which attests to a long history of decentered politics, the commemorative history of Hanoi insists on a tightly centripetal pattern: beginning in 1010, political power began to emanate from the center, and throughout the realm, from the innermost reaches of the capital to the most remote areas of the periphery, it radiated in a smooth and uniform way. The commemorative history describes Hanoi as the center, the heart, and the hub of Vietnam. It presents Hanoi as a distillation of the country's past and an encapsulation of its future. As the Research Committee pointed out: "Once control over Hanoi is gained, the independence and unity of our entire country are bound to come about."[150]

Epilogue

This project began with two assumptions. The first is that new renditions of the past are an essential part of decolonization. Because of circumstances unique to Vietnam, historical writing played an especially critical role: in precolonial times each dynasty created its own historiographical corpus, and in colonial times French scholars and Francophile Vietnamese added their own imprint. The historiographical canon inherited briefly by revolutionaries in 1945 and more permanently in 1954 *demanded* a response. The second assumption is that because the Vietnamese declared their independence following decades of anticolonial struggle, a revolution, and nine years of military conflict to prevent the recolonization of their country, the necessity of rejecting the cultural legacies of France was much more urgent than in nonrevolutionary settings. As the Viet Minh were in the process of defeating the French militarily, political and intellectual elites laid the foundations for the cultural wars to come. In 1953, before the French had actually surrendered, revolutionary leaders established the Committee for Literary, Historical, and Geographical Research and charged historians with the task of writing a general history of Vietnam. Although in this book I explore several dimensions of postcolonial historiography, I am most concerned with why the new national history took more than thirty years to complete, despite the historians' dedication to finishing it. The political and administrative dynamics of the delay remain more or less opaque, but one thing is clear: representations of the national past had to correspond with the political and intellectual exigencies of postrevolutionary and postcolonial times, and these were constantly in flux. The fluidity of the present, in other words, continually imposed new requirements on the past. In addition to the insistence that the past legitimate the present, specific conceptual problems also arose. My research has been structured by the intellectual conundrums that blocked the completion of the new standard text.

With their first publications in 1954, Trần Huy Liệu, Minh Tranh, Nguyễn Đổng Chi, Nguyễn Công Bình, Văn Tân, and many others set out to "construct history" (*xây dựng lịch sử*). They also committed themselves to the idea of "new history" (*lịch sử mới*); but the meaning of this apparently oxymoronic expression was unclear. For most, it meant rewriting the past according to Marxist paradigms—but few agreed on how Marxism should be understood. These disagreements were further complicated by the fact that the Vietnamese rarely read the work of Marx himself but depended instead on Stalin's codification of his theories, as well as those of Engels and Lenin. Furthermore, the Vietnamese overwhelmingly rejected the idea of class conflict as a critical historical force and often looked to "Marxism" as a way to legitimate and consolidate the postrevolutionary state.

For many postcolonial writers, new history meant eroding the traditional barrier between scholars, on the one hand, and rice farmers, miners, fisherfolk, and factory workers, on the other, so that the idea of "the author" could be radically reconceived. Those who had figured as the passive objects of traditional narratives would become acting subjects. To others, new history meant undermining bourgeois ideas of authorship: rather than claim sole proprietorship of their work, new historians often worked in collectivities that made intellectual ownership impossible to discern. Or, instead of living cloistered lives, as traditional historians had done, new historians functioned as normal people actively engaged in daily life. After all, unlike dynastic chroniclers, French colonial historians, or colonialist Vietnamese, postcolonial historians wanted their work to represent the experiences of ordinary people—not the privileges of a reclusive elite. To include new voices, they had to devise new methods for conducting research and new modes of analysis and interpretation.

Many historians believed that the newness of new history lay in its determination to displace the existing canon. Paradoxically, as they tried to distance their work from that of their dynastic predecessors, official historians unconsciously established closer ties. That was the case initially, at least; by the late 1950s they overtly embraced the dynastic tradition they had earlier scorned. In an aside, one could remark that the postcolonial ambivalence toward the precolonial past was apparent in other settings as well. For instance, revolutionaries rejected the monarchy, of course, but they also recognized that the signs of imperial power were still potent. After the August Revolution, Trần Huy Liệu actually traveled from Hanoi to the Nguyễn capital in Hue to claim the imperial seal and imperial regalia from the exemperor Bảo Đại.

Although they came to appreciate the solemn dignity of dynastic texts, new historians wanted to avoid the circular notions of history and time that informed them. Borrowing historical models that originated in the Soviet Union, they explored linear and evolutionary approaches to the past. Ultimately, though, as the years of debate about one model or another generated nothing substantial, new historians drew even more extensively from the traditional canon, especially the fifteenth-century chronicle by Ngô Sĩ Liên. Most notably, they rehabilitated the idea that dynastic chronologies rather than modes of production provided the most reasonable means to periodize the past. Although they incorporated elements of precolonial histories into their work, new historians also altered the content of traditional forms. Rather than focus on peace, order, and prosperity in the countryside, as court historians always hoped to do (these conditions verified imperial power), new historians stressed the rebelliousness of peasants but claimed that foreign aggressors were the target of their wrath.

New historians' relationship to precolonial culture, in other words, was not merely polemic. As for the French, new historians condemned virtually every aspect of the occupation, especially their cultural and intellectual norms; but they also invoked those norms, directly and indirectly, to substantiate their own research. New historians, I have noted, sought to reconstruct the national past in progressive, linear terms as opposed to the traditionally cyclical ones. For the Vietnamese, those patterns were inextricably linked to the French, so new historians turned at first to Stalin's five-stage model of history. Its rigidity, however, and the extreme plasticity with which it could be applied negated its potential value. At a deeper level, as well, the evolutionary idea of history conflicted with some cherished ideals. Evolutionary models of history established that Vietnamese society was like any other: it progressed from one stage of development to the next. Having endured the contempt of the French, Vietnamese scholars found such formulations assuring because they made it possible to demythologize the history of France. And yet, these ideas were also troubling in that they crushed the deeply embedded sense that Vietnamese history was unique. Criticizing universal and evolutionary models for rewriting the past, one Vietnamese writer remarked: "History is a crystallization."[1]

New history was also animated by unspoken concerns. Because of the political differences that divided the Vietnamese during the French occupation, World War II, and the postwar interventions of Japan, Nationalist China, Britain, France, the United States, the People's Republic of China, and the Soviet Union—intrusions that transformed domestic conflicts into a true catastrophe—one could imagine that the hostility that official historians felt toward some Vietnamese stemmed from political disputes. To a great degree it did, but the enmity also derived from unacknowledged and less transparent sources. To be more precise: much of what new historians hoped to accomplish had already been achieved. In fact, in many ways, the figures whom they most reviled—the Catholic converts Huỳnh Tịnh Của and Trương Vĩnh Ký, the modernist collaborator Phạm Quỳnh, and the conservative collaborator Trần Trọng Kim—had already become the cultural innovators that new historians wanted to be. Their "reactionary" predecessors and contemporaries had already compiled anthologies of popular culture, invented new kinds of historical narrative, and, by developing the romanized script *quốc ngữ* and disseminating it throughout Vietnam, they had created a vast new reading public. Because this system of writing was originally devised by Catholic missionaries, for centuries it was dismissed as a sign of cultural treason. Thanks to the contributions of "lackeys" and "traitors," however, the romanized script became a rich and viable medium that twentieth-century revolutionaries appropriated and transformed into one of their more powerful tools. Because new historians claimed that only they could conceive of, let alone realize, such "antifeudal" and "anticolonial" goals, the accomplishments of "reactionary" scholars were all the more galling.

What, in the end, did new historians gain from their labor? First, their works address a range of topics that dynastic historians could not have foreseen. Second, unlike their precolonial and colonial predecessors, they managed to make the icons of classical culture accessible to new generations of Vietnamese. After the revolution, the Research Committee and the Institute of History diligently translated the main chronicles and great literary works that had been redacted in classical Chinese, mainly, and in *nôm* to a lesser degree, into romanized Vietnamese. In this way they bridged the cultural gap between the present and past. Third, historians also rebutted the accusations of the French and, earlier, the Chinese, that Vietnam had no real culture of its own. Those familiar with postcolonial studies have encountered this scenario innumerable times because all colonized peoples have suffered a similar kind of debasement. In postcolonial times, writers, politicians, painters, musicians, and scholars are in some way obliged to insist on what the colonizers denied. New historians were aware of the cultural legacies of Vietnam and wanted their contemporaries to know about that heritage and claim it as their own. Using historical narrative as an anticolonial instrument, they also rescued the Vietnamese past from its traditionally peripheral status. They demolished the clichés of French colonial historiography and, in the process, disengaged their own past from the tyranny of Sinitic paradigms. Finally, in a mytho-historiographical coup, new historians pinpointed national origins. Well into the 1950s and 1960s, most Vietnamese traced their origins to the third century B.C.E., at the earliest, and, more likely, to the first century B.C.E. By the 1970s, however, many believed that national origins dated to the third *millennium* B.C.E., and in Vietnam today the date of 2879 B.C.E. is probably universally known.

In addition to being blocked by the problem of narration, the new general history was stymied by other concerns. How could historians write the history of Vietnam when they were unsure what the term "Vietnamese" actually meant? Clearly, the problem of identity was a concern not only to postcolonial Vietnamese. Modernity itself and, more to the point, the colonial powers had thoroughly altered traditional ideas of community. In the case of Vietnam, treaties between France and China, France and Britain, and France and Siam, as well as the whimsical precision of a surveyor's line, resulted in new boundaries and new definitions of inside and out. Traditionally, the idea of Vietnam was linked to the ethnic Vietnamese; over time its meaning broadened, but not in a way that was uniformly understood. In the mid-1950s, leading scholars had to point out that when they said "Vietnam" they did not mean ethnic Vietnamese alone. These caveats, they must have believed, required an explanation because usually they then identified the four or five groups that they believed constituted the non-Việt part of Vietnam.

The ethnographic studies of the 1950s through 1970s were of tremendous interest to historians because, without some consensus—without a shared understanding of who, exactly, was Vietnamese—they could not proceed with the general history. Ultimately, the delay caused by questions of belonging may have been a fortunate one from the perspective of the state, for the ethnographic and historiographical processes themselves helped to create a new sense of nation. As ethnographers recorded kinship patterns, the details of material life, and ritual observances and religion, they established the evidence necessary for an inclusive—or expansionist—rendition of the past. In other words, ethnographers not only recorded what they saw, they also introduced minorities to new, more "standard" practices. Thus, the very attempt to redact the past in a way that was mindful of difference also provided ways to suppress the heterogeneity of the present; and the possibility of a genuinely multivocal past metamorphosed into a more univocal one. It was fine, even necessary, to recognize and organize ethnic differences, but differences were not supposed to be disruptive (as is currently the case in the central highlands). By now, a slogan that first cropped up in the 1950s and 1960s has become an unavoidable cliché: within the "great Vietnamese national family" there are fifty-four ethnic groups (not four or five!) who live together as "siblings," as brothers and sisters, one might add, from the same colossal womb.

So that these siblings could benefit from ever closer ties, the DRV developed aggressive programs to transfer ethnic Vietnamese from the delta to the highlands and to shift minorities from their original habitats to new ones. These measures were carried out with great fervor for political reasons, it is clear, but also because economic transformations were based on the transplantation of people. By relocating ethnic Vietnamese, the government established cooperativized wet-rice farming in places that were previously uncultivated or where different agricultural techniques had prevailed, and they expanded the production of plantation crops. Ethnic Vietnamese with technical training as well as unskilled laborers were also moved into the highlands so that they could supervise or assist in the process of industrialization. Even though they had traditionally resided in the delta, ethnic Vietnamese gradually became the dominant group, both numerically and culturally, in the midlands and mountains; and after national reunification in 1976, this process accelerated in the North and South. Ethnographic research did not initiate these changes, but it accompanied and contributed to them. Even more than geographic and environmental changes, education played a major role in altering individual and collective identities. Members of all ethnic groups were urged to see themselves in nationalistic terms and to repress earlier patterns of thinking. Finally, the propagation of a common language (Vietnamese) and script was supposed to bind these siblings together. In the 1930s, it is true, revolutionaries were officially committed to multicultural policies, particularly to the creation and maintenance of ethnic autonomous zones. After 1976, the autonomous zones were abolished, but in a gesture that appeared to hint at a genuinely multicultural state the SRV translated official histories and official decrees into minority languages. On this point I have argued that these kinds of endeavors did not defer to minority cultures; on the contrary, they merely promoted the interests of the state.

Significantly, histories published in the 1950s through 1970s largely avoided the topic of Nam Tiến (the Southern Advance), the process through which ethnic Vietnamese annexed and colonized what are now the country's central and southern parts. Or, I should say, they avoided the topic of Nam Tiến as it is traditionally understood. Instead, they reintroduced the same term, Nam Tiến, but used it to describe the final stages of the "Anti-American War." In other words, new historians converted the expression that most clearly encapsulates the history of Vietnamese imperialism into a term that expresses the eruption of purely defensive, self-protective measures — even though the new Nam Tiến was aimed against other Vietnamese as well as the United States. Just as postcolonial historians overlooked Vietnam's annexation of the Center and South, they never acknowledged the history of what we might call Sơn Tiến, the Advance into (annexation of) the Mountains.

In their early publications, new historians criticized the elitism of dynastic chronicles, meaning their habit of recounting only the interests and activities of the court and the details of politics. By being more attuned to culture, new historians believed, they could overcome these deficiencies and produce, instead, a much more inclusive and comprehensive sense of the past. For a number of reasons, this endeavor, too, delayed the completion of the standard history. The devotion to cultural studies was expected to bring official histories closer to "the people," but instead their initial explorations led them toward China. "Vietnamese culture," as it was conventionally understood, meant high culture — literary works that reinterpreted or even reproduced Chinese classics. It referred to works written in classical Chinese, or *nôm*, the demotic script that reflected Vietnamese pronunciation but still depended on classical Chinese. Initially, then, the quest for what was authentically Vietnamese led new historians to what they saw as the principal source of inauthenticity. Abandoning conventional views that underscored the complex intermingling of Chinese and Vietnamese traditions, they began to discuss new ways of conceptualizing culture. They focused on what they believed would be pure and authentic: folklore, folktales, folkways — in short, rural culture.

Although this approach brought historians out of the shadow cast by Chinese culture, it made them confront a new set of problems. Genuinely popular culture often regarded constituted authority in unflattering and even contemptuous terms. From the perspective of many villagers, no matter how government officials had gained their credentials — by passing Confucian exams, by waving the red flag, by waging war against the French — they were always corrupt or corruptible and eager to exploit. For postcolonial officials, this view of authority had to be wiped out, so new historians focused not on popular culture in a generic sense but on "representative" examples. In this way, popular culture that demonstrated love of community, love of labor, fierce patriotism, and love of the state above all took the place of illegitimate and "unrepresentative" — that is, antistatist — forms. In other words, when postcolonial scholars and officials praised "the people," and they did this quite often, they left their suspicions unspoken; and always they referred in still more laudatory tones to the brilliant leadership of Chairman Ho, the party, and the government. Without sage leadership, they often remarked, the genius of "the people" would never be expressed.

Given its variety, its fluidity, and its ability to subvert, popular culture could not be canonized in an indiscriminate way. It had to be tailored and refined to fit the needs of the present. The acceptable, "representative" parts of popular culture provided the core for what became known as national essence. Whereas folkways suggested differences and variation, the idea of national essence was supposed to make all Vietnamese the same: united, indomitable, and ready to repel foreign aggressors. During the American War, these clichés were potent and made it easier, it seems, to rally Vietnamese to the anti-American cause. Once the war was over, however, the images of combat and heroic acts of resistance were more or less buried: with the two Vietnams united into one, more pacific images came to the fore. In place of national essence and its obsession with military glory, the cult of antiquity, which culminated in the idea of the family-state, provided a more unitary or at least integrative way of imagining the past and managing the present.

Like colonial officials, postcolonial administrators disparaged traditional notions of time and were determined to establish new ones. Days, they emphasized, were marked by the solar calendar and the clock, not by lunar schedules nor by sunrises and sunsets. Like days, years, too, sequentially unfolded, and life-cycle events — births, for example, and deaths — occurred in a unique, specific, and unrepeatable year, not in astrological cycles. More important than reconceiving time in the hourly, daily, and annual sense was the reconstruction of historical time and the attachment of new meanings to the past. Historians were not only obliged to analyze and recite; their responsibility, the committee declared, was to scientifically study "the beautiful work" of their ancestors so that the people would esteem their collective past.[2] As Văn Tân later wrote, history was supposed to encourage patriotic feelings and thoughts.[3]

This aspect of the postcolonial government's historical mission was carried out most ostentatiously through the rituals of commemoration. Through these elaborate didactic campaigns, all Vietnamese were supposed to learn the general trajectory of the national past, recognize its most distinguished moments, and honor their ancestor's heroic acts. In the 1950s and 1960s, there was a wild profusion of commemorative events that not only cued people to remember but taught them what and how to remember. Pedagogical displays to honor a heroic ancestor or celebrate one glorious battle or another required extensive organization. Because the Research Committee and the Institute of History alone could not arrange them, they supplied the intellectual content, as it were, while other organs of state, such as the Ministry of Culture, worked out the logistics. Although these rituals of state were devised by those on top and imposed on those below, they were officially treated as expressions of popular culture. So successful were these didactic campaigns that some observers have interpreted the level of historical literacy in Vietnam as evidence of an almost mystical reverence for a shared national past. I have argued that the skill with which bureaucrats and scholars made their views of the past the normative ones should not be mistaken as a sign of spontaneous and collective reflection.

In 1960, the great commemorative extravaganza to celebrate the 950th anniversary of the founding of Hanoi brought all these elements together. By locating the origins of the national capital in Hanoi in the year 1010, the commemoration washed away the imprecision of the past; it glossed over the complications of historical geography and completely erased the political dynamics that normally had limited the government's reach. Moreover, the commemorative literature proclaimed, since its founding in 1010 Hanoi had been the single legitimate center of authority, the source of centralized rule, and the country's cultural and economic hub. The Nguyễn emperors, it acknowledged, had undermined the political centrality of Hanoi, but they did so only temporarily and superficially, it claimed, because "the people" had never supported them. As it celebrated Hanoi's nearly ten centuries of political, cultural, and economic supremacy, the 1960 commemoration also responded to earlier debates about the relative worth of rural communities versus urban ones. Engaging in these debates, official historians briefly identified villages as the site of indigenous and therefore authentic culture; they implied, at the same time, that foreign and therefore inauthentic culture existed only in cities. The commemorative celebrations apparently settled that dispute and further extinguished southern impressions of the past. Hanoi, the center of government and symbol of the state, was the true locus of culture and power.

List of Abbreviations

AFIMA   Association pour l'instruction morale des Annamites (Association for the Moral Instruction of Annamites)

BEFEO   *Bulletin de l'École Française d'Extrême-Orient* (*Bulletin of the French School of the Far East*)

BNCVSĐ   Ban nghiên cứu Văn Sử Địa (Committee for Literary, Historical, and Geographical Research). For the journal's first and second issues only, the discipline of history (*sử*) appeared first: BNCSĐV.

CCP   Chinese Communist Party

CPSU   Communist Party of the Soviet Union

CPVN   Communist Party of Vietnam

DRV   Democratic Republic of Vietnam

DTH   *Tạp chí Dan tộc học* (*Journal of Ethnography*)

EFEO   École Française d'Extrême-Orient (French School of the Far East)

FLPH   Foreign Languages Publishing House

GMD   Guomindang (Chinese Nationalist Party)

HĐVSĐ   Hoạt động Sử Địa Văn or Hoạt động Văn Sử Địa (Activities in Literature, History, and Geography, a section of *VSĐ*, *Journal of Literary, Historical, and Geographical Research*)

HĐVSĐQT   Hoạt động Sử Địa Văn quốc tế, Hoạt động Sử Địa Văn ở ngoài quốc tế, or Hoạt động Văn Sử Địa quốc tế (International Activities in Literature, History, and Geography, a section of *VSĐ*, *Journal of Literary, Historical, and Geographical Research*)

JCH   *Journal of Contemporary History*

JMH   *Journal of Modern History*

JSEAS   *Journal of Southeast Asian Studies*

ICP   Indochinese Communist Party

LDP   Lao động Party, abbreviation for Đảng Lao động Việt Nam (Vietnamese Labor Party; often mistranslated as Vietnamese Workers' Party)

LSTĐ   *Lịch sử thủ đô Hà Nội* (*The History of the Capital of Hanoi*)

NCLS	*Tập san Nghiên cứu Lịch sử* (nos. 1–12), *Nghiên cứu Lịch sử* (nos. 13–105; 130–present), or *Tạp chí Nghiên cứu Lịch sử* (nos. 106–129) (*Journal of Historical Research*)
NFLS	National Front for the Liberation of the South (also known as the NLF, National Liberation Front; in American sources often referred to as VC, meaning "Viet Cong")
PRC	People's Republic of China
RVN	Republic of Vietnam
SRV	Socialist Republic of Vietnam
TCNCLS	Tạp chí Nghiên cứu Lịch sử (Editorial board of *Journal of Historical Research*)
TSNCLS	Tập san Nghiên cứu Lịch sử (Editorial board of *Journal of Historical Research*)
TTKH	Tin tức, Tin tức khoa học lịch sử, Tin tức hoạt động khoa học lịch sử, or Tin tức hoạt động sử học (News in Historical Studies, a section of *NCLS, Journal of Historical Research*)
TTKHNN	Tin tức khoa học lịch sử nước ngoài (Foreign News in Historical Studies, a section of *NCLS, Journal of Historical Research*)
VNF	*The Vietnam Forum*
VNS	*Vietnamese Studies*
VNSS	*Viet Nam Social Sciences*
VSĐ	*Tập san Nghiên cứu Sử Địa Văn* (nos. 1–2) or *Tập san Nghiên cứu Văn Sử Địa* (nos. 3–48) (*Journal of Literary, Historical, and Geographical Research*)
VSH	Viện Sử học (Institute of History)

Notes

INTRODUCTION: POSTCOLONIAL VISIONS

Note: All translations are mine unless otherwise indicated.

1 "Fatherland Front" is the more usual translation of Mặt trận Tổ quốc Việt Nam, but it is an unfortunate one in that it misses the clear emphasis on generations of ancestors (*tổ*). Ban nghiên cứu Văn Sử Địa (hereafter BNCVSĐ), "Trách nhiệm của chúng ta," *Tập san Nghiên cứu Văn Sử Địa* (hereafter VSĐ) 3 (October 1954): 3–6. Nguyễn Minh, "Ôn lại cuộc khởi nghĩa của Hai Bà Trưng," *VSĐ* 5 (February 1955): 48–52. Minh Tranh, "Những bài học đại đoàn kết bảo về tổ quốc trong lịch sử nước ta," *VSĐ* 10 (September–October 1955): 1–7.

2 This confusion between peace, war, and war to preserve peace cropped up on numerous occasions. See, for example, Trần Huy Liệu, "Vấn đề công tác và tổ chức khoa học đã được đề ra trong Quốc hội khóa thứ sáu," *VSĐ* 24 (January 1957): 1–5.

3 BNCVSĐ (1953–1959) and Viện Sử học (hereafter VSH), which superceded the committee in 1959.

4 *Orientalism* (New York: Pantheon, 1978) and *Culture and Imperialism* (New York: Vintage, 1993).

5 See, for example, Alfred Schreiner, *Abrégé de l'histoire d'Annam* (Saigon: Imprimerie Coudurier and Montégout, 1906), pp. 10–14.

6 *Metahistory: The Historical Imagination in Nineteenth-Century Europe* (Baltimore: Johns Hopkins University Press, 1973) and *Tropics of Discourse* (Baltimore: Johns Hopkins University Press, 1978).

7 David Marr, *Vietnamese Tradition on Trial, 1920–1945* (Berkeley: University of California Press, 1981), p. 91.

8 Ibid., p. 211.

9 Patricia Pelley, "The History of Resistance and the Resistance to History in Post-Colonial Vietnam," in *Essays into Vietnamese Pasts,* ed. K. W. Taylor and John K.

Whitmore (Ithaca: Cornell University Southeast Asia Program, 1995), pp. 232–45.

10 These discussions appeared in *VSĐ*, published from 1954 to 1959, and *Tập san Nghiên cứu Lịch sử* (hereafter *NCLS*), published since 1959.

1. CONSTRUCTING HISTORY

1 The original titles are *Lịch triều hiến chương loại chí, Dương trình ký kiến, Đại Nam thực lục, Khâm định Việt sử thông giám cương mục,* and *Đại Nam nhất thống chí,* respectively.

2 *Cours d'histoire annamite* (Saigon: Imprimerie du Gouvernement, 1875, 1877). Truong Buu Lam, *New Lamps for Old: The Transformation of the Vietnamese Administrative Elite* (Singapore: Institute of Southeast Asian Studies, 1982), p. 31.

3 Trần Văn Thược and Ngô Văn Minh, *Manuel d'histoire d'Annam,* 5th ed. (Hanoi: Édition Nam-Ky, 1939). Dương Quảng Hàm, *Leçons d'histoire d'Annam* (Hanoi: Le Van Tan, 1936).

4 "Annamites" is the term used by colonial writers to refer to all Vietnamese. Dương Quảng Hàm, *Leçons d'historie,* p. 5. Emphasis added.

5 The Vietnamese titles of the two journals are *Tập san Nghiên cứu Văn Sử Địa* published by the Research Committee, and *Tập san Nghiên cứu Lịch sử,* published by the Institute of History. For excerpts of the relevant decree (34 QN/TU), see BNCVSĐ, "Để chuẩn bị tiến lên một giai đoạn mới—Tổng kết công tác Ban nghiên cứu Văn Sử Địa từ ngày thành lập đến nay," *VSĐ* 48 (January 1959): 2. Trần Huy Liệu provided additional details in "Công tác của Ban nghiên cứu Văn Sử Địa trong một năm qua," *VSĐ* 35 (December 1957): 1–9, as did the editorial committee of *NCLS* in "Kỷ niệm năm thứ 20 quyết định của Trung ương Đảng thành lập Ban nghiên cứu Lịch sử, Địa lý, Văn học," *NCLS* 152 (October 1973): 1–4.

6 "Tổng kết công tác của Ban nghiên cứu Văn Sử Địa trong một năm qua và đề án công tác năm 1956," *VSĐ* 14 (February 1956): 3. On self-criticism, see "Hoạt động Văn Sử Địa," (Activities in Literature, History, and Geography, hereafter "HĐVSĐ"), *VSĐ* 11 (November 1955): 78–81.

7 This decree was promulgated on September 4, 1956. Trần Huy Liệu, "Kiểm điểm công tác của BNCVSĐ năm 1956 và đề án công tác năm 1957," *VSĐ* 23 (November-December 1956): 1–9. The usual translation for Đảng Lao động is "Workers' Party," but the term *lao động* refers, in fact, to the abstract category of labor rather than to the workers who perform it.

8 BNCVSĐ, "Hoan nghênh nghị quyết của Quốc hội về việc thành lập Uỷ ban Khoa học," *VSĐ* 41 (June 1958): 1–6 and *VSĐ* 48 (January 1959): 1–10.

9 "HĐVSĐ," *VSĐ* 11: 78–80. Without explaining the nature of their cooperation, the survey also listed the Ngái as one of the minority groups with which committee historians had worked.

10 "Tin tức khoa học lịch sử nước ngoài" (News in Historical Studies in Foreign Countries, hereafter "TTKHNN"), *NCLS* 3 (May 1959): 90.

11 Minh Tranh, "Vấn đề tiêu chuẩn để phân định những thời kỳ lịch sử nước ta," *VSĐ* 5 (February 1955): 18–19. Trần Huy Liệu, "Vấn đề công tác và tổ chức khoa học đã được đề ra trong Quốc hội Khóa thứ sáu," *VSĐ* 24 (January 1957): 1–5, and T. H. L. (most likely Trần Huy Liệu), "Tinh thần tranh đấu để bảo vệ độc lập và hoa bình của dân tộc Việt Nam," *VSĐ* 6 (March–April 1955): 1–8.

12 Lê Xuân Phương, "Mưa ở nước ta ảnh hưởng đến việc trồng trọt như thế nào?" *VSĐ* 30 (July 1957): 70–76. Minh Tranh, "Sử học phải phục vụ cách mạng như thế nào?" *NCLS* 3 (May 1959): 1–8. BNCVSĐ, "Trách nhiệm của chúng ta," *VSĐ* 3 (October 1954): 5. *VSĐ* 48: 2–3.

13 BNCVSĐ, "Khoa học lịch sử và công tác cách mạng," *VSĐ* 1 (June 1954): 2–7. Văn Tân, "Vấn đề viết văn học sử Việt Nam," *VSĐ* 17 (May 1956): 5–17. Trần Huy Liệu, "Đi sâu vào những đặc điểm của xã hội Việt Nam," *VSĐ* 26 (March 1957): 1–2. Minh Tranh, *NCLS* 3: 8. "Kỷ niệm Lê Văn Hưu, một sử gia đầu tiên của Việt Nam," *NCLS* 1 (March 1959): 6. VSH, "Tích cực đẩy mạnh việc học tập chủ nghĩa Mác—Lê-nin một cách hệ thống trong cán bộ sử học," *NCLS* 8 (October 1959): 8.

14 "Trích diễn văn khai mạc hội nghị tổng kết công tác 7 năm của Viện Sử học ngày 7-1-1961 của đồng chí Trần Huy Liệu, Viện trưởng Viện Sử học," *NCLS* 23 (February 1961): 2–3.

15 Trần Huy Liệu, "Một vài nét đặc biệt về Đảng Cộng sản Đông Dương," *VSĐ* 12 (December 1955): 4–18. See also *VSĐ* 14: 12.

16 "Lại một vấn đề nêu ra! Những cuộc vận động Đông Du, Đông Kinh nghĩa thục, Duy Tân . . . là phong trào tư sản hay tiền tư sản?" *VSĐ* 11 (November 1955): 35–38.

17 Tập san Nghiên cứu Lịch sử (Editorial Board of Journal of Historical Research, hereafter TSNCLS), "Các bạn đọc thân mến," *NCLS* 1 (March 1959): 2.

18 Ban biên tập, "Tổng kết cuộc trưng cầu ý kiến bạn độc của *Tập san Nghiên cứu Lịch sử*," *NCLS* 25 (April 1961): 1–13.

19 "Việc đào tạo cán bộ sử học ở Liên Xô," *VSĐ* 13 (January 1956): 71–75.

20 Hải Khách, "Góp ý kiến về việc đào tạo và bồi dưỡng cán bộ sử học," *NCLS* 4 (June 1959): 7–11. Trần Huy Liệu, "Công tác sử học bắt đầu đi vào cán bộ và nhân dân," *NCLS* 5 (July 1959): 1–5. VSH, "Công tác sử học bắt đầu đi vào cán bộ và nhân dân," *NCLS* 7 (September 1959): 1–2.

21 Trần Huy Liệu, "Sưu tầm tài liệu lịch sử," *NCLS* 9 (November 1959): 1–6, and "Việc xây dựng lịch sử các địa phương, các xí nghiệp, các ngành, cần đi vào tổ chức," *NCLS* 40 (July 1962): 3–5.

22 *NCLS* 5: 3.

23 *NCLS* 8: 6. Tổ lịch sử địa phương, "Một dịp tốt để sưu tầm tài liệu lịch sử cách mạng ở địa phương," *NCLS* 48 (March 1963): 1. "Đề án thành lập Hội những người công tác sử học," *NCLS* 79 (September 1965): 1. "Bản dự thảo điều lệ Hội những người công tác sử học Việt Nam," *NCLS* 79: 63. Phan Gia Bền, "Tiến tới

thành lập Hội Sử học nhằm góp phần đẩy mạnh hơn nữa công tác khoa học lịch sử," *NCLS* 82 (January 1966): 5–6.

24 Trần Huy Liệu et al., *Lịch sử Việt Nam,* 2 vols. (Hanoi: Social Sciences, 1971, 1985).

25 See, for example, *VSĐ* 23: 2–4 and the entire issue of *NCLS* 16 (July 1960), which was devoted to the "informal discussion" on slavery.

26 TSNCLS, "Những đề mục nghiên cứu năm 1962," *NCLS* 34 (January 1962): 1–2.

27 Văn Tân, "Đã đến lúc tạm kết thúc cuộc tranh luận về vấn đề 'Có nên liệt những bài văn do người Việt Nam trước kia viết bằng chữ Hán vào văn học dân tộc của ta không'?" *VSĐ* 23 (November–December 1956): 10–23.

28 "Tin tức hoạt động khoa học lịch sử" (hereafter "TTKH") *NCLS* 13 (April 1960): 74–76.

29 In April and May 1960, Prime Minister Pham Van Dong attended the symposium on slavery. In January 1961, General Vo Nguyen Giap attended a conference on the accomplishments of the Research Committee and the Institute of History and the institute's goals.

30 This suggestion appears at the beginning of Nguyễn Đổng Chi's "Nên phân chia thời đại lịch sử nước ta như thế nào?" *VSĐ* 3 (October 1954): 71.

31 "Vấn đề chế độ chiếm hữu nô lệ ở Việt Nam," *VSĐ* 7 (May–June 1955): 5–26.

32 "Bàn thêm về vấn đề chống sùng bái cá nhân," *VSĐ* 19 (July 1956): 5–6.

33 "Cố gắng tiến tới thống nhất nhận định về Đông Kinh nghĩa thục," *NCLS* 81 (December 1965): 31–37.

34 "Vấn đề thời kỳ lịch sử Việt Nam," *VSĐ* 5 (February 1955): 62–67.

35 *VSĐ* 1: 5.

36 "Thử tìm sử liệu Việt Nam trong ngữ ngôn," *VSĐ* 1 (June 1956): 57–58.

37 *VSĐ* 3: 3–5.

38 "Cần đi sâu và rộng hơn nữa vào những chuyên đề," *VSĐ* 46 (November 1958): 1–6.

39 *Đại Việt sử ký* and *Đại Việt sử ký toàn thư.*

40 *NCLS* 1: 3–7. Lê Văn Hưu did not readily lend himself to commemoration. There were no records indicating the date of his death, the event most crucial to ancestral rites. In terms of biographical data, the only solid clues concerned his place (but not date) of birth: Phủ Lý village in Đông Sơn district, Thanh Hóa province; the date when he passed the civil service exams (1247); and his service at the National Institute of History beginning in 1259. Moreover, there were no material traces to which the commemorative events could be attached: early in the fifteenth century, Vietnamese have often affirmed, Ming invaders either destroyed his work or spirited it away.

41 *VSĐ* 46: 1–6.

42 *Đại Việt sử ký toàn thư, Khâm định Việt sử thông giám cương mục,* and *Đại Nam nhất thống chí,* respectively. "Dân tộc Việt Nam thành hình từ bao giờ?" *VSĐ* 5 (February 1955): 5–16. The source for his discussion for the Hùng kings was Lê Tắc's *An Nam chí lược.* "Giỗ tổ Hùng Vương," *VSĐ* 17 (May 1956): 1–4.

43 He specifically cited *An Nam chí nguyên* (by Cao Hùng Trưng, a.k.a. Gao Xiong-

cheng) and crucial works from the Nguyễn dynasty: *Đại Nam thực lục* and *Lịch triều hiến chương loại chí*. "Một số tài liệu về địa tô phong kiến trong lịch sử Việt Nam," *VSĐ* 15 (March 1956): 36–50.

44 The revised and original texts are *Tân đính hiệu bình Việt điện u linh tập* and *Việt điện u linh tập*. "Quyển *Trưởng Nam* ở Việt Nam có từ bao giờ?" *VSĐ* 32 (September 1957): 42–50. His particular focus, Nguyễn Hữu Chỉnh's role in the uprising, drew from *Hoàng Lê nhất thống chí*. "Thử đánh giá Nguyễn Hữu Chỉnh," *VSĐ* 46 (November 1958): 29–42.

45 The more prominent contributors included Chu Thiên, Chương Thâu, Hoa Bằng, Phạm Trọng Điềm, Tôn Quang Phiệt, Trần Văn Giáp, and Trần Quốc Vượng. Romanized Vietnamese versions of Phan Bội Châu's works were published in 1955 (*Tự phê phán*), 1957 (*Phan Bội Châu niên biểu*), and 1958 (*Việt Nam vong quốc sử*). Nguyễn Trãi's *Quốc âm thi tập* appeared in 1957, his *Dư địa chí* in 1960, and *Quân Trung từ mệnh tập* in 1961. Quốc ngữ versions of Lê Quý Đôn's *Kiến văn tiểu lục* appeared in 1963 and of *Phủ biên tạp lục* in 1964. By 1960 the first twenty volumes (*Tiền biên* and *Chính biên*) of the Nguyễn chronicle *Khâm định Việt sử thông giám cương mục* were complete, as was Phan Huy Chú's *Lịch triều hiến chương loại chí*.

46 *VSĐ* 46: 1–6.

47 Bruce Lockhart (personal communication) has noted that this strategy underscores the differences between the DRV's and RVN's approach to a Sinitic past. Whereas northern translators typically omitted Chinese characters (only recently, in fact, have they begun to include them), southern translators normally published bilingual editions, presenting characters and *quốc ngữ* on facing pages.

48 The excerpt was taken from volume 38 of *Lịch triều hiến chương loại chí*. Phan Huy Chú "Vấn đề ruộng đất trong triều nhà Lê," *VSĐ* 2 (n.d.): 53–67.

49 Đào Duy Anh, "Văn hóa Đông Sơn hay văn hóa Lạc Việt?" *VSĐ* 1 (June 1954): 14–29. Văn Tân, "Bàn góp vào công trình tìm tòi nguồn gốc dân tộc Việt Nam," *NCLS* 9 (September 1959): 26–39. Nguyễn Lương Bích, "Không sùng bái học giả thực dân, cần nhận rõ và phê phán những sai lầm, thiếu sót của họ trong khảo cổ học," *NCLS* 11 (February 1969): 72–88. Trần Huy Liệu (*VSĐ* 14: 1–14) specifically criticized Robequain's *Évolution économique* (1939) and Gourou's *Les Paysans du delta tonkinois* (1936) and *L'Utilisation du sol en Indochine* (1940).

50 The titles in French are *Économie agricole*, *Revue indochinoise*, and *Bulletin économique de l'Indochine*. Indications of the postcolonial dependence on colonial sources abound. For particularly striking examples: see Văn Tạo, "Công cuộc khai thác thuộc địa của thực dân Pháp ở Việt Nam và sự phát triển của giai cấp công nhân Việt Nam," *VSĐ* 11 (November 1955): 54–64; Phan Gia Bền, "Tư bản Pháp với thủ công nghiệp Việt Nam," *VSĐ* 37 (February 1958): 18–33; Nguyễn Công Bình, "Tình hình và đặc tính của giai cấp tư sản Việt Nam thời Pháp thuộc," *VSĐ* 41 (June 1958) through *VSĐ* 46 (November 1958); and Đặng Việt Thanh, "Giai cấp công nhân Việt Nam hình thành từ bao giờ?" *NCLS* 6 (August 1959): 11–22.

51 Ironically, during a time when committee historians dogmatically maintained that, from North to South, Vietnam was a single united land, Nguyễn Khắc Đạm reprinted this letter in "Hoạt động Văn Sử Địa quốc tế" (International Activities in Literature, History, and Geography, hereafter "HĐVSĐQT"), *VSĐ* 43 (August 1958): 96–97.

52 Văn Tân, "Ai đã thống nhất Việt Nam? Nguyễn Huệ hay Nguyễn Ánh?" *NCLS* 51 (June 1963): 3–11.

53 The titles in Vietnamese are *Đông Dương tạp chí, Trí tân, Phụ nữ tân văn,* and *Nam Phong tạp chí.*

54 *Việt Nam sử lược,* 2 vols. (Saigon: Bộ Giáo Dục, 1971).

55 "Lực lượng sản xuất và quan hệ sản xuất trong cuộc khủng hoảng của xã hội phong kiến Việt Nam," *VSĐ* 1 (June 1954): 35–56. Tenuous from the beginning, Trần Đức Thảo's ties to the Research Committee did not long endure; only the first several issues of *Văn Sử Địa* included examples of his work.

56 "Bóc trần quan điểm thực dân và phong kiến trong quyển *Việt Nam sử lược* của Trần Trọng Kim," *VSĐ* 6: 20–37, *VSĐ* 14: 1–14, and "Đánh giá cuộc Cách mạng Tây Sơn và vai trò lịch sử của Nguyễn Huệ," *VSĐ* 14 (February 1956): 30–44.

57 *VSĐ* 7: 6.

58 "Sự phát triển của chế độ phong kiến nước ta và vai trò của Hồ Quý Ly trong cuối thế kỷ XIV và đầu thế kỷ XV," *VSĐ* 11 (November 1955): 5–19.

59 Trần Trọng Kim makes this point most forcefully in *Việt Nam sử lược,* pp. 127–29.

60 David Marr treats these issues in detail in "Ethics and Politics," in *Vietnamese Tradition on Trial, 1920–1945* (Berkeley: University of California Press, 1981), pp. 101–35.

61 The Japanese occupation of Indochina began in December 1940, but because of the agreement between the Japanese and the Vichy government in France, the Japanese left the French colonial government basically intact until the coup of March 1945. Bảo Đại, the last of the Nguyễn emperors, abrogated the treaty of protectorate with France and became head of the (nominally) independent Empire of Vietnam. Following the counsel of his new Japanese patrons, Bảo Đại asked Trần Trọng Kim to serve in the place of Phạm Quỳnh, who had resigned. Revolutionaries despised Bảo Đại for having collaborated with the Japanese, and they scorned Trần Trọng Kim as his opportunistic assistant. Their agonistic relations were neatly enacted after the revolution, when Trần Huy Liệu, the senior historian to be, traveled to Hue to strip Bảo Đại and Trần Trọng Kim of the imperial regalia. Dương Trung Quốc has compiled a richly detailed chronology of this period in *Việt Nam: Những sự kiện lịch sử 1858–1945, tập IV (1936–1945)* (Hanoi: Social Sciences, 1989).

62 Marr, *Tradition on Trial,* p. 107.

63 Trần Huy Liệu et al., *Tài liệu tham khảo lịch sử Cách mạng cận đại Việt Nam (1956–1958), Lịch sử tám mươi năm chống Pháp (1957–1961), Cách mạng tháng Tám (1960), Cách mạng tháng Tám: Tổng khởi nghĩa ở Hà Nội và ở các địa phương (1960),* and *Lịch sử thủ đô Hà Nội (1960).*

64 *VSĐ* 1: 2–7.

65 Because of his central role in the dissident Nhân văn–Giai phẩm Affair, Phan Khôi's involvement with the Research Committee was exceedingly brief. In 1958, in fact, he was formally denounced by a member of the committee. Nevertheless, he managed to formulate some of postcolonial historiography's enduring concerns. Nguyễn Đổng Chi,"Quan điểm phản động, phản khoa học của Phan Khôi phải chăng là học mót của Hồ Thích?" *VSĐ* 41 (June 1958): 7–24.

66 He identified *Đại Việt sử ký toàn thư* and *Khâm định Việt sử thông giám cương mục* as the two main chronicles. *VSĐ* 1: 57–58.

67 "Đại hội Đảng Cộng sản Liên Xô lần thứ XX và vấn đề nghiên cứu lịch sử Đảng," *VSĐ* 22 (October 1956): 31–44.

68 Arif Dirlik, *Revolution and History: The Origins of Marxist Historiography in China, 1919–1937* (Berkeley: University of California Press, 1978).

69 He specifically cited two journals, *Tập san Đại học* and *Học tập*, and Đào Duy Anh's *Lịch sử Việt Nam*, which official historians then (in the mid-1950s) viewed skeptically. Nguyễn Lương Bích translated and summarized this article, which appeared originally in the Chinese journal *Historical Research* (*Lishi Yanjiu*). Nguyễn Lương Bích, "Các nhà sử học Trung Hoa giới thiệu công tác của các nhà sử học Việt Nam," *VSĐ* 34 (November 1957): 56–58.

70 BNCVSĐ, "Đảng Lao động Việt Nam, Đảng khoa học," *VSĐ* 15 (March 1956): 9.

71 *Leçons d'histoire d'Annam*, pp. 217–18.

72 *VSĐ* 1: 4.

73 Phan Khôi, *VSĐ* 1: 57–58. Trần Huy Liệu, *VSĐ* 14: 1–14.

74 "Duy vật lịch sử là cơ sở lý luận của khoa học lịch sử," *VSĐ* 6 (March–April 1955): 76–83.

75 Minh Tranh, *VSĐ* 5: 17–30.

76 "Một vài vấn đề trong việc bình luận nhân vật lịch sử," *VSĐ* 3: 58–70.

77 *VSĐ* 14: 1–14.

78 *VSĐ* 34: 57–58.

79 *NCLS* 8: 1–15.

80 This cliché was first introduced by T. H. L. in *VSĐ* 6: 1–8.

81 One can appreciate the persistence of this debate in Nguyễn Đổng Chi, *VSĐ* 3: 71–75; Văn Tân, "Để góp phần xây dựng quyển thông sử Việt Nam—mấy ý kiến đối với mấy bộ sách lịch sử đã xuất bản," *VSĐ* 47 (December 1958): 70–81; Cao Xuân Phổ, "Góp ý kiến về quyển sách *Giáo khoa Lịch sử lớp 9 phổ thông tập I*," *NCLS* 54 (September 1963): 48–52; and Trương Hữu Quýnh, "Vài ý kiến bàn thêm về vấn đề phân kỳ lịch sử," *NCLS* 100 (July 1967): 40–43.

82 Minh Tranh, *VSĐ* 5: 17–30.

83 *VSĐ* 5: 62–67.

84 The Russian-language original was translated into Vietnamese as *Duy vật biện chứng pháp từ điển*. "Lịch sử là gì?" *VSĐ* 5 (February 1955): 60–61. Although Russian-language sources were sometimes translated directly into Vietnamese, more typically the Vietnamese versions were based on Chinese translations of Russian-language originals.

85 "Dialectical and Historical Materialism," in *The History of the Communist Party*

of the Soviet Union (Bolsheviks), Short Course, ed. Central Committee, Communist Party of the Soviet Union (B) (New York: International Publishers, 1939), pp. 105–31.

86 Nguyễn Lương Bích, "Mấy nhận xét về nền khảo cổ học của thực dân Pháp ở Việt Nam trước đây," *NCLS* 4 (June 1959): 12–24. Long Điền and Vạn Thành, "Góp ý kiến với bài 'Mấy nhận xét về nền khảo cổ học của thực dân Pháp ở Việt Nam trước đây' của ông Nguyễn Lương Bích," *NCLS* 6 (August 1959): 60–65.

87 "Mấy điểm rút ra từ cuộc tọa đàm vừa rồi," *NCLS* 16 (July 1960): 1.

88 "Một vài nét về vấn đề ruộng đất trong lịch sử Việt Nam," *VSĐ* 2 (n.d.): 32–52, and "Phong trào nông dân trong lịch sử xã hội phong kiến nước ta," *VSĐ* 3 (October 1954): 6–21. He reiterated this position in *Sơ thảo lược sử Việt Nam,* vol. 1 (Hanoi: Bộ Giáo Dục, 1954), pp. 8–13.

89 *VSĐ* 17: 1.

90 Keith Taylor describes Âu Lạc as the legendary kingdom founded by Thục Phán (who reigned as An Dương Vương). See "Lac Lords," in *The Birth of Vietnam* (Berkeley: University of California Press, 1983), pp. 1–44. Đào Duy Anh's article, which originally appeared in *Tập san Văn học Nghệ thuật,* was cited by Văn Tân in "Cần có một quan niệm nhất trí về chế độ chiếm hữu nô lệ ở Việt Nam," *NCLS* 16 (July 1960): 8.

91 *Sơ thảo lịch sử Việt Nam,* vol. 1, pp. 14–22. His counterarguments appeared in *VSĐ* 2: 32–52, *VSĐ* 3: 6–21, and *VSĐ* 7: 5–26.

92 *VSĐ* 3: 71–75. Later, slightly retreating from this view, Nguyễn Đổng Chi cited the Muong folktale "One Hundred Eggs" as potential evidence of slavery—as it was practiced by the Muong themselves, not the Việt. "Vấn đề chiếm hữu nô lệ ở Việt Nam qua ý nghĩa một truyện cổ tích," *VSĐ* 18 (June 1956): 53–63.

93 *NCLS* 16: 7–9.

94 "Trống đồng với chế độ chiếm hữu nô lệ ở Việt Nam," *VSĐ* 15 (March 1956): 30–35.

95 "Nhận định về mấy kiến khác nhau trong vấn đề chế độ nô lệ ở Việt Nam," *VSĐ* 24 (January 1957): 19–30 and *VSĐ* 25 (February 1957): 51–59.

96 In several sections of "HĐVSĐQT," Nguyễn Lương Bích discussed Korean, Chinese, and Japanese debates on slavery: *VSĐ* 29 (June 1957): 66–67, *VSĐ* 30 (July 1957): 61–69, and *VSĐ* 36 (January 1958): 61–68.

97 "Mấy ý kiến thêm về chủ trương lịch sử Việt Nam không có thời kỳ chế độ nô lệ của ông Đào Duy Anh," *VSĐ* 32 (September 1957): 9–18. "Lịch sử Việt Nam có hay không có thời kỳ chiếm hữu nô lệ?" *VSĐ* 35 (December 1957): 34–46.

98 According to Văn Tân, who cited the *Soviet Journal of Asian Studies* (*Sovetskoe vostokovedenie*) 8 (1958), Deopik ("Đê-ô-pích") traced the practice of slavery to the third-century B.C.E. kingdom of Âu Lạc.

99 *NCLS* 16: 7–9.

100 Văn Tân, "Vài ý kiến về vấn đề chế độ chiếm hữu nô lệ ở Việt Nam," *NCLS* 13 (April 1960): 22–40.

101 The two principal works are *Lịch sử chế độ cộng sản nguyên thủy ở Việt Nam* (1960) and *Lịch sử chế độ phong kiến Việt Nam,* 3 vols. (1960–1961). Trần Quốc

Vượng and Chu Thiên summarized their position in "Xã hội Việt Nam có trải qua một thời kỳ của chế độ chiếm hữu nô lệ hay không?" *NCLS* 16 (July 1960): 10–36.

102 *NCLS* 16: 1–3. "Cuộc tọa đàm về vấn đề chế độ chiếm hữu nô lệ ở Việt Nam," *NCLS* 16: 4–6.

103 *NCLS* 16: 7–9.

104 "Xã hội Việt Nam đã thực sự trải qua thời kỳ chế độ chiếm hữu nô lệ," *NCLS* 16 (July 1960): 37–51.

105 *NCLS* 16: 5.

106 These statements are based on the arguments of Trần Văn Giáp, Đào Tử Khai, Nguyễn Lương Bích, Minh Tranh, Văn Tân, and Mạc Đường as articulated in *NCLS* 16: 37–51 and "Sự phát triển của sức sản xuất đã quyết định sự hình thành quan hệ chiếm hữu nô lệ ở Viiệt Nam thời cổ đại," *NCLS* 16: 52–61.

107 *NCLS* 16: 1–2.

108 The assaults and counterassualts continued throughout the next few months. See *NCLS* 35–40 (February–July 1962).

109 Mai Hòa, "Những điều nghi vấn của chúng tôi về chế độ chiếm hữu nô lệ ở Việt Nam," *NCLS* 62 (May 1964): 13–15. Nguyễn Đức Nghinh, "Thử bàn về đặc điểm của chế độ nô tỳ thời Lê sơ," *NCLS* 90 (September 1966): 39–45. Nguyễn Đổng Chi, "Chế độ nô tỳ thời Lê sơ và tác dụng của các phong trào quần chúng ở thế kỷ XIV và đầu thế kỷ thứ XV," *NCLS* 99 (June 1967): 34–40.

110 *VSĐ* 1: 35–49 and "Bài hịch tướng sĩ của Trần Hưng Đạo và xã hội Việt Nam trong thời kỳ thịnh của chế độ phong kiến," *VSĐ* 5 (February 1955): 31–39.

111 *VSĐ* 2: 32–52 and *VSĐ* 3: 6–21. *VSĐ* 3: 71–75.

112 "Sê-rép-nin" in Vietnamese. L. V. Cherepnin, *Những giai đoạn chính của phát triển chế độ phong kiến ở Nga*, trans. Nguyễn Khắc Đam (1956). Vương Hoàng Tuyên, "Một vài ý kiến về nguyên nhân hình thành của nhà nước phong kiến trung ương tập quyền ở Việt Nam," *NCLS* 4 (June 1959): 59–65. Chiêm Tế, "Thử tìm những đặc điểm phát triển lịch sử của xã hội phong kiến Việt Nam," *NCLS* 5 (July 1959): 6–19.

113 Nguyễn Hồng Phong presented less-conformist views in "Vấn đề ruộng đất trong lịch sử chế độ phong kiến Việt Nam," *NCLS* 1 (March 1959): 42–55, and *NCLS* 2 (April 1959): 26–53; "Trở lại vấn đề nguyên nhân hình thành của nhà nước phong kiến trung ương tập quyền tại Việt Nam," *NCLS* 5 (July 1959): 78–80, and "Sự phát triển của kinh tế hàng hóa và vấn đề hình thành của chủ nghĩa tư bản ở Việt Nam dưới thời phong kiến," *NCLS* 9 (November 1959): 7–25.

114 BNCVSĐ, "Cách mạng tháng Tám và vấn đề ruộng đất," *VSĐ* 2 (n.d.): 3–8.

115 *NCLS* 1: 42–55.

116 *NCLS* 1: 3–7.

117 In his studies of Marxist historiography in China (in the generation that preceded decolonization in Vietnam), Arif Dirlik identifies similar problems. "Feudal" conditions, he observes, referred variously to military and bureaucratic localism, patriarchal family organization, and the dominance of Confucian thought (*Revolution and History*, p. 74).

118 *VSĐ* 7: 5–26.

119 "Đờ-ru-giư-nin" in Vietnamese. N. M. Druzinin, *Sự hình thành chủ nghĩa tư bản ở Nga*, trans. Hướng Tân (pen name of Lê Toại).

120 Nguyễn Hồng Phong identified the Vietnamese as the relevant actors (*NCLS* 5: 78–80 and *NCLS* 9: 7–10); Chiêm Tế implied that the Vietnamese were essentially passive (*NCLS* 5: 6–19), as did Vương Hoàng Tuyên, "Một vài ý kiến về sự manh nha của yếu tố tư bản chủ nghĩa trong xã hội phong kiến Việt Nam," *NCLS* 15 (June 1960): 4–10.

121 *The Asiatic Mode of Production* (Oxford: Basil Blackwell, 1989), p. 330.

122 This summary draws from O'Leary, *The Asiatic Mode* (p. 9) and Germaine Hoston, *Marxism and the Crisis of Development in Prewar Japan* (Princeton: Princeton University Press, 1986), p. 129. In Vietnamese, Plekhanov is rendered "Pờ-lê-kha-nốp," Madyar becomes "Mát-gia," and Varga "Vác-ga."

123 O'Leary, *The Asiatic Mode*, pp. 7–11. Wittfogel appears as "Vít-tơ-phô-ghen" in Vietnamese.

124 Dirlik, *Revolution and History*, pp. 191–99. Hoston, *Marxism and the Crisis of Development*, pp. 127–78.

125 *VSĐ* 7: 12–13.

126 "Phương thức sản xuất châu Á là gì?" *NCLS* 53 (August 1963): 2–10, and *NCLS* 54 (September 1963): 18–26.

127 Nguyễn Lương Bích's citations underscored the circuitousness of Marxism's transmission to Vietnam. To quote from Marx's prefatory remarks, he cited a Vietnamese translation of a French translation of the German-language original. His access to the work of Plekhanov also depended on French translations. *NCLS* 53: 2–3. Riazanov appears in Vietnamese as "Ri-a-zô-nốp."

128 *NCLS* 53: 3–4. Rendered in Vietnamese, the names are "Xa-pha-nốp" and "Quách Mạt Nhược."

129 In *Marxism and the Crisis of Development* (p. 145), Hoston makes no reference to a 1928 conference devoted to this topic; instead, she comments that Japanese Marxists began to address the question of the AMP after the Leningrad Conference in 1931.

130 *NCLS* 53: 4. Iolk is "Ôn-cờ" in Vietnamese.

131 *NCLS* 53: 5. In Vietnamese, the names are "Cô-va-lốp" (Kovalev), "Stru-vê" (Strouve), "Ap-đi-ép" (Avdiev), "Phạm Văn Lan" (Fan Wenlan), "Hầu Ngoại Lư" (Hou Wailu), and "Lã Chấn Vũ" (Lu Zhenyu).

132 *NCLS* 53: 6–8. Based on material in *Three Hundred Years of Oriental Studies in Russia*, ed. L. I. Chernorutskaya, trans. A. I. Cuprin et al. (Moscow: Institute of Oriental Studies, 1997), I am assuming that Alexander Andreevich Guber, the Soviet specialist in Southeast Asian Studies, is the scholar Trần Huy Liệu had in mind when he referred to Professor "Gu-bê." I would like to thank Professor A. Y. Drogov for having brought this work to my attention. Among Soviet historians, evidently only A. I. Tyumenev ("Chiu-mê-nép") objected to the new plan. In Vietnamese, Dong Shuye is "Đồng Thư Nghiệp."

133 *NCLS* 53: 8.

134 For this passage he cited two versions of Lenin's *Marx-Engels: Marxism,* the Viet-namese translation published in Hanoi (1959) and the French one issued by the Foreign Languages Publishing House in Moscow (1954). *NCLS* 53: 8–10.

135 *NCLS* 53: 24.

136 NCLS, "1961," *NCLS* 22 (January 1961): 2–5.

137 "Đối với bài 'Về quyển *Lịch sử chế độ phong kiến Việt Nam tập I*' của ông Trần Quốc Vượng và ông Hà Văn Tấn," *NCLS* 40: 22–30. *NCLS* 54: 48–52. *NCLS* 100: 40–43.

138 Phan Huy Lê, Trần Quốc Vượng, Hà Văn Tấn, and Lương Ninh, *Lịch sử Việt Nam,* vol. 1 (Hanoi: Đại Học Và Trung Học Chuyên Nghiệp, 1983).

139 *VSĐ* 23: 1–9.

140 *VSĐ* 36 (January 1958) through *VSĐ* 48 (January 1959); *NCLS* 11 (February 1960) through *NCLS* 34 (January 1962).

141 Both *Văn Sử Địa* and *Nghiên cứu Lịch sử* covered these connections in "HDVSD," "HDVSDQT," "TTKH," and "TTKHNN."

142 Trần Huy Liệu, "Chúng tôi đã thấy gì ở kho sử liệu của Liên Xô?" *VSĐ* 4: 44–45. Minh Tranh, "Những bài học của Cách mạng Nga 1905 và Việt Nam," *VSĐ* 13 (January 1956): 19–40.

143 "HDVSDQT," *VSĐ* 2 (n.d.): 74–76; *VSĐ* 3: 3–5.

144 Phan Gia Bền, *La Recherche historique en République démocratique du Vietnam* (Hanoi: Éditions Scientifiques, 1965), p. 81.

145 Trần Huy Liệu, "Cuộc chiến tranh chống Mỹ cứu nước của nhân dân Việt Nam gắn liền với phong trào phản chiến đang dâng lên ở nước Mỹ," *NCLS* 81 (December 1965): 1–2.

146 Oliver W. Wolters, "Historians and Emperors in Vietnam and China: Comments Arising Out of Le Van Huu's History, Presented to the Tran Court in 1272," in *Perceptions of the Past in Southeast Asia,* ed. Anthony Reid and David Marr (Singapore: Heinemann, 1979), pp. 80–82.

147 Truong Buu Lam discusses this edict, "Chiếu Cần Vương," in *Patterns of Vietnamese Response to Foreign Intervention, 1858–1900* (New Haven: Yale University Council on Southeast Asia Studies, 1967), pp. 116–20. David Marr does so as well in *Vietnamese Anticolonialism 1885–1925* (Berkeley: University of California Press, 1971), pp. 44–51.

148 I would identify the key texts as Lewis Henry Morgan's *Ancient Society,* Friedrich Engels's *The Origin of the Family, Private Property, and the State,* Vladimir Lenin's *Materialism and Empiriocriticism* and *Imperialism: The Highest Stage of Capitalism,* and Josef Stalin's *Marxism and the National Question, Marxism and Linguistics, Problems of Leninism,* and *Dialectical and Historical Materialism*

149 The more prominent examples are V. I. Avdiyev, L. V. Cherepnin, D. V. Deopik, B. D. Grekov, Y. S. Iolk, M. O. Kosven, V. N. Nikiforov, F. N. Nikiplov, A. M. Pankratova, N. V. Pigulevskaia, G. V. Plekhanov, G. Safarov, V. V. Strouve, A. I. Tyumenev, and E. M. Zhukov.

150 Văn Tân, Nguyễn Linh, Lê Văn Lan, Nguyễn Đổng Chi, and Hoàng Hưng, *Thời đại Hùng Vương,* 2nd ed. (Hanoi: Social Sciences, 1976).

151 See, for example, Trần Đức Thảo, *VSĐ* 1: 49; BNCVSĐ, *VSĐ* 3: 4; Minh Tranh, *VSĐ* 3: 20; and Trần Huy Liệu, "Phong trào cách mạng trong giai đoạn thứ hai từ sau Đại chiến I đến năm 1930 do giai cấp nào lãnh đạo?" *VSĐ* 3 (October 1954): 22–26.

152 Phạm Huy Thông, "Our Stone Age: From the Mount Do Industry to the Hoa Binh Industry," *Vietnamese Studies* (hereafter *VNS*) 46 (1974): 9.

2. THE LAND OF THE VIỆT AND VIỆT NAM

1 The great synthetic volume of Eugène Teston and Maurice Percheron instantiates this view in exemplary fashion. See *L'Indochine moderne: Encyclopédie administrative, touristique, artistique et économique* (Paris: Librairie de France, 1931).

2 "Danh mục các thành phần dân tộc Việt Nam," *Tạp chí Dân tộc học* (hereafter *DTH*) 1 (1980): 78–83.

3 For example, see H. N., "The Neo-Colonialist Political Structure," *VNS* 31 (1971): 76.

4 Đặng Nghiêm Vạn, "An Outline of the Thai in Vietnam," *VNS* 32 (1972): 172, 184. This translation summarizes the material he presented in "Sơ bộ bàn về quá trình hình thành các nhóm dân tộc Tày Thái ở Việt Nam. Mối quan hệ với các nhóm ở Nam Trung Quốc và Đông Dương," *NCLS* 108 (March 1968): 24–37.

5 Lã Văn Lô, "Brief Survey of the Tay Nung," *VNS* 41 (1973): 19.

6 Eugène Cazenave, "Les Travaux publics," in *Un Empire colonial français: L'Indochine*, ed. Georges Maspero, vol. 2 (Paris: G. Van Oest, 1930), p. 236.

7 E. Chassigneux, "Géographie de l'Indochine," in *Un Empire colonial français: L'Indochine*, ed. Georges Maspero, vol. 1 (Paris: G. Van Oest, 1929), p. 47.

8 Đặng Nghiêm Vạn, *VNS* 32: 154. See also Peter Zinoman, *The Colonial Bastille: A History of Imprisonment in Vietnam, 1862–1940* (Berkeley: University of California Press, 2001).

9 Quoted in Nguyễn Đức Hợp, "The Thai," *VNS* 15 (1968): 147.

10 Jean Chesneaux, *The Vietnamese Nation: Contribution to a History*, trans. Malcolm Salmon (Sydney: Current Books, 1966), pp. 113–14.

11 Henri Brenier, "L'Indochine économique," in *Un Empire colonial français: L'Indochine*, ed. Georges Maspero, vol. 2 (Paris: G. Van Oest, 1930), p. 214.

12 Chassigneux, "Géographie de l'Indochine," p. 34.

13 Pierre Huard, "The Blackening of Teeth in Eastern Asia and Indochina," in *Vietnamese Ethnographic Papers* (New Haven: Human Relations Area Files, 1953), p. 5.

14 Paul Doumer, *Situation de l'Indochine* (Hanoi, F. N. Schneider, 1902), p. 2.

15 Chassigneux, "Géographie de l'Indochine," p. 37.

16 Việt Chung, "National Minorities and Nationality Policy in the DRV," *VNS* 15 (1968): 6–7, 11.

17 Lã Văn Lô, "Ba mươi năm thực hiện chính sách dân tộc của Đảng," *NCLS* 10 (January 1960): 68–76.

18 Việt Chung, *VNS* 15: 11–12.

19 The Executive Committee, which included Nguyễn Ái Quốc (the future Ho Chi Minh), Trường Chinh, Hoàng Văn Thụ, Hoàng Quốc Việt, and Phùng Chí Kiên, represented the party's Central Committee. Dương Trung Quốc, *Việt Nam: Những sự kiện lịch sử, 1858–1945, tập IV (1936–1945)* (Hanoi: Social Sciences, 1989), pp. 137–39.

20 Đặng Nghiêm Vạn, "The Khmu in Vietnam," *VNS* 36 (1973): 85.

21 From a cynical perspective based on the SRV's behavior after 1975, it is easy to interpret Lê Quảng Ba's "memories" as yet another attempt to portray majority-minority relations in terms of friendship and mutual respect when the historical experience has been considerably different. In a similarly cynical vein, one could argue that the precise timing of his memoirs (1968) responded to the crisis of the American War, which made the support of highland peoples so crucial again. See "Reminiscences of Underground Revolutionary Work," *VNS* 15 (1968): 39, 49.

22 For a thorough (and thoroughly skeptical) reading of ICP statements, see Walker Connor, *The National Question in Marxist-Leninist Theory and Strategy* (Princeton: Princeton University Press, 1984). Connor also offers a broad and very useful overview of the legal standing of minorities according to the constitutions of 1946, 1959, and 1976; the Labor Party Platform of 1951; the First Three-Year Plan (1958–1960); and the various Five-Year Plans, which began in 1961. Because Connor's work is based exclusively on English-language sources, however, it is impossible to know how critical Vietnamese terms have been translated.

23 David Marr, *Vietnam 1945: The Quest for Power* (Berkeley: University of California Press, 1995), p. 496.

24 Mặt trận liên hiệp quốc dân Việt Nam in Vietnamese.

25 As noted in the previous chapter, the Lao Dong Party is often incorrectly translated as the Workers' Party, even though *lao động* means labor, not laborers.

26 Quoted by Việt Chung in *VNS* 15: 12–13.

27 Khu tự trị Tây Bắc in Vietnamese. Nguyễn Thành, "Vấn đề chữ của dân tộc Thái," *VSĐ* 39 (April 1958): 65. Nguyễn Khắc Viện, "Directives and Resolutions of the DRVN Government and the Vietnam Workers' Party on National Education," *VNS* 30 (1971): 176.

28 Some of this material is discussed in greater detail in my "'Barbarians' and 'Younger Brothers': The Remaking of Race in Postcolonial Vietnam," *Journal of Southeast Asian Studies* (hereafter *JSEAS*) 29, no. 2 (1998): 374–91.

29 Literally, *người* means "the body." *VSĐ* 1: 59. "Thử tìm sử liệu Việt Nam trong ngữ ngôn," *VSĐ* 1 (June 1954): 57–61, *VSĐ* 2 (n.d.): 68–73, and *VSĐ* 3 (October 1954): 40–49. As noted in the previous chapter, because of his dissident acts, Phan Khôi's connections to the committee were extremely brief.

30 Within the more general category of Mọi, he included Lô-ô, Đá-vách, and Ja-đê. *VSĐ* 2: 69.

31 Bruce Lockhart, "Looking Down from a Tightrope: Ethnology in Vietnam" (unpublished manuscript), 1986.

32 Nguyễn Đổng Chi, "Nên phân chia thời đại lịch sử nước ta như thế nào?" *VSĐ* 3 (October 1954): 71–75.

33 He designated the Kinh, Muong, Thai, Tho, Mán, Meo, and Rhade as the "more important" groups. From this list of names, only Kinh, Muong, Thai, and Tho were included in the statement of 1979. "Dân tộc Việt Nam thành hình từ bao giờ?" *VSĐ* 5 (February 1955): 8.

34 "Việt Nam là một khối thống nhất từ Bắc đến Nam," *VSĐ* 5 (February 1955): 1.

35 *VSĐ* 5: 5–16.

36 *Marxism and the National Question* (Moscow: Foreign Languages Publishing House [hereafter FLPH], 1950).

37 *Nations and Nationalisms since 1780: Programme, Myth, Reality* (Cambridge: Cambridge University Press, 1990), p. 2.

38 "Việt Nam là một dân tộc đang mạng mẽ tiến lên," *VSĐ* 8 (July 1955): 2–3.

39 *VSĐ* 8: 1–3.

40 Decision 230-SL, which established the Thai-Meo Autonomous Zone, was issued in April 1955. Decision 268-SL, which created the Viet Bac Autonomous Zone, was announced in August 1956. In this zone, the Tay and Nung were the two main groups. Việt Chung, *VNS* 15: 17–18.

41 *VNS* 15: 152–54.

42 Việt Chung mentioned in particular Tây Kỳ (meaning "Western Unit") in the central highlands, and ethnic-based states for the Thai in the northwest, for the Nung in the northeast, and for the Muong on the edge of the Red River delta. *VNS* 15: 8.

43 The figure of twelve appears in Việt Chung, *VNS* 15: 17; the figure of nineteen occurs in Nông Ích Thùy's "Vấn đề đặt chữ và cải tiến chữ các dân tộc," *VSĐ* 21 (September 1956): 85–87.

44 *Fortune Is a Woman: Gender and Politics in the Thought of Niccoló Machiavelli* (Princeton: Princeton University Press, 1984). I would like to thank John Najemy for bringing this book to my attention.

45 This decision was issued in 1955. Cited by Việt Chung, *VNS* 15: 17.

46 *VNS* 15: 155.

47 "Những tiêu chuẩn để nhận định sự thành hình dân tộc," *VSĐ* 12 (December 1955): 29–40.

48 Trần Huy Liệu, "Từ Mục Nam quan đến mũi Cà Mâu, Việt Nam là khối thống nhất." Trần Huy Liệu, "Tổng kết công tác của Ban nghiên cứu Văn Sử Địa trong một năm qua và đề án công tác năm 1956," *VSĐ* 14 (February 1956): 2.

49 "Việt Bắc," published originally in *Việt Bắc* (Hanoi: Văn Hóa, 1954). My translation is based on a subsequent edition, *Việt Bắc* (Hanoi: Văn Nghệ, 1955), pp. 138–42.

50 Nguyễn Lương Bích, "HDVSDQT," *VSĐ* 26 (March 1957): 64–65.

51 Unattributed, "Thành lập Uỷ ban Khoa học Nhà nước," *VSĐ* 47 (December 1958): 1. See also TSNCLS, "Cùng các bạn đọc thân mến," *NCLS* 1 (March 1959): 101.

52 *VSĐ* 47: 1.

53 Nguyễn Lương Bích, "Mấy nét sơ lược về dân tộc học Mác-xít." *VSĐ* 47 (December 1958): 15.

54 Eugène Pittard, *Les Races et l'histoire: Introduction ethnologique à l'histoire* (Paris: Renaissance du livre, 1924).

55 "Góp ý kiến về công tác dân tộc học ở Việt Nam trong giai đoạn hiện tại," *NCLS* 3 (May 1959): 18.

56 On ethnographic studies in China, see, for example, "Tình hình công tác điều tra lịch sử và xã hội dân tộc thiểu số ở Trung Quốc trong mấy năm gần đây," *NCLS* 2 (April 1959): 88–89, and Lã Văn Lô, "Ngành dân tộc học mới của Trung Quốc," *NCLS* 11 (February 1960): 89–96. Soviet studies were introduced in Cao Văn Biền, "Hoạt động của Viện các dân tộc Châu Á của Liên Xô," *NCLS* 31 (October 1961): 66. The work of Czech and East German ethnographers was discussed by Lã Văn Lô, "Hai nhà dân tộc học Tiệp Khắc và Cộng hòa dân chủ Đức tại Việt Nam" and "Vài nét sơ lược về công tác dân tộc học ở Tiệp Khắc và Cộng hòa dân chủ Đức," both articles in *NCLS* 35 (February 1962).

57 "Sự phát triển dân tộc học ở Triều Tiên sau ngày giải phóng," trans. Trương Như Ngạn, *NCLS* 5 (July 1959): 93–95. Cao Văn Biền, "Hội nghị Quốc tế lần thứ Sáu của các nhà dân tộc học và nhân loại học," *NCLS* 27 (June 1961): 73–74. The ethnographer's name was rendered Kim Huân Cúc.

58 "Chế độ *côn hương* ở vùng Thái khu tự trị Thái-Mèo," *NCLS* 27 (June 1961): 63–67. "Mấy nét tình hình và nhận xét về chế độ *quảng* trong dân tộc Tày ở Hà Giang," *NCLS* 44 (November 1962): 17–26. "Sơ lược tìm hiểu mối quan hệ giữa các ngành Nùng ở Việt Nam," *NCLS* 45 (December 1962): 38–44.

59 "Bàn thêm về lịch sử Lai Châu," *NCLS* 62 (May 1964): 60–63. "Sơ lược về sự thiên di của các bộ tộc Thái vào Tây Bắc Việt Nam," *NCLS* 78 (September 1965): 40–48.

60 He looked specifically at the Zao, Thai, Bahnar, Meo, Lô Lô, and Ê Dê in "Hôn nhân và gia đình của một số dân tộc thiểu số ở Việt Nam," *NCLS* 26 (May 1961): 66–77. "Lịch sử di cư và tên gọi của người Mèo," *NCLS* 30 (September 1961): 54–58.

61 "Quá trình phát triển của các cộng đồng người là tiến từ bộ lạc lên bộ tộc, từ bộ tộc lên dân tộc, hay là tiến thẳng từ bộ lạc lên dân tộc?" *NCLS* 49 (April 1963): 10–19.

62 The collection of Thai chronicles (*Quám tô mương*) was published in 1960. *Dân tộc học là gì?* (1960) addressed questions of theory and method. The survey was published as *Các dân tộc miền núi Bắc Trung Bộ*.

63 "Tìm hiểu về nguồn gốc lịch sử của người Cao Lan," *NCLS* 55 (October 1963): 58–64. "Thử bàn về ba bộ tộc Tày, Nùng, Thái ở Việt Nam đã hình thành như thế nào?" *NCLS* 60 (March 1964): 46–56. "Tìm hiểu về tôn giáo tín ngưỡng ở vùng Tày, Nùng, Thái," *NCLS* 75 (June 1965): 55–64. "Lịch sử xã hội nguyên thủy của người Tày qua truyền thuyết 'Pú lương quân,'" *NCLS* 65 (August 1964): 57–63. "Bước đầu nghiên cứu nhà cửa của người Tày," *NCLS* 58 (January 1964): 54–62. "Bước đầu tìm hiểu về thơ ca cổ truyền của người Tày," *NCLS* 79 (October 1966): 41–51.

64 Lã Văn Lô, *NCLS* 10: 69.

65 "Nghiên cứu về sự cư trú và nhà ở của người Dao ở Việt Nam," *NCLS* 9 (Novem-

ber 1959): 80–86. "Quan hệ công xã trong các tộc thiểu số miền Bắc trước và sau Cách mạng tháng Tám," *NCLS* 18 (September 1960): 38–45. "Xã hội và ruộng đất ở vùng Mường trước Cách mạng tháng Tám," *NCLS* 37 (April 1962): 49–56, and *NCLS* 38 (May 1962): 38–44. "Tìm hiểu về người Rục ở miền núi tỉnh Quảng Bình," *NCLS* 48 (March 1963): 32–44. "Các loại hình kinh tế văn hóa và nền văn hóa vật chất của các dân tộc thiểu số Bắc Trung Bộ," *NCLS* 54 (September 1963): 29–45.

66 "Nguồn gốc lịch sử và sự di cư của người Mán ở Việt Nam," *NCLS* 5 (July 1959): 81–86. The problem of terminology strikes again! *Mán* is based on the root *man*, which means "savage." Like the term "Mọi," discussed above, "Mán" was usually a generic and pejorative term, but in some cases it may have been used in a specific (and possibly nonpejorative) way.

67 Those formerly known as Mán were reclassified as (1) Sán Chay and (2) Thai from the Tay-Thai segment of the Austro-Asian family; (3) Hmong, (4) Zao, and (5) Pà Thẻn from the Hmong-Zao segment of the Austro-Asian family; (6) La Chí and (7) Pu Péo from the Kadai or Cờ Lao segment of the Austro-Asian family; (8) Sán Dìu from the Han segment of the Sino-Tibetan family; and (9) Lô Lô from the Tibeto-Birman segment of the Sino-Tibetan family. *Tạp chí Dan tộc học* (hereafter *DTH*) 1 (1980): 78–83.

68 Lê-vin (M. G. Lewin), "Tài liệu dân tộc học và nhân loại học là tài liệu lịch sử," trans. Cao Văn Biền, *NCLS* 29 (August 1961): 28–33.

69 Nguyễn Thành, "Vấn đề chữ của dân tộc Thái," *VSĐ* 39 (April 1958): 53–66, *VSĐ* 40 (May 1958): 35–48, and *VSĐ* 41 (June 1958): 43–55. The Chinese model was relevant for other researchers, as well. Nguyễn Khắc Đạm, for one, translated articles from a Chinese journal on the task of "inventing" (*sáng chế*) and "improving" (*cải tiến*) the written languages of ethnic minorities. Nguyễn Khắc Đạm, "HDVSDQT," *VSĐ* 45 (October 1958): 93.

70 Lã Văn Lô, "Mấy ý kiến về hướng nghiên cứu dân tộc học," *NCLS* 15 (June 1960): 19–24.

71 Incongruously, he also complimented the "enlightened policies" of the party and government that allowed each of the "more than sixty" nationalities (*dân tộc*) to establish its own autonomous zone. "Vấn đề đặt chữ và cải tiến chữ các dân tộc," *VSĐ* 21 (September 1956): 85–89.

72 Chassigneux, "Géographie de l'Indochine," p. 37.

73 Đan Đức Lợi, "Vấn đề đặt chữ cho các dân tộc chưa có văn tự," *VSĐ* 29 (June 1957): 83. See also Nông Ích Thùy's "Vấn đề chọn tiếng phương ngôn cơ sở và âm tiêu chuẩn trong việc đặt chữ cho các dân tộc," *VSĐ* 36 (January 1958): 91.

74 *VSĐ* 39: 53–66.

75 The word "compatriot," with its emphasis on the patriline, fails to convey the matrilineal sense of *đồng bào thiểu số* because *đồng bào* literally means "womb." *VSĐ* 19 (July 1956): 74–79.

76 "Tiếng Mường và mối liên quan về nguồn gốc giữa người Mường, người Kinh," *VSĐ* 42 (July 1958): 68–75.

77 "Tên gọi của người Mường và mối quan hệ giữa tên gọi của người Mường với

người Việt," *NCLS* 32 (November 1961): 47–54. Chân Thành, "Truyện thần thoại Mường có thể chứng minh sự tồn tại chế độ chiếm hữu nô lệ trong lịch sử Việt Nam không?" *VSĐ* 36 (January 1958): 75–79.

78 "Quanh vấn đề An-dương vương Thục Phán hay là truyền thuyết 'Cẩu chủa cheng vùa' của đồng bào Tày," *NCLS* 50 (May 1963): 48–57, and *NCLS* 51 (June 1963): 58–62.

79 T. H. L., "Tinh thần tranh đấu để bảo vệ độc lập và hoa bình của dân tộc Việt Nam," *VSĐ* 6 (March–April 1955): 1–8.

80 Trần Huy Liệu offered a preview of this historiographical trend in "Ôn lại quá trình đấu tranh chống xâm lược của các dân tộc thiểu số ở Việt Nam," *VSĐ* 7 (May–June 1955): 42–57.

81 Đỗ Thiện, "Một vài nét về lịch sử tỉnh Lai Châu chống thực dân Pháp đầu thế kỷ XX," *NCLS* 45 (December 1962): 33–37. Văn Khôi, "Góp mấy ý kiến về bài 'Một vài nét về lịch sử tỉnh Lai Châu (khu tự trị Tây Bắc) chống thực dân Pháp đầu thế kỷ XX' của bạn Đỗ Thiện," *NCLS* 47 (February 1963): 53–54. Hoài Nam, "Cuộc khởi nghĩa năm kỷ dậu (1909) của dân tộc Mường ở Hòa Bình," *NCLS* 47 (February 1963): 55–59. Lã Văn Lô, "Bước đầu nghiên cứu về chế độ xã hội ở vùng Tày, Nùng, Thái dưới thực dân Pháp," *NCLS* 68 (November 1964): 38–46. Mạc Đường, "Chủ nghĩa đế quốc xâm lược vào Tây Nguyên và lịch sử đấu tranh của các dân tộc Tây Nguyên chống đế quốc," *NCLS* 70 (January 1965): 38–50.

82 "Một vài nhận xét về đặc điểm truyền thống bất khuất của đồng bào Thượng," *NCLS* 76 (July 1965): 28–38.

83 My approach to the "tradition of resistance to foreign aggression" is indebted to the work of Mary Douglas in *Purity and Danger* (New York: Praeger, 1966), pp. 1–6, 114–28, 140–58.

84 *NCLS* 10: 68.

85 Nguyễn Khắc Đạm, "HDVSDQT," *VSĐ* 45 (October 1958): 93; and Nguyễn Khắc Đạm, "TTKHNN," *NCLS* 2 (April 59): 88–89.

86 *NCLS* 3: 17.

87 *VNS* 15: 18.

88 "Góp một số ý kiến về vấn đề cấu tạo nội dung lịch sử Việt Nam theo quan điểm đa dân tộc," *NCLS* 48 (March 1963): 50–56; and "Vấn đề cấu tạo nội dung lịch sử Việt Nam theo quan điểm đa dân tộc," *NCLS* 50 (May 1963): 7–10.

89 In Vietnamese, the names are Uỷ ban Khoa học Xã hội Việt Nam and Viện Dân tộc học.

90 Hue Tam Ho Tai, "Our Fathers' House," in *Radicalism and the Origins of the Vietnamese Revolution* (Cambridge: Harvard University Press, 1992), pp. 10–56; David G. Marr, "Language and Literacy," in *Vietnamese Tradition on Trial, 1920–1945* (Berkeley: University of California Press, 1981), pp. 136–89; and Nguyễn Khắc Viện, *VNS* 30: 166. The Vietnamese name is Hội Truyền ba Quốc ngữ.

91 Nguyễn Văn Mệnh et al., *Tiếng Việt thực hành, Giáo trình sơ giản* (Hanoi: Bộ Đại Học, 1988), pp. 1–2.

92 This discussion of assimilationist politics in the DRV does not mean to imply that conditions in the RVN were better. Indeed, the Saigon government also set out

to homogenize the social domain by abolishing customary courts, resettling minorities in "protected areas," and transplanting ethnic Vietnamese (from areas controlled by the National Liberation Front [NLF] as well as immigrants from the DRV) to the highlands. The reactions of minority peoples to the initiatives of the RVN were generally negative and culminated (1964–1965) in a series of revolts led by the Rhade, many of whom had worked with the French. The Saigon-based government retaliated by executing the leaders of the rebellions. See Peter Kunstadter, "Vietnam: Introduction," in *Southeast Asian Tribes, Minorities, and Nations*, vol. 2 (Princeton: Princeton University Press, 1967), pp. 680–82.

93 "The Zao Are Coming Down to the Lowlands," *VNS* 15 (1968): 181.

94 Bế Viết Đẳng, "The Process of Resettlement of Nomadic People for Sedentary Farming in Mountainous Regions," *Viet Nam Social Sciences* (hereafter *VNSS*) 1–2 (1987): 78.

95 Đặng Nghiêm Vạn, *VNS* 36: 74; Bế Viết Đẳng, "The Zao in Vietnam," *VNS* 40 (1973): 77.

96 *VNS* 36: 73.

97 The devastating effects of commercial logging have become only more apparent in the past few decades. Official statistics demonstrate that for the period 1980–1990, government revenue from logging multiplied by fifty, from two hundred million to ten billion *đồng*. *Số liệu thống kê Cộng hòa Xã hội Chủ nghĩa Việt Nam* (Hanoi: Thống Kê, 1991), p. 12.

98 An Thu identified the settler simply as Monpezat (*VNS* 15: 177–78).

99 *VNS* 15: 185–86.

100 *VNS* 15: 181–83. *VNS* 15: 19.

101 An Thu, *VNS* 15: 185

102 *VNS* 15: 19; *VNS* 36: 134.

103 Mai Quang, "Viet Bac: From Cradle of the Revolution to Autonomous Zone," *VNS* 41: 160–61.

104 Huu Tho, "Storming the Hills," *VNS* 72 (1982): 151–53. So esteemed were the cassava's "thousand fruits" that Tố Hữu devoted to them a prize-winning poem, "Tình khoai sắn," in *Việt Bắc* (Hanoi: Văn Nghệ, 1955), p. 105.

105 Huu Tho, *VNS* 72: 154.

106 Đặng Nghiêm Vạn specifically mentioned Tam Van. *VNS* 32: 148, 160.

107 *VNS* 15: 28–29.

108 Đặng Nghiêm Vạn, *VNS* 36: 72.

109 Đặng Nghiêm Vạn, *VNS* 32: 160–65.

110 Hoang Thuy Nguyen, "Preventive Medicine in the DRVN: Problems and Achievements," *VNS* 34 (1972): 99.

111 *VNS* 36: 74.

112 Huu Tho, *VNS* 72: 161.

113 "A Survey of the Meo," *VNS* 36 (1973): 22.

114 *VNS* 15: 184.

115 *VNS* 32: 194–96.

116 *VNS* 15: 35–36.

117 *VNS* 15: 20.

118 *VNS* 36: 59.

119 *VNS* 36: 65, 134.

120 All quotations are from *The Constitution of the Democratic Republic of Vietnam* (Hanoi: FLPH, 1960), pp. 13–14.

121 *VNS* 15: 15, 6.

122 *VNS* 32: 15, 9, 10.

123 *VNS* 36: 135.

124 "Danh mục các thành phần dân tộc Việt Nam," *DTH* 1 (1980): 78–83.

125 Vương Hoàng Tuyên, "Some Ethnic Groups Only Just Saved from Extinction Living in Remote Parts of the Northwest," *VNS* 36 (1973): 143–95.

126 Former Mọi were reclassified as Muong, Hre, Stieng, Kotu, Jeh Trieng, Ma, Co, Chơ Ro, Jarai, Ede, Raglai, or Chu-Ru. Those known formerly as Mán were reclassifed as Thai, Sán Chay, Hmong, Zao, Pà Thẻn, La Chí, Pu Péo, Sán Dìu, or Lô Lô. *DTH* 1: 78–83.

127 I have based these statements on the descriptive entries for "Hmông" and "Pà Thẻn" in Đặng Nghiêm Vạn, Chu Thái Sơn, and Lưu Hùng, *Ethnic Minorities in Vietnam* (Hanoi: The Gioi, 1993), pp. 234, 239.

128 These include the Xrê, Hà-lăng, Trong, Ve, Cao Lan, Pu Nà, Thuy, Meo, Tống, Ho Roi, and Tu Dí. I base this statement on a comparison of the lists of ethnic groups provided in *The Socialist Republic of Vietnam: Basic Data* (Hanoi: FLPH, 1978) and *DTH* 1: 78–83.

129 The names of the groups included in the 1960 survey (but omitted from the proclamation of 1979) include the Cao Lan, Han, Meo, Cò Sung, Duy, Khùa, Mày, Puộc, Qúy Châu, Thu Lao, U Ní, Xạ Phang, Xá Phó, and Xo. "Mountain Regions and National Minorities," *VNS* 15 (1968).

130 Việt Chung, *VNS* 15: 5–6.

131 The other groups integrated into the Kohu are the Nốp, Cơ-don, Chil, Tơ-ring, and Lát. The new location given for the Kohu included Lâm Đồng, Bình Thuận, Ninh Thuận, and Khánh Hòa provinces. *DTH* 1: 78–83; *The Socialist Republic of Vietnam*, p. 39.

132 Both the Mon-Khmer and Tay-Thai, I should point out, belonged to the Austro-Asian family. *The Socialist Republic of Vietnam*, p. 39; Đặng Nghiêm Vạn et al., *Ethnic Minorities in Vietnam*, p. 124.

133 Đặng Nghiêm Vạn et al., *Ethnic Minorities in Vietnam*, p. 124.

134 The new groups included the Cóc Mùn, Cóc Ngáng, Dìu Miền, Đại Bản, Động, Kiềm Miền, Kìm Mùn, Làn Tẻn, Lô Gang, Mán, Quần Chẹt, Quần Trắng, Sơn Đầu, Tiểu Bản, Thanh Y, Trại, and Xá. Of the former groups, some of the Mán were reclassified as Sán Chay, some of the Trại became Sán Dìu, and some of the Xá became Kháng. *DTH* 1: 80–82.

135 Compare An Thu, *VNS* 15: 181 and Bế Viết Đẳng, *VNS* 40: 40, with Đặng Nghiêm Vạn et al., *Ethnic Minorities in Vietnam*, p. 149.

136 Compare Bế Viết Đẳng, *VNS* 40: 46 with Đặng Nghiêm Vạn et al., *Ethnic Minorities in Vietnam*, pp. 3–4. The 1979 Decision 121 placed the Zao language within

the (newly created) Hmong-Zao subgroup of the Austro-Asian family, a family that also includes Việt-Muong, Môn-Khmer, Tay-Thai, and Kadai-Cờ Lao.

137 An Thu, *VNS* 15: 181.

138 All quotations are from *Constitution of the Socialist Republic of Vietnam* (Hanoi: FLPH, 1981), pp. 12–15.

139 These observations stem from a series of visits to the Museum of Fine Arts, 1987–1994. Since then, the Museum of Ethnology has opened in Hanoi.

140 The expression is from Steven Lavine, "Audience, Ownership, and Authority: Designing Relations between Museums and Communities," in *Museums and Communities: The Politics of Public Culture*, ed. Ivan Karp, Christine Mullen Kreamer, and Steven D. Lavine (Washington, D.C.: Smithsonian Institution Press, 1992), p. 146.

141 Trần Thức, "Mỹ thuật Lý-Trần-Lê-Nguyễn," in *Bảo tàng Mỹ thuật Việt Nam*, ed. Nguyễn Văn Chung (Hanoi: Văn Hóa, 1986), pp. 49–51.

142 The suppression of southern history is apparent at every turn and is expressed in formulations such as this: "The revolutionary movement under the leadership of the party and Chairman Ho forced the imperialists to recognize that Vietnam was a single united nation, not the separate entities of North, Center, and South" (*VSĐ* 8: 1–2). In their zeal to represent the past in monolithic terms, postcolonial scholars implied that only the imperialists thought of Vietnam in regional terms, even though this was not at all the case. The Vietnamese themselves, including those who fought with the revolution and even those who composed the revolutionary government's official texts, frequently made the same distinctions. To be fair, though, it is important to note that in converting regional divisions into the specific political and administrative entities of Tonkin, Annam, and Cochinchina, the colonial government institutionalized these differences in fundamentally new ways.

143 *VNS* 36: 59.

3. NATIONAL ESSENCE AND THE FAMILY-STATE

1 The Hội truyền bá chữ quốc ngữ was organized in 1939. "Nhân dịp kỷ niệm Cách mạng tháng Tám, điểm qua quá trình công tác tư tưởng và văn hóa của Đảng," *NCLS* 6 (August 1959): 1–10. See also Peter Weiss, *Notes on the Cultural Life of the Democratic Republic of Vietnam* (New York: Dell, 1970).

2 Among the members of the Standing Committee (Ban Thường vụ Trung ương Đảng) were Trường Chinh, Hoàng Văn Thụ, and Hoàng Quốc Việt. Dương Trung Quốc notes that this meeting was held in the village of Võng La (Đông Anh, Phúc Yên). Dương Trung Quốc, *Việt Nam: Những sự kiện lịch sử 1848–1945, tập IV: 1936–1945* (Hanoi: Social Sciences, 1989), pp. 190–93.

3 No exact title is given; this text is simply referred to as the "Đề cương Văn hóa Việt Nam." *NCLS* 6: 7.

4 *NCLS* 6: 7–8.

5 Members of the association (Hội Văn hóa cứu quốc) included Học Phi, Nguyên

Hồng, Nguyễn Huy Tưởng, and Nam Cao. These two gatherings are described alternately as congresses (*đại hội*) and conferences (*hội nghị*) in official chronologies. See, for example, VSH, *Việt Nam: Những sự kiện 1945–1986* (Hanoi: Social Sciences, 1990), pp. 29, 42. The variations in nomenclature may account for some of the discrepancies that researchers are likely to uncover. Some sources identify the National Conference on Culture of 1948 as the first (rather than the second) and make no mention of a National Congress on Culture having taken place in 1946.

6 *Chủ nghĩa Mác với vấn đề văn hóa Việt Nam*. In later editions, the title was slightly revised: *Chủ nghĩa Mác và văn hóa Việt Nam* (Hanoi: Sự Thật, 1974).

7 The original titles are, respectively, *Sự thật, Nhân dân, Quân đội Nhân dân, Nghiên cứu Van Sử Địa, Học tập, Tổ quốc,* and *Văn nghệ*. The best English-language study of the Ministry of Culture is Kim Ninh, "Revolution, Politics, and Culture in Socialist Vietnam, 1945–1965" (Ph.D. dissertation, Yale University, 1996).

8 These congresses were held in 1943, 1948 (2), 1957, 1960, 1962, and 1968. Lê Thành Khôi discusses some of these events in "La Vie culturelle," in *Socialisme et développement au Việt Nam* (Paris: Presses Universitaires de France, 1978), pp. 282–309.

9 In addition to the ICP and the Labor Party (Lao động), other parties were also involved in disseminating new culture: Communist (Cộng sản), Democratic (Dân chủ), and Socialist (Xã hội). The front organizations included the Viet Minh, Liên hiệp, Liên Việt, Tổ quốc, and Mặt trận dân tộc giải phóng miền Nam. The Good Studying, Good Teaching movement is mentioned in Communist Party of Vietnam (hereafter CPVN), *The Fourth National Congress* (Hanoi: FLPH, 1977), p. 100.

10 Viện Sử học, *Việt Nam: Những sự kiện, 1945–1986,* pp. 25, 27, 41, 53, 103, 115, 117–118, 121–122, 130, 266–67, 277, 307, 316.

11 Ibid., pp. 210, 212–14, 216–17.

12 Lê Thành Khôi, *Socialisme et développement,* pp. 283–85.

13 The original titles are *Đất nước đứng lên, Truyện anh Lục, Nam bộ mến yêu, Lên công trường, Truyện Tây Bắc, Ngôi sao,* and *Người chiến sĩ*. These details have been culled from a variety of sources: Phan Khôi, "Phê bình lãnh đạo Văn nghệ" (from *Giai phẩm mùa thu,* vol. 1), reprinted in *Trăm hoa đua nở trên đất bắc,* ed. Võ Văn Ái (Paris: Quê Mẹ, 1983), pp. 59–72; Nguyễn Khắc Viện and Hữu Ngọc, *Vietnamese Literature: Historical Background and Texts* (Hanoi: FLPH, n.d.); and Thai Quang Trung, *Collective Leadership and Factionalism: An Essay on Ho Chi Minh's Legacy* (Singapore: Institute of Southeast Asian Studies, 1985).

14 In addition to the work by Võ Văn Ái, see Georges Boudarel, *Cent fleurs écloses dans la nuit du Việt Nam* (Paris: Éditions Jacques Bertoin, 1991). A condensed and preliminary version of Boudarel's work has also been translated into English: "Intellectual Dissidence in the 1950s: The Nhân văn—Giai phẩm Affair," *VNF* 13 (1990): 154–174.

15 Lê Thành Khôi, *Socialisme et développement,* p. 285.

16 I find the more common translation for this campaign, Down to the People, to be less accurate and needlessly partial to events that later happened in China.

17 Anonymous, *Economic Restoration and Cultural Development in the DRV, 1955–1957* (Hanoi: FLPH, 1958), pp. 36–37.

18 *Bàn về Văn hóa và Văn nghệ.* Ho Chi Minh, *Collected Works,* vol. 4 (Hanoi: FLPH, 1960), p. 326.

19 For a time (1957–1959), Đặng Việt Thanh was affiliated with the Committee for Literary, Historical, and Geographical Research, but later he joined the Institute of Philosophy. "Cách mạng tháng Tám và cách mạng văn hóa," *NCLS* 18 (September 1960): 31–37.

20 Lê Thành Khôi, *Socialisme et développement,* p. 309; Weiss, *Notes on Cultural Life,* p. 155.

21 CPVN, *Fourth National Congress,* pp. 44, 29, 54–56, 97–107, 228.

22 J. A. S. Grenville, *A History of the World in the Twentieth Century,* vol. 2 (Cambridge: Harvard University Press, 1997), pp. 491–507.

23 John King Fairbank and Merle Goldman, *China: A New History* (Cambridge: Harvard University Press, 1998), pp. 378–80.

24 "Con người mới Việt Nam, nền văn hóa Việt Nam," *NCLS* 3 (1981): 1–3.

25 CPVN, *Political Report of the Fifth National Congress* (Hanoi: FLPH, 1982), pp. 82–99.

26 The relevant works are *Nam quốc sơn ha,* Lý Thường Kiệt's famous affirmation of Vietnamese identity; *Hịch tướng sĩ,* the plea from Trần Hưng Đạo to fight against the Mongols; *Quốc ngữ thi tập,* Chu Văn An's collection of poems in the national language; and *Việt điện u linh tập,* Lý Tế Xuyên's compilation of tales about Vietnamese spirits. The celebrated works of Nguyễn Trãi include "Bình Ngô đại cáo," *Quân trung từ mệnh tập, Ức Trai thi tập,* and *Quốc âm thi tập.* The Vietnamese title for the poem written by Đoàn Thị Điểm is "Chinh phụ ngâm."

27 Nguyễn Khắc Viện and Hữu Ngọc, *Vietnamese Literature,* p. 332.

28 Among the novels most frequently discussed were *Phạm Công Cúc Hoa, Nhị độ mai, Lục súc tranh công, Truyện Thạch Sanh, Chử Đồng Tử, Trạng Quỳnh, Tống Trân Cúc Hoa, Phạm Tải—Ngọc Hoa, Truyện Trinh thử,* and *Hạnh Thục Ca.* The more prominent participants in these discussions were Hằng Phương, Văn Tân, Trương Chính, Hoa Bằng, Võ Xuân Phố, Nguyễn Đổng Chi, Mai Hanh, Ninh Viết Giao, and Đặng Việt Thanh.

29 A number of writers have discussed this practice. See, for example, Nguyễn Thị Định, *No Other Road to Take,* trans. Mai Elliot (Ithaca: Cornell University Southeast Asia Program, 1976); Truong Buu Lam, *New Lamps for Old: The Transformation of the Vietnamese Administrative Elite* (Singapore: Institute of Southeast Asian Studies, 1982); and David Marr, "Language and Literacy," in *Vietnamese Tradition on Trial, 1920–1945* (Berkeley: University of California Press, 1981), pp. 136–90.

30 Precisely for this reason, Trương Vĩnh Ký became the subject of an extended discussion initiated by Nguyễn Anh. "Vài ý kiến về Trương Vĩnh Ký," *NCLS* 57

(December 1963): 17–27. Although postcolonial writers despised his sycophantic behavior vis-à-vis the French, they could not condemn him in absolutist terms because of his importance to the development of *quốc ngữ*, a medium that anticolonial activists appropriated for literacy campaigns. Among those who participated in the discussion of Trương Vĩnh Ký were Chu Quang Trứ, Hồ Song, Mai Hanh, Mẫn Quốc, Nguyễn Khắc Đạm, Nguyễn Kim Thư, Nguyễn Thành Hằng, and Tô Minh Trung. The discussion was formally brought to a close by Trần Huy Liệu in "Nhận định về Trương Vĩnh Ký," *NCLS* 63 (June 1964): 29–31.

31 *Nam phong tạp chí* was published in Hanoi (1917–1934). Shawn McHale in "Printing, Power, and the Transformation of Vietnamese Culture, 1925–1945" (Ph.D. dissertation, Cornell University, 1995), Hue-Tam Ho Tai in *Radicalism and the Origins of the Vietnamese Revolution* (Cambridge: Harvard University Press, 1992), and David Marr in *Tradition on Trial* have commented insightfully on the development and dissemination of *quốc ngữ* and the creation of a new reading public. Stephen O'Harrow has written an essential piece on the political controversy surrounding Phạm Quỳnh and the importance of his contributions to *quốc ngữ*: "French Colonial Policy Towards Vernacular Language Development and the Case of Pham Quynh," in *Aspects of Vernacular Languages in Asian and Pacific Societies,* comp. Nguyen Dang Liem (Honolulu: University of Hawai'i Southeast Asian Studies Program, 1973), pp. 113–35.

32 Hồng Hạnh, "Sự thống nhất về tính chất phản động của Phạm Quỳnh trong lĩnh vực chính trị và văn học," *VSĐ* 48 (December 1958): 60–81.

33 Minh Tranh, "Một vấn đề về văn học sử Việt Nam: Có thể liệt những bài văn yêu nước do người Việt Nam trước kia viết bằng chữ Hán vào văn học dân tộc của ta không?" *VSĐ* 6 (March–April 1955): 9–19.

34 Three scholars, Văn Tân, Vũ Ngọc Phan, and Nguyễn Đổng Chi, dominated this discussion but many others joined in, including Hằng Phương, Hồng Bích, Lê Thước, Lê Trọng Khánh, Lê Tùng Sơn, Lý Trần Quý, Nguyễn Huệ Chi, Nguyễn Lộc, Nguyễn Minh Văn, Nguyễn Thế Phương, Nguyễn Tư Hoành, and Trương Chính. Nguyễn Minh Văn raised the problem of evaluating translations and adaptations in "Có thể xếp loại văn dịch những tác phẩm chữ Hán do người Việt Nam viết vào văn học Việt Nam không?" *VSĐ* 7 (May–June 1955): 58–61.

35 The relevant journal was *Trí tân*. The respondents included Dương Quảng Hàm, Ngô Tất Tố, and Trần Văn Giáp. Văn Tân, "Đã đến lúc tạm kết thúc cuộc tranh luận về vấn đề 'Có nên liệt những bài văn do người Việt Nam trước kia viết bằng chữ Hán vào văn học dân tộc của ta không?'" *VSĐ* 23 (November–December 1956): 10–23.

36 Nguyễn Đức Đàn argued that the issue required further discussion in "Vài nét về Nguyễn Dữ và tập *Truyền kỳ mạn lục*," *VSĐ* 24 (January 1957): 31–44. Subsequently, in his review of Trương Chính's and Huỳnh Lý's book on Vietnamese literature, Văn Tân himself remarked that the status of Vietnamese literature written in Chinese was still unclear. "Mấy nhận xét về quyển *Lược khảo lịch sử văn học Việt Nam* của nhóm Lê Quý Đôn," *VSĐ* 30 (July 1957): 9.

37 Paul Bourde, "Les Écoles du Tonkin," *Les Temps* 2 (October 1889): 2, and "L'Enseignement en Indo-Chine," *Le Temps* 2 and 17 (October 1889): 1–2.

38 Văn Tân et al., *Sơ thảo lịch sử văn học Việt Nam*, 5 vols (Hanoi: Văn Sử Địa and Sử Học, 1957–1960).

39 Vũ Ngọc Phan, "Người nông dân Việt Nam trong truyện cổ tích," *VSĐ* 4 (January 1955): 25.

40 The chronicle in question is the *Toàn thư*. O. W. Wolters, "Possibilities for a Reading of the 1293–1357 Period in the Vietnamese Annals," *VNF* 11 (Winter–Spring 1988): 92–137.

41 Alexander B. Woodside, "Central Việt Nam's Trading World in the Eighteenth Century as Seen in Lê Quý Đôn's *Frontier Chronicles*," in *Essays into Vietnamese Pasts*, ed. K. W. Taylor and John K. Whitmore (Ithaca: Cornell University Southeast Asia Program, 1995), pp. 157–72.

42 Alexander B. Woodside, *Vietnam and the Chinese Model* (Cambridge: Harvard University Council on East Asian Studies, 1988), pp. 25–30.

43 Maurice Blanchot, "La Parole quotidienne," in *L'Entretien infini* (Paris: Gallimard, 1969), pp. 355–66. I would like to thank James T. Siegel for having brought this text to my attention.

44 "Giảng văn về ca dao cổ của nông dân đấu tranh," *VSĐ* 1 (June 1954): 62–70. This article prompted a lively discussion on the meaning and merits of folk culture as well as specific examples of *ca dao*. The participants included Minh Tranh, Vũ Ngọc Phan, Hằng Phương, Văn Tân, and Nguyễn Đổng Chi.

45 Writers such as Ngô Quân Miện, Ngọc Lân, Nguyễn Hồng Phong, Ninh Viết Giao, Trần Hữu Chí, Trương Chính, and Văn Tân debated the meaning of the folktales *Thằng Bờm* and *Truyện Trê Cóc*.

46 In addition to numerous articles and monographs, Văn Tân also published two surprising anthologies, *Tiếng cười Việt Nam* (on Vietnamese humor) in 1957 and *Văn học trào phúng Việt Nam* (on Vietnamese satire) in 1958. Vũ Ngọc Phan also published extensively and a number of his anthologies, including *Truyện cổ tích Việt Nam*, *Dân ca Việt Nam* (both published in 1955) and *Tục ngữ và dân ca Việt Nam* (1956) became standard texts; repeatedly they have been revised and reissued. Nguyễn Đổng Chi also distinguished himself with his many articles, but his two most important works are *Lược khảo về thần thoại Việt Nam* (1956) and the five-volume monolith *Kho tàng truyện cổ tích Việt Nam* (1957–1974).

47 The original titles are *Việt điện u linh tập*, *Lĩnh nam trích quái*, *Truyền kỳ mạn lục*, *Thiên Nam ngữ lục*, and *Tân đính hiệu bình Việt điện u linh tập*. For help in translating the titles, I have relied on Nguyễn Khắc Viện and Hữu Ngọc, *Vietnamese Literature*, pp. 65, 223–25, 259–61, 268–78; Keith Taylor, "Sources for Early Vietnamese History," in *The Birth of Vietnam* (Berkeley: University of California Press, 1983), pp. 349–59; Huỳnh Sanh Thông, "Folk History in Vietnam," *VNF* 5 (Winter–Spring 1985): 66–80; and Maurice Durand, *Imagerie populaire vietnamienne* (Paris: École Française d'Extrême-Orient, 1960).

48 The original titles are *Contes et légendes annamites*, *Légendes historiques de l'Annam et du Tonkin*, and *Les Chants et les traditions populaires des Annamites*.

Nguyen Van Phong, *La Société vietnamienne de 1882 à 1902 d'après des auteurs français* (Paris: Presses Universitaires de France, 1971).

49 *Le Paysan tonkinois à travers le parler populaire* (Hanoi: Éditions Alexandre de Rhodes, 1930).

50 *Kho tàng truyện cổ tích Việt Nam,* vol. 1 (Hanoi: Văn Sử Địa, 1957).

51 Lê Thước, "Một tài liệu văn sử: Chính khí ca Việt Nam," *NCLS* 73 (April 1965): 21–29.

52 "Vấn đề ruộng đất, vấn đề nông dân và thắng lợi của cách mạng Việt Nam," *VSĐ* 42 (July 1958): 3–10. For an alternative view of land reform, see Edwin Moise, *Land Reform in China and North Vietnam* (Chapel Hill: University of North Carolina Press, 1983).

53 "Nông dân trong thời kỳ phong kiến có tinh thần yêu nước và ý thức dân tộc hay không?" *NCLS* 80 (November 1965): 6–14.

54 Among the many authors who argued this point, and in addition to those cited below, I would emphasize Minh Tranh, "Phong trào nông dân trong lịch sử xã hội phong kiến nước ta," *VSĐ* 3 (October 1954): 6–21; Trần Huy Liệu, "Cuộc kháng chiến cứu nước của đồng bào miền Nam hiện nay là một cuộc chiến tranh nhân dân," *NCLS* 64 (July 1964): 1–6; and Văn Tân, "Mấy ý kiến về vấn đề khởi nghĩa nông dân trong lịch sử Việt Nam," *NCLS* 74 (May 1965): 17–20.

55 Hoài Giang, "Hồi thế kỷ XVIII trước khởi nghĩa Tây Sơn, tại sao các cuộc khởi nghĩa nông dân khác đều thất bại?" *NCLS* 75 (June 1965): 29–36.

56 "Vấn đề chiếm hữu nô lệ ở Việt Nam qua ý nghĩa một truyện cổ tích," *VSĐ* 18 (June 1956): 53–63; *NCLS* 80: 6–14.

57 Nguyễn Hồng Phong's two articles were published in *NCLS* 1 (March 1959) and *NCLS* 2 (April 1959). See also Trương Hoàng Châu, "Mấy vấn đề về đấu tranh giai cấp của nông dân trong xã hội phong kiến Việt Nam," *NCLS* 41 (August 1962): 29–41, and Chu Lương Tiêu, "Tính chất chống phong kiến của chiến tranh nông dân,"*NCLS* 78 (September 1965): 56–59.

58 Many of Trần Huy Liệu's articles in *Văn Sử Địa* emphasized this aim. Articles signed collectively by the Research Committee or the Institute of History also stressed this imperative. See, for example, BNCVSĐ, "Khoa học lịch sử và công tác cách mạng," *VSĐ* 1 (June 1954): 2–7.

59 *VSĐ* 3: 6–21.

60 "Góp ý kiến vào việc tìm hiểu văn học nhân dân của ta," *VSĐ* 4 (January 1955): 6–24.

61 The common expression "the enlightened leadership of Chairman Ho, the Party, and the [national] government" is "lãnh đạo sáng suốt của Hồ Chủ tịch, Đảng và Chính phủ" in Vietnamese.

62 "Những tiếng phản kháng của phụ nữ nông thôn trong dân ca Việt Nam," *VSĐ* 6 (March–April 1955): 38–53.

63 The Vietnamese dictionary prepared by the Institute of Linguistics includes the term *folklor* [*sic*] but omits *phong tục học*. Viện Ngôn ngữ học (Institute of Linguistics), *Từ điển tiếng Việt* (Hanoi: Social Sciences, 1988), p. 388.

64 This section further develops ideas that I originally presented in "The History

of Resistance and the Resistance to History in Postcolonial Constructions of the Past," in *Essays into Vietnamese Pasts,* ed. K. W. Taylor and John K. Whitmore (Ithaca: Cornell University Southeast Asia Program, 1995), pp. 232–45.

65 Carol Gluck, *Japan's Modern Myths* (Princeton: Princeton University Press, 1985).

66 An Khê, "Quốc tuý và Văn minh," *Tạp chí Nam phong* 78 (December 1932): 453–58. In their studies of the 1920s, 1930s, and 1940s, both Hue-Tam Ho Tai (*Radicalism,* pp. 10–56) and David Marr (*Tradition on Trial,* pp. 45–55) discuss the interest of Vietnamese scholars in national essence.

67 David Marr, "World War II and the Vietnamese Revolution," in *Southeast Asia under Japanese Occupation,* ed. Alfred W. McCoy (New Haven: Yale University Council on Southeast Asia Studies, 1980), p. 115.

68 Nguyễn Hồng Phong, *Tìm hiểu tính cách dân tộc* (Hanoi: Social Sciences, 1963).

69 For postcolonial scholars, the key texts were Treitschke's *History of Germany in the Nineteenth Century* (5 vols., 1879–1894) and Renan's *What Is a Nation?* (1882).

70 *Marxism and the National Question* (Moscow: FLPH, 1950), pp. 20–21.

71 T. H. L., "Tinh thần tranh đấu để bảo vệ độc lập và hoa bình của dân tộc Việt Nam," *VSĐ* 6 (March–April 1955): 1–8.

72 Dương Minh, "Đồng bào theo Phật giáo ở miền Nam đang tiếp tục truyền thống anh dũng, bất khuất của dân tộc," *NCLS* 53 (August 1963): 1. Mạc Đường, "Chủ nghĩa đế quốc Mỹ xâm lược vào Tây Nguyên và lịch sử đấu tranh của các dân tộc Tây Nguyên chống đế quốc," *NCLS* 70 (January 1965): 38–50. Nguyễn Đổng Chi, "Một vài nhận xét về đặc điểm truyền thống bất khuất của đồng bào Thượng," *NCLS* 76 (July 1965): 28–38.

73 Nguyễn Khánh Toàn, "Những điều cần chú ý hiện nay trong khi bàn về phương pháp luận sử học, *NCLS* 90 (September 1966): 1–7. John Whitmore has commented on the "immortal spirit" in "Communism and History in Vietnam," in *Vietnamese Communism in Comparative Perspective,* ed. William Turley (Boulder: Westview Press, 1980), pp. 11–44.

74 "Archetypes and Repetition," in *The Myth of the Eternal Return,* trans. Willard Trask (Princeton: Princeton University Press, 1973), pp. 3–48.

75 "Chúng ta đương sống những ngày oanh liệt nhất, vinh quang nhất của lịch sử dân tộc ta," *NCLS* 75 (June 1965): 1.

76 Stalin, *Marxism and the National Question,* p. 16.

77 BNCVSĐ, "Âm mưu cản bước tiến của lịch sử nhất định sẽ bị nghiến nát," *VSĐ* 19 (July 1956): 3.

78 BNCVSĐ, "Việt Nam là một dân tộc đang mạng mẽ tiến lên," *VSĐ* 8 (July 1955): 5.

79 Trần Huy Liệu, "Việt Nam thống nhất trong quá trình đấu tranh cách mạng," *VSĐ* 9 (August 1955): 53–64.

80 "Introduction," "External Boundaries," and "The System at War with Itself," in *Purity and Danger* (New York: Praeger Press, 1966), pp. 1–6, 114–28, 140–58.

81 BNCVSĐ, "Lịch sử thủ đô và lịch sử dân tộc," *VSĐ* 4 (January 1955): 1.

82 Claude Lefort, *The Political Forms of Modern Society: Bureaucracy, Democracy, Totalitarianism,* ed. John B. Thompson (Boston: MIT Press, 1986), p. 16.

83 George Kahin, "Bombing the North Will Save the South" and "The Decision for

Sustained Bombing," in *Intervention: How America Became Involved in Vietnam* (New York: Anchor Books, 1987), pp. 260–305.

84 *NCLS* 75: 1–3.

85 "Archetypes and Repetition" and "The Terror of History," in *The Myth of the Eternal Return*, pp. 3–48, 139–62.

86 "Death, Time, and History: Volkish Utopia and Its Transcendence," in *Masses and Man: Nationalist and Fascist Representations of Reality* (Detroit: Wayne State University Press, 1987), pp. 69–86.

87 Hội văn nghệ dân gian (Popular Culture Association). The proceedings of the conference at which the association was founded were published in *Những ý kiến về văn học nghệ thuật dân gian Việt Nam* (Hanoi: Social Sciences, 1969).

88 "The Revival of Village Traditions in the Rural Areas of the Red River Delta," paper presented at the conference "Vietnam and Asia," sponsored by the Vietnam Center at Texas Tech University, April 1998.

89 This section expands on "The Cult of Antiquity in Postcolonial Vietnam," a paper I presented at the annual meeting of the Association for Asian Studies, Honolulu, April 1996.

90 Nguyễn Đổng Chi, "Nên phân chia thời đại lịch sử nước ta như thế nào?" *VSĐ* 3 (October 1954): 71–75. Trần Huy Liệu, "Dân tộc Việt Nam thành hình từ bao giờ?" *VSĐ* 5 (February 1955): 5–16.

91 T. H. L., *VSĐ* 6: 1–8.

92 "Những tiêu chuẩn để nhận định sự thành hình dân tộc," *VSĐ* 12 (December 1955): 29–40.

93 *VSĐ* 5: 5–16.

94 "Vấn đề viết văn học sử Việt Nam," *VSĐ* 17 (May 1956): 5–17.

95 "Cần đi sâu và rộng hơn nữa vào những chuyên đề," *VSĐ* 46 (November 1958): 1–6.

96 Burton Watson, trans., *Records of the Grand Historian*, 2 vols. (New York: Columbia University Press, 1961).

97 Keith Taylor expresses this view when he notes that Chinese sources provide the only textual evidence for Vietnamese history before the tenth century (*Birth of Vietnam*, p. 349). See also Edward H. Schafer, *The Vermilion Bird: T'ang Images of the South* (Berkeley: University of California Press, 1967).

98 Charles Higham, "The Discovery of the Bronze Age," in *The Bronze Age of Southeast Asia* (Cambridge: Cambridge University Press, 1996), pp. 17–38. The key texts he cites for Vietnam are M. H. Parmentier, "Anciens tambours de bronze," *Bulletin de l'École Française d'Extreme-Orient* (hereafter *BEFEO*) 18 (1918): 18–30; V. Goloubew, "L'Age du bronze au Tonkin et dans le nord-Annam," *BEFEO* 29 (1929): 1–46; and O. R. T. Janse, *The Ancient Dwelling Site of Dong-Son*, vol. 3 of *Archaeological Research in Indo-China* (Cambridge: Harvard University Press, 1958). In the passage that follows, I have summarized the evidence presented by Higham.

99 Đào Duy Anh, "Văn hóa Đông Sơn hay văn hóa Lạc Việt?" *VSĐ* 1 (June 1954): 14–29.

100 Lê Văn Hữu presented *Đại Việt sử ký* to the Trần emperor Thánh Tông in 1272; *An Nam chí lược* was completed around 1340 by Lê Tắc, who expatriated to China, and *Đại Việt sử lược* was probably finished in the 1380s. Émile Gaspardone, "Matériaux pour servir à l'histoire d'Annam," *BEFEO* 29 (1929): 63–106, and "Bibliographie annamite," *BEFEO* 34 (1934): 1–152; and Keith Taylor, "Sources for Early Vietnamese History," in *Birth of Vietnam*, pp. 349–59.

101 "Assertions of Cultural Well-Being in Fourteenth-Century Vietnam," in *Two Essays on Đại Việt in the Fourteenth Century* (New Haven: Yale University Council on Southeast Asia Studies, 1988), pp. 3–53. The fifteenth-century chronicle is *Đại Việt sử ký toàn thư*.

102 Keith Taylor makes this point about Vietnam's "chronological equality" with China in *Birth of Vietnam*, pp. 309–11.

103 On the topic of this poem, a good deal of contradictory information has surfaced. Some sources—Chu Văn Tấn, for example—have claimed that Ho Chi Minh wrote the poem (in Chinese) when he was in the mountains of Viet Bac. Others have stated that he *composed* and *recited* the poem without actually writing it down. Some insist that the poem was written, not only composed, but that no copies of it survive; and at least one source mentions that a copy of the poem is on display in the Museum of the Revolution. See, for example, Chu Văn Tấn, *Reminiscences on the Army for National Salvation*, trans. Mai Elliot (Ithaca: Cornell University Southeast Asia Program, 1974).

104 "Giỗ tổ Hùng Vương," *VSĐ* 17 (May 1956): 1–4.

105 To support this historiographical move, I imagine, Mai Hanh wrote an article on the process through which mythological characters became historical. He cited specifically the example of Trạng Quỳnh, who was not originally a historical figure but who, with time, became one (*trở thành nhân vật lịch sử*). "Giá trị Truyện Trạng Quỳnh," *VSĐ* 21 (September 1956): 35–48.

106 *VSĐ* 17: 4.

107 *VSĐ* 17: 5–17.

108 "Giọt lệ bể dâu (Tang hải lệ đàm)," trans. Trịnh Đình Rư, *VSĐ* 43 (August 1958): 80–88.

109 *VSĐ* 46: 1–6.

110 In making this claim, he cited *Việt sử lược*, the thirteenth-century text, instead of the fifteenth-century *Toàn thư*, the source to which postcolonial scholars were becoming increasingly partial. "Xã hội nước Văn Lang và xã hội nước Âu Lạc," *NCLS* 20 (November 1960): 23–33.

111 He spoke with Hoài Thanh and Cao Huy Đỉnh (*Cultural Life of the DRV*, p. 5).

112 *VSĐ* 17: 2.

113 Văn Tân, Hà Văn Tấn, Hoàng Lương, and Đỗ Xuân Trạch discussed this topic in *NCLS* 2 (April 1959) through *NCLS* 7 (September 1959).

114 "Vài ý kiến về bài 'Xã hội nước Văn Lang và xã hội nước Âu Lạc' (bàn với ông Văn Tân)," *NCLS* 26 (May 1961): 32–42 and *NCLS* 27 (June 1961): 35–48.

115 Among those present were Hà Huy Giáp, Nguyễn Đức Quỳ, Trần Huy Liệu, Đào

Tử Khai, Nguyễn Đỗ Cung, and Văn Tân. These details were recounted by the editorial board in TCNCLS, "Nên nghiên cứu vấn đề thời đại Hồng Bàng," *NCLS* 97 (April 1967): 5–6, and by Văn Tân, Nguyễn Linh, Lê Văn Lan, Nguyễn Đổng Chi, and Hoàng Hưng in *Thời đại Hùng vương* (Hanoi: Social Sciences, 1976), pp. 26–27.

116 Văn Tân, "Vấn đề thời đại Hùng vương trong lịch sử dân tộc Việt Nam," *NCLS* 98: 16–29. Nguyễn Linh, "Vài suy nghĩ về việc tìm hiểu thời đại Hồng Bàng," *NCLS* 100: 32–39. Đào Tử Khải, "Những bước phát triển lớn của thị tộc Hồng Bàng có hay không và nhận vật Hùng vương trong lịch sử dân tộc chúng ta," *NCLS* 101: 41–45. Hoàng Thị Châu, "Tìm hiểu từ 'Phụ đạo' trong truyền thuyết về Hừng vương," *NCLS* 102: 22–28. Trương Hoàng Châu, "Nền văn hóa khảo cổ học duy nhất trong thời đạI đồng thau Việt Nam và vấn đề nước Văn Lang của Hùng vương," *NCLS* 105: 35–41.

117 Hồng Việt discussed Vietnamese ancient history in relation to Marx, Engels, and Lenin (*NCLS* 106); Lê Văn Lan, Phạm Văn Kinh, and Hoàng Hưng analyzed the archaeological traces of the Hùng kings (*NCLS* 107); Trần Huy Bá researched the Hùng dynasty (*NCLS* 108); Nguyễn Linh approached the Hùng kings as descendants of the mythical Chinese ruler Shen Nong (*NCLS* 111) and delved into the subject of Văn Lang (*NCLS* 112).

118 The results of these conferences were summarized in a number of places, including the *Journal of Archaeology* (*Tạp chí Khảo cổ học*) and Văn Tân et al., *Thời đại Hùng vương*, pp. 28–29.

119 Phạm Huy Thông, "Ba lần dựng nước," *Học tập* 21, no. 237 (September 1975): 63–72, 76.

120 *Radicalism*, pp. 196–98; *Tradition on Trial*, pp. 131–34.

121 Vo Nguyen Giap, *Unforgettable Months and Years*, trans. Mai Van Elliot (Ithaca: Cornell University Southeast Asia Program, 1975), 27.

122 *VSĐ* 17: 1–2.

123 Lã Văn Lô, "Ba mươi năm thực hiện chính sách dân tộc của Đảng," *NCLS* 10 (January 1960): 69.

124 In a review of Jean Chesneaux's generally sympathetic *Contribution à l'histoire de la nation vietnamienne*, Trần Huy Liệu criticized Chesneaux for being unnecessarily attentive to conflict between Vietnamese and ethnic minorities. "Một vài nhận xét về quyển *Cống hiến vào lịch sử của dân tộc Việt Nam* của Jean Chesneaux," *VSĐ* 22 (October 1956): 3–15.

125 Because some crucial ideas were missing from the English translation, I have re-translated certain passages. "Trong vòng tay của Mẹ hiền Tổ quốc, các thế hệ nối tiếp nhau của 54 dân tộc lớn nhỏ anh em trong đại gia đình dân tộc Việt Nam từ bao đời nay đã sát cánh bên nhau, đồng cam cộng khổ, cùng đổ mồ hôi và xương máu bảo vệ và xây dựng quê hương . . . ," *Việt Nam: Quê hương tôi / Vietnam: My Homeland* (Hanoi: Sự Thật and Vietnamtourism, 1989), pp. 8–9.

1 *Collective Memory,* trans. Francis J. Ditter Jr. and Vida Yazdi Ditter (New York: Harper Colophon Books, 1980).

2 Natalie Zemon Davis and Randolph Starn, "Introduction," *Representations* 26 (spring 1989): 4.

3 *The Ritual Process: Structure and Anti-Structure* (New York: Aldine, 1969).

4 In Vietnamese the three enclosures are known as the *Kinh thành, Hoàng thành,* and *Tử Cấm thành.*

5 Hue-Tam Ho Tai, *Radicalism and the Origins of the Vietnamese Revolution* (Cambridge: Harvard University Press, 1992), p. 110.

6 The zodiac consisted of two distinct cycles that, combined, produced the sixty-year cycle. The ten heavenly stems (*thập can*) are *giáp, ất, bính, đinh, mậu, kỷ, canh, tân, nhâm,* and *quý.* The twelve earthly branches (*thập nhị chi*) are rat (*tý*), ox (*sửu*), tiger (*dần*), hare (*mão*), dragon (*thìn*), snake (*ty*), horse (*ngọ*), sheep (*mùi*), monkey (*thân*), cock (*dậu*), dog (*tuất*), and pig (*họi*). According to this pattern of succession, *giáp tý* (also the year of the rat) is the first year of the cycle and *quý họi* (the year of the pig) is the sixtieth. Vietnamese methods for dating also recognized the movement of the sun. The solar year (of 365 days) was divided into twenty-four segments known as *khi,* half of which were considered even and half of which were considered odd. The twenty-four *khi* were named after natural events that occurred during that time of the year: astronomical events such as the beginning of seasons, equinoxes, or solstices; meteorological events such as intense heat or mild heat, heavy snow or light snow; and biological facts such as the "waking of worms." Two consecutive *khi* formed one solar month (*tháng*). See Hoang Xuan Han, "Calendars and Vietnamese Calendar," *VNS* 76 (1985): 69–81; and Joseph Needham, "Ancient Calendars" and "Calendrical and Planetary Astronomy," in *Mathematics and the Sciences of the Heavens and the Earth,* vol. 3 of *Science and Civilization in China* (Cambridge: Cambridge University Press, 1959, 1992), pp. 194–96, 390–408.

7 Bruce Lockhart, personal communication.

8 See, for example, Nguyễn Q. Thắng and Nguyễn Bá Thế, *Từ điển nhân vật lịch sử Việt Nam,* rev. ed. (Ho Chi Minh City: Văn Hóa, 1993).

9 O. W. Wolters, "Assertions of Cultural Well-Being in Fourteenth-Century Vietnam," in *Two Essays on Đại Việt in the Fourteenth Century* (New Haven: Yale University Council on Southeast Asia Studies, 1988), pp. 3–53.

10 Trần Huy Liệu, "Đánh gía cho đúng những anh hùng dân tộc của chúng ta," *VSĐ* 1 (June 1954): 30–34. Văn Tạo translated Jian Bozan (Tiễn Bá Tán in Vietnamese), "Một vài vấn đề trong việc bình luận nhân vật lịch sử," *VSĐ* 3 (October 1954): 58–70. Trần Huy Liệu, "Chúng tôi đã thấy những gì ở kho sử liệu của Liên Xô?" *VSĐ* 4 (January 1955): 35–46.

11 BNCVSĐ, "Hồ Chủ tịch và thời đại chúng ta," *VSĐ* 7 (May–June 1955): 1–4.

12 Worse yet, according to Sha Ying (Sa Anh in Vietnamese), Hu Shi (Hồ Thích) also believed in pragmatism, an "extremely reactionary philosophy of the Ameri-

can bourgeoisie." "Tác dụng của quần chúng nhân dân và cá nhân trong lịch sử: Bình luận cả quan điểm phản động của Hồ Thích," trans. Phạm Trọng Điềm, *VSĐ* 10 (September–October 1955): 73–85.

13 Trần Huy Liệu, "Giỗ tổ Hùng vương," *VSĐ* 17 (May 1956): 1–4.

14 "Chống sùng bái cá nhân, nhưng cần nhận rõ vai trò cá nhân trong lịch sử," *VSĐ* 18 (June 1956): 1–13.

15 "Bàn thêm về vấn đề chống sùng bái cá nhân," *VSĐ* 19 (July 1956): 5–9.

16 In addition to discussing the work of Nguyễn Trãi, he mentioned the two Trưng sisters, Lý Bôn, Mai Thúc Loan, Phùng Hưng, Ngô Quyền, Trần Hưng Đạo, Lê Lợi, and Nguyễn Huệ. Others quickly added the Hùng kings and Lady Triệu to the list. "Nguyễn Trãi, một nhà ái quốc tiêu biểu cho lòng nhân nghĩa và ý chí hòa bình của nhân dân ta trong đầu thế kỷ XV," *VSĐ* 20 (August 1956): 7–20.

17 Unattributed, "Đại hội Đảng Cộng sản Liên Xô lần thứ XX và vấn đề nghiên cứu lịch sử Đảng," *VSĐ* 22 (October 1956): 31–44.

18 Nhất Nguyên, "Chủ nghĩa Mác–Lê-nin bàn về nhân vật lịch sử," *NCLS* 14 (May 1960): 11–23.

19 The occasions identified here reflect only a sampling of the people and events commemorated by official historians.

20 Davis and Starn, "Introduction," 3.

21 David Marr has discussed earlier views of the heroic pantheon in "Perceptions of the Past," in *Vietnamese Tradition on Trial, 1920–1945* (Berkeley: University of California Press, 1985), pp. 252–87.

22 The following comparisons are based, in part, on O. W. Wolters's "Historians and Emperors in Vietnam and China: Comments Arising Out of Le Van Huu's History, Presented to the Tran Court in 1272," in *Perceptions of the Past in Southeast Asia*, ed. Anthony Reid and David Marr (Singapore: Heinemann, 1979), pp. 69–89.

23 Alexander B. Woodside, *Vietnam and the Chinese Model* (Cambridge: Harvard University Council on East Asian Studies, 1971, 1988), p. 12.

24 David Marr, *Vietnamese Anticolonialism 1885–1925* (Berkeley: University of California Press, 1971), p. 168.

25 Hồ Quý Ly, Nguyễn Trường Tộ, Phan Thanh Giản, Trương Vĩnh Ký, Phan Chu Trinh, and Lưu Vĩnh Phúc. TSNCLS, "Đánh giá một số nhân vật lịch sử," *NCLS* 23 (February 1961): 5–7.

26 Ngô Hàm in Vietnamese. "Bàn về vấn đề đánh giá nhân vật lịch sử," *NCLS* 41 (August 1962): 42–51. "Xung quanh việc kỷ niệm các danh nhân trong nước," *NCLS* 44 (November 1962): 1–2.

27 Sarah Womack has developed similar lines of thought in "The Remaking of a Legend: Women and Patriotism in the Hagiography of the Trưng Sisters," *Crossroads: An Interdisciplinary Journal of Southeast Asian Studies* 9, no. 2 (1996): 31–50.

28 Unless indicated otherwise, the source for the above quotations is Keith Weller Taylor, *The Birth of Vietnam* (Berkeley: University of California Press, 1983), pp. 334–37.

29 From a 1960 edition of Lý Tế Xuyên's *Việt Điện u linh tập,* quoted in Taylor, *Birth of Vietnam,* p. 337.

30 The Vietnamese translation of this statement by Nguyễn Minh is "Lịch sử loài người là lịch sử đấu tranh giai cấp . . . Nhân dân Việt Nam và nhân dân Trung Quốc cùng với nhau chống bọn phong kiến Trung Quốc." "Ôn lại cuộc khởi nghĩa của Hai Bà Trưng," *VSĐ* 5 (February 1955): 48–51.

31 Dương Minh, "Nhân dịp kỷ niệm hai Bà — Thử xét xem nguyên nhân gì khiến cuộc kháng chiến của Trưng Trắc và Trưng Nhị phải thất bại," *NCLS* 36 (March 1962): 3–6.

32 vsh, *Việt Nam: Những sự kiện 1945–1986* (Hanoi: Social Sciences, 1990), p. 212. Trần Huy Liệu, "Ba mươi năm đấu tranh của phụ nữ Việt Nam dưới sự lãnh đạo của Đảng," *NCLS* 13 (April 1960): 1–12.

33 Her memoirs provide unusual insights into the movement in the South; see *No Other Road to Take,* trans. Mai Elliot (Ithaca: Cornell University Southeast Asia Program, 1976).

34 Văn Tân, "Chuẩn bị kỷ niệm 1930 năm Hai Bà Trưng tuẫn tiết," *NCLS* 142 (January–February 1972): 6–9; Vũ Tuấn Sán, "Cuộc khởi nghĩa Hai Bà Trưng tại thủ đô Hà Nội," *NCLS* 149 (March–April 1973): 41–50. Lê Thước and Trần Huy Bá, "Tấm bia đá trước sân đền Hai Bà Trưng ở Hà Nội," *NCLS* 149 (March–April 1973): 51–54.

35 "Archetypes and Repetition" in *The Myth of the Eternal Return,* trans. Willard Trask (Princeton: Princeton University Press, 1974), pp. 3–48.

36 Citing the memoirs of Vo Nguyen Giap, Marr notes that in Hanoi in 1945, revolutionaries promoted Altars for the Ancestral Land (Bàn thờ Tổ quốc) (*Tradition on Trial,* p. 133).

37 Trần Đức Thảo, "Bài hịch tướng sĩ của Trần Hưng Đạo và xã hội Việt Nam trong thời kỳ thịnh của chế độ phong kiến," *VSĐ* 5 (February 1955): 31–40.

38 Trần Huy Liệu, "Vai trò lịch sử của Trần Quốc Tuấn," *VSĐ* 10 (September–October 1955): 8–17.

39 They mentioned the battles of Chương Dương, Hàm Tử, Vạn Kiếp, and Vân Đồn. Nguyễn Văn Dị and Văn Lang, "Nghiên cứu về trận Bạch Đằng năm 1288," *NCLS* 43 (October 1962): 27–36.

40 They specifically cited Minh Tranh's *Sơ thảo lược sử Việt Nam;* Đào Duy Anh's *Lịch sử Việt Nam;* Trần Quốc Vượng and Hà Văn Tấn's *Lịch sử chế độ phong kiến Việt Nam;* Hoàng Thúc Trâm's *Trần Hưng Đạo;* and Chu Thiên's *Chống quân Nguyên.*

41 Trùng Hưng was Trần Nhân Tông's reign name. Trần Huy Liệu, "Kỷ niệm 675 năm trận chiến thắng Bạch Đằng," *NCLS* 50 (May 1963): 1–6.

42 This point was made even more emphatically by Nguyễn Ngọc Thụy, "Về con nước triều trong trận Bạch Đằng 1288," *NCLS* 63 (June 1964): 36.

43 *NCLS* 50: 6.

44 See, for example, Văn Tân, "Bàn thêm về nguyên nhân khiến cho cuộc kháng chiến chống quân Mông Cổ hồi thế kỷ XIII đi đến thắng lợi," *NCLS* 66 (September 1964): 2–7, and *NCLS* 67 (October 1964): 39–45; Đào Duy Anh, "Tìm các

đèo Khâu Cấp và Nội Bàng trên đường dụng binh của Trần Hưng Đạo," *NCLS* 66 (September 1964): 36–38; and Văn Tân, "Nhân dịp kỷ niệm 680 năm chiến thắng Bạch Đằng: Thử tìm hiểu thêm nguyên nhân và ý nghĩa lịch sử của cuộc chiến thắng quân Mông Cổ hồi thế kỷ XIII," *NCLS* 107 (February 1968): 19–24. On the first battle of Bạch Đằng, see Chương Dương, "Kỷ niệm 1030 năm chiến thắng Bạch Đằng lần thứ nhất," *NCLS* 125 (August 1969): 60–63.

45 I would like to thank Nola Cooke for her comments on an earlier draft of this section.

46 Minh Tranh, *VSĐ* 20: 7–20.

47 Dương Quảng Hàm, *Leçons d'histoire d'Annam* (Hanoi: Imprimerie Le Van Tan, 1936), p. 68.

48 *VSĐ* 20: 8–9.

49 *Bình Ngô đại cáo* in Vietnamese.

50 *VSĐ* 20: 7. Minh Tranh's impressions of Nguyễn Trãi and the morality text (*Gia huấn ca*) are not universally shared. Nguyen Tran Huan and Maurice Durand, for example, argue that its vocabulary suggests a much later date of composition, possibly not before the eighteenth century. Unlike Minh Tranh, who stresses Nguyễn Trãi's activism, these same two critics emphasize different aspects of his career. "Some of Nguyen Trai's subjects (love of the country and of a quiet life, distaste for the rough-and-tumble of the court, integrity, rectitude, etc.) are to be found in the great Chinese poets of the T'ang and Sung, notably Po Chu-i. But his especial favorite, often most delightfully treated, is the pleasure of *otium* or idleness, in the Latin (i.e., the nonpejorative) sense of the word. This is the discriminating idleness of the cultured man." Maurice Durand and Nguyen Tran Huan, *An Introduction to Vietnamese Literature*, trans. D. M. Hawke (New York: Columbia University Press, 1985), pp. 58–64.

51 *VSĐ* 20: 20.

52 Trần Huy Liệu, "Nguyễn Trãi, một nhà đại chính trị, đại văn hào Việt Nam," *VSĐ* 21 (September 1956): 1–21. The ceremony, held on September 19, prompted a spate of commemorative texts: Lê Thước and Trương Chính, "Thử xét lại cái án Nguyễn Trãi," *VSĐ* 24 (January 1957): 63–72; Nguyễn Hồng Phong, "Tìm hiểu *Gia huấn ca*," *VSĐ* 27 (April 1957): 4–21, and *VSĐ* 29 (June 1957): 23–39; Đào Tứ Minh, "Một vài ý kiến về vấn đề phiên âm và giải thích thơ *Quốc âm* của nhà đại văn hào Nguyễn Trãi," *VSĐ* 36 (January 1958): 80–90; and Phạm Trọng Điềm, "Một vài ý kiến trao đổi với bạn Đào Tứ Minh về vấn đề phiên âm và chú giải cuốn *Quốc âm thi tập*," *VSĐ* 38 (March 1958): 70–81.

53 *VSĐ* 21: 1.

54 *VSĐ* 21: 3.

55 *VSĐ* 21: 21.

56 Dương Quảng Hàm, *Leçons d'histoire*, p. 69.

57 TSNCLS, "Nguyễn Trãi, một nhân vật vĩ đại trong lịch sử Việt Nam," *NCLS* 42 (September 1962): 1–7. Văn Tân, "Bàn thêm về Nguyễn Trãi, một lãnh tụ của khởi nghĩa Lam Sơn," *NCLS* 44 (November 1962): 9–16; "Nguyễn Trãi có sang Trung Quốc hay không?" *NCLS* 53 (August 1963): 11–15; and "Tư tưởng nhân văn của

Nguyễn Trãi," *NCLS* 54 (September 1963): 2–9. Lê Thước, "Một số chữ in sai về thơ văn Nguyễn Trãi trong *Ức-trai di tập*," *NCLS* 66 (September 1964): 32–35. Thanh Ba, "Bàn thêm về quan điểm của Nguyễn Trãi trong vấn đề chiến tranh và hòa bình," *NCLS* 69 (December 1964): 34–38. Hoài Phương, "Tìm hiểu nguồn gốc tư tưởng nhân dân của Nguyễn Trãi," *NCLS* 80 (November 1965): 2–5. Lê Văn Kỳ, "Tư tưởng 'dân' của Nguyễn Trãi với chúng ta," *NCLS* 81 (December 1965): 19–30.

58 Trần Huy Liệu, "Kỷ niệm Nguyễn Trãi trong cuộc đánh Mỹ cứu nước của chúng ta hiện nay," *NCLS* 102 (September 1967): 12–13, 63.

59 Văn Tân, "550 năm ngày khởi nghĩa Lam Sơn," *NCLS* 106 (January 1968): 1–2.

60 Viện Văn học, *Nguyễn Trãi: Khí phách và tinh hoa của dân tộc* (Hanoi: Social Sciences, 1980).

61 *Leçons d'histoire,* pp. 103–5.

62 Minh Tranh, Trần Huy Liệu, Nguyễn Lương Bích, and others were responsible for the initial excavations, published in *VSĐ* 14. Commemorative festivities were reported in *NCLS* 119 (February 1969): 64 and *NCLS* 130 (January–February 1970): 1–3.

63 "Khởi nghĩa Tây Sơn và sự hình thành dân tộc Việt Nam," *VSĐ* 24 (January 1957): 6–18.

64 "Những yếu tố thắng lợi của trận lịch sử Đống Đa," *VSĐ* 38 (March 1958): 1–7.

65 Between 1963 and 1969, many authors, including Trần Văn Giáp (*NCLS* 46), Văn Tân (*NCLS* 60 and *NCLS* 119), and Duy Minh (*NCLS* 83), contributed to this discussion

66 *Lịch sử Việt Nam,* vol. 1 (Hanoi: Social Sciences, 1971), pp. 337–68.

67 "Việt Nam thống nhất trong quá trình đấu tranh cách mạng," *VSĐ* 9 (August 1955): 53.

68 BNCVSĐ, "Âm mưu cản bước tiến của lịch sử nhất định sẽ bị nghiến nát," *VSĐ* 19 (July 1956): 3.

69 Mona Ozouf has examined the power of commemorative events to repress the past in "The Festival in the French Revolution," in *Constructing the Past: Essays in Historical Methodology,* ed. Jacques LeGoff and Pierre Nora (Cambridge: Cambridge University Press, 1985), pp. 181–97.

70 *On Revolution* (New York: Viking Press, 1965): 13–52.

71 "Vấn đề ruộng đất trong Cách mạng Việt Nam," *VSĐ* 2 (n.d.): 9–31.

72 BNCVSĐ, "Cách mạng tháng Tám và vấn đề ruộng đất," *VSĐ* 2 (n.d.): 3–8.

73 BNCVSĐ, "Quan hệ Việt-Xô trong quá trình cách mạng," *VSĐ* 16 (April 1956): 5–6.

74 The Vietnamese title was given as *Điều tra về chân tướng của nước Nga. VSĐ* 16: 2.

75 *VSĐ* 16: 3.

76 This narrative obscures the fact that the Soviet Union officially recognized the DRV only after the People's Republic of China did the same.

77 "chúng ta càng thấy rõ mối tình Việt-Xô là tình anh em ruột thịt cùng sống trong đại gia đình xã hội chủ nghĩa." *VSĐ* 16: 4–5.

78 Phan Bội Châu, *Phan Bội Châu niên biểu*, trans. Vinh Sinh and Nicholas Wicken-den, *Overturned Chariot: The Autobiography of Phan-Bội-Châu* (Honolulu: University of Hawaiʻi Press, 1999), pp. 245–46.

79 "Nghị quyết Hội nghị Trung ương lần thứ tám với cuộc Cách mạng tháng Tám," *VSĐ* 30 (July 1957): 1–4.

80 "Cách mạng tháng Mười và Cách mạng Việt Nam," *VSĐ* 33 (October 1957): 1–18.

81 A number of writers have effectively explored this theme. See Marr, *Tradition on Trial;* Hue-Tam Ho Tai, *Radicalism;* and Shawn McHale, "Printing, Power, and the Transformation of Vietnamese Culture, 1920–1945" (Ph.D. dissertation, Cornell University, 1995).

82 In January 1960, the entire issue of *NCLS* was devoted to commemorative reflections on the ICP. The timing was determined, in part, by the fact that the ICP was founded in 1930 and, less directly, to a resolution of the Second Party Congress (convened in 1951). The timing was also linked to global events, as the Institute of History in Hanoi attributed its own commemorative gestures to the Fifth International Congress on the History of Workers' Movements and Communism, held in Bucharest (August 25–September 2, 1959). Nguyễn Hồng Phong, "Sự thành lập Đảng Cộng sản Đông Dương là một bước vĩ đại trong lịch sử cách mạng cận đại Việt Nam," *NCLS* 10 (January 1960): 3, 91.

83 *VSĐ* 33: 3.

84 The names of these organizations in Vietnamese are, respectively, Đông Dương Cộng sản Đảng, An Nam Cộng sản liên đoàn, Đảng Cộng sản Việt Nam, Đông Dương Cộng sản Đảng liên đoàn, Tân Việt Cách mạng Đảng, and Đảng Cộng sản Đông Dương. Huỳnh Kim Khánh, *Vietnamese Communism, 1925–1945* (Ithaca: Cornell University Press, 1982), pp. 63, 113–29; Hue-Tam Ho Tai, *Radicalism,* pp. 224–32; David Marr, *Vietnam 1945: The Quest for Power* (Berkeley: University of California Press, 1995).

85 VSH, "Vấn đề Đảng sử," *NCLS* 10 (January 1960): 1.

86 *NCLS* 10: 3–4.

87 *NCLS* 10: 27.

88 The (other) Indochinese Communist Party, the Federated Indochinese Communist Party, and the Annamese Communist Federation were among the contenders he mentioned. *NCLS* 10: 20, 27.

89 Chiến, "Đi sâu vào Cách mạng Việt Nam," *VSĐ* 1 (June 1954): 8–13. Pen names of writers who were affiliated with the Research Committee are provided in Văn Tạo and Nguyễn Quang Ân, eds., *Ban Văn Sử Địa, 1953–1959* (Hanoi: Social Sciences and Nhân Văn Quốc Gia, 1993), but no references to "Chiến" appear.

90 Although Chiến did not elaborate on who specifically was included in the "gang of Trotskyists," his readers would have understood whom he had in mind: Hồ Hữu Tường, Huỳnh Văn Phương, Lương Đức Thiệp, Nguyễn An Ninh, Phan Văn Hùm, Tạ Thu Thâu, and others who were associated with such publications as *Le Nhà quê, La Vérité, La Lutte,* and *La Cloche fêlée*—in other words, revolutionaries from the South. A number of writers offer detailed descriptions of these tensions: Marr, " 'Stalinists' and 'Trotskyists,' " in *Tradition on Trial,* pp.

387–400; Huỳnh Kim Khánh, "The Internationalist Wilderness," in *Vietnamese Communism,* pp. 198–231; Hue-Tam Ho Tai, "The Rise of Trotskyism," in *Radicalism,* pp. 232–43; Nguyễn Q. Thắng and Nguyễn Bá Thế, *Từ điển Nhân vật lịch sử Việt Nam;* and Ngo Van, *Viêt-Nam 1920–1945: Révolution et contre-révolution sous la domination coloniale,* 2nd ed. (Paris: L'Insomniaque, 1996).

91 The Viet Minh Front, as I have noted, was created in 1941 by the party's Central Committee as a mechanism for uniting all Vietnamese, regardless of class, in the common struggle against France and Japan. With the party's official dissolution in 1945, however, its ability to control the Viet Minh diminished. The appearance of a second front organization, Liên Việt, in May 1946 seems to have further complicated the chain of revolutionary command. In any case, the new front absorbed what was left of the Viet Minh in March 1951. BNCVSĐ, "Cách mạng tháng Tám và công tác nghiên cứu lịch sử," *VSĐ* 43 (August 1958): 1–2.

92 "Quá trình thành lập Mặt trận Việt Minh và thắng lợi của Mặt trận trong Cách mạng tháng Tám," *VSĐ* 43 (August 1958): 3.

93 "Vài nét về quá trình xây dựng và phát triển của Nhà nước cách mạng Việt Nam," *VSĐ* 48 (January 1959): 11–27.

94 "Cách mạng tháng Tám và kháng chiến là một cuộc cách mạng quần chúng dưới sử lãnh đạo của Đảng," *VSĐ* 44 (September 1958): 1–5.

95 He applied the Maoist three-stage model this way: the first phase (1858–1919) was led by the feudalists; the second phase (1918–1930) was led by the petit bourgeoisie; and the third phase (1930–1945) was led by the proletariat. Explaining the Leninist two-stage model of revolution, Trần Huy Liệu merely noted that the first phase was led by feudalists against the French and that the second stage pitched the proletariat against the imperialists and feudalists. *VSĐ* 2: 9–31.

96 In Vietnamese, these are Đông Du, Đông Kinh nghĩa thục, and Duy Tân. "Phong trào cách mạng trong giai đoạn thứ hai từ sau đại chiến I đến năm 1930 do giai cấp nào lãnh đạo?" *VSĐ* 3 (October 1954): 22–26.

97 Trường Chinh, "The Resistance Will Win," in *Primer for Revolt: The Communist Takeover of Viet-Nam* (New York: Frederick A. Praeger, 1963), pp. 81–213. Văn Tạo, *VSĐ* 48: 11–27.

98 "Xung quanh cái chết của Hoàng Diệu và việc thất thủ thành Hà Nội năm 1882," *VSĐ* 16 (April 1956): 25–37.

99 "Mấy nét đặc biệt về Cách mạng tháng Tám," *VSĐ* 20 (August 1956): 1–6. Emphasis added.

100 Greg Lockhart, *Nation in Arms: The Origins of the People's Army of Vietnam* (Sydney: Allen and Unwin, 1989), pp. 252–63. The full text of the law was published as *Agrarian Reform Law* (Hanoi: FLPH, 1955).

101 Although this detail and the following quotation come from Christine White, "Agrarian Reform and National Liberation in the Vietnamese Revolution 1920–1957" (Ph.D. dissertation, Cornell University, 1981), p. 224, she is not likely to agree with the interpretation presented here.

102 Edwin Moise, *Land Reform in China and North Vietnam* (Chapel Hill: University of North Carolina Press, 1983), p. 178.

103 White, "Agrarian Reform," pp. 264–78.

104 Ibid., pp. 283–91.

105 The text of the letter appeared in Ho Chi Minh's *Selected Works*, vol. 4 (Hanoi: FLPH, 1960), pp. 190–93.

106 White, "Agrarian Reform," p. 406a.

107 *Lịch sử tám mươi năm chống Pháp*, 3 vols. (Hanoi: Văn Sử Địa and Viện Sử Học, 1957–1961).

108 His memoirs "Phong trào cách mạng qua văn thơ," published in *VSĐ* 27–47 and in *NCLS* 1–29, opened with the fall of Hanoi. The diaries on which his memoirs are based were written in Chinese, so when Trần Huy Liệu quoted himself he had to translate his own words into *quốc ngữ*, the romanized script. In this sense Trần Huy Liệu was not anomalous; other revolutionaries, including Ho Chi Minh, also began their careers writing in Chinese and concluded them writing in *quốc ngữ*.

109 "Phấn đấu để trở nên một đảng viên cộng sản (hồi ký)," *NCLS* 10 (January 1960): 77–90. In other contexts, as well, Trần Huy Liệu undermined the party's monopoly of revolutionary history. "The Tân Việt Party," he remarked in his memoirs, "was different from the Revolutionary Youth Party, but it was equally red." *VSĐ* 29 (June 1957): 1–18.

110 See Hue-Tam Ho Tai's illuminating essay on this theme, "Monumental Ambiguity: The State of Commemoration of Hồ Chí Minh," in *Essays into Vietnamese Pasts* ed. K. W. Taylor and John K. Whitmore (Ithaca: Cornell University Southeast Asia Program, 1995), pp. 272–88.

111 For English-speaking readers, this view has been most succinctly expressed in Thomas Hodgkin, *Vietnam: The Revolutionary Path* (New York: St. Martin's Press, 1983). Because Hodgkin based this work on interviews he conducted in January to April 1974 at the Institute of History, it can reasonably be regarded as a synthesis of official historiography as it stood at that time.

112 This paragraph sums up a short and quirky but important essay by Ngo Vinh Long, "Rewriting Vietnamese History," *Journal of Contemporary Asia* 10, no. 3 (1980): 286–92.

113 Trần Huy Liệu et al., *Lịch sử thủ đô Hà Nội* (hereafter *LSTĐ*) (Hanoi: Sử Học, 1960). Articles leading up to the commemorative volume were written by Hoa Bằng (*NCLS* 14), Trần Quốc Vượng (*NCLS* 15 and 17), and Trần Huy Liệu (*NCLS* 19).

114 These volumes, which provided more details on the prehistory of the region around Hanoi, include Hoàng Đạo Thúy, *Phố phường Hà Nội xưa* (1974) and *Người và cảnh Hà Nội* (1982); Trần Quốc Vượng and Vũ Tuấn Sán, *Hà Nội nghìn xưa* (1975); *Vietnamese Studies* 48 (1977); Nguyễn Vinh Phúc and Trần Huy Bá, *Đường phố Hà Nội* (1979); and *Địa chí văn hóa dân gian Thăng Long—Đông Đô—Hà Nội* (1991).

115 Nguyễn Lương Bích, "Lời nói đầu," *LSTĐ*, pp. 5–9.

116 Cited in Lê Thành Khôi, *Histoire du Việt Nam des origines à 1858* (Paris: Sudestasie, 1981), p. 145.

117 Trần Quốc Vượng and Nguyễn Vĩnh Long argued that Hanoi became a separate district in the fifth century, during the Liu Song dynasty (Lưu Tống in Vietnamese). "Hanoi: De la préhistoire au 19e siècle," *Études vietnamiennes* 48 (1977): 16.

118 See Keith W. Taylor, "Authority and Legitimacy in Eleventh-Century Vietnam," *The Vietnam Forum* (hereafter *VNF*), 12 (1988): 20–59, and "Surface Orientations in Vietnam: Beyond Histories of Nation and Region," *Journal of Asian Studies* 59, no 4 (1988): 949–78.

119 *LSTĐ*, p. 8. See also BNCVSĐ, "Lịch sử thủ đô và lịch sử dân tộc," *VSĐ* 4 (January 1955): 1–5 for an earlier manifestation of this view.

120 Nguyễn Lương Bích, "Thủ đô Hà Nội từ đầu thế kỷ XI tới đầu thế kỷ XV," *LSTĐ*, pp. 13–56.

121 *LSTĐ*, pp. 16–17.

122 *LSTĐ*, p. 21.

123 *LSTĐ*, p. 56.

124 Nguyễn Lương Bích, "Thủ đô Hà Nội từ đầu thế kỷ XV đến cuối thế kỷ XIX," *LSTĐ*, pp. 57–91.

125 *LSTĐ*, pp. 71–75.

126 Nguyễn Phước Tương, "Cảng thị Hội An: Trung tâm trung chuyển của con đường tơ lụa và gốm sứ quốc tế xuyên đại dương trong thế kỷ XVI-XVIII," *Văn hóa Hội An* 2 (1998): 15–23.

127 He specifically mentions 1663, 1695, 1717, 1754, and 1773. *LSTĐ*, p. 76.

128 *LSTĐ*, pp. 80–86.

129 Mai Hanh, "Thực dân Pháp đánh chiếm Hà Nội và xây dựng thành phố thuộc địa," *LSTĐ*, pp. 93–122, and "Tình hình văn hóa, kinh tế, chính trị và các phong trào cách mạng ở Hà Nội," *LSTĐ*, pp. 123–210.

130 *LSTĐ*, p. 93.

131 *LSTĐ*, p. 106.

132 *LSTĐ*, pp. 112–13.

133 *LSTĐ*, p. 124.

134 *Hanoi pendant la période héroique* (Paris: P. Geuthner, 1929). There is a rich literature on colonial urbanism. Two impressive collections of essays are Nezar AlSayyad, ed. *Forms of Dominance: On the Architecture and Urbanism of the Colonial Enterprise* (Aldershot, Eng.: Avebury, 1992), and Robert Ross and Gerard J. Telkamp, eds. *Colonial Cities* (Dordrecht, Netherlands: Leiden University Press, 1985). Gwendolyn Wright offers some illuminating comments on this topic in "Indochina: The Folly of Grandeur," in *The Politics of Design in French Colonial Urbanism* (Chicago: University of Chicago Press, 1991), pp. 161–233.

135 Nguyễn Việt, "Hà Nội trong cách mạng tháng Tám và trong kháng chiến toàn quốc," *LSTĐ*, pp. 213–64; Phan Gia Bền, "Hà Nội giải phóng và xây dựng kinh tế xã hội chủ nghĩa," *LSTĐ*, pp. 265–95; Võ Văn Nhung, "Hà Nội tiến mạnh lên chủ nghĩa xã hội về các mặt chính trị, văn hóa, xã hội," *LSTĐ*, pp. 296–332; and Mai Hanh, "Thủ đô Hà Nội trong tương lai," *LSTĐ*, pp. 333–35.

136 In terms of contemporary scholarship (and the work of Pierre Nora, most no-

tably) these details clearly resonate with the literature linked to landscape and memory.

137 Việt Nam Cách mạnh đồng minh hội, or Việt cách. Nguyễn Việt maintains that while these groups were in China they received support from the French and Japanese. Although this claim may be empirically valid, I have seen no other evidence to support it.

138 *LSTĐ*, p. 227.

139 *LSTĐ*, p. 252.

140 *LSTĐ*, p. 265.

141 *LSTĐ*, pp. 266–67. Incidentally, the "Trại" were not included in Decision 121, issued March 2, 1979, which identified the fifty-four ethnic groups in Vietnam. Apparently they were reclassified as a subgroup of the Zao.

142 *LSTĐ*, p. 269.

143 *LSTĐ*, pp. 278–95.

144 Because these details of postcolonial bureaucracy are not well known, I provide here the original Vietnamese names: Uỷ ban hành chính Hà Nội, Đội công tác hành chính, Ban cán sự hành chính quận, Ban đại diện hành chính khu phố, Ban đại biểu dân phố, Ban bảo về dân phố, Hội đồng nhân dân thành phố, Ban đại diện Uỷ ban quân chính, Uỷ ban hành chính quận, Uỷ ban hành chính xã, Tổng liên đoàn lao động, Liên hiệp công đoàn Hà Nội, Liên hiệp thanh niên, Liên hiệp phụ nữ, Liên hiệp công thương, Mặt trận Tổ quốc, Mặt trận Tổ quốc trung ương, and Ban chấp hành Đoàn Thanh niên lao động Việt Nam của Hà Nội. *LSTĐ*, pp. 296–99.

145 *LSTĐ*, p. 321.

146 *NCLS* 19: 2.

147 *Nhân cách phụ nữ Việt Nam hiện đại* (Hanoi: Mai Linh, 1943). I would like to thank Shawn McHale for bringing this work to my attention.

148 *Behind the Lines—Hanoi* (New York: Harper and Row, 1967), p. 108.

149 John B. Thompson, "Introduction," in Claude Lefort, *The Political Forms of Modern Society: Bureaucracy, Democracy, Totalitarianism* (Boston: MIT Press, 1986), p. 6.

150 BNCVSĐ, *VSĐ* 4: 3.

EPILOGUE

1 Lê Văn Kỳ, "Tư tưởng 'dân' của Nguyễn Trãi với chúng ta," *NCLS* 81 (December 1965): 19.

2 BNCVSĐ, "Khoa học lịch sử và công tác cách mạng," *VSĐ* 1 (June 1964): 5; "Trách nhiệm của chúng ta," *VSĐ* 3 (October 1954): 5.

3 "Vấn đề viết văn học sử Việt Nam," *VSĐ* 17 (May 1956): 5–17. See also Minh Tranh, "Sử học phải phục vụ cách mạng như thế nào?" *NCLS* 3 (May 1959): 1–8.

Selected Bibliography

AlSayyad, Nezar, ed. *Forms of Dominance: On the Architecture and Urbanism of the Colonial Enterprise.* Aldershot, Eng.: Avebury, 1992.

Anderson, Benedict. *Imagined Communities.* Rev. ed. 1983; London: Verso, 1991.

Anderson, Perry. "The Asiatic Mode of Production." In *Lineages of the Absolutist State* (London: Verso, 1974). 462–549.

An-đơ-rê-ép (N. D. Anduriev). "Vấn đề bình thường hóa cách phát âm tiếng Việt Nam." *VSĐ* 18 (June 1956): 29–37.

An Khê. "Quốc tuý và Văn minh." *Tạp chí Nam phong* 78 (December 1932): 453–58.

An Thu. "The Zao Are Coming Down to the Lowlands." *VNS* 15 (1968): 175–87.

Arendt, Hannah. *On Revolution.* New York: Viking, 1965.

Arvon, Henri. *Marxist Esthetics.* Trans. Helen Lane. Ithaca: Cornell University Press, 1973.

Aymonier, Émile. "L'Enseignement en Indo-Chine." *Le Temps* 17 October (1889): 1.

Bạch Hào. "Cuộc khởi nghĩa của nông dân Tây Sơn qua một ít bức thư của người ngoại quốc đã ở Việt Nam đương thời." *VSĐ* 14 (February 1956): 69–74.

Bakhtin, Mikhail. *The Dialogic Imagination.* Ed. Michael Holquist. Trans. Caryl Emerson and Michael Holquist. Austin: University of Texas Press, 1981.

Ban biên tập. "Tổng kết cuộc trưng cầu ý kiến bạn đọc của *Tập san Nghiên cứu lịch sử.*" *NCLS* 25 (April 1961): 1–13.

"Bản dự thảo điều lệ Hội những người công tác sử học Việt Nam." *NCLS* 79 (October 1965): 63.

Ban nghiên cứu Văn Sử Địa (BNCVSĐ). "Âm mưu cản bước tiến của lịch sử nhất định sẽ bị nghiền nát." *VSĐ* 19 (July 1956): 1–4.

———. "Cách mạng tháng Tám và công tác nghiên cứu lịch sử." *VSĐ* 43 (August 1958): 1–2.

———. "Cách mạng tháng Tám và vấn đề ruộng đất." *VSĐ* 2 (n.d.): 3–8.

———. "Đảng Lao động Việt Nam, Đảng khoa học." *VSĐ* 15 (March 1956): 1–9.

———. "Để chuẩn bị tiến lên một giai đoạn mới—Tổng quết công tác Ban nghiên cứu Văn Sử Địa từ ngày thành lập đến nay." *VSĐ* 48 (January 1959): 1–10.

———. "Hoan nghênh nghị quyết của Quốc hội về việc thành lập Uỷ ban Khoa học." *VSĐ* 41 (June 1958): 1–6 and *VSĐ* 48 (January 1959): 1–10.

———. "Hồ Chủ tịch và thời đại chúng ta." *VSĐ* 7 (May–June 1955): 1–4.

———. "Khoa học lịch sử và công tác cách mạng." *VSĐ* 1 (June 1954): 2–7.

———. "Lịch sử thủ đô và lịch sử dân tộc." *VSĐ* 4 (January 1955): 1–5.

———. "Quan hệ Việt-Xô trong quá trình cách mạng." *VSĐ* 16 (April 1956): 1–6.

———. "Trách nhiệm của chúng ta." *VSĐ* 3 (October 1954): 3–5.

———. "Việt Nam là một dân tộc đang mạnh mẽ tiến lên." *VSĐ* 8 (July 1955): 1–5.

———. "Việt Nam là một khối thống nhất từ Bắc đến Nam." *VSĐ* 5 (February 1955): 1–4.

Ban trù bị hội nghị phương pháp luận sử học. "Những gợi ý về một số chuyên đề trong hội nghị phương pháp luận sử học." *NCLS* 83 (February 1966): 4–17.

Bartosek, Karel. "Czechoslovakia: The State of Historiography." *JCH* 2 (January 1967): 143–55.

Berman, Marshall. *Adventures in Marxism.* London: Verso, 1999.

Bế Viết Đẳng. "The Process of Resettlement of Nomadic People for Sedentary Farming in Mountainous Regions." *VNSS* 1–2 (1987): 76–85.

———. "The Zao in Vietnam." *VNS* 40 (1973): 40–83.

Black, Cyril, ed. *Rewriting Russian History.* 2nd ed. 1956; New York: Vintage Books, 1962.

Blanchot, Maurice. "La Parole quotidienne." In *L'Entretien infini.* Paris: Gallimard, 1969. 355–66.

Boudarel, Georges. *Cent fleurs écloses dan la nuit du Vietnam: Communisme et dissidence, 1954–1956.* Paris: Éditions Jacques Bertoin, 1991.

———. "Intellectual Dissidence in the 1950s: The Nhân văn—Giai phẩm Affair." *VNF* 13 (1990): 154–74.

Boudarel, Georges et al., eds. *La Bureaucratie au Vietnam.* Paris: L'Harmattan, 1983.

Bourde, Paul. "L'Enseignement en Indo-chine." *Le Temps* 17 October (1889): 1–2.

———. "Les Écoles du Tonkin," *Les Temps* 2 October (1889): 2.

Brenier, Henri. "L'Indochine économique." In *Un Empire colonial français: L'Indochine,* ed. Georges Maspero. Vol. 2. Paris: G. Van Oest, 1930. 137–216.

Brownlee, John B., ed. *History in the Service of the Japanese Nation.* Toronto: University of Toronto–York University Joint Centre on Modern East Asia, 1983.

Bùi Đình Thanh. *Hai mươi năm nước Việt Nam Dân chủ Cộng hoà.* Hanoi: Sử Học, 1965.

———. "Một số kinh nghiệm qua các bản tham luận tại hội nghị chuyên đề lịch sử địa phương." *NCLS* 41 (August 1962): 3–7.

———. "Từ chương trình mười điểm đến cương lĩnh chính trị của Mặt trận dân tộc giải phóng miền Nam Việt Nam." *NCLS* 116 (November 1968): 24–38.

Bùi Quang Tung and Nguyễn Hương, trans. *Le Đại Việt et ses voisins d'après le "Đại Việt sử ký toàn thư."* Annotated by Nguyễn Thế Anh. Paris: L'Harmattan, 1990.

Cadière, Léopold. *Croyances and pratiques religieuses des Annamites.* Hanoi: Imprimerie d'Extrême-Orient, 3 vols., 1944–1957.

Cẩm Giang. "Bức thư mở cẩm." *NCLS* 7 (September 1959): 82–87.

Cao Văn Biền. "Hoạt động của Viện các dân tộc châu Á của Liên Xô." *NCLS* 31 (October 1961): 66.

———. "Hội nghị Quốc tế lần thứ sáu của các nhà dân tộc học và nhân loại học." *NCLS* 27 (June 1961): 73-74.

Cao Văn Lượng. "Vấn đề liên minh công nông trong cuộc cách mạng dân tộc dân chủ ở miền Nam Việt Nam hiện nay." *NCLS* 64 (July 1964): 23-28.

Cao Xuân Phổ. "Góp ý kiến về quyển sách *Giáo khoa Lịch sử lớp 9 phổ thông tập I*." *NCLS* 54 (September 1963): 48-52.

Cazenave, Eugène. "Les Travaux publics." In *Un Empire colonial français: L'Indochine*, ed. Georges Maspero. Vol. 2. Paris: G. Van Oest, 1930. 217-41.

Certeau, Michel de. *The Writing of History*. Trans. Tom Conley. New York: Columbia University Press, 1988.

Chambers, Ross. *Room for Maneuver: Reading (the) Oppositional (in) Narrative*. Chicago: University of Chicago Press, 1991.

Chân Thành. "Truyện thần thoại Mường có thể chứng minh sự tồn tại chế độ chiếm hữu nô lệ trong lịch sử Việt Nam không?" *VSĐ* 36 (January 1958): 75-79.

Chassigneux, E. "Géographie de l'Indochine." In *Un Empire colonial français: L'Indochine*, ed. Georges Maspero. Vol. 1. Paris: G. Van Oest, 1929. 4-52.

Chernorutskaya, L. I., ed. *Three Hundred Years of Oriental Studies in Russia*. Trans. A. I. Cuprin et al. Moscow: Institute of Oriental Studies, 1997.

Chesneaux, Jean. *The Vietnamese Nation: Contribution to a History*. Trans. Malcolm Salmon. Sydney: Current Books, 1966.

Chiêm Tế. "Cách mạng tháng Tám là một bộ phận của cách mạng thế giới." *NCLS* 18 (September 1960): 21-30.

———. "Thử tìm những đặc điểm phát triển lịch sử của xã hội phong kiến Việt Nam." *NCLS* 5 (July 1959): 6-19.

———. "Vài nét về tư tưởng và hoạt động của Hồ Chủ tịch liên quan tới sự nghiệp giải phóng của các dân tộc bị áp bức." *NCLS* 132 (May-June 1970): 33-47.

Chiến. "Đi sâu vào Cách mạng Việt Nam." *VSĐ* 1 (June 1954): 8-13.

Chomsky, Noam. *Intellectuals and the State*. Baarn, Netherlands: Wereldvenster, 1978.

Chu Lương Tiêu. "Tính chất chống phong kiến của chiến tranh nông dân." *NCLS* 78 (September 1965): 56-59.

Chương Dương. "Kỷ niệm 1030 năm chiến thắng Bạch Đằng lần thứ nhất." *NCLS* 125 (August 1969): 60-63.

Chu Thiên. "Nhân dịp kỷ niệm 180 năm ngày mất của Lê Quý Đôn (1726-1783), đính chính một số chú thích sai về lịch sử trong một bài thơ hoài cổ của ông: 'Cổ lộng thành.'" *NCLS* 59 (February 1964): 50-52.

Chu Văn Tấn. *Reminiscences on the Army for National Salvation*. Trans. Mai Elliot. Ithaca: Cornell University Southeast Asia Program, 1974.

Clifford, James. *The Predicament of Culture*. Cambridge: Harvard University Press, 1988.

Communist Party of Vietnam (CPVN). *The Fourth National Congress*. Hanoi: FLPH, 1977.

———. *Political Report of the Fifth National Congress*. Hanoi: FLPH, 1982.

Connor, Walker. *The National Question in Marxist-Leninist Theory and Strategy*. Princeton: Princeton University Press, 1984.

Constitution of the Democratic Republic of Vietnam. Hanoi: FLPH, 1960.

Constitution of the Socialist Republic of Vietnam. Hanoi: FLPH, 1981.

Cowan, C. D. and Oliver Wolters, eds. *Southeast Asian History and Historiography*. Ithaca: Cornell University Press, 1976.

"Cuộc tọa đàm về vấn đề chế độ chiếm hữu nô lệ ở Việt Nam." *NCLS* 16 (July 1960): 4–6.

"Đại hội Đảng Cộng sản Liên Xô lần thứ XX và vấn đề nghiên cứu lịch sử Đảng." *VSĐ* 22 (October 1956): 31–44.

Đan Đức Lợi. "Vấn đề đặt chữ cho các dân tộc chưa có văn tự." *VSĐ* 29 (June 1957): 81–83.

Đặng Đức Siêu et al. *Việt Nam: Di tích và thắng cảnh*. Danang: Danang Press, 1991.

Đặng Nghiêm Vạn. "Dien Bien Phu: Some Ethnohistorical Data." *VNS* 43 (1973): 7–23.

———. "The Khmu in Vietnam." *VNS* 36 (1973): 62–140.

———. "An Outline of the Thai in Vietnam." *VNS* 32 (1972): 143–96.

———. "Sơ bộ bàn về quá trình hình thành các nhóm dân tộc Tày Thái ở Việt Nam. Mối quan hệ với các nhóm ở Nam Trung Quốc và Đông Dương." *NCLS* 108 (March 1962): 24–37.

———. "Sơ lược về sự thiên di của các bộ tộc Thái vào Tây Bắc Việt Nam." *NCLS* 78 (September 1965): 40–48.

Đặng Nghiêm Vạn, Chu Thái Sơn, and Lưu Hùng. *Ethnic Minorities in Vietnam*. Hanoi: The Gioi, 1993.

Đặng Việt Thanh. "Cách mạng tháng Tám và cách mạng văn hóa." *NCLS* 18 (September 1960): 31–37.

———. "Giai cấp công nhân Việt Nam hình thành từ bao giờ?" *NCLS* 6 (August 1959): 11–22.

"Danh mục các thành phần dân tộc Việt Nam." *DTH* 1 (1980): 78–83.

Daniels, Glyn. *The Idea of Prehistory*. Baltimore: Penguin Books, 1964.

Đào Duy Anh. "Tìm các đèo Khâu Cấp và Nội Bàng trên đường dụng binh của Trần Hưng Đạo." *NCLS* 66 (September 1964): 36–38.

———. "Văn hóa Đông Sơn hay văn hóa Lạc Việt?" *VSĐ* 1 (June 1954): 14–29.

Đào Tử Khải. "Những bước phát triển lớn của thị tộc Hồng Bàng có hay không và nhân vật Hùng vương trong lịch sử dân tộc chúng ta." *NCLS* 101 (August 1967): 41–45.

Đào Tứ Minh. "Một vài ý kiến về vấn đề phiên âm và giải thích thơ *Quốc âm* của nhà đại văn hào Nguyễn Trãi." *VSĐ* 36 (January 1958): 80–90.

Đào Tùng. "Nhân dịp kỷ niệm 50 năm tác phẩm thiên tài của Lê-nin: Giá trị lớn của tác phẩm thiên tài: *Chủ nghĩa duy vật và chủ nghĩa phê phán kinh nghiệm* của Lê-nin đối với cuộc đấu tranh tư tưởng hiện nay." *NCLS* 8 (October 1959): 41–57.

Davis, Natalie Zemon, and Randolph Starn, eds. *Representations* 26 (Spring 1989).

"Đề án thành lập Hội những người công tác sử học Việt Nam." *NCLS* 79 (October 1965): 1.

DeFrancis, John. *Colonialism and Language Policy in Vietnam*. New York: Mouton, 1977.

Điệp Đình Hoa. "Vài ý kiến về bài 'Xã hội nước Văn Lang và xã hội nước Âu Lạc' (bàn với ông Văn Tân)." *NCLS* 27 (June 1961): 35–48.

Đinh Gia Khánh. "The Cultural, Social, and Political Significance of the Study of Folklore." *VNSS* 2 (1984): 89–97.

Dirlik, Arif. *Revolution and History: The Origins of Marxist Historiography in China, 1919–1937.* Berkeley: University of California Press, 1978.

Đỗ Thiện. "Bàn thêm về lịch sử Lai Châu." *NCLS* 62 (May 1964): 60–63.

———. "Một vài nét về lịch sử tỉnh Lai Châu (khu tự trị Tây Bắc) chống thực dân Pháp đầu thế kỷ XX." *NCLS* 45 (December 1962): 33–37.

Douglas, Mary. *Purity and Danger*. New York: Praeger, 1966.

Doumer, Paul. *Situation de l'Indochine*. Hanoi: F. N. Schneider, 1902.

Đỗ Xuân Trạch. "Một vài ý kiến về những nhận định của ông Văn Tân đối với vấn đề tô-tem của người Việt nguyên thủy." *NCLS* 7 (September 1959): 94–97.

Duiker, William J. *The Comintern and Vietnamese Communism*. Athens: Ohio University Center for International Studies, 1975.

———. *The Communist Road to Power in Vietnam*. 2nd ed. 1981; Boulder: Westview Press, 1996.

———. "Hanoi Scrutinizes the Past: The Marxist Evaluation of Phan Boi Chau and Phan Chu Trinh." *Southeast Asia* 1, no. 3 (1970): 243–54.

———. *Vietnam: Revolution in Transition*. 2nd ed. Boulder: Westview Press, 1995.

Dunn, Stephen. *The Rise and Fall of the Asiatic Mode of Production*. London: Routledge and Kegan Paul, 1982.

Dương Minh. "Đồng bào theo Phật giáo ở miền Nam đang tiếp tục truyền thống anh dũng, bất khuất của dân tộc." *NCLS* 53 (August 1963): 1.

———. "Nhân dịp kỷ niệm hai Bà: Thử xét xem nguyên nhân gì khiến cuộc kháng chiến của Trưng Trắc và Trưng Nhị phải thất bại." *NCLS* 36 (March 1962): 3–6.

———. "Thử tìm hiểu phương pháp sưu tầm tài liệu của Lê Quý Đôn." *NCLS* 61 (April 1964): 2–5.

Dương Quảng Hàm. *Leçons d'histoire d'Annam*. Hanoi: Le Van Tan, 1936.

Dương Trung Quốc. *Vietnam: Những sự kiện lịch sử 1958–1945, tập IV (1936–1945)*. Hanoi: Social Sciences, 1989.

Durand, Maurice. *Imagerie populaire vietnamienne*. Paris: École Française d'Extrême-Orient, 1960.

Durand, Maurice, and Nguyen Tran Huan. *An Introduction to Vietnamese Literature*. Trans. D. M. Hawke. New York: Columbia University Press, 1985.

Duy Minh. "Vai trò của khởi nghĩa nông dân trong quá trình phát triển của dân tộc." *NCLS* 81 (December 1965): 3–7.

———. "Vài ý kiến về cuốn *Tây Sơn thủy mạt khảo* của Đào Nguyên Phổ." *NCLS* 83 (February 1966): 45–48.

Economic Restoration and Cultural Development in the DRV. Hanoi: FLPH, 1958.

Eliade, Mircea. *The Myth of the Eternal Return*. Trans. Willard Trask. Princeton: Princeton University Press, 1974.

————. *Images and Symbols.* Trans. Philip Mairet. New York: Sheed and Ward, 1961.

Elias, Norbert. *Time: An Essay.* Oxford: Blackwell, 1992.

Enteen, George M. "Soviet Historians Review Their Own Past: The Rehabilitation of M. N. Pokrovsky." *Soviet Studies* 20, no. 3 (January 1969): 306–20.

————. *The Soviet Scholar-Bureaucrat.* University Park: Pennsylvania State University Press, 1978.

Evans, Grant. "Central Highlanders of Vietnam." In *Indigenous Peoples of Asia,* ed. R. H. Barnes, Andrew Gray, and Benedict Kingsbury. Ann Arbor: Association for Asian Studies, 1995. 247–71.

Fairbank, John King, and Merle Goldman. *China: A New History.* Cambridge: Harvard University Press, 1998.

Fanon, Frantz. *Studies in a Dying Colonialism.* Trans. H. Chevalier. Harmondsworth: Penguin, 1970.

Feuerwerker, Albert, and S. Cheng. *Chinese Communist Studies of Modern Chinese History.* Cambridge: Harvard University East Asia Research Center, 1970.

Foucault, Michel. *The Order of Things.* New York: Random House, 1970.

Engels, Friedrich. *Origin of the Family, Private Property and the State in the Light of the Researches of Lewis H. Morgan.* New York: International Publishers, 1942.

Gaspardone, Émile. "Bibliographie annamite." *BEFED* 34, Part 1 (1934): 1–152.

————. "Matériaux pour servir à l'histoire d'Annam." *BEFED* 29:1 (1929): 63–106.

Ginzburg, Carlo. *The Cheese and the Worms: The Cosmos of a Sixteenth-Century Miller.* Trans. John Tedeschi and Anne Tedeschi. Baltimore: Johns Hopkins University Press, 1980.

Gluck, Carol. *Japan's Modern Myths.* Princeton: Princeton University Press, 1985.

Goscha, Christopher E. *Thailand and the Southeast Asian Networks of the Vietnamese Revolution, 1885–1954.* Surrey, Eng.: Curzon, Nordic Institute of Asian Studies, 1999.

Gosselin, Charles. *L'Empire d'Annam.* Paris: Librairie Académique Didier, 1904.

Gouldner, Alvin. *The Two Marxisms: Contradictions and Anomalies in the Development of Theory.* New York: Seabury Press, 1980.

Greenblatt, Stephen. *Marvellous Possessions.* Chicago: University of Chicago Press, 1991.

Grenville, J. A. S. *A History of the World in the Twentieth Century.* Vol. 2. Cambridge: Harvard University Press, 1997.

Hải Khách. "Góp ý kiến về việc đào tạo và bồi dưỡng cán bộ sử học." *NCLS* 4 (June 1959): 7–11.

————. "Nhân dịp kỷ niệm 33 năm ngày thành lập Đảng: Đảng Cộng sản Việt Nam thành lập trong một bối cảnh lịch sử nào?" *NCLS* 47 (February 1963): 1–2.

Halbwachs, Maurice. *Collective Memory.* Trans. Francis J. Ditter Jr. and Vida Yazdi Ditter. New York: Harper Colophon, 1980.

Hà Văn Tấn. "Trở lại vấn đề tô-tem của người Việt." *NCLS* 4 (June 1959): 66–79.

Heine-Geldern, Robert. *Conceptions of State and Kingship in Southeast Asia.* Ithaca: Cornell University Southeast Asia Program, 1956.

Hémery, Daniel. *Hồ Chí Minh: De l'Indochine au Vietnam.* Paris: Gallimard, 1990.

Hickey, Gerald Cannon. *Free in the Forest: Ethnohistory of the Vietnamese Central Highlands, 1954–1976.* New Haven: Yale University Press, 1982.

————. "Some Aspects of Hill Tribe Life in South Vietnam." In *Southeast Asian Tribes, Minorities, and Nations,* ed. Peter Kunstadter. Vol. 1. Princeton: Princeton University Press, 1967. 745–70.

Higham, Charles. *The Bronze Age of Southeast Asia.* Cambridge: Cambridge University Press, 1996.

Hirst, Paul, and Barry Hindess. *Pre-Capitalist Modes of Production.* 1975; London: Routledge and Kegan Paul, 1979.

H. N. "The Neo-Colonialist Political Structure." *VNS* 31 (1971): 43–82.

Hoa Bằng. "Nhân đọc cuốn *Cổ tích và thắng cảnh Hà Nội,* thử tìm hiểu về thành Thăng Long qua Lý, Trần, Lê và các cửa ô ở cuối thế kỷ thứ XVIII." *NCLS* 14 (May 1960): 73–78.

————. "Tài liệu tham khảo về Văn miếu (Quốc tử giám) Hà Nội." *NCLS* 127 (October 1969): 46–56.

Hoài Giang. "Hồi thế kỷ XVIII trước khởi nghĩa Tây Sơn, tại sao các cuộc khởi nghĩa nông dân khác đều thất bại?" *NCLS* 75 (June 1965): 29–36.

Hoài Nam. "Cuộc khởi nghĩa năm kỷ dậu (1909) của dân tộc Mường ở Hòa Bình." *NCLS* 47 (February 1963): 55–59.

Hoài Phương. "Tìm hiểu nguồn gốc tư tưởng nhân dân của Nguyễn Trãi." *NCLS* 80 (November 1965): 2–5.

Hoàng Hưng. "Vấn đề Hùng vương và khảo cổ học." *NCLS* 108 (March 1968): 18–23.

Hoàng Linh, trans. "Tổng kết cuộc thảo luận vấn đề quy luật kinh tế cơ bản của chủ nghĩa phong kiến trong tạp chí *Vấn đề lịch sử* của Liên Xô." *VSĐ* 10 (September-October 1955): 36–42.

Hoàng Lương. "Bàn góp thêm vấn đề tô-tem của người Việt nguyên thủy." *NCLS* 5 (July 1959): 69–77.

Hoàng Thị Châu. "Tìm hiểu từ 'Phụ đạo' trong truyền thuyết về Hùng vương." *NCLS* 102 (September 1967): 22–28.

Hoang Thuy Nguyen. "Preventive Medicine in the DRVN: Problems and Achievements." *VNS* 34 (1973): 87–122.

Hoang Tu Dong. "Complementary Education for Adults." *VNS* 30 (1971): 23–46.

Hoang Xuan Han. "Calendars and Vietnamese Calendar." *VNS* 76 (1985): 69–81.

Hobsbawm, Eric J. *Nations and Nationalism since 1780: Programme, Myth, Reality.* Cambridge: Cambridge University Press, 1990.

Ho Chi Minh. *Selected Works.* 4 vols. Hanoi: FLPH, 1960.

————. *Thủ đô Hà Nội phải là thành phố gương mẫu.* Hanoi: Sự Thật, 1985.

Hodgkin, Thomas. *Vietnam: The Revolutionary Path.* New York: St. Martin's Press, 1983.

Hồng Hạnh. "Sự thống nhất về tính chất phản động của Phạm Quỳnh trong lĩnh vực chính trị và văn học." *VSĐ* 48 (January 1959): 60–81.

Hồng Quang. "Kỷ niệm sinh nhật Mác: Chủ nghĩa Mác—Lê-nin bất diệt." *NCLS* 38 (May 1962): 1–7.

————. "Nhân ngày kỷ niệm thành lập Đảng: Mấy ý nghĩ về vấn đề nghiên cứu ý nghĩa và tác dụng lịch sử của Xô-viết Nghệ Tĩnh." *NCLS* 35 (February 1962): 5–10.

————. "Những vấn đề của lịch sử cận hiện đại đã được đề xuất và nghiên cứu trong 7 năm qua." *NCLS* 21 (December 1960): 18–27.

Hồng Việt. "Học tập Mác—Ăng-ghen, Lê-nin trong công tác nghiên cứu lịch sử cổ đại." *NCLS* 106 (January 1968): 38–43.

Hoston, Germaine. *Marxism and the Crisis of Development in Prewar Japan.* Princeton: Princeton University Press, 1986.

Huard, Pierre. "The Blackening of Teeth in Eastern Asia and Indochina." In *Vietnamese Ethnographic Papers.* New Haven: Human Relations Area Files, 1953. n.p.

Huu Tho. "Storming the Hills." *VNS* 72 (1982): 149–58.

Hữu Thùy. "Nhân dịp kỷ niệm ngày quốc khánh Liên Xô: Vài nét về công tác sử học ở Liên Xô trong thời gian sáu năm qua (1956–1961)." *NCLS* 45 (December 1962): 55–61.

Huỳnh Kim Khánh. *Vietnamese Communism, 1925–1945.* Ithaca: Cornell University Press, 1982.

Huỳnh Sanh Thông. "Folk History in Vietnam." *VNF* 5 (winter–spring 1985): 66–80.

————. "Frogs and Toads as Vietnamese Peasants." *VNF* 1 (winter–spring 1983): 70–84.

Kahin, George. *Intervention: How America Became Involved in Vietnam.* New York: Anchor Books, 1987.

Keep, John L. H. *Moscow's Problems of History: A Select Critical Bibliography of the Soviet Journal "Voprosy Istorii," 1956–1985.* Toronto: University of Toronto Institute of Soviet and East European Studies, 1986.

Kelly, Michael. "Tran Duc Thao's Materialist Inversion." In *Modern French Marxism* (Baltimore: Johns Hopkins University Press, 1982). 160–64.

Kim Huân Cúc. "Sự phát triển dân tộc học ở Triều Tiên sau ngày giải phóng." Trans. Trương Như Ngạn. *NCLS* 5 (July 1959): 93–95.

Kohl, Philip L., and Clare Fawcett, eds. *Nationalism, Politics, and the Practice of Archaeology.* Cambridge: Cambridge University Press, 1995.

Koschmann, J. Victor, Oiwa Keibo, and Yamashita Shinji, eds. *International Perspectives on Yanagita Kunio and Japanese Folklore Studies.* Ithaca: Cornell University East Asia Program, 1985.

Kunstadter, Peter, ed. *Southeast Asian Tribes, Minorities, and Nations.* 2 vols. Princeton: Princeton University Press, 1967.

"Kỷ niệm Lê Văn Hưu, một sử gia đầu tiên của Việt Nam." *NCLS* 1 (March 1959): 3–7.

Lafont, Pierre-Bernard, ed. *Les Frontières du Vietnam.* Paris: L'Harmattan, 1989.

Lâm Hà. "Một số tài liệu về địa tô phong kiến trong lịch sử Việt Nam." *VSĐ* 15 (March 1956): 36–50.

Lâm Tâm. "Hôn nhân và gia đình của một số dân tộc thiểu số ở Việt Nam." *NCLS* 26 (May 1961): 66–77.

————. "Lịch sử di cư và tên gọi của người Mèo." *NCLS* 30 (September 1961): 54–58.

————. "A Survey of the Meo." *VNS* 36 (1973): 7–61.

———. "Tên gọi của người Mường và mối quan hệ giữa tên gọi của người Mường với người Việt." *NCLS* 32 (November 1962): 47–54.

Lã Văn Lô. "Ba mươi năm thực hiện chính sách dân tộc của Đảng." *NSLS* 10 (January 1960): 68–76.

———. "Brief Survey of the Tay Nung." *VNS* 41 (1973): 7–39.

———. "Bước đầu nghiên cứu nhà cửa của người Tày." *NCLS* 58 (January 1964): 54–62.

———. "Bước đầu nghiên cứu về chế độ xã hội ở vùng Tày, Nùng, Thái dưới thực dân Pháp." *NCLS* 68 (November 1964): 38–46.

———. "Bước đầu tìm hiểu về thơ ca cổ truyền của người Tày." *NCLS* 79 (October 1966): 41–51.

———. "Hai nhà dân tộc học Tiệp Khắc và Cộng hòa dân chủ Đức tại Việt Nam." *NCLS* 35 (February 1962): 58–59.

———. "Lịch sử xã hội nguyên thủy của người Tày qua truyền thuyết 'Pú lương quân.' " *NCLS* 65 (August 1964): 57–63.

———. "Mấy ý kiến về hướng nghiên cứu dân tộc học." *NCLS* 15 (June 1960): 19–24.

———. "Ngành dân tộc học mới của Trung Quốc." *NCLS* 11 (February 1960): 89–96.

———. "Thử bàn về ba bộ tộc Tày, Nùng, Thái ở Việt Nam đã hình thành như thế nào?" *NCLS* 60 (March 1964): 46–56.

———. "Tìm hiểu về nguồn gốc lịch sử của người Cao Lan." *NCLS* 55 (October 1963): 58–64.

———. "Tìm hiểu về tôn giáo tín ngưỡng ở vùng Tày, Nùng, Thái." *NCLS* 75 (June 1965): 55–64.

———. "Vài nét sơ lược về công tác dân tộc học ở Tiệp Khắc và Cộng hòa dân chủ Đức." *NCLS* 35 (February 1962): 59–61.

Lavine, Steven D. "Audience, Ownership, and Authority: Designing Relations between Museums and Communities." In *Museums and Communities: The Politics of Public Culture,* ed. Ivan Karp, Christine Mullen Kreamer, and Steven D. Lavine. Washington, D.C.: Smithsonian Institution Press, 1992. 137–57.

Lefort, Claude. *The Political Forms of Modern Society: Bureaucracy, Democracy, Totalitarianism.* Ed. John B. Thompson. Boston: MIT Press, 1986.

Lê Khôi. "Kỷ niệm lần thứ 90 năm sinh G. Đi-mi-tờ-rốp (1882–1972): Những trang sử cuộc đời một người cộng sản lỗi lạc." *NCLS* 145 (July–August 1972): 18–22.

Lê Quảng Ba. "Reminiscences of Underground Revolutionary Work." *VNS* 15 (1968): 25–56.

Lê Thành Khôi. *Histoire du Việt Nam des origines à 1858.* Paris: Sudestasie, 1981.

———. *Socialisme et développement au Việt Nam.* Paris: Presses Universitaires de France, 1978.

Lê Thị Nhâm Tuyết. "Village Festivals in Traditional Vietnamese Society." *VNSS* 4 (1985): 41–50.

Lê Thước. "Một số chữ in sai về thơ văn Nguyễn Trãi trong *Ức Trai di tập.*" *NCLS* 66 (September 1964): 32–35.

———. "Một tài liệu văn sử: Chính khí ca Việt Nam." *NCLS* 73 (April 1975): 21–29.

Lê Thước and Trần Huy Bá. "Tấm bia đá trước sân đền Hai Bà Trưng ở Hà Nội." *NCLS* 149 (March–April 1973): 51–54.

Lê Thước and Trương Chính. "Thử xét lại cái án Nguyễn Trãi." *VSĐ* 24 (January 1957): 63–72.

Lê Văn Hảo. "Ethnological Studies and Research in Vietnam." *VNS* 32 (1972): 9–48.

Lê Văn Kỳ. "Tư tưởng 'dân' của Nguyễn Trãi với chúng ta." *NCLS* 81 (December 1965): 19–30.

Lê Văn Lan and Phạm Văn Kỉnh. "Di tích khảo cổ trên đất Phong Châu, địa bàn gốc của các vua Hùng." *NCLS* 107 (February 1968): 34–46.

Lê-vin (M. G. Lewin). "Tài liệu dân tộc học và nhân loại học là tài liệu lịch sử." Trans. Cao Văn Biền. *NCLS* 29 (August 1961): 28–33.

Lê Xuân Phương. "Mưa ở nước ta ảnh hưởng đến việc trồng trọt như thế nào?" *VSĐ* 30 (July 1957): 70–76.

"Lịch sử là gì?" *VSĐ* 5 (February 1955): 60–61.

Li Tana. *Nguyễn Cochinchina: Southern Vietnam in the Seventeenth and Eighteenth Centuries.* Ithaca: Cornell University Southeast Asia Program, 1998.

Lockhart, Bruce. "Đổi mới in Vietnamese Historiography: Re-evaluating the Nguyễn Dynasty." Unpublished manuscript, 2000.

———. *The End of the Vietnamese Monarchy.* New Haven: Yale University Council on Southeast Asia Studies, 1993.

———. "Looking Down from a Tightrope: Ethnology in Vietnam." Unpublished manuscript, 1986.

Lockhart, Greg. *Nation in Arms: The Origins of the People's Army of Vietnam.* Sydney: Allen and Unwin, 1989.

Long Điền and Vạn Thành. "Góp ý kiến với bài 'Mấy nhận xét về nền khảo cổ học của thực dân Pháp ở Việt Nam trước đây' của ông Nguyễn Lương Bích." *NCLS* 6 (August 1959): 60–65.

Mạc Đường. "Các loại hình kinh tế văn hóa và nền văn hóa vật chất của dân tộc thiểu số Bắc Trung Bộ." *NCLS* 54 (September 1963): 29–45.

———. "Chủ nghĩa đế quốc xâm lược vào Tây Nguyên và lịch sử đấu tranh của các dân tộc Tây Nguyên chống đế quốc." *NCLS* 70 (January 1965): 38–50.

———. "Nghiên cứu về sự cư trú và nhà ở của người Dao ở Việt Nam." *NCLS* 9 (November 1959): 80–86.

———. "Nguồn gốc lịch sử và di cư của người Mán ở Việt Nam." *NCLS* 5 (July 1959): 81–86.

———. "Quan hệ công xã trong các tộc thiểu số miền Bắc trước và sau Cách mạng tháng Tám." *NCLS* 18 (September 1960): 38–45.

———. "Tìm hiểu về người Rục ở miền núi tỉnh Quảng Bình." *NCLS* 48 (March 1963): 32–44.

———. "Xã hội và ruộng đất ở vùng Mường trước Cách mạng tháng Tám." *NCLS* 37 (April 1962): 49–56 and *NCLS* 38 (May 1962): 38–44.

———. "Xung quanh vấn đề chiếm hữu nô lệ có hay không ở Việt Nam?" *NCLS* 17 (August 1960): 54–69.

Mai Hanh. "Giá trị *Truyện Trạng Quỳnh.*" *VSĐ* 21 (September 1956): 35–48 and *VSĐ* 22 (October 1956): 56–63.

———. "Trương Định: người anh hùng tiêu biểu cho tinh thần chống ngoại xâm của nhân dân miền Nam Việt Nam thời cận đại." *NCLS* 66 (September 1964): 59–62.

Mai Hòa. "Những điều nghi vấn của chúng tôi về chế độ chiếm hữu nô lệ ở Việt Nam." *NCLS* 62 (May 1964): 13–15.

Mai Quang. "Viet Bac: From Cradle of the Revolution to Autonomous Zone." *VNS* 41 (1973): 136–66.

Marr, David G. *Vietnamese Anticolonialism 1885–1925.* Berkeley: University of California Press, 1971.

———. *Vietnamese Tradition on Trial, 1920–1945.* Berkeley: University of California Press, 1981.

———. *Vietnam 1945: The Quest for Power.* Berkeley: University of California Press, 1995.

———. "World War Two and the Vietnamese Revolution." In *Southeast Asia under Japanese Occupation,* ed. Alfred W. McCoy. New Haven: Yale University Council on Southeast Asia Studies, 1980. 104–31.

Masaya Shiraishi. "The Background to the Formation of the Tran Trong Kim Cabinet in April 1945: Japanese Plans for Governing Vietnam." In *Indochina in the 1940s and 1950s,* ed. Takashi Shiraishi and Motoo Furuta. Ithaca: Cornell University Southeast Asia Program, 1992. 113–41.

Maspero, Henri. *Études d'histoire d'Annam.* Hanoi: École Française d'Extrême-Orient, 1916.

Masson, André. *Hanoi pendant la période héroique.* Paris: P. Geuthner, 1929.

Mazour, Anatole G., and Herman E. Bateman. "Recent Conflicts in Soviet Historiography." *JMH* 24, no. 1 (March 1952): 56–68.

McAlister, John T. "Mountain Minorities and the Viet Minh: A Key to the Indochina War." In *Southeast Asian Tribes, Minorities, and Nations,* ed. Peter Kunstadter. Vol. 2. Princeton: Princeton University Press, 1967. 771–844.

McHale, Shawn. "Printing, Power, and the Transformation of Vietnamese Culture, 1920–1945." Ph.D. dissertation, Cornell University, 1995.

McLellan, David. *Marxism after Marx: An Introduction.* 3rd ed. London: Macmillan, 1998.

Minh Cương (Meng Qun). "Duy vật lịch sử là cơ sở lý luận của khoa học lịch sử." *VSĐ* 6 (March–April 1955): 76–83.

Minh Tranh. "Cách mạng tháng Tám và kháng chiến là một cuộc cách mạng quần chúng dưới sự lãnh đạo của Đảng." *VSĐ* 44 (September 1958): 1–5.

———. "Cần đi sâu và rộng hơn nữa vào những chuyên đề." *VSĐ* 46 (November 1958): 1–6.

———. "Chống sùng bái cá nhân, nhưng cần nhận rõ vai trò cá nhân trong lịch sử." *VSĐ* 18 (June 1956): 1–13.

———. "Góp ý kiến vào việc tìm hiểu văn học nhân dân của ta." *VSĐ* 4 (January 1955): 6–24.

———. "Khởi nghĩa Tây Sơn và sự hình thành dân tộc Việt Nam." *VSĐ* 24 (January 1956): 6–18.

———. "Một vài nét về vấn đề ruộng đất trong lịch sử Việt Nam." *VSĐ* 2 (n.d.): 32–52.

———. "Một vấn đề về văn học sử Việt Nam: Có thể liệt những bài văn yêu nước do người Việt Nam trước kia viết bằng chữ Hán vào văn học dân tộc của ta không?" *VSĐ* 6 (March–April 1955): 9–19.

———. "Nguyễn Trãi, một nhà ái quốc tiêu biểu cho lòng nhân nghĩa và ý chí hòa bình của nhân dân ta trong đầu thế kỷ XV." *VSĐ* 20 (August 1956): 7–20.

———. "Những bài học của Cách mạng Nga 1905 và Việt Nam." *VSĐ* 13 (January 1956): 19–40.

———. "Những bài học đại đoàn kết bảo vệ tổ quốc trong lịch sử nước ta." *VSĐ* 10 (September–October 1955): 1–7.

———. "Phong trào nông dân trong lịch sử xã hội phong kiến nước ta." *VSĐ* 3 (October 1954): 6–21.

———. *Sơ thảo lược sử Việt Nam.* 2 vols. Hanoi: Bộ Giáo dục and Văn Sử Địa, 1954–1955.

———. "Sử học phải phục vụ cách mạng như thế nào?" *NCLS* 3 (May 1959): 1–8.

———. "Sự phát triển của chế độ phong kiến nước ta và vai trò của Hồ Quý Ly trong cuối thế kỷ XIV và đầu thế kỷ XV." *VSĐ* 11 (November 1955): 5–19.

———. "Vấn đề chế độ chiếm hữu nô lệ ở Việt Nam." *VSĐ* 7 (May–June 1955): 5–26.

———. "Vấn đề ruộng đất, vấn đề nông dân và thắng lợi của cách mạng Việt Nam." *VSĐ* 42 (July 1958): 3–10.

———. "Vấn đề thời kỳ trong lịch sử Việt Nam." *VSĐ* 5 (February 1955): 62–67.

———. "Vấn đề tiêu chuẩn để phân định những thời kỳ lịch sử nước ta." *VSĐ* 5 (February 1955): 17–30.

———. "Xã hội Việt Nam trong thế kỷ XVIII và những phong trào nông dân khởi nghĩa." *VSĐ* 14 (February 1956): 15–29.

Moise, Edwin. *Land Reform in China and Vietnam.* Chapel Hill: University of North Carolina Press, 1983.

Mosse, George. *Masses and Man: Nationalist and Fascist Representations of Reality.* Detroit: Wayne State University Press, 1987.

———. *The Nationalization of the Masses.* New York: Howard Fertig, 1975.

"Một số tư liệu về Cách mạng tháng Mười Nga đối với cách mạng Việt Nam." *NCLS* 103 (October 1967): 33–44.

National Committee for the International Symposium on the Ancient Town of Hoi An. *Ancient Town of Hoi An.* 2nd ed. Hanoi: The Gioi, 1993.

Needham, Joseph. *Mathematics and the Sciences of the Heavens and the Earth.* Vol. 3 of *Science and Civilization in China.* 1959; Cambridge: Cambridge University Press, 1992.

Ngô Hàm. "Bàn về vấn đề đánh giá nhân vật lịch sử." *NCLS* 41 (August 1962): 42–51.

Ngo Van. *Viêt-Nam 1920–1945: Révolution et contre-révolution sous la domination coloniale.* 2nd ed. Paris: L'Insomniaque, 1996.

Ngo Vinh Long. "Rewriting Vietnamese History." *Journal of Contemporary Asia* 10, no. 3 (1980): 286–92.

Nguyễn Anh. "Vài ý kiến về Trương Vĩnh Ký." *NCLS* 57 (December 1963): 17–27.

Nguyen Ba Khoach, Allen J. Riedy, and Truong Buu Lam, eds. *An Annotated Index of the Journals "Van Su Dia" (1954–1959) and "Nghien cuu lich su" (1959–1981).* Honolulu: University of Hawai'i Center for Asian and Pacific Studies, 1984.

Nguyễn Bình Minh. "Cuộc biểu tình Duyên Hà—Tiên Hưng trong dịp kỷ niệm ngày Lao động quốc tế 1-5-1930." *NCLS* 50 (May 1963): 43–47.

Nguyễn Công Bình. " 'Muốn cứu nước và giải phóng dân tộc không có con đường nào khác con đường cách mạng vô sản' (Lời Hồ Chủ tịch)." *NCLS* 162 (May–June 1975): 3–6.

———. "Nhân dịp kỷ niệm ngày tạ thế của Hoàng Hoa Thám, lãnh tụ nông dân Yên Thế: Tinh chất cuộc khởi nghĩa Yên Thế." *VSĐ* 48 (January 1958): 28–43.

———. "Tình hình và đặc tính của giai cấp tư sản Việt Nam thời Pháp thuộc." *VSĐ* 41 (June 1958) through *VSĐ* 46 (November 1958).

Nguyễn Đổng Chi. "Chế độ nô tỳ thời Lê sơ và tác dụng của các phong trào quần chúng ở thế kỷ XIV và đầu thế kỷ thứ XV." *NCLS* 99 (June 1967): 34–40.

———. *Kho tàng truyện cổ tích Việt Nam.* 5 vols. Hanoi: Văn Sử Địa, Sử Học, and Social Sciences, 1957–1974.

———. "Một vài nhận xét về đặc điểm truyền thống bất khuất của đồng bào Thượng." *NCLS* 76 (July 1965): 28–38.

———. "Nên phân chia thời đại lịch sử nước ta như thế nào?" *VSĐ* 3 (October 1954): 71–75.

———. "Nông dân trong thời kỳ phong kiến có tinh thần yêu nước và ý thức dân tộc hay không?" *NCLS* 80 (November 1965): 6–14.

———. "Quan điểm phản động, phản khoa học của Phan Khôi phải chăng là học mót của Hồ Thích?" *VSĐ* 41 (June 1958): 7–24.

———. "Quyền *Trưởng Nam* ở Việt Nam có từ bao giờ?" *VSĐ* 31 (September 1957): 42–50.

———. "Thử đánh giá Nguyễn Hữu Chỉnh." *VSĐ* 46 (November 1958): 29–42.

———. "Vấn đề chiếm hữu nô lệ ở Việt Nam qua ý nghĩa một truyện cổ tích." *VSĐ* 18 (June 1956): 53–63.

———. "Vấn đề sử dụng tài liệu văn học dân gian." *NCLS* 63 (June 1964): 48–53.

Nguyễn Đức Đàn. "Vài nét về Nguyễn Dữ và tập *Truyền kỳ mạn lục.*" *VSĐ* 24 (January 1957): 31–44.

Nguyễn Đức Hợp. "The Thai." *VNS* 15 (1968): 137–64.

Nguyễn Đức Nghinh. "Thử bàn về đặc điểm của chế độ nô tỳ thời Lê sơ." *NCLS* 90 (September 1966): 39–45.

Nguyễn Hồng Phong. "Cách mạng tháng Tám và chủ nghĩa xã hội." *NCLS* 29 (August 1961): 1–6.

———. "Nhân dịp mừng thọ Hồ Chủ tịch 70 tuổi: Đồng chí Nguyễn Ái Quốc với lý luận của chủ nghĩa Lê-nin về vấn đề dân tộc và dân tộc thuộc địa." *NCLS* 14 (May 1960): 1–10.

———. "Sự phát triển của kinh tế hàng hóa và vấn đề hình thành của chủ nghĩa tư bản ở Việt Nam dưới thời phong kiến." *NCLS* 9 (November 1959): 7–25.

———. "Sự thành lập Đảng Cộng sản Đông Dương là một bước ngoặt vĩ đại trong lịch sử cách mạng cận đại Việt Nam." *NCLS* 10 (January 1960): 6–29.

———. "Tìm hiểu *Gia huấn ca*." *VSĐ* 27 (April 1957): 4–21 and *VSĐ* 29 (June 1957): 23–39.

———. *Tìm hiểu tính cách dân tộc*. Hanoi: Social Sciences, 1963.

———. "Trở lại vấn đề nguyên nhân hình thành của nhà nước phong kiến trung ương tập quyền tại Việt Nam." *NCLS* 5 (July 1959): 78–80.

———. "Vấn đề ruộng đất trong lịch sử chế độ phong kiến Việt Nam." *NCLS* 1 (March 1959): 42–55 and *NCLS* 2 (April 1959): 26–53.

Nguyễn Khắc Đạm. "Góp ý kiến cùng hai bạn Nguyễn Văn Dị và Văn Lang về bài 'Nghiên cứu về trận Bạch Đằng năm 1288.'" *NCLS* 47 (February 1963): 51–51.

———. "Hai mươi năm lớn lên của thư viện Viện Sử học." *NCLS* 153 (November-December 1973): 63–64.

Nguyễn Khắc Viện. "Directives and Resolutions of the DRVN Government and the Vietnam Workers' Party on National Education." *VNS* 30 (1971): 163–203.

Nguyễn Khắc Viện and Hữu Ngọc. *Vietnamese Literature: Historical Background and Texts*. Hanoi: FLPH, n.d.

Nguyễn Khánh Toàn. "Bốn mươi năm dưới ngọn cờ quang vinh của chủ nghĩa Mác—Lê-nin." *NCLS* 130 (January-February 1970): 4–16.

———. "Chân lý của Lê-nin mãi mãi sáng ngời. Cuộc khủng hoảng của thế giới tư bản." *NCLS* 155 (March-April 1974): 3–14.

———. "Dưới lá cờ của chủ nghĩa Mác—Lê-nin, có Đảng tiền phong của giai cấp công nhân lãnh đạo, dân tộc Việt Nam trở nên một lực lượng cách mạng lớn của thời đại anh hùng của chúng ta." *NCLS* 160 (January-February 1975): 3–7.

———. "Dưới lá cờ vĩ đại của Lê-nin, tiến lên!" *NCLS* 144 (May-June 1972): 1–8.

———. "Hồ Chủ tịch, nhà kiến trúc sư thiên tài của lịch sử Việt Nam hiện đại." *NCLS* 144 (May-June 1972): 9–11.

———. "Kỷ niệm một trăm năm ngày xuất bản quyển *Tư bản* của Các Mác." *NCLS* 102 (September 1967): 1–11.

———. "Kỷ niệm năm mươi năm *Bản án chế độ thực dân Pháp*—Một sự kiện lịch sử, một nhát cuốc đầu tiên đào mồ chôn chủ nghĩa thực dân." *NCLS* 161 (March-April 1975): 3–17.

———. "Nhân kỷ niệm năm mươi năm thành lập Liên bang Cộng hòa xã hội chủ nghĩa xô-viết: Thắng lợi lịch sử vĩ đại." *NCLS* 147 (November-December 1972): 1.

———. "Những điều cần chú ý hiện nay trong khi bàn về phương pháp luận sử học." *NCLS* 90 (September 1966): 1–7.

Nguyễn Lân. "Vấn đề thống nhất cách phát âm tiếng Việt." *VSĐ* 19 (July 1956): 74–79.

Nguyễn Linh. "Phải chăng Hùng vương thuộc dòng dõi Thần Nông." *NCLS* 111 (June 1968): 24–35.

———. "Vài suy nghĩ về việc tìm hiểu thời đại Hồng Bàng." *NCLS* 100 (July 1967): 32–39.

———. "Về sự tồn tại của nước Văn Lang." *NCLS* 112 (July 1968): 19–32.

Nguyễn Lương Bích. "Bảy năm công tác dân tộc học ở Việt Nam." *NCLS* 21 (December 1961): 41–45.

———. "Cuộc thảo luận của các nhà sử học Liên Xô về công tác biên tập của tạp chí *Vấn đề lịch sử.*" *VSĐ* 13 (January 1956): 66–70.

———. "Giới thiệu mấy nét về dòng họ Nguyễn Trãi, Nguyễn Thiện Thuật, Nguyễn Văn Cừ." *NCLS* 119 (February 1969): 59–63.

———. "Góp ý kiến về công tác dân tộc học ở Việt Nam trong giai đoạn hiện tại." *NCLS* 3 (May 1959): 17–29.

———. "Không sùng bái học giả thực dân, cần nhận rõ và phê phán những sai lầm, thiếu sót của họ trong khảo cổ học." *NCLS* 11 (February 1960): 72–88.

———. "Lịch sử Việt Nam có hay không có thời kỳ chiếm hữu nô lệ?" *VSĐ* 35 (December 1957): 34–46.

———. "Mấy nét sơ lược về dân tộc học Mác-xít." *VSĐ* 47 (December 1958): 15–33.

———. "Mấy nhận xét về nền khảo cổ học của thực dân Pháp ở Việt Nam trước đây." *NCLS* 4 (June 1959): 12–24.

———. "Mấy ý kiến thêm về chủ trương lịch sử Việt Nam không có thời kỳ chế độ nô lệ của ông Đào Duy Anh." *VSĐ* 32 (September 1957): 9–18.

———. "Nguyên nhân thành bại của Cách mạng Tây Sơn." *VSĐ* 14 (February 1956): 45–50.

———. "Nhận định về mấy kiến khác nhau trong vấn đề chế độ nô lệ ở Việt Nam." *VSĐ* 24 (January 1957): 19–30 and *VSĐ* 25 (February 1957): 51–59.

———. "Những tiêu chuẩn để nhận định sự thành hình dân tộc." *VSĐ* 12 (December 1955): 29–40.

———. "Phương thức sản xuất châu Á là gì?" *NCLS* 53 (August 1963): 2–10 and *NCLS* 54 (September 1963): 18–26.

———. "Quá trình phát triển của các cộng đồng người là tiến từ bộ lạc lên bộ tộc, từ bộ tộc lên dân tộc, hay là tiến thẳng từ bộ lạc lên dân tộc?" *NCLS* 49 (April 1963): 10–19.

———. "Sự phát triển của sức sản xuất đã quyết định sự hình thành quan hệ chiếm hữu nô lệ ở Việt Nam thời cổ đại." *NCLS* 16 (July 1960): 52–61.

———. "Việc đào tạo cán bộ sử học ở Liên Xô." *VSĐ* 13 (January 1956): 71–74.

Nguyễn Minh. "Ôn lại cuộc khởi nghĩa của Hai Bà Trưng." *VSĐ* 5 (February 1955): 48–51.

Nguyễn Minh Văn. "Có thể xếp loại văn dịch những tác phẩm chữ Hán do người Việt vào văn học Việt Nam không?" *VSĐ* 7 (May–June 1955): 58–61.

Nguyễn Ngọc Huy and Tạ Văn Tài. *The Lê Code: Law in Traditional Vietnam.* 3 vols. Athens: Ohio University Press, 1987.

Nguyễn Ngọc Quế and Nguyễn Xuân Kỳ. "Cách mạng Cu-ba." *NCLS* 105 (December 1967): 50–56.

Nguyễn Ngọc Thụy. "Về con nước triều trong trận Bạch Đằng 1288." *NCLS* 63 (June 1964): 36.

Nguyễn Phước Tương. "Cảng thị Hội An: Trung tâm trung chuyển của con đường tơ lụa và gốm sứ quốc tế xuyên đại dương trong thế kỷ XVI-XVIII." *Văn hóa Hội An* 2 (1998): 15–23.

Nguyễn Q. Thắng and Nguyễn Bá Thế. *Từ điển Nhân vật lịch sử Việt Nam*. Rev. ed. Ho Chi Minh City: Văn hóa, 1993.

Nguyễn Quang Ngọc. "The Revival of Village Traditions in the Rural Areas of the Red River Delta." Paper presented at the conference "Vietnam and Asia," sponsored by the Vietnam Center at Texas Tech University, April 1998.

Nguyễn Tài Cung et al. *Việt Nam: Quê hương tôi / Vietnam: My Homeland*. Hanoi: Sự Thật and Vietnamtourism, 1989.

Nguyễn Thành. "Vấn đề chữ của dân tộc Thái." *VSĐ* 39 (April 1958): 53–66, *VSĐ* 40 (May 1958): 35–48, and *VSĐ* 41 (June 1958): 43–55.

Nguyễn Thế Phương. "Tiếng Mường và mối liên quan về nguồn gốc giữa người Mường, người Kinh." *VSĐ* 42 (July 1958): 68–75.

Nguyễn Thị Định. *No Other Road to Take*. Trans. Mai Elliot. Ithaca: Cornell University Southeast Asia Program, 1976.

Nguyễn Tuấn Liêu. "Mấy nét tình hình và nhận xét về chế độ quằng trong dân tộc Tày ở Hà Giang." *NCLS* 44 (November 1962): 17–26.

Nguyễn Văn Chung, ed. *Bảo tàng Mỹ thuật Việt Nam*. Hanoi: Văn Hóa, 1986.

Nguyễn Văn Dị and Văn Lang. "Bàn thêm về trận Bạch Đằng năm 1288." *NCLS* 49 (April 1963): 37–45.

———. "Nghiên cứu về trận Bạch Đằng năm 1288." *NCLS* 43 (October 1962): 27–36.

Nguyễn Văn Khoa. "Chế độ 'côn hươn' ở vùng Thái khu tự trị Thái-Mèo." *NCLS* 27 (June 1961): 63–67.

Nguyễn Văn Ký. *La Société vietnamienne face à la modernité*. Paris: L'Harmattan, 1995.

Nguyễn Văn Mệnh et al. *Tiếng Việt thực hành, Giáo trình sơ giản*. Hanoi: Bộ Đại học, 1988.

Nguyen Van Phong. *La Société vietnamienne de 1882 à 1902 d'après les écrits des auteurs français*. Paris: Presses universitaires de France, 1971.

Nguyễn Xuân Hoè. "Nước ta có qua chế độ nô lệ không?" *VSĐ* 11 (November 1955): 75–77.

Nguyệt Hương. "Phụ nữ miền Nam Việt Nam trong đấu tranh chống Mỹ-ngụy." *NCLS* 137 (March–April 1971): 25–34.

Nhất Nguyên. "Chủ nghĩa Mác—Lê-nin bàn về nhân vật lịch sử." *NCLS* 14 (May 1960): 11–23.

"Những ngày hội nghị kỷ niệm Cách mạng 1905–1907 lần thứ 50 ở Mạc-tư-khoa do Viện Hàn lâm khoa học Liên Xô triệu tập." *VSĐ* 13 (January 1956): 4–6.

Ni-kíp-lốp (F. N. Nikiplov). "Bàn về mấy qui luật chung của sự biến chuyển từ chế độ chiếm hữu nô lệ sang chế độ phong kiến trong các nước khác nhau." Trans. Tư Huyền. *VSĐ* 30 (July 1957): 41–52.

Ninh, Kim Ngoc Bao. "Revolution, Politics, and Culture in Socialist Vietnam, 1945–1965." Ph.D. dissertation, Yale University, 1996.

Nông Ích Thùy. "Vấn đề chọn tiếng phương ngôn cơ sở và âm tiêu chuẩn trong việc đặt chữ cho các dân tộc." *VSĐ* 36 (January 1958): 91.

———. "Vấn đề đặt chữ và cải tiến chữ các dân tộc." *VSĐ* 21 (September 1956): 85–89.

Nong Trung. "Sơ lược tìm hiểu mối quan hệ giữa các ngành Nùng ở Việt Nam." *NCLS* 45 (December 1962): 38–44.

Nora, Pierre, ed. *Les Lieux de mémoire.* Paris: Gallimard, 1984.

Odlozilik, Otakar. "Modern Czechoslovak Historiography." *Slavonic and East European Review* 30, no. 75 (June 1952): 376–92.

O'Harrow, Stephen. "French Colonial Policy towards Vernacular Language Development and the Case of Pham Quynh." In *Aspects of Vernacular Languages in Asian and Pacific Societies,* comp. Nguyen Dang Liem. Honolulu: University of Hawai'i Southeast Asian Studies Program, 1973. 113–35.

———. "Men of Hu, Men of Han, Men of the Hundred Man." *BEFEO* 75 (1986): 249–66.

———. "Nguyen Trai's *Binh Ngo Dai Cao* of 1428: The Development of a Vietnamese National Identity." *JSEAS* 10, no. 1 (1978): 159–74.

O'Leary, Brendan. *The Asiatic Mode of Production.* Oxford: Basil Blackwell, 1989.

Ooms, Herman. *Tokugawa Ideology: Early Constructs, 1570–1680.* Princeton: Princeton University Press, 1985.

Ozouf, Mona. "The Festival in the French Revolution." In *Constructing the Past: Essays in Historical Methodology,* ed. Jacques LeGoff and Pierre Nora. Cambridge: Cambridge University Press, 1985. 181–97.

Pelley, Patricia M. "'Barbarians' and 'Younger Brothers': The Remaking of Race in Postcolonial Vietnam." *JSEAS* 29, no. 2 (1998): 374–91.

———. "The Cult of Antiquity in Postcolonial Vietnam." Paper presented at the annual meeting of the Association for Asian Studies, Honolulu, April 1996.

———. "The History of Resistance and the Resistance to History in Postcolonial Constructions of the Past." In *Essays into Vietnamese Pasts,* ed. K. W. Taylor and John K. Whitmore. Ithaca: Cornell University Southeast Asia Program, 1995. 232–45.

———. "Writing Revolution: The New History in Postcolonial Vietnam." Ph.D. dissertation, Cornell University, 1993.

Phạm Huy Thông. "Ba lần dựng nước." *Học tập* 21, no. 237 (September 1975): 63–72, 76.

———. "Our Stone Age: From the Mount Do Industry to the Hoa Binh Industry." *VNS* 46 (1974): 9–49.

Phạm Ngọc Liễn. "Góp một số ý kiến về vấn đề cấu tạo nội dung lịch sử Việt Nam theo quan điểm đa dân tộc." *NCLS* 48 (March 1963): 50–56.

Phạm Quỳnh. *Le Paysan tonkinois à travers le parler populaire.* Hanoi: Éditions Alexandre de Rhodes, 1930.

Phạm Trọng Điềm. "Một vài ý kiến trao đổi với bạn Đào Tứ Minh về vấn đề phiên âm và chú giải cuốn *Quốc âm thi tập.*" *VSĐ* 38 (March 1958): 70–81.

Phan Bội Châu. *Phan Bội Châu niên biểu.* Trans. Vinh Sinh and Nicholas Wickenden. *Overturned Chariot: The Autobiography of Phan Bội Châu.* Honolulu: University of Hawai'i Press, 1999.

Phan Gia Bền. "Cuộc khởi nghĩa Ong Kẹo—Kô-ma-đăm (1901–1937) và cuộc khởi nghĩa Phò Cà-đuột (1901–1903)." *NCLS* 137 (March–April 1971): 18–24.

———. "Một vài suy nghĩ về vấn đề nâng cao chất lượng công trình nghiên cứu sử học." *NCLS* 69 (December 1964): 3–14.

————. *La Recherche historique en République démocratique du Vietnam*. Hanoi: Éditions Scientifiques, 1965.

————. "Tiến tới thành lập Hội Sử học nhằm góp phần đẩy mạnh hơn nữa công tác khoa học lịch sử." *NCLS* 82 (January 1966): 5–6.

————. "Tư bản Pháp với thủ công nghiệp Việt Nam." *VSĐ* 37 (February 1958): 18–33.

Phan Gia Bền and Nguyễn Khắc Đạm. "Tài liệu tham khảo về lịch sử đường sắt Hải Phòng-Côn Minh." *VSĐ* 20 (August 1956): 33–49.

Phan Huy Chú. "Vấn đề ruộng đất trong triệu nhà lê." Trans. and adapted by Phạm Trọng Điềm. *VSĐ* 2 (n.d.): 53–67.

Phan Huy Lê. "Bàn thêm mấy vấn đề phong trào nông dân Tây Sơn." *NCLS* 49 (April 1963): 20–26 and *NCLS* 50 (May 1963): 36–42.

Phan Huy Lê, Trần Quốc Vượng, Hà Văn Tấn, and Lương Ninh. *Lịch sử Việt Nam.* Vol. 1. Hanoi: Đại Học và Trung Học Chuyên Nghiệp, 1983.

Phan Khôi. "Phê bình lãnh đạo Văn nghệ." In *Trăm hoa đua nở trên đất bắc,* ed. Võ Văn Ái. Paris: Quê Mẹ, 1983. 59–72.

————. "Thử tìm sử liệu Việt Nam trong ngữ ngôn." *VSĐ* 1 (June 1954): 57–61, *VSĐ* 2 (n.d.): 68–73, and *VSĐ* 3 (October 1954): 40–49.

Phan Manh Hung. "Fortieth Anniversary of the *Outline of the Cultural Revolution of Vietnam.*" *VNSS* 1 (1984): 118–19.

Phan Ngọc Liên and Nguyễn Văn Đức. "Công xã Pa-ri với cách mạng Việt Nam." *NCLS* 137 (March–April 1971): 4–17.

Piggot, Stuart. *Approach to Archaeology*. New York: McGraw-Hill, 1965.

Pitkin, Hannah. *Fortune Is a Woman: Gender and Politics in the Thought of Niccoló Machiavelli*. Princeton: Princeton University Press, 1984.

Post, Ken. *Revolution, Socialism and Nationalism in Vietnam*. 5 vols. Aldershot, Eng.: Dartmouth, 1989–1990.

Pundeff, Marin. "Bulgarian Historiography, 1942–1958." *American Historical Review* 66 (April 1961): 682–93.

Quang Chính. "Vấn đề cấu tạo nội dung lịch sử Việt Nam theo quan điểm đa dân tộc." *NCLS* 50 (May 1963): 7–10.

Quốc Chấn. "Phong trào nông dân hay phong trào dân tộc?" *VSĐ* 36 (January 1958): 69–74.

Reid, Anthony, ed. *Slavery, Bondage and Dependency in Southeast Asia*. New York: St. Martin's Press, 1983.

Renan, Ernest. *Qu'est-ce qu'une nation? et autres écrits politiques*. Ed. Raoul Giradet. Paris: Imprimerie nationale, 1996.

Ross, Robert, and Gerard J. Telkamp, eds. *Colonial Cities*. Dordrecht, Netherlands: Leiden University Press, 1985.

Ryszka, Franciszek. "Poland: Some Recent Re-evaluations." *JCH* 2 (January 1967): 107–23.

Sa Anh (Sha Ying). "Tác dụng của quần chúng nhân dân và cá nhân trong lịch sử: Bình luận cả quan điểm phản động của Hồ Thích [Hu Shi]." Trans. Phạm Trọng Điềm. *VSĐ* 10 (September–October 1955): 73–85.

Said, Edward. *Beginnings*. New York: Columbia University Press, 1975.

————. *Culture and Imperialism.* New York: Vintage, 1993.

————. *Orientalism.* New York: Pantheon, 1978.

Salemink, Oscar. "The King of Fire and Vietnamese Ethnic Policy in the Central Highlands." In *Development or Domestication? Indigenous Peoples of Southeast Asia,* ed. Donald McCaskill and Ken Kampe. Chiang Mai: Silk Worm, 1997. 488–535.

Salisbury, Harrison. *Behind the Lines—Hanoi.* New York: Harper and Row, 1967.

Schafer, Edward H. *The Vermilion Bird: T'ang Images of the South.* Berkeley: University of California Press, 1967.

Schreiner, Alfred. *Abrégé de l'histoire d'Annam.* Saigon: Imprimerie Coudurier and Montégout, 1906.

Schwartz, Vera. "Memory, Commemoration, and the Plight of China's Intellectuals." *Wilson Quarterly* (August 1989): 120–29.

Scott, James C. *Seeing Like a State.* New Haven: Yale University Press, 1998.

Smith, Bardwell and H. B. Reynolds, eds. *The City as a Sacred Center: Essays on Six Asian Contexts.* Leiden, Netherlands: E. J. Brill, 1987.

Smith, Ralph. *Viet-Nam and the West.* Ithaca: Cornell University Press, 1968, 1971.

Socialist Republic of Vietnam: Basic Data. Hanoi: FLPH, 1978.

Số liệu thống kê Cộng hòa Xã hội Chủ nghĩa Việt Nam. Hanoi: Thống kê, 1991.

Soviet Orientology and Studies in the History of Colonialism. Moscow: Nauka, 1968.

Spivak, Gayatri Chakravorty. "Can the Subaltern Speak?" In *Marxism and the Interpretation of Culture,* ed. Cary Nelson and Lawrence Grossberg. Urbana: University of Illinois Press, 1988. 271–313.

Stalin, Josef. "Dialectical and Historical Materialism." In *The History of the Communist Party of the Soviet Union (Bolsheviks), Short Course,* ed. Central Committee, Communist Party of the Soviet Union (B). New York: International Publishers, 1939. 105–31.

————. *Marxism and the National Question.* Moscow: FLPH, 1950.

Tai, Hue-Tam Ho. "Monumental Ambiguity: The State of Commemoration of Hồ Chí Minh." In *Essays into Vietnamese Pasts,* ed. K. W. Taylor and John K. Whitmore. Ithaca: Cornell University Southeast Asia Program, 1995. 272–88.

————. *Radicalism and the Origins of the Vietnamese Revolution.* Cambridge: Harvard University Press, 1992.

Tap chí Nghiên cứu Lịch sử (TCNCLS). "1970: Năm những ngày lễ lớn." *NCLS* 130 (January–February 1970): 1–3.

————. "20-8-1964: Một trăm năm ngày mất của Trương Định." *NCLS* 65 (August 1964): 6.

————. "Chuẩn bị kỷ niệm 900 năm thành lập Văn miếu-Quốc tử giám Hà Nội." *NCLS* 127 (October 1969): 5–6.

————. "Để kỷ niệm ngày thành lập Mặt trận dân tộc giải phóng miền Nam Việt Nam." *NCLS* 116 (November 1968): 1, 38.

————. "Hai ngày kỷ niệm, một ý nghĩa." *NCLS* 145 (July–August 1972): 1.

————. "Hồ Chủ tịch vĩ đại của Đảng ta và dân tộc ta." *NCLS* 132 (May–June 1970): 3–6, 120.

————. "Kỷ niệm năm thứ 20 quyết định của Trung ương Đảng thành lập Ban nghiên cứu Lịch sử, Địa lý, Văn học." *NCLS* 152 (October 1973): 1–4.

————. "Kỷ niệm 150 năm ngày sinh Ăng-ghen: Người đã cùng Mác sáng lập ra chủ nghĩa xã hội khoa học." *NCLS* 135 (November–December 1970): 1–2.

————. "Kỷ niệm 25 năm ngày toàn quốc kháng chiến chống thực dân Pháp." *NCLS* 141 (November–December 1971): 1–2.

————. "Mấy ngày kỷ niệm của năm 1971." *NCLS* 137 (March–April 1971): 1–3.

————. "Nên nghiên cứu vấn đề thời đại Hồng Bàng." *NCLS* 97 (April 1967): 5–6.

————. "Nhân ngày kỷ niệm thành lập Mặt trận dân tộc giải phóng miền Nam Việt Nam." *NCLS* 129 (December 1969): 1–2.

————. Những cán bộ công tác sử học chúng ta trước 4 ngày kỷ niệm lớn năm 1970." *NCLS* 124 (July 1969): 1–2.

Tập san Nghiên cứu Lịch sử (TSNCLS). "Các bạn đọc thân mến." *NCLS* 1 (March 1959): 1–2.

————. "Đánh giá một số nhân vật lịch sử." *NCLS* 23 (February 1961): 5–7.

————. "Mấy vấn đề khoa học của Cách mạng tháng Tám cần đi sâu nghiên cứu." *NCLS* 18 (September 1960): 1–20.

————. "Nguyễn Trãi, một nhân vật vĩ đại trong lịch sử Việt Nam." *NCLS* 42 (September 1962): 1–7.

————. "Những đề mục nghiên cứu năm 1962." *NCLS* 34 (January 1962): 1–2.

————. "1961." *NCLS* 22 (January 1961): 5–7.

Tạ Văn Tài. "Ethnic Minorities and the Law in Traditional Vietnam." *VNF* 5 (1985): 22–36.

Taylor, Keith W. "Authority and Legitimacy in Eleventh-Century Vietnam." *VNF* 12 (1988): 20–59.

————. *The Birth of Vietnam*. Berkeley: University of California Press, 1983.

————. "Đại Việt and the Rise of Thăng Long." In *Explorations in Early Southeast Asian History: The Origins of Southeast Asian Statecraft*, ed. Kenneth R. Hall and John K. Whitmore. Ann Arbor: University of Michigan Center for South and Southeast Asian Studies, 1976. 149–203.

————. "Looking Behind the Vietnamese Annals: Lý Phát Mã and Lý Nhật Tôn in the *Việt sử lược* and the *Toàn thư*." *VNF* 7 (1986): 47–69.

————. "Nguyen Hoang and the Beginning of Vietnam's Southward Expansion." In *Southeast Asia in the Early Modern Era*, ed. Anthony Reid. Ithaca: Cornell University Press, 1993. 42–65.

————. "Surface Orientations in Vietnam: Beyond Histories of Nation and Region," Journal of Asian Studies 57, no. 4 (1998): 949–78.

————. "Vietnamese Confucian Narratives." Paper presented at "Rethinking Confucianism in Asia at the End of the Twentieth Century," organized by the Center for Chinese Studies, University of California at Los Angeles, May 28–June 1, 1999.

Teston, Eugène, and Maurice Percheron. *L'Indochine moderne: Encyclopédie administrative, touristique, artistique et économique*. Paris: Librairie de France, 1931.

Thai Quang Trung. *Collective Leadership and Factionalism: An Essay on Ho Chi Minh's Legacy*. Singapore: Institute of Southeast Asian Studies, 1985.

Thanh Ba. "Bàn thêm về quan điểm của Nguyễn Trãi trong vấn đề chiến tranh và hòa bình." *NCLS* 69 (December 1964): 34–38.

Thanh Ha. "The Languages of National Minorities and the Creation or Improvement of Their Scripts." *VNS* 15 (1968): 121–36.

"Thành lập Uỷ ban Khoa học Nhà nước." *VSĐ* 47 (December 1958): 1–14.

Thayer, Carlyle A. *War by Other Means: National Liberation and Revolution in Viet-Nam, 1954–1960.* Sydney: Allen and Unwin, 1989.

T. H. L. "Tinh thần tranh đấu để bảo vệ độc lập và hoa bình của dân tộc Việt Nam." *VSĐ* 6 (March–April 1955): 1–8.

Thongchai Winichakul. *Siam Mapped: A History of the Geo-Body of a Nation.* Honolulu: University of Hawai'i Press, 1994.

Tiền Bá Tán (Jian Bozan). "Một vài vấn đề trong việc bình luận nhân vật lịch sử." Trans. Văn Tạo. *VSĐ* 3 (October 1954): 58–70.

"Tinh hình công tác điều tra lịch sử và xã hội dân tộc thiểu số ở Trung Quốc trong mấy năm gần đây." *NCLS* 2 (April 1959): 88–89.

Tòa soạn Tạp chí Nghiên cứu Lịch sử. "Về bài 'Ảnh hưởng Cách mạng Trung Quốc đối với sự chuyển biến tư tưởng của Phan Bội Châu.'" *NCLS* 48 (March 1963): 45.

Tố Hữu. *Việt Bắc.* Hanoi: Văn Nghệ, 1955.

Tổ lịch sử địa phương. "Một dịp tốt để sưu tầm tài liệu lịch sử cách mạng ở địa phương." *NCLS* 48 (March 1963): 1.

Tonnesson, Stein. *The Vietnamese Revolution of 1945.* London: Public Records and Information Office, 1991.

Trần Đức Thảo. "Bài hịch tướng sĩ của Trần Hưng Đạo và xã hội Việt Nam trong thời kỳ thịnh của chế độ phong kiến." *VSĐ* 5 (February 1955): 31–39.

———. "Lực lượng sản xuất và quan hệ sản xuất trong cuộc khủng hoảng của xã hội phong kiến Việt Nam." *VSĐ* 1 (June 1954): 35–49.

Trần Hà. "Xung quanh trận Bạch Đằng năm 1288." *NCLS* 46 (January 1963): 60–66.

Trần Huy Liệu. "Ba mươi năm đấu tranh của phụ nữ Việt Nam dưới sự lãnh đạo của Đảng." *NCLS* 13 (April 1960): 1–12.

———. "Bàn thêm về vấn đề chống sùng bái cá nhân." *VSĐ* 19 (July 1956): 5–9.

———. "Bóc trần quan điểm thực dân và phong kiến trong quyển *Việt Nam sử lược* của Trần Trọng Kim." *VSĐ* 6 (March–April 1955): 20–37.

———. "Cách mạng tháng Mười và Cách mạng Việt Nam." *VSĐ* 33 (October 1957): 1–18.

———. "Chúng ta đương sống những ngày oanh liệt nhất, vinh quang nhất của lịch sử dân tộc ta." *NCLS* 75 (June 1965): 1–3.

———. "Chúng tôi đã thấy những gì ở kho sử liệu của Liên Xô?" *VSĐ* 4 (January 1955): 35–46.

———. "Công tác của Ban nghiên cứu Văn Sử Địa trong một năm qua." *VSĐ* 35 (December 1957): 1–9.

———. "Công tác sử học bắt đầu đi vào cán bộ và nhân dân." *NCLS* 5 (July 1959): 1–5.

———. "Cuộc chiến tranh chống Mỹ cứu nước của nhân dân Việt Nam gắn liền với phong trào phản chiến đang dâng lên ở nước Mỹ." *NCLS* 81 (December 1965): 1–2.

———. "Cuộc kháng chiến cứu nước của đồng bào miền Nam hiện nay là một cuộc chiến tranh nhân dân." *NCLS* 64 (July 1964): 1–6.

———. "Cuộc khởi nghĩa của Phan Đình Phùng, tiêu biểu của phong trào văn thân 1885–1889." *VSĐ* 45 (October 1958): 1–14.

———. "Đánh gía cho đúng những anh hùng dân tộc của chúng ta." *VSĐ* 1 (June 1954): 30–34.

———. "Đánh giá cuộc Cách mạng Tây Sơn và vai trò lịch sử của Nguyễn Huệ." *VSĐ* 14 (February 1956): 30–44.

———. "Dân tộc Việt Nam thành hình từ bao giờ?" *VSĐ* 5 (February 1955): 5–16.

———. "Đi sâu vào những đặc điểm của xã hội Việt Nam." *VSĐ* 26 (March 1957): 1–2.

———. "Giới thiệu một vài ý kiến của cụ Phan Bội Châu về sử học." *NCLS* 104 (November 1967): 2–5.

———. "Giỗ tổ Hùng vương." *VSĐ* 17 (May 1956): 1–4.

———. "Hai nước Việt Nam và Trung Quốc trong lịch sử hiện đại." *NCLS* 67 (October 1964): 1.

———. "Kiểm điểm công tác của BNCVSĐ năm 1956 và đề án công tác năm 1957." *VSĐ* 23 (November–December 1956): 1–9.

———. "Kỷ niệm 675 năm trận chiến thắng Bạch Đằng." *NCLS* 50 (May 1963): 1–6.

———. "Kỷ niệm 950 năm thành lập thủ đô Hà Nội." *NCLS* 19 (October 1960): 1–2 and *NCLS* 20 (November 1960): 74–78.

———. "Kỷ niệm Nguyễn Trãi trong cuộc đánh Mỹ cứu nước của chúng ta hiện nay." *NCLS* 102 (September 1967): 12–13, 63.

———. "Lại một vấn đề nêu ra! Những cuộc vận động Đông Du, Đông Kinh nghĩa thục, Duy Tân . . . là phong trào tư sản hay tiền tư sản?" *VSĐ* 11 (November 1955): 35–38.

———. *Lịch sử tám mươi năm chống Pháp.* 3 vols. Hanoi: Văn Sử Địa and Sử Học, 1957–1961.

———. "Mấy điểm cần đi sâu vào cuộc Yên Thế khởi nghĩa." *VSĐ* 37 (February 1958): 1–4.

———. "Mấy điểm rút ra từ cuộc tọa đàm vừa rồi." *NCLS* 16 (July 1960): 1–3.

———. "Mấy nét đặc biệt về Cách mạng tháng Tám." *VSĐ* 20 (August 1956): 1–6.

———. "Một vài nét đặc biệt về Đảng Cộng sản Đông Dương." *VSĐ* 12 (December 1955): 4–18.

———. "Một vài nhận xét về quyển *Cống hiến vào lịch sử của dân tộc Việt Nam* của Jean Chesneaux." *VSĐ* 22 (October 1956): 3–15.

———. "Nghị quyết Hội Trung ương lần thứ tám với cuộc Cách mạng tháng Tám." *VSĐ* 30 (July 1957): 1–4.

———. "Nguyễn Trãi, một nhà đại chính trị, đại văn hào Việt Nam." *VSĐ* 21 (September 1956): 1–21.

———. "Nhận định về Trương Vĩnh Ký." *NCLS* 63 (June 1964): 29–31.

———. "Nhân dịp kỷ niệm Cách mạng tháng Tám, điểm qua quá trình công tác tư tưởng và văn hóa của Đảng." *NCLS* 6 (August 1959): 1–10.

———. "Nhân dịp kỷ niệm cuộc Tổng khởi nghĩa tháng Tám triển vọng của cuộc đấu tranh giải phóng miền Nam nước ta hiện nay." *NCLS* 113 (August 1968): 1–3.

———. "Nhân dịp kỷ niệm 16 năm toàn quốc kháng chiến: Đề ra việc viết lịch sử kháng chiến." *NCLS* 45 (December 1962): 1–2.

———. "Nhân dịp kỷ niệm toàn quốc kháng chiến: Điểm lại thuyết ba giai đoạn của chúng ta." *VSĐ* 34 (November 1957): 1–5.

———. "Những yếu tố thắng lợi của trận lịch sử Đống Đa." *VSĐ* 38 (March 1958): 1–7.

———. "Ôn lại quá trình đấu tranh chống xâm lược của các dân tộc thiểu số ở Việt Nam." *VSĐ* 7 (May–June 1955): 42–57.

———. "Phan Bội Châu, tiêu biểu cho những cuộc vận động yêu nước ở Việt Nam đầu thế kỷ XX." *NCLS* 105 (December 1967): 1–10.

———. "Phấn đấu để trở nên một đảng viên cộng sản (hồi ký)." *NCLS* 10 (January 1960): 77–90.

———. "Phong trào cách mạng qua văn thơ." *VSĐ* 27 (April 1957) through *VSĐ* 47 (December 1958) and *NCLS* 1 (March 1959) through *NCLS* 29 (August 1961).

———. "Phong trào cách mạng trong giai đoạn thứ hai từ sau đại chiến I đến năm 1930 do giai cấp nào lãnh đạo?" *VSĐ* 3 (October 1954): 22–26.

———. "Sưu tầm tài liệu lịch sử." *NCLS* 9 (November 1959): 1–6.

———. "Tổng kết công tác của BNCVSĐ trong một năm qua và đề án công tác năm 1956." *VSĐ* 14 (February 1956): 1–4.

———. "Triển vọng công tác sử học năm 1960." *NCLS* 11 (February 1960): 1.

———. "Vài nét về tình hình khoa học lịch sử trên thế giới hiện nay." *VSĐ* 39 (April 1958): 1–7.

———. "Vai trò lịch sử của Trần Quốc Tuấn." *VSĐ* 10 (September–October 1955): 8–17.

———. "Vấn đề công tác và tổ chức khoa học đã được đề ra trong Quốc hội khoá thứ sáu." *VSĐ* 24 (January 1957): 1–5.

———. "Vấn đề ruộng đất trong Cách mạng Việt Nam." *VSĐ* 2 (n.d.): 9–31.

———. "Việc xây dựng lịch sử các địa phương, các xí nghiệp, các ngành, cần đi vào tổ chức." *NCLS* 40 (July 1962): 3–5.

———. "Việt Nam thống nhất trong quá trình đấu tranh cách mạng." *VSĐ* 9 (August 1955): 53–64.

———. "Xung quanh cái chết của Hoàng Diệu và việc thất thủ thành Hà Nội năm 1882." *NCLS* 39 (August 1962): 1–4.

———. "Xung quanh cái chết của Hoàng Diệu và việc thất thủ thành Hà Nội năm 1882." *VSĐ* 16 (April 1956): 25–37.

———. "Xung quanh việc kỷ niệm các danh nhân trong nước." *NCLS* 44 (November 1962): 1–2.

Trần Huy Liệu et al. *Lịch sử thủ đô Hà Nội.* Hanoi: Sử Học, 1960.

Trần Lanh, trans. "Ý kiến của một số nhà sử học Trung Quốc về bài 'Bàn về mấy quy luật chung của sự biến chuyển từ chế độ nô lệ sang chế độ phong kiến trong các nước khác nhau' của F. N. Ni-kíp-lốp." *VSĐ* 36 (January 1958): 18–31.

Trần Minh Thư. "Cố gắng tiến tới thống nhất nhận định về Đông Kinh nghĩa thục." *NCLS* 81 (December 1965): 31–37.

Trần Quốc Vượng. "Địa lý lịch sử miền Hà Nội (trước thế kỷ thứ XI)." *NCLS* 15 (June 1960): 48–57 and *NCLS* 17 (August 1960): 44–53.

———. "The Legend of Ông Dóng from the Text to the Field." In *Essays into Vietnamese Pasts,* ed. K. W. Taylor and John K. Whitmore. Ithaca: Cornell University Southeast Asia Program, 1995. 13–41.

Trần Quốc Vượng and Chu Thiên. "Xã hội Việt Nam có trải qua một thời kỳ của chế độ chiếm hữu nô lệ hay không?" *NCLS* 16 (July 1960): 10–36.

Trần Quốc Vượng and Hà Văn Tấn. *Lịch sử chế độ cộng sản nguyên thủy ở Việt Nam.* Hanoi: Bộ Giáo Dục, 1960.

———. *Lịch sử chế độ phong kiến Việt Nam.* Vol. 1. Hanoi: Bộ Giáo Dục, 1960.

———. "Về quyển *Lịch sử chế độ cộng sản nguyên thủy ở Việt Nam* (trả lời ông Văn Tân)." *NCLS* 37 (April 1962): 43–48.

———. "Về quyển *Lịch sử chế độ phong kiến Việt Nam* tập I (trả lời ông Văn Tân)." *NCLS* 39 (June 1962): 55–64.

Trần Quốc Vượng and Nguyễn Vĩnh Long. "Hanoi: De la préhistoire au 19e siècle." *Études vietnamiennes* 48 (1977): 9–59.

Trần Thanh Mại. "Giảng văn về ca dao cổ của nông dân đấu tranh." *VSĐ* 1 (June 1954): 62–70.

Trần Thức, "Mỹ thuật Lý-Trần-Lê-Nguyễn." In *Bảo tàng Mỹ thuật Việt Nam,* ed. Nguyễn Văn Chung. Hanoi: Văn Hóa, 1986. 49–51.

Trần Trọng Kim. *Việt Nam sử lược.* 2 vols. Saigon: Bộ Giáo Dục, 1971.

Trần Văn Giáp. "Nhân dịp kỷ niệm chiến thắng Đống Da: Nguyễn Huệ với bia tiến sĩ ở Văn miếu Hà Nội." *NCLS* 46 (January 1963): 4–20.

———. "Trống đồng với chế độ chiếm hữu nô lệ ở Việt Nam." *VSĐ* 15 (March 1956): 30–35.

Trần Văn Thược and Ngô Văn Minh. *Manuel d'histoire d'Annam.* 5th ed. Hanoi: Édition Nam-Ky, 1939.

"Trích diễn văn khai mạc hội nghị tổng kết công tác 7 năm của Viện Sử học ngày 7-1-1961 của đồng chí Trần Huy Liệu, Viện trưởng Viện Sử học." *NCLS* 23 (February 1961): 1–4.

Trinh Van Thao. *Vietnam: Du confucianisme au communisme.* Paris: L'Harmattan, 1990.

Trung Chính. "Kỷ niệm năm mươi năm Phạm Hồng Thái hy sinh vì việc nước." *NCLS* 158 (September–October 1974): 16–26.

———. "Kỷ niệm sáu mươi năm ngày sinh đồng chí Nguyễn Văn Cừ, một cán bộ lãnh đạo Đảng trong thời kỳ 1938–1940." *NCLS* 145 (July–August 1972): 7–17.

———. "Thử tìm xem Hồ Chủ tịch tiếp thu chủ nghĩa Lê-nin và truyền bá vào Việt Nam như thế nào?" *NCLS* 132 (May–June 1970): 48–55.

Truong Buu Lam. *New Lamps for Old: The Transformation of the Vietnamese Administrative Elite.* Singapore: Institute of Southeast Asian Studies, 1982.

————. *Patterns of Vietnamese Response to Foreign Intervention, 1858–1900*. New Haven: Yale University Council on Southeast Asia Studies, 1967.

Trường Chinh. *Chủ nghĩa Mác và văn hóa Việt Nam*. Hanoi: Sự Thật, 1974.

————. "The Resistance Will Win." In *Primer for Revolt: The Communist Takeover of Viet-Nam*. New York: Frederick A. Praeger, 1963. 81–213.

Trương Hoàng Châu. "Mấy vấn đề về đấu tranh giai cấp của nông dân trong xã hội phong kiến Việt Nam." *NCLS* 41 (August 1962): 29–41.

————. "Nền văn hóa khảo cổ học duy nhất trong thời đại đồng thau Việt Nam và vấn đề nước Văn Lang của Hùng vương." *NCLS* 105 (December 1967): 35–41.

Trương Hữu Quýnh. "Vài ý kiến bàn thêm về vấn đề phân kỳ lịch sử." *NCLS* 100 (July 1967): 40–43.

Trương Ngọc Khang, Nguyễn Khách, and Tạ Xuân Linh. "Nhân ngày thành lập mặt trận dân tộc giải phóng miền Nam Việt Nam: Dân tộc Cor Trà Bồng trước cuộc khởi nghĩa ngày 28-8-1959." *NCLS* 148 (January–February 1973): 11–25.

Trương Vĩnh Ký. *Cours d'histoire annamite*. Saigon: Imprimerie du Gouvernement, 1875.

Tucker, Robert C., ed. *The Marx-Engels Reader*. 2nd ed. New York: Norton, 1972.

Turley, William S., ed. *Vietnamese Communism in Comparative Perspective*. Boulder: Westview Press, 1980.

Turner, Bryan S. *Marx and the End of Orientalism*. London: Allen and Unwin, 1978.

Turner, Victor. *The Ritual Process: Structure and Anti-Structure*. Ithaca, NY: Cornell University Press, 1977.

T. X. "Ngày giỗ Ngô Thì Nhậm." *NCLS* 121 (April 1969): 60–62.

————. "Tài liệu về cuộc kháng chiến của Trương Định." *NCLS* 77 (August 1965): 44–55.

"Vấn đề thời kỳ trong lịch sử Việt Nam." *VSĐ* 5 (February 1955): 62–67.

Văn Lạc. "Nhân dịp kỷ niệm 4 năm cuộc Cách mạng Cu-ba: Quá trình xâm lược của Mỹ vào Cu-ba từ hơn một thế kỷ nay." *NCLS* 47 (February 1963): 3–12.

Văn Khôi. "Góp mấy ý kiến về bài 'Một vài nét về lịch sử tỉnh Lai Châu chống thực dân Pháp đầu thế kỷ XX' của bạn Đỗ Thiện." *NCLS* 47 (February 1963): 53–54.

Văn Phong. "Tính chất xã hội Việt Nam và Cách mạng tháng Tám." *VSĐ* 20 (August 1956): 21–32.

Văn Tân. "Ai đã thống nhất Việt Nam? Nguyễn Huệ hay Nguyễn Ánh?" *NCLS* 51 (June 1963): 3–11.

————. "Bàn góp vào công trình tìm tòi nguồn gốc dân tộc Việt Nam." *NCLS* 9 (November 1959): 26–39.

————. "Bàn thêm về nguyên nhân khiến cho cuộc kháng chiến chống quân Mông Cổ hồi thế kỷ XIII đi đến thắng lợi." *NCLS* 66 (September 1964): 2–7 and *NCLS* 67 (October 1964): 39–45.

————. "Bàn thêm về Nguyễn Trãi, một lãnh tụ của khởi nghĩa Lam Sơn." *NCLS* 44 (November 1962): 9–16.

————. "Cần có một quan niệm nhất trí về chế độ chiếm hữu nô lệ ở Việt Nam." *NCLS* 16 (July 1960): 7–9.

———. "Chuẩn bị kỷ niệm 1930 năm Hai Bà Trưng tuẫn tiết." *NCLS* 142 (January–February 1972): 6–9.

———. "Đã đến lúc tạm kết thúc cuộc tranh luận về vấn đề 'Có nên liệt những bài văn do người Việt Nam trước kia viết bằng chữ Hán vào văn học dân tộc của ta không?'" *VSĐ* 23 (November–December 1956): 10–23.

———. "Để góp phần xây dựng quyển thông sử Việt Nam—Mấy ý kiến đối với mấy bộ sách lịch sử đã xuất bản." *VSĐ* 47 (December 1958): 70–81.

———. "Đối với bài 'Về quyển *Lịch sử chế độ phong kiến Việt Nam* tập I' của ông Trần Quốc Vượng và Hà Văn Tấn." *NCLS* 40 (July 1962): 22–30.

———. "550 năm ngày khởi nghĩa Lam Sơn." *NCLS* 106 (January 1968): 1–2.

———. "Hai mươi lăm năm nước Việt Nam dân chủ cộng hòa." *NCLS* 134 (September–October 1970): 1–4.

———. "Kỷ niệm 530 năm ngày Nguyễn Trãi bị tru di." *NCLS* 145 (July–August 1972): 2–6.

———. "Kỷ niệm hai trăm năm khởi nghĩa nông dân do anh em Tây Sơn lãnh đạo." *NCLS* 136 (January–February 1971): 1–8.

———. *Lịch sử Việt Nam (sơ giản)*. Hanoi: Sử Học, 1963.

———. "Lục súc tranh công." *VSĐ* 16 (April 1956): 38–50.

———. "Mấy nhận xét về chiến thắng Đống Đa năm 1789 do Nguyễn Huệ chỉ huy." *NCLS* 119 (February 1969): 4–12.

———. "Mấy nhận xét về quyển *Lược khảo lịch sử văn học Việt Nam* của nhóm Lê Quý Đôn." *VSĐ* 30 (July 1957): 8–26.

———. "Mấy ý kiến về vấn đề khởi nghĩa nông dân trong lịch sử Việt Nam." *NCLS* 74 (May 1965): 17–20.

———. "Nguyễn Đình Chiểu, một nhà trí thức yêu nước nồng nàn, một nhà thơ lỗi lạc của dân tộc Việt Nam." *NCLS* 143 (March–April 1972): 1–10.

———. "Nguyễn Huệ đã cả phá quân xâm lược Xiêm ở Rạch Gầm-Xoài Mút như thế nào?" *NCLS* 60 (March 1964): 3–10.

———. "Nguyễn Trãi có sang Trung Quốc hay không?" *NCLS* 53 (August 1963): 11–15.

———. "Nhân dịp kỷ niệm 680 năm chiến thắng Bạch Đằng: Thử tìm hiểu thêm nguyên nhân và ý nghĩa lịch sử của cuộc chiến thắng quân Mông Cổ hồi thế kỷ XIII." *NCLS* 107 (February 1968): 12–24.

———. "Phê bình quyển *Lịch sử chế độ cộng sản nguyên thủy ở Việt Nam* của ông Trần Quốc Vượng và ông Hà Văn Tấn." *NCLS* 35 (February 1962): 35–46.

———. "Phê bình quyển *Lịch sử chế độ phong kiến Việt Nam* tập I của ông Trần Quốc Vượng và ông Hà Văn Tấn." *NCLS* 36 (March 1962): 38–49.

———. "Quá trình tiến hành công tác mặt trận của Đảng ta." *NCLS* 139 (July–August 1971): 1–7.

———. "Thử tìm hiểu cống hiến của Lê Hoàn đối với lịch sử dân tộc Việt Nam hồi thế kỷ X." *NCLS* 140 (September–October 1971): 1–6.

———. "Trả lời ông Trần Quốc Vượng và ông Hà Văn Tấn." *NCLS* 38 (May 1962): 22–30.

———. "Từ Cách mạng tháng Tám 1945 đến cuộc tổng tiến công và nổi dậy đại thắng mùa xuân năm 1975." *NCLS* 163 (July–August 1975): 3–6.

———. "Tư tưởng nhân văn của Nguyễn Trãi." *NCLS* 54 (September 1963): 2–9.

———. "Vài ý kiến đối với nhận định của ông Đào Duy Anh về vấn đề tô-tem của người Việt nguyên thủy." *NCLS* 2 (April 1959): 10–25.

———. "Vài ý kiến về vấn đề chế độ chiếm hữu nô lệ ở Việt Nam." *NCLS* 13 (April 1960): 22–40.

———. "Vấn đề thời đại Hùng vương trong lịch sử dân tộc Việt Nam." *NCLS* 98 (May 1967): 16–19.

———. "Vấn đề văn học cổ điển Việt Nam." *VSĐ* 42 (July 1958): 11–26.

———. "Vấn đề viết văn học sử Việt Nam." *VSĐ* 17 (May 1956): 5–17.

———. "Xã hội nước Văn Lang và xã hội nước Âu Lạc." *NCLS* 20 (November 1960): 23–33.

———. "Xã hội Việt Nam đã thực sự trải qua thời kỳ chế độ chiếm hữu nô lệ." *NCLS* 16 (July 1960): 37–51.

Văn Tân et al. *Sơ thảo lịch sử văn học Việt Nam.* 5 vols. Hanoi: Văn Sử Địa and Sử Học, 1957–1960.

Van Tân, Nguyễn Linh, Lê Văn Lan, Nguyễn Đổng Chi, and Hoàng Hưng. *Thời đại Hùng vương.* Hanoi: Social Sciences, 1976.

Văn Tạo. "Con người mới Việt Nam nền văn hóa Việt Nam." *NCLS* 3 (1981): 1–3.

———. "Công cuộc khai thác thuộc địa của thực dân Pháp ở Việt Nam và sự phát triển của giai cấp công nhân Việt Nam." *VSĐ* 11 (November 1955): 54–64.

———. "Hồ Chủ tịch và tình ruột thịt Bắc Nam." *NCLS* 149 (March–April 1973): 1–12.

———. "Hồ Chủ tịch và truyền thống dân tộc." *NCLS* 132 (May–June): 7–32.

———. "Hội nghị Khoa học nhân dịp kỷ niệm lần thứ 30 ngày thành lập nước Việt Nam dân chủ cộng hòa tại Mát-scơ-va tháng 9-1975." *NCLS* 164 (September-October 1975): 80.

———. "Nhân ngày quốc khánh: Phát huy chủ nghĩa anh hùng cách mạng để xây dựng con người mới xã hội chủ nghĩa Việt Nam." *NCLS* 151 (July–August 1973): 1–5.

———. "Quá trình thành lập Mặt trận Việt Minh và thắng lợi của Mặt trận trong Cách mạng tháng Tám." *VSĐ* 43 (August 1958): 3–18.

———. "Vài nét về quá trình xây dựng và phát triển của Nhà nước cách mạng Việt Nam." *VSĐ* 48 (January 1959): 11–27.

Văn Tạo and Nguyễn Quang Ân, eds. *Ban Văn Sử Địa, 1953–1959.* Hanoi: Social Sciences and Nhân Văn Quốc Gia, 1993.

Vasavakul, Thaveeporn. "Schools and Politics in South and North Vietnam." Ph.D. dissertation, Cornell University, 1994.

Viện Ngôn ngữ học. *Từ điển tiếng Việt.* Hanoi: Social Sciences, 1988.

Viện Sử học Việt Nam (VSH). "Công tác sử học bắt đầu đi vào cán bộ và nhân dân," *NCLS* 7 (September 1959): 1–2.

———. *Lịch sử Việt Nam.* 2 vols. Hanoi: Social Sciences, 1971, 1985.

———. "Nhân dịp kỷ niệm Cách mạng tháng Mười lần 42: Tích cực đẩy mạnh việc học tập chủ nghĩa Mác—Lê-nin một cách hệ thống trong cán bộ sử học." *NCLS* 8 (October 1959): 1–15.

————. "Tích cực đẩy mạnh việc học tập chủ nghiã Mác—Lê-nin một cách hệ thống trong cán bộ sử học." *NCLS* 8 (October 1959): 1–15.

————. "Trích đăng bản báo cáo về công tác sử học đọc tại Hội nghị chuyên đề ngày 24, 25, 26 tháng 5 năm 1962 tại Hà Nội." *NCLS* 40 (July 1962): 6–21.

————. "Vấn đề Đảng sử." *NCLS* 10 (January 1960): 1–5.

————. *Việt Nam: Những sự kiện 1945–1986.* Hanoi: Social Sciences, 1990.

Viện Văn học. *Nguyễn Trãi: Khí phách và tinh hoa của dân tộc.* Hanoi: Social Sciences, 1980.

Việt Chung. "National Minorities and Nationality Policy in the DRV." *VNS* 15 (1968): 3–23.

Vo Nguyen Giap. *Unforgettable Months and Years.* Trans. Mai Van Elliot. Ithaca: Cornell University Southeast Asia Program, 1975.

Võ Văn Ái, ed. *Trăm hoa đua nở trăn đất bắc.* Paris: Quê Mẹ, 1983.

Vũ Ngọc Phan. "Người nông dân Việt Nam trong truyện cổ tích." *VSĐ* 4 (January 1955): 25–34.

————. "Những tiếng phản kháng của phụ nữ nông thôn trong dân ca Việt Nam." *VSĐ* 6 (March–April 1955): 38–53.

————. *Tục ngữ, ca dao, dân ca Việt Nam.* 8th ed. Hanoi: Social Sciences, 1978.

Vucinich, Wayne S. "Postwar Yugoslav Historiography." *JMH* 23, no. 1 (March 1951): 41–57.

Vương Hoàng Tuyên. "Một vài ý kiến về nguyên nhân hình thành của nhà nước phong kiến trung ương tập quyền ở Việt Nam." *NCLS* 4 (June 1959): 59–65.

————. "Một vài ý kiến về sự manh nha của yếu tố tư bản chủ nghĩa trong xã hội phong kiến Việt Nam." *NCLS* 15 (June 1960): 4–10.

————. "Some Ethnic Groups Only Just Saved from Extinction Living in Remote Parts of the Northwest." *VNS* 36 (1973): 141–95.

Vũ Tuấn Sán. "Cuộc khởi nghĩa Hai Bà Trưng tại thủ đô Hà Nội." *NCLS* 149 (March–April 1973): 41–50.

Watson, Burton. *Records of the Grand Historian.* 2 vols. New York: Columbia University Press, 1961.

Weber, Eugen. *Peasants into Frenchmen: The Modernization of Rural France.* Stanford: Stanford University Press, 1976.

Weiss, Peter. *Notes on the Cultural Life of the Democratic Republic of Vietnam.* New York: Dell, 1970.

White, Christine. "Agrarian Reform and National Liberation in the Vietnamese Revolution, 1920–1957." Ph.D. dissertation, Cornell University, 1981.

White, Hayden. *Metahistory: The Historical Imagination in Nineteenth-Century Europe.* Baltimore: Johns Hopkins University Press, 1973.

————. *Tropics of Discourse.* Baltimore: Johns Hopkins University Press, 1978.

Whitmore, John K. "Communism and History in Vietnam." In *Vietnamese Communism in Comparative Perspective,* ed. William S. Turley. Boulder: Westview Press, 1980. 11–44.

Wolters, O. W. "Assertions of Cultural Well-Being in Fourteenth-Century Vietnam."

In *Two Essays on Đại Việt in the Fourteenth Century.* New Haven: Yale Council on Southeast Asia Studies, 1988. 3–53.

———. "Historians and Emperors in Vietnam and China: Comments Arising Out of Le Van Huu's History, Presented to the Tran Court in 1272." In *Perceptions of the Past in Southeast Asia,* ed. Anthony Reid and David Marr. Singapore: Heinemann, 1979. 69–89.

———. *History, Culture, and Region in Southeast Asian Perspectives.* Ithaca: Cornell University Southeast Asia Program, 1999.

———. "Possibilities for a Reading of the 1293–1357 Period in the Vietnamese Annals." *VNF* 11 (winter–spring 1988): 92–137.

Womack, Sarah. "The Remaking of a Legend: Women and Patriotism in the Hagiography of the Trưng Sisters." *Crossroads* 9, no. 2 (1996): 31–50.

Woodside, Alexander B. "Central Việt Nam's Trading World in the Eighteenth Century as Seen in Lê Quý Đôn's *Frontier Chronicles.*" In *Essays into Vietnamese Pasts,* Ithaca: Cornell University Southeast Asia Program, 1995). 157–72.

———. "Classical Primordialism and Frontier Universalism in Vietnamese Confucianism." Paper presented at "Rethinking Confucianism in Asia at the End of the Twentieth Century," organized by the Center for Chinese Studies, University of California at Los Angeles, May 28–June 1, 1999.

———. *Community and Revolution in Modern Vietnam.* Boston: Houghton Mifflin, 1976.

———. "Conceptions of Change and of Human Responsibility for Change in Late Traditional Vietnam." In *Moral Order and the Question of Change: Essays on Southeast Asian Thought,* ed. David K. Wyatt and Alexander Woodside. New Haven: Yale University Council on Southeast Asia Studies, 1982.

———. "Early Ming Expansionism (1407–1427): China's Abortive Conquest of Vietnam." *Papers on China* 17 (1963): 1–37.

———. *Vietnam and the Chinese Model.* 1971; Cambridge: Harvard University Council on East Asian Studies, 1988.

Wright, Gwendolyn. "Indochina: The Folly of Grandeur." In *The Politics of Design in French Colonial Urbanism.* Chicago: University of Chicago Press, 1991. 161–233.

X. X. "Dư luận nước ngoài đối với bộ *Lịch sử Việt Nam.*" *NCLS* 154 (January–February 1974): 73–74.

Zinoman, Peter. *The Colonial Bastille: A History of Imprisonment in Vietnam, 1862–1940.* Berkeley: University of California Press, 2001.

Index

26, 28, 35, 39, 41–44, 60–61, 69, 78–80, 82–83; 87–88, 93, 134, 170, 235–44; and delay in producing new standard text, 8, 59, 69, 113, 235–44; and denial of the South, 6, 31, 39, 244; as dialogue, 15, 26; fluidity of, 41, 104–9; international audience of, 62–63; and political legitimation, 12; and the state, 7, 20–23, 87

Ngo Dinh Diem, 4, 35, 153, 185, 192, 202, 205, 216, 229

Ngô Quyền, 159, 177, 191. *See also* Bạch Đằng

Ngo Sĩ Liên, 29, 65–66, 151–52, 178–80, 184, 237. *See also* Traditional canon

Ngô Thì Nhậm, 175–76

Ngô Văn Minh, 19

Nguyễn Công Bình, 29, 34, 236

Nguyễn Đình Chiểu, 36, 176

Nguyễn Đổng Chi, 28, 30, 236; on culture, 134, 136–38; on ethnic differences, 80, 93; on historical periodization, 49, 52–53

Nguyễn Du, 166; *The Tale of Kĩều*, 126, 129, 142

Nguyễn Dữ, 134

Nguyễn Đức Hợp, 83, 85

Nguyễn dynasty, 126, 190, 203, 217, 243; Bảo Đại, 1, 3, 237; Đông Khanh, 17; Gia Long, 39, 133, 166; Hàm Nghi, 63; Minh Mạng, 133, 212; Tự Đức, 17, 30, 40

Nguyễn dynasty histories and historians, 17, 31–32, 190, 217. *See also* Traditional canon

Nguyễn Hoàng. *See* Nguyễn lords

Nguyễn Huệ. *See* Tây Sơn

Nguyễn Hồng Phong, 53, 139, 200

Nguyễn Huy Tưởng, 119

Nguyễn Khắc Đạm, 34, 87, 94

Nguyễn Khuyến, 36

Nguyễn Kim Anh, 178

Nguyễn Lân, 91

Nguyễn Linh, 154–55

Nguyễn lords, 32, 133, 190–92, 216; Nguyễn Hoàng, 31, 39

Nguyễn Lương Bích, 33, 231; on ethnographic research, 85–88, 94; on Hanoi, 211–17; on historical periodization, 49, 56–58, 63; on national origins, 147–48

Nguyễn Minh, 180, 182

Nguyễn Ngọc, 118

Nguyễn Quang Ngọc, 146

Nguyễn Thành, 91

Nguyễn Thế Phương, 92

Nguyễn Thị Định, 181

Nguyễn Thiện Thuật, 175

Nguyễn Thượng Hiền, 153

Nguyễn Trãi, 30, 125, 159, 173–74, 176–78, 185–89, 191; *Family Instructions*, 187; *Proclamation of Victory over the Wu*, 186. *See also* Lam Sơn

Nguyễn Trường Tộ, 26

Nguyễn Tuấn Liêu, 88

Nguyễn Văn Cừ, 176

Nguyễn Văn Di, 183–84

Nguyễn Văn Khoa, 88

Nguyễn Việt, 221–24

Nhân Dân. *See The People*

Nhân văn–Giai phẩm, 120

Nôm, 30, 32

Nông Ích Thùy, 90

Nông Trung, 88

North Korea, 61, 88

N'Trang Lớng Movement, 174

Nung, 70, 75–76, 88–89, 93–94, 102

October Revolution, 173–74, 176, 194–96

Ơ Đu, 104

O'Leary, Brendan, 54–55

One-Pillared Pagoda, 29, 67

Pankratova, Anna, 49

Paris Commune, 175

Parmentier, Henri, 149

Party Congresses, 111, 113, 121, 125, 146

Pả Thẻn, 105

Peace-loving spirit, 11

PATRICIA PELLEY IS ASSISTANT PROFESSOR OF HISTORY

AT TEXAS TECH UNIVERSITY.

Library of Congress Cataloging-in-Publication Data

Pelley, Patricia M.

Postcolonial Vietnam : new histories of the national past / Patricia M. Pelley.

p. cm.— (Asia Pacific; A John Hope Franklin Center Book)

Includes bibliographical references and index.

ISBN 0-8223-2984-0 (cloth : alk. paper) — ISBN 0-8223-2966-2 (pbk. : alk. paper)

1. Vietnam—History—1975–   I. Title.   DS556.5 .P45   2002

959.704'4—dc21   2002002593

7731

DATE DUE